Born in Chatham, Kent, **HENRY STEDMAN** has been writing guide-books for over fifteen years now and is the author or co-author of half a dozen titles, including Trailblazer's *Kilimanjaro*, *Hadrian's Wall Path* and all three books in the *South-West Coast Path series* as well as *The Bradt Guide to Palestine* and the *Rough Guides* to *Indonesia* and *Southeast Asia*. When not travelling or writing, Henry lives in Hastings editing other people's guidebooks, maintaining his Kilimanjaro website and arranging climbs on the mountain through his company, Climb Mount Kilimanjaro.

This **sixth edition** of *Coast to Coast Path* was researched and updated by **CHRIS SCOTT** and **BRYN THOMAS**.

**Authors**

**Coast to Coast Path** First edition: 2004; this sixth edition: 2014

**Publisher** Trailblazer Publications
The Old Manse, Tower Rd, Hindhead, Surrey, GU26 6SU, UK
info@trailblazer-guides.com, www.trailblazer-guides.com

**British Library Cataloguing in Publication Data**
A catalogue record for this book is available from the British Library

**ISBN 978-1-905864-57-7**

© **Trailblazer** 2004, 2006, 2008, 2010, 2012, 2014: Text and maps

**Series Editor**: Anna Jacomb-Hood  **Editors**: Nicky Slade and Jane Thomas
**Additional research**: Anna Jacomb-Hood, Nicky Slade and Caroline Gray
**Illustrations**: © Nick Hill (pp63-4)  **Photographs (flora)**: © Bryn Thomas (BT)
**All other photographs**: © CS = Chris Scott, HS = Henry Stedman, JM = Jim Manthorpe
**Cartography**: Nick Hill  **Layout**: Bryn Thomas  **Index**: Jane Thomas

The maps in this guide were prepared from out-of-Crown-
copyright Ordnance Survey maps amended and updated by Trailblazer.

## Acknowledgements

Thanks to contributors and for updates sent by letter and email from: John Beckwith, Ben
Bennetts, Michael Brewster, Gerri Burgess, Chizzer Childs and Mand, Mark & Chesney, Sue
& Andrew Cooper, Ian Cramp, Elaine Davenport, Mark Faust & Sara Fischer, Volker Gring-
muth, Robert Hall, John Harding, Mats Heder, John Hedrick, Colin Honeybone, Elizabeth,
Chris Ingram, Phill Kuehnle, Colin Lindsay, Andrew & Harriet Napier, Tony Oldershaw, Jean
Oliphant, Bob & Fiona Parker, Renford Paris, Edith Peters, Colin Ryman, Brian Shaw, Colin
Shepherd, Ken & Alison Smedley, Marilyn Smith, Mary & George Southern, Natalie Stevens,
Bob Story, Philippa & Michael Sutton, Jean Thornton, Rick Toyer, Sjef and Valentijn
Verpaalen, Ian Walker & Steve, Richard Ward, Michele & Andy Webb, Fiona Werge, Harry
Whitehouse and John Woolston. Thanks also to Stuart Greig, Chris Scott for route research and
detailed map work, Nick Hill for cartography, Anna Jacomb-Hood and Caroline Gray for addi-
tional research, and Nicky Slade and Jane Thomas for editing and proofreading.

## A request

The author and publisher have tried to ensure that this guide is as accurate and up to date
as possible. Nevertheless, things change. If you notice any changes or omissions, please
write to Trailblazer (address above) or email us at ▣ info@trailblazer-guides.com. A free
copy of the next edition will be sent to persons making a significant contribution.

## Warning: hill walking can be dangerous

Please read the notes on when to go (pp14-6) and outdoor safety (pp81-5). Every effort has
been made by the author and publisher to ensure that the information contained herein is as
accurate and up to date as possible. However, they are unable to accept responsibility for
any inconvenience, loss or injury sustained by anyone as a result of the advice and information given in this guide.

**Photos – Front cover**: Striding Edge (© HS). **Previous page**: Beginning the climb up
Lining Crag (© CS). **Opposite**: On the trail between Helvellyn and Patterdale (© HS) in
summer and **overleaf**, early in winter (© BT)

Updated information will be available on: ▣ **www.trailblazer-guides.com**.

Printed on chlorine-free paper by D'Print (☎ +65-6581 3832), Singapore

# Coast to Coast
## PATH

**109 large-scale maps & guides to 33 towns and villages**
**PLANNING – PLACES TO STAY – PLACES TO EAT**
**ST BEES TO ROBIN HOOD'S BAY**

HENRY STEDMAN

**Sixth edition researched and updated by**
**CHRIS SCOTT & BRYN THOMAS**

with contributions by
Stuart Greig, David & Maria Bull,
Noel Cox and Chris Foster

## TRAILBLAZER PUBLICATIONS

# Contents

# PART 4: ROUTE GUIDE AND MAPS

Contents

## ABOUT THIS BOOK

This guidebook contains all the information you need. The hard work has been done for you so you can plan your trip from home without the usual pile of books, maps and guides.

When you're all packed and ready to go, there's comprehensive public transport information to get you to and from the trail and 109 detailed maps and town plans to help you find your way along it. The guide includes:

● All standards of accommodation with reviews of campsites, bunkhouses, hostels, B&Bs, guesthouses and hotels
● Walking companies if you want an organised tour and baggage-carrying services if you just want your luggage carried
● Itineraries for all levels of walkers
● Answers to all your questions: when to go, degree of difficulty, what to pack, and how much the whole walking holiday will cost
● Walking times and GPS waypoints
● Cafés, pubs, tearooms, takeaways, restaurants and shops for buying supplies
● Rail, bus and taxi information for all villages and towns along the path
● Street plans of the main towns: St Bees, Grasmere, Shap, Orton, Kirkby Stephen, Reeth, Richmond, Grosmont and Robin Hood's Bay
● Historical, cultural and geographical background information

## MINIMUM IMPACT FOR MAXIMUM INSIGHT

*Man has suffered in his separation from the soil and from other living creatures ... and as yet he must still, for security, look long at some portion of the earth as it was before he tampered with it.* **Gavin Maxwell**, *Ring of Bright Water*, 1960

Why is walking in wild and solitary places so satisfying? Partly it is the sheer physical pleasure: sometimes pitting one's strength against the elements and the lie of the land. The beauty and wonder of the natural world and the fresh air restore our sense of proportion and the stresses and strains of everyday life slip away. Whatever the character of the countryside, walking in it benefits us mentally and physically, inducing a sense of well-being, an enrichment of life and an enhanced awareness of what lies around us.

All this the countryside gives us and the least we can do is to safeguard it by supporting rural economies, local businesses, and low-impact methods of farming and land-management, and by using environmentally sensitive forms of transport – walking being pre-eminent.

In this book there is a detailed and illustrated chapter on the wildlife and conservation of the region and a chapter on minimum-impact walking, with ideas on how to tread lightly in this fragile environment; by following its principles we can help to preserve our natural heritage for future generations.

# INTRODUCTION

In devising a walk that would span the north of England from the Cumbrian coast to the North Sea, the legendary fell walker, guidebook writer and illustrator, Alfred Wainwright, created an enduring concept that 40 years later continues to inspire hikers in ever-growing numbers.

Despite not being an official National Trail with all the support that entails, the Coast to Coast path has almost certainly become the most popular long-distance footpath in England. At about 190 miles (see box p18) it's not the longest in the country and certainly doesn't, as some mistakenly think, cross the country at its widest point. It makes no claim to being especially tough (though we can safely predict that those who attempt it in one go will find it sufficiently challenging). Nor does it, unlike the long-distance paths that run alongside Hadrian's Wall or Offa's Dyke, follow any ancient construction or border.

> **It's almost certainly become the most popular long-distance path in England**

In truth, the Coast to Coast is but one of an infinite number of routes that could be devised by joining the various footpaths and byways to form a trail across northern England and in doing so providing those who follow it with a snapshot of the country.

But what a magnificent snapshot that is! Around two-thirds of the walk is spent in the national parks of the Lake District, the Yorkshire Dales and the North York Moors. These parks encompass the most dramatic upland scenery in England, from its highest fells to its largest lakes, some of its most beautiful woods and parts of its bleakest, barest moors. The walk also passes through areas alive with some of Britain's rarest wildlife, including red squirrels and otters, and even skirts around the eyrie of England's last surviving golden eagle.

> **Around two-thirds of the walk is spent in national parks**

Furthermore, where man has settled on the trail he has, on the whole, worked in harmony with nature to produce some of England's finest villages, from idyllically situated Grasmere to unspoilt Egton Bridge. The trail itself is a further example of this harmony; these paths and bridleways have existed for centuries and though man-made, do not feel or look like an imposition on the landscape but are very much part of it.

By the beach at St Bees, 'Mile Zero' (**above**) is clearly marked. It's become a tradition to collect a pebble, carry it with you as a keepsake and then drop it into the North Sea at Robin Hood's Bay (**below**) to mark your journey's end. (© CS)

While these paths and villages continue to thrive under the steady stream of Coast to Coasters, in other places nature has reclaimed the poignant ruins of mills and mines, ancient Iron Age sites and mysterious stone circles which between them bear witness to thousands of years of human endeavour. They punctuate the path and provide absorbing highlights along the way.

But the walker on the Coast to Coast path experiences additional, unquantifiable rewards. There is the pleasure of acquiring a developing level of fitness, the satisfaction of unravelling a route-finding conundrum and the relief when a hard-won day finally ends at the doorstep of a cosy B&B or in a centuries-old hostelry. Most memorably, it's the cheery camaraderie shared by your fellow pilgrims bound for Robin Hood's Bay and the window into the lives of the people who live and work in this fabulous landscape that stay with you as you transit the country from coast to coast.

## Wainwright's Coast to Coast path

The Coast to Coast path owes its existence to one man: Alfred Wainwright. It was in 1972 that Wainwright, already renowned for his exquisitely illustrated guides to walking in the Lake District, finally completed a trek across the width of England along a path of his own devising. It was an idea that he had been kicking around for a time: to cross his native land on a route that, as far as he was aware, would 'commit no offence against privacy nor trample on the sensitive corns of landowners and tenants'. The result of his walk, a guidebook, was originally printed by his long-time publishers, *The Westmoreland Gazette*, the following year. It proved hugely successful. Indeed, a full twenty years after the book was first published, a television series of the trail was also made in which

Wainwright himself starred, allowing a wider public to witness first-hand his wry, abrupt, earthy charm.

**It was in 1972 that Wainwright finally completed a trek across the width of England along a path of his own devising**

Wainwright reminds people in his book that his is just **one of many such trails** across England that could be devised, and since Wainwright's book other Coast to Coast walks have indeed been established. Yet it is still *his* trail that is by far and away the most popular, and in order to distinguish it from the others, it is now commonly known as Wainwright's Coast to Coast path.

The route has been amended slightly since 1973 mostly because, though careful to try to use only public rights of way, in a few places Wainwright's original trail actually intruded upon private land. Indeed, even today the trail does in places cross private territory and it's only due to the largesse of the landowners that the path has remained near-enough unchanged throughout its course.

Though the trail passes through three national parks, crosses the Pennine Way and at times joins with both the Lyke Wake Walk and the Cleveland Way, it's not itself one of the 15 national trails in the UK, nor is it likely to become one anytime soon. What is certain is that despite this lack of official support, the Coast to Coast has become one of the most popular of Britain's long-distance paths, with estimates of up to 10,000 people attempting it annually.

---

Wainwright's 'AW' monogram on a fingerpost on the North Yorks Moors.

❏ **Mr Coast to Coast – Alfred Wainwright**

The popular perception of the man who devised the Coast to Coast path is that of a gruff, anti-social curmudgeon with little time for his fellow men, though one who admittedly knew what he was doing when it came to producing guidebooks. It's an unflattering portrait, but one that the man himself did little to destroy. Indeed, many say that he deliberately cultivated such a reputation in order to make himself unapproachable, thus allowing him to continue enjoying his beloved solitary walks without interruptions from the cagoule-clad masses who trudged the fells in his wake. Yet this unflattering and rather dull two-dimensional description disguises a very complex man: artist, father, divorcé, pipe smoker, accountant, part-time curator at Kendal Museum, TV personality, romantic and cat-lover.

Alfred Wainwright was born in Blackburn on 17 January 1907, to a hardworking, impoverished mother and an alcoholic father. Bright and conscientious, his early years gave little clue to the talents that would later make him famous, though his neat handwriting – a feature of his guidebooks – was frequently praised by his teachers. Leaving school to work in accounts at the Borough Engineer's Office in Blackburn Town Hall, he regularly drew cartoons to entertain his colleagues. When, in December 1931, he married Ruth Holden, it seemed that Wainwright's life was set upon a course of happy – if humdrum – conformity. Wainwright, however, never saw it like that. In particular, he quickly realised that his marriage had been a mistake.

*(Continued overleaf)*

*(Continued from p9)*  Wainwright felt stifled and bored with his home life; feelings that not even the arrival of a son, Peter, could erase. His wife, though loyal, good and obedient, left Wainwright unfulfilled and any trace of romantic love that had been in the marriage at the beginning quickly drained away.

To escape the misery at home, Wainwright threw himself into his new-found hobby, fellwalking. He first visited the Lakes in 1930 and soon after was making detailed notes and drawings on the walks he made. Initially, these visits were few and far between, but a move to Kendal ten years later to take up a position as an accounting assistant allowed Wainwright to visit the Lakes virtually every weekend. Yet it wasn't until the early 1950s that Wainwright struck upon the idea of shaping his copious notes and drawings into a series of walking guides. The idea wasn't a new one: guides to the Lakes had existed since at least the late 18th century and previous authors had included such literary luminaries as William Wordsworth. Where Wainwright's guides differed, however, was in their detail and the unique charm of their production.

For Wainwright was a publisher's dream: his writing was concise and laced with a wry humour, his ink sketches were delightful, and every page was designed by the author himself, with the text justified on both sides (and without hyphens!) around the drawings. As a result, all the publisher really needed to do was crank up the printing press, load in the paper, and hey presto! They had another bestseller on their hands.

His first seven books, a series of guides to the Lakeland fells, took fourteen years to produce and by the end he had built up quite a following amongst both walkers and those who simply loved the books' beauty. Further titles followed, including one on the Pennine Way (a walk that he seemed to have enjoyed rather less than the others, possibly because at one point he had needed to be rescued by a warden after falling into a bog). As an incentive to walkers, however, he offered to buy a pint for every reader who completed the entire walk, telling them to put it on his bill at the Border Hotel at the end of the Pennine Way. The Coast to Coast was the follow-up to the Pennine Way, with the research starting in 1971 and the book published in 1973. It was a project that Wainwright seemed to have derived much greater enjoyment from (though, unfortunately, there was no offer of a free drink this time!).

While all this was going on, however, Wainwright's private life was in turmoil. Though his homelife with Ruth remained as cold as ever, Wainwright had found the love of his life in Betty McNally, who had visited him in his office on official matters sometime in 1957. For Wainwright, it was love at first sight, and he began courting Betty soon after. They married eventually in 1970, and by all accounts this union provided Wainwright with the contentment and happiness he had so signally failed to find in his first marriage. She also accompanied Wainwright on his forays into television, where his gruff, no-nonsense charm proved a big hit.

At the time of their marriage Wainwright, already 63, promised Betty ten happy years. In the event, he was able to provide her with 21, passing away on Sunday, January 20, 1991. His last wish, fulfilled two months later by Betty and his long-time friend Percy Duff, was to have his ashes scattered on Hay Stacks. At the end of his autobiography, *Ex-Fellwanderer*, he sums his life up thus:

*I have had a long and wonderful innings and enjoyed a remarkable immunity from unpleasant and unwelcome incidents. ... I never had to go to be a soldier, which I would have hated. I never had to wear a uniform, which I also would have hated. ... I was never called upon to make speeches in public nor forced into the limelight; my role was that of a backroom boy, which suited me fine. I never went bald, which would have driven me into hiding. ... So, all told, I have enjoyed a charmed life, I have been well favoured. The gods smiled on me since the cradle. I have had more blessings than I could ever count.*

# How difficult is the Coast to Coast path?

Undertaken **in one go** the Coast to Coast path is a long, tough walk. Despite the presence of some fairly steep gradients, every mile is 'walkable' and no mountaineering or climbing skills are necessary. All you need is some suitable clothing, a bit of money, a backpack full of determination and a half-decent pair of calf muscles. In the 190-odd miles from seashore to seashore you'll have ascended and of course descended the equivalent height of Mount Everest.

That said, the most common complaint we've received about this book, particularly from North American readers, is that it doesn't emphasise how tough it can be. So

**From seashore to seashore you'll have ascended and of course descended the equivalent height of Mount Everest**

let us be clear: **the Coast to Coast is a tough trek**, **particularly if undertaken in one go**. Ramblers describe it as 'challenging' and they're not wrong. When walkers begin to appreciate just how tough the walk can be, what they're really discovering is the reality of covering a daily average of just over 14 miles or 23km, *day after day*, for two weeks, in fair weather or foul and while nursing a varying array of aches and pains. After all, how often do any of us walk 14 miles in a day, let alone continuously for *two weeks*?

The Lake District, in particular, contains many steep sections that will test you to the limit; however, there are also plenty of genteel tearooms and

Looking west along the escarpment of the North York Moors from near Clay Bank Top. (JM).

Hillwalkers on Red Pike (see p109), seen from High Stile, on the high route between Ennerdale Bridge and Borrowdale. (© JM).

accommodation options in this section should you prefer to break your days into easier sections.

The topography of the eastern section is less extreme, though the number of places with accommodation drops too, and for a couple of days you may find yourself walking 15 miles or more in order to reach a town or village on the trail that has somewhere to stay.

Regarding safety, there are few places on the regular trail where it would be possible to fall from a great height, save perhaps for the cliff walks that book-end the walk. On some of the high-level Lakeland alternatives (see p123 and p133), however, there is a chance of being blown off a ridge. In 2009 a walker suffered this fate and broke his ankle, as did the rescuer who came in a helicopter, though sustaining such a serious injury by being blown over is highly unusual. The greatest danger to trekkers is, perhaps, the likelihood of **losing the way**, particularly in the Lake District with its greater chance of poor visibility, bad weather and a distinct **lack of signposting**. A compass and knowing how to use it is vital, as is appropriate clothing for inclement weather and most importantly of all, a pair of boots which you ease on each morning with a smile not a grimace.

Not pushing yourself too hard is important, too, as this leads to fatigue with all its inherent dangers, not least poor decision making. In case all this deters you from the walk bear in mind that in 2009 a 71-year-old finished the walk for the fifth time, and a 7-year-old girl once completed the walk with her father – and they all managed it in 13 days! At the same time young men with all the right kit and a previous crossing under their belt were finished after storming across to Shap in three days.

## How long do you need?

We've heard about an athlete who completed the entire Coast to Coast path in just 37 hours and a walker who managed it in eight days. We also know somebody who did it in ten and another guy who did four four-day stages over four years. Continuously or over several visits, for most people, the Coast to Coast trail takes a minimum of 14 walking days, in other words an average distance of just over 14 miles (23km) a day. Indeed, even with a fortnight in

**For most people, the Coast to Coast trail takes a minimum of 14 walking days**

INTRODUCTION

The view down the hidden valley of Bannerdale, near Angle Tarn above Patterdale. (© JM).

which to complete the trail, many people still find it tough going, and it doesn't really allow you time to look around places such as Grasmere or Richmond which can deserve a day in themselves. So, if you can afford to build a couple of rest days into your itinerary or even break it up into shorter stages over several weeks, you'll be very glad you did.

Of course, if you're fit there's no reason why you can't go a little faster if that's what you want to do, though you'll end up having a different sort of trek to most of the other people on the route. For where theirs is a fairly relaxing holiday, yours will be more of a sport as you try to reach the finishing line on schedule. There's nothing wrong with this approach, though you obviously won't see as much as those who take their time; *chacun à son goût*, as the French probably say. However, what you mustn't do is try to push yourself beyond your body's ability; such punishing challenges often end prematurely in exhaustion, injury or, at the absolute least, an unpleasant time.

When deciding how long to allow for their trek, those intending to camp and carry their own luggage shouldn't underestimate just how much a heavy pack can wear you down. On pp34-5 there are some suggested itineraries covering different walking speeds. If you've only got a few days, don't try to walk it all; concentrate, instead, on one area such as the Lakes or North York Moors. You can always come back and attempt the rest of the walk another time.

See pp34-5 for some suggested itineraries covering different walking speeds

# When to go

## SEASONS

Britain is a notoriously wet country and the north-west of England is an infamously damp part of it. Rare indeed is the trekker who manages to walk the Coast to Coast path without suffering at least one day of rain; three or four days per trek is more likely, even in summer. That said, it's equally unlikely that

Average max/min temperatures – Richmond

you'll spend a fortnight in the area and not see any sun at all, and even the most cynical of walkers will have to admit that, during the walking season at least, there are more sunny days than showery ones. That **walking season**, by the way, starts at Easter and builds to a crescendo in August, before quickly tailing off in September. By the end of that month there are few trekkers on the trail, and in late October many places close down for the winter.

### Spring

Find a couple of dry weeks in springtime and you're in for a treat. The wild flowers are beginning to come into bloom, lambs are skipping in the meadows and the grass is green and lush. Of course, finding a dry fortnight in spring (around the end of March to mid-June) is not easy but occasionally there's a mini-heatwave at this time. Another advantage will be fewer trekkers on the trail so finding accommodation without booking is relatively easy. Easter is the exception, the first major holiday in the year when people flock to the Lake District and other national parks.

### Summer

Summer, on the other hand, can be a bit *too* busy and, in somewhere like the Lakes over a weekend in August, at times depressingly congested. Still, the chances of a prolonged period of sunshine are of course higher at this time of year than any other, the days are much longer and the heather is in bloom, too, turning the hills a fragrant purple. If you like the company of other trekkers summer will provide you with the opportunity of meeting scores of them, though do remember that you'll need to book your accommodation well in advance or be prepared to camp occasionally. Despite the higher-than-average chance of sunshine, take clothes for any eventuality – it's bound to rain at some point.

### Autumn

September can be a wonderful time to walk; many of the families have returned home and the path is clear although accommodation gets filled up in early

September by a wave of older visitors who've been waiting for the new school term. The weather is usually sunny, too, at least at the beginning of September. By the end of the month the weather will begin to get a little wilder and the nights will start to draw in. For most mortals the walking season is almost at an end.

## Winter

A few people trek the Coast to Coast in winter, putting up with the cold, damp conditions and short days for the chance to experience the trail without other tourists and maybe even under snow. Much of the accommodation will be closed too but whilst it may also be a little more dangerous to walk at this time, particularly on the high-level routes through the Lakes, if you find yourself walking on one of those clear, crisp, wintry days it will all seem absolutely worth it.

## RAINFALL

At some point on your walk, it will rain; if it doesn't, it's fair to say that you haven't really lived the full Coast to Coast experience properly. At nearly 4.7 metres (185 inches), the hills over Borrowdale on Stage 2 record the **highest rainfall in England**; a staggering eight times more than the south-east of England, for example! The question, therefore, is not whether you will be rained on, but how often and how hard. But as long as you dress accordingly and take note of the safety advice given on pp81-5, this shouldn't be a problem.

Average rainfall – Richmond

Do, however, think twice about tackling some of the high-level alternatives if the weather is bad and visibility poor, and don't do so on your own.

## DAYLIGHT HOURS

If walking in autumn, winter or early spring, you must take account of how far you can walk in the available light. It won't be possible to cover as many miles as you would in summer. Remember though, that you'll get a further 30-45 minutes of usable light before sunrise and after sunset depending on the weather. In June, because the path is in the far north of England, those coming

Hours of daylight – Richmond

from the south may be surprised that there's enough light for walking until at least 10pm. Conversely, in early spring, late autumn and winter you'll be equally amazed how quickly the nights draw in.

❏ **FESTIVALS AND ANNUAL EVENTS**

Thanks largely to its undying appeal with tourists, **Grasmere** has become something of a mecca for those interested in those peculiarly Lakeland sports such as fell running, and Cumberland and Westmoreland wrestling.

In addition to the events outlined below, all kinds of **agricultural shows** take place annually in towns and villages on the Coast to Coast trail. These shows are an integral and traditional part of life all over rural England and particularly in the Lake District. Too numerous to list here, details of all the shows can be found by looking at the websites of the places concerned. For further information about events in the southern Lake District see 🖳 http://applications.southlakeland.gov.uk/eventsearch.

Being aware of the bigger festivals is also useful when planning your walk as there's a good chance that available accommodation will be all the more in demand should you turn up on a busy weekend. For example early June's Appleby Horse Fair (🖳 www.applebyfair.org) can drain accommodation opportunities in Kirkby Stephen and Orton.

**January to March**
Grasmere hosts an annual Art and Book Festival (🖳 www.wordsworth.org.uk; click on What's on) at one of Wordsworth's old houses, Dove Cottage (or at a hotel very nearby). The festival usually takes place in January, is residential and consists of lectures, surgeries and workshops.

**April to June**
The villages of Swaledale, which include Keld, Muker, Thwaite, Gunnerside and Reeth, hold an annual music festival (Swaledale Festival); this usually takes place at the end of May to early June. The festival has an annual theme (eg stringed instruments), and in addition to the music there are all kinds of other activities from art exhibitions and guided walking trails to craft workshops; information can be found and tickets bought on the dedicated website 🖳 www.swaledale-festival.org.uk. Another event in June is the Swaledale Marathon (🖳 www.swaledaleoutdoorclub.org.uk; click on Swaledale Marathon) so accommodation in the area can dry up.

Robin Hood's Bay hosts a folk music weekend (🖳 www.robin-hoods-bay.co.uk – click on What's on), usually on the first or second weekend of June.

**July to September**
Richmond Live (🖳 www.richmondlive.org) is a pop music festival usually held over one weekend in late July or early August. Some readers have advised that if you want a quiet night's sleep, Richmond can be well worth avoiding at this time.

The Grasmere Lakeland Sports and Show (🖳 www.grasmeresports.com) has taken place every year since 1868, except during World Wars I and II. Held on August Bank Holiday Sunday, sports featured include wrestling, tug-of-war, hound-trailing and the more recent addition of mountain biking.

After the walk many people will head for Whitby to catch a train or bus. If you're there at the end of August consider staying on for Whitby Folk Week (🖳 www.whitbyfolk.co.uk) when the pubs and other venues are abuzz with fiddles and bodhrans.

**October to December**
If you happen to be in Robin Hood's Bay in winter don't miss the Victorian weekend (🖳 www.robin-hoods-bay.co.uk – click on What's on) at the beginning of December, where the town turns out in 19th-century costume. It's all good fun, with quizzes, recitals, concerts and demonstrations, and it's all in aid of charity too.

## Practical information for the walker

### ROUTE FINDING

The presence of signposts and waymarking varies along the path. Once over the Pennines and into Yorkshire the trail becomes fairly well signposted and finding the way shouldn't be a problem. In the Lakes, on the other hand, there are few Coast to Coast signposts and you'll have to rely on the descriptions in this book to find the way. For much of the time the path is well-trodden and obvious, though of course there are situations where there are a number of paths to choose from, and other occasions where the ground is so boggy no clear path is visible at all. Misty conditions are another problem, particularly in the Lake District. In these instances a compass or GPS will help you move in the right direction or follow the correct path. (See the box on pp91-3 for more details.)

In the Lakes in particular there are a number of high-level alternatives to the main route, and on a clear day fit trekkers should consider taking them. Though obviously more tiring, the rewards in terms of the views and sense of achievement are all worthwhile.

### GPS

*I never carried a compass, preferring to rely on a good sense of direction... I never bothered to understand how a compass works or what it is supposed to do ... To me a compass is a gadget, and I don't get on well with gadgets of any sort.*
**Alfred Wainwright**

While Wainwright's acolytes may scoff, other walkers will accept GPS technology as an inexpensive, well-established if non-essential, navigational aid. To cut a long story short, within a minute of being turned on and with a clear view of the sky, **GPS receivers** will establish your position as well as elevation in a variety of formats, including the British OS grid system, anywhere on earth to an accuracy of within a few metres. These days, most **smartphones** have a GPS receiver built in and mapping software available to run on it (see p46).

One thing must be understood however: **treating GPS as a replacement for maps, a compass and common sense is a big mistake**. Every electronic device is susceptible to battery failure or some electronic malfunction that might leave you in the dark. GPS is primarily a navigational aid or backup to conventional route finding and, in almost all cases, is best used in conjunction with a paper map. At its most basic level a GPS stops you exacerbating navigational errors and saves you time in correcting them. Newer units may come with some inbuilt mapping, but while it's possible to buy **digital mapping** (see box p46) to import into a regular GPS unit with sufficient storage capacity, it might be considered as practical as having internet on a mobile phone – you still end up scrolling and zooming across a tiny screen.

### Using GPS with this book – tracklog and waypoints

The easiest way to avoid getting lost is to install a **tracklog** of the route on either a GPS unit or a smartphone running GPS. A tracklog is a continuous line like a path that appears on your GPS screen; all you have to do is keep on that line. If you lose it on the screen you can zoom out until it reappears and walk towards it. To download the GPS tracklog on which this sixth edition's maps are based, see the Trailblazer website – 🖥 www.trailblazer-guides.com.

Where a tracklog is a continuous line, **waypoints** are single points like cairns. This book identifies key waypoints on the route maps. It's anticipated you won't tramp along day after day, ticking off the book's waypoints, transfixed by the screen on your GPS or smartphone; the route description and maps are more than adequate most of the time. Only when you're unsure of your position or which way to go might you feel the need to even turn on the unit for a quick affirmation. You'll find more waypoints across bleak mountain and moorland sections where the walk can degenerate into a prolonged stumble through thick mist.

The book's waypoints correlate to the list on pp258-63 which gives the OS grid reference and a description. You can either simply read off the nearest presumed waypoint from the list as and when the need arises and work out where you are in relation to it or, less confusingly, key it in as a new point and press

---

❏ **Just how long is Wainwright's Coast to Coast path?**

The figure of **191$^1$/$_2$ miles** has been bandied around for years as this is close to the 190 miles which Wainwright's original edition quoted back in 1972. Disregarding the fact that these days his exact route is no longer followed, for this guidebook each stage was logged using a suitably calibrated GPS odometer and after editing the final tally showed the actual distance walked to be around **189$^1$/$_2$ miles** (305km) via the most used routes.

This, of course, doesn't account for walking to the pub or B&Bs off the track, going the wrong way and even, as some Pythagorians like to consider, the fact that walking up and down hills technically covers more ground than if the terrain was flat.

The precise total length of Wainwright's Coast to Coast (and doubtless many other long-distance paths) is not of great import in the big picture as you'll walk the walk, but a day's true distance is something worth knowing when psyching yourself up for a long stage. Other guides, maps and local signposts will show differing distances, often constrained to fit the immutable figure estimated by Alfred Wainwright. This is the first Coast to Coast path guidebook to use satellite technology to closely estimate the actual distance walked.

'go to'. As there will probably be only a handful of times you need to do this, for most that will suffice but, with less margin for keystroke error, you can download the complete list as a GPS-readable .gpx file of grid references (but with no descriptions) from 🖳 www.trailblazer-guides.com

In the Lakes there's little in the way of Coast to Coast signposting but once over the Pennines and into Yorkshire the trail is well signposted.

Using GPS with this book, be it a track-log, all the waypoints or just the key way-points, is *an option*. Without them you could find yourself staggering around a mist-clad moor, or ambling confidently down the wrong path. With GPS, when the need arises, you can reliably establish your position in relation to the path, or quickly find out how far and in what direction it is to a known point on the trail.

It's worth repeating that 98% of people who've ever walked the Coast to Coast did so without GPS so there's no need to rush out and buy one – or a new GPS-enabled smartphone. Your spending priorities ought to be on good waterproofs and above all, footwear. However, correctly using this book's GPS data could get you back on track and dozing in front of the pub fire-place or tucked up in bed all the sooner.

For more on how not to lose your way, see pp91-3.

In 2012 the Wainwright Society announced agreements had been made to mark fingerposts at public road crossings with a special C2C logo featuring Wainwright's 'AW' monogram. By late 2013 not many were yet in evidence.

## ACCOMMODATION

From one coast to the other, businesses and families alike today owe a lot to Wainwright's inspired concept. Smaller towns and villages as well as isolated farms far from the reliable Lakeland honeypots have come to rely on accom-modating and feeding the seasonal flow of coastbound walkers.

The route guide (Part 4) lists a fairly comprehensive selection of places to stay along the trail. The three main options are: camping, staying in hostels/ bunkhouses, or using B&Bs/pubs/hotels. Few people stick to just one of these the whole way, preferring, for example, to camp most of the time but spend every third night in a hostel, or perhaps take a hostel where possible but splash out on a B&B or hotel every once in a while.

The table on pp36-7 provides a snapshot of what type of accommodation and services are available in each of the towns and villages, while the tables on pp34-5 provide some suggested itineraries. The following is a brief introduction as to what to expect from each type of accommodation.

## Camping

It's possible to camp all along the Coast to Coast path, though few people do so every night. You're almost bound to get at least one night where the rain falls relentlessly, sapping morale; it's then that most campers opt to spend the next night drying out in a hostel or B&B somewhere. There are, however, many advantages with camping. It's more economical, for a start, with most campsites charging somewhere between £4 and £8. Best of all there's **rarely any need to book**, except possibly in the very high season, and even then you'd be highly unlucky not to find somewhere, even if it means camping discreetly in the woods. The campsites vary and you get what you pay for: some are just pub gardens or a farmer's spare field with basic toilet/shower facilities; others are full-blown caravan sites with security access codes and sparkling ablutions blocks and a few spaces put aside for tents. Showers are usually available, occasionally for a fee, though more often than not for free. Note that most youth hostels on the Coast to Coast path no longer accept campers (Borrowdale does). Note, too, that some of the bigger towns such as Richmond and Grasmere do not have recognised campsites, with the nearest being at least three miles away.

**Wild camping** (ie camping not in a regular campsite; see p79) is also possible along the route but please don't do so in a field without first gaining permission from the landowner. Some good wild camping locations include the level areas surrounding mountain lakes such as Innominate Tarn (on the high route to Borrowdale), Grisedale Tarn (out of Grasmere) and Angle Tarn (two miles from Patterdale). Further east old mine ruins, such as those on the high route to Reeth, provide good shelter and 'cover' as well as patches of level grass and nearby running water. Beyond there, wild camping might be misconstrued as 'vagrancy' so woodland or plantations will be your best bet.

Remember that camping, wild or 'tame', is not an easy option, especially for a solo walker. Walked continuously, the route is wearying enough without carrying the means to sleep and cook with you. Should you decide to camp at campsites, consider employing one of the baggage-carrying companies mentioned on pp28-9, though this does mean the loss of spontaneity which is the whole point of camping, and of course they can't deliver to Angle Tarn!

## Bunkhouses and camping barns

A bunkhouse and a camping barn are different things. In most cases a **camping barn** is pretty much what it sounds like: an old barn in the corner of a farmer's field with a couple of wooden benches to sleep on; sleeping bags and usually sleeping mats are thus necessary, though bedding is provided in many of the YHA-franchised camping barns. A camping barn is probably the nearest non-campers will get to sleeping outside, while at the same time providing shelter from the elements. Note also that camping barns are sometimes booked for sole occupancy and thus it is essential to call in advance to check availability.

**Bunkhouses** can be much more agreeable places, with fluffed-up bedding, bathrooms you'd be happy to show to your parents and even kitchen and lounge areas. The description 'bunkhouse' is often used in place of 'small hostel' or 'independent hostel' to distinguish a private enterprise from lodgings under the

YHA banner (see below) which can sometimes be huge properties with scores of beds, hyperactive school groups and, depending on your age, unhappy memories of a long-gone institutional past.

## Hostels

Youth hostels are plentiful along the Coast to Coast path and if you haven't visited one recently – and thus the words 'youth' and 'hostel' still conjure up images of limited opening hours, crowded dorms, lousy food and staff who really wish you'd move on – we advise you to take a second look. Hostels, whether owned by the Youth Hostel Association (YHA) or independent, offer some of the best-located and most interesting accommodation along the path. In fact there are now as many independent hostels as YHA ones along the Coast to Coast path, several having passed from YHA into private ownership in recent years as the YHA reviews its portfolio of properties.

### ❑ Should you book your accommodation in advance?

With the trend in recession-beating 'staycations' and the general rise in the popularity of walking holidays, the Coast to Coast path could be entering something of a boom time and some have predicted that accommodation may struggle to cope. In the high season of **June to August**, unless camping, it's essential you have your night's accommodation secured. Nothing is more deflating than arriving at the end of a long day only to find that you've then got to walk another few miles or even take a detour off the route, because everywhere is booked up.

How soon you start booking is up to you but doing so the night before is no longer dependable. If you start booking **up to six months** in advance you'll have a good chance of getting precisely the accommodation you want. Booking so early does leave you vulnerable to changing circumstances of course, but with enough notice it's likely your deposit will be returned as they can easily fill your bed; ask on booking.

Outside the high season and away from weekends, as long as you're **flexible** and willing to take what's offered, you might get away with booking just a couple of weeks or even just days in advance. Having said that, some establishments we've spoken to told us that May and September were in fact their busiest months, early September being dubbed 'Saga week' when older hikers return to the hills once the schools have re-absorbed all the kids. However, **weekends** are busy everywhere, especially in **the Lakes** and in places like Keld or Blakey Moor where conveniently close accommodation is limited.

If you've left it too late and can only get accommodation for parts of the walk but are set on a certain period, **consider camping** to fill in the gaps. It's not to everyone's taste and it helps if you already own the gear, but it can save you money which you can lavish on yourself later without guilt and, if using a baggage service, they can cart the gear from door to door at no extra effort to yourself.

If you're planning on staying in hostels the same applies, though do be careful when travelling out of high season as many **hostels** close during the week and shut altogether from around November to February. Once again, it's well worth booking in advance. Campers, whatever time of year, should always be able to find somewhere to pitch their tent, though ringing in advance can't hurt and will at least confirm that the campsite is still open.

Despite the name, anyone of any age can join the YHA. This can be done at any hostel, or by contacting the **Youth Hostels Association of England and Wales** (☎ 01629 592700 or 0800 0191 700, 🖳 www.yha.org.uk). The cost of a year's membership is £20 for an adult (£15 if you pay by Direct Debit), £10/5 for anyone under 26. Having secured your membership, youth hostels are easy to book, either online or by phone through the contact details above. Since non-members have to pay £3 more per night it is worth joining if you expect to stay in a YHA hostel for more than six nights in a year. You'll also get free wi-fi.

Hostels come equipped with a whole range of facilities, from drying rooms to washing machines, televisions to pool tables and fully equipped kitchens. Some have a shop selling a selection of groceries, snacks and souvenirs and may even have internet access. Many offer breakfast and/or dinner (of varying quality), some offer a packed lunch, and several have a licence to sell alcohol. They are also great places to meet fellow walkers, swap stories and compare blisters.

❑ **Information for foreign visitors**

● **Currency** The British pound (£) comes in notes of £100, £50, £20, £10 and £5, and coins of £2 and £1. The pound is divided into 100 pence (usually referred to as 'p', pronounced 'pee') which come in silver coins of 50p, 20p 10p and 5p and copper coins of 2p and 1p.

● **Rates of exchange** Up-to-date exchange rates can be found at 🖳 www.xe.com/ucc.

● **Business hours** Most **shops** and main **post offices** are open at least from Monday to Friday 9am-5pm and Saturday 9am-12.30pm. Many choose longer hours and some open on Sundays as well. However, some also close early one day a week, often Wednesday or Thursday. **Banks** are usually open 10am-4pm Monday to Friday.

    **Pub** opening hours have become more flexible – up to 24 hours a day seven days a week – so each pub may have different times. However, most pubs on the Coast to Coast route continue to follow the traditional 11am to 11pm and some still close in the afternoon.

● **National (Bank) holidays** Most businesses are shut on 1 January, Good Friday (March/April), Easter Monday (March/April), the first and last Monday in May, the last Monday in August, 25 December and 26 December.

● **School holidays** School holiday periods in England are generally as follows: a one-week break late October, two weeks around Christmas, a week mid-February, two weeks around Easter, a week in late May and from late July to early September.

● **Documents** If you are a member of a National Trust organisation in your country bring your membership card as you should be entitled to free entry to National Trust properties and sites in the UK.

● **Travel/medical insurance** The European Health Insurance Card (EHIC) entitles EU nationals (on production of the EHIC card) to necessary medical treatment under the UK's National Health Service while on a temporary visit here. However, this is not a substitute for proper medical cover on your travel insurance for unforeseen bills and for getting you home should that be necessary. Also consider cover for loss or theft of personal belongings, especially if you're camping or staying in hostels, as there will be times when you'll have to leave your luggage unattended.

● **Weights and measures** The European Commission is no longer attempting to ban the pint or the mile: so, in Britain, milk can be sold in pints (1 pint = 568ml), as can beer in pubs, though most other liquid including petrol (gasoline) and diesel is sold

Weighed against these advantages is the fact that even though many hostels now have rooms with two to four beds you may have to share your night with a heavy snorer. A couple of the hostels also suffer from uncomfortably small dorms when they're full. Some rooms now have en suite facilities but in others you have to share a shower room and in a couple of cases facilities may be limited. Nor is it possible to stay in hostels every night on the trail, for there are some areas where hostels don't exist and when they do they're occasionally at least a mile or two off the path.

If you're travelling out of the main season (particularly between November and February) you may find some hostels are shut to walkers during the week, or completely. Even in high season some are not staffed during the day and walkers may have to wait until 5pm before checking in, though you may be able to access the kitchen and leave luggage in a secure room before 5pm. And finally, the cost of staying in a hostel, once breakfast has been added on, is in many

in litres. Distances on road and path signs will also continue to be given in miles (1 mile = 1.6km) rather than kilometres, and yards (1yd = 0.9m) rather than metres.

The population remains split between those who still use inches (1 inch = 2.5cm), feet (1ft = 0.3m) and yards and those who are happy with millimetres, centimetres and metres; you'll often be told that 'it's only a hundred yards or so' to somewhere, rather than a hundred metres or so.

Most food is sold in metric weights (g and kg) but the imperial weights of pounds (lb: 1lb = 453g) and ounces (oz: 1oz = 28g) are often displayed too. The weather – a frequent topic of conversation – is also an issue: while most forecasts predict temperatures in centigrade (C), many people continue to think in terms of fahrenheit (F; see temperature chart on p14 for conversions).

● **Time** During the winter the whole of Britain is on Greenwich Meantime (GMT). The clocks move one hour forward on the last Sunday in March, remaining on British Summer Time (BST) until the last Sunday in October.

● **Smoking** Smoking in enclosed public places is banned. The ban relates not only to pubs and restaurants, but also to B&Bs, hostels and hotels. These latter have the right to designate one or more bedrooms where the occupants can smoke, but the ban is in force in all enclosed areas open to the public – even in a private home such as a B&B. Should you be foolhardy enough to light up in a no-smoking area, which includes pretty well any indoor public place, you could be fined £50, but it's the owners of the premises who suffer most if they fail to stop you, with a potential fine of £2500.

● **Telephones** The international access code for Britain is +44, followed by the area code minus the first 0, and then the number you require. To call a number with the same area code as the landline phone you are calling from you can omit the area code. It's cheaper to phone at weekends and after 6pm and before 8am on weekdays. **Mobile phone reception** is better than you think. Even in the Lakes you're often actually quite close to a town and on high ground where a weak signal can often be picked up. It's said the Vodaphone network works best across rural northern England followed by O2 or EE.

● **Internet access** See p27.

● **Emergency services** For police, ambulance, fire and mountain rescue dial ☎ 999 (or the EU standard number ☎ 112).

instances not that much cheaper (from £17-27 for YHA members) than staying in a B&B, especially if you're walking with someone.

## Bed and breakfast

Bed and Breakfasts (B&Bs) are a great British institution and many of those along the Coast to Coast are absolutely charming, with buildings often three or four hundred years old. Older owners often treat you as surrogates for their long-departed offspring and enjoy nothing more than looking after you.

As the name suggests, they provide you with a bed in a private room, and breakfast – a hearty, British-style cooked one unless you specify otherwise beforehand – though they range in style enormously. Most B&Bs have en suite rooms and/or rooms with either private or shared facilities. En suite facilities often mean a shower squeezed into a room but with private/shared facilities there may be a bath, which is what most walkers prefer at the end of a long day, and the bathroom is never more than a few feet away. These rooms usually contain either a double bed (known as a double room), or two single beds (known as a twin room). Family rooms are for three or more people. Solo trekkers should take note: single rooms are not so easy to find so you'll often end up occupying a double room, for which you'll have to pay a single occupancy supplement (see below).

**Smoking** is banned in all enclosed places open to the public in England but places to stay are able to designate rooms for smokers, so do check this if it's important to you.

Some B&Bs provide an **evening meal**; if not, there's often a pub or sometimes a restaurant nearby or, if it's far, the owner may give you a lift to and from the nearest place with food.

**B&B rates and booking** B&Bs in this guide start at around £30 per person for the most basic accommodation to over £40 for the most luxurious en suite places in a popular tourist haunt like Grasmere. Most charge around £30-35 per person. A typical **single occupancy supplement** is between £10 and £20. An evening meal (usually around £10-15) is sometimes provided, but you may need to book in advance. Packed lunches are often available too for around £5.

Some B&Bs have their own website and offer online/email booking but for the majority you will need to phone. Most places ask for a **deposit** (about 50%) which is generally non-refundable if you cancel at short notice. Some places may charge 100% if the booking is for one night only. Always let the owner know as soon as possible if you have to cancel your booking so they can offer the bed to someone else.

Larger places take credit or debit cards. Most smaller B&Bs accept only cheques by post or payments by bank transfer for the deposit; the balance can be settled with cash or a cheque.

## Guesthouses, hotels, pubs and inns

A guesthouse offers bed and breakfast but should have a better class of décor and more facilities such as offering evening meals and a lounge for guests. However, they are unlikely to offer room service, unlike a hotel.

**Pubs and inns** may also offer bed and breakfast accommodation and tariffs are no more than in a regular B&B. However, you need to be prepared for a noisier environment, especially if your room is above the bar.

**Hotels** do usually cost more, however, and some might be a little displeased by a bunch of muddy trekkers turning up. Most places on the walk, particularly in the quieter towns and villages, are used to seeing trekkers, make a good living from them and welcome them warmly. Prices in hotels and pubs start at around £35 per person.

## FOOD AND DRINK

### Breakfast

Stay in a B&B/guesthouse/hotel and you'll be filled to the gills each morning with a cooked English breakfast. This can consist of a bowl of cereal followed by a plateful of eggs, bacon, sausages, mushrooms, tomatoes, and possibly baked beans or black pudding, with toast and butter, and all washed down with coffee, tea and/or juice. Enormously satisfying the first time you try it, by the fourth or fifth morning you may start to prefer the lighter continental breakfast or porridge, which most establishments now offer.

Alternatively, and especially if you're planning an early start, you might like to request a packed lunch instead of this filling breakfast and just have a cup of coffee before you leave.

The youth hostels mentioned in this guide offer breakfast; usually it's a good meal but they charge an additional £5-6.

### Lunch

Your B&B host or youth hostel can usually provide a packed lunch at an additional cost, though of course there's nothing to stop you preparing your own. There are some fantastic locally made cheeses and pickles that can be picked up along the way, as well as some wonderful bakers still making bread in the traditional manner (the bakeries in Kirkby Stephen, see p164, and Reeth, see p190, spring to mind). Alternatively, stop in a pub.

see p164 ... see p190

---

#### ❏ Is a full English breakfast healthy?

You've paid for the bed, it's understandable you want the breakfast too, and enough breakfast to fuel you down the trail all the way to lunch. But is the traditional 'FEB' the way to go? Most probably not which is why you begin to gag at the very idea after a few days. The former national dish never recovered from the muesli revolution of the 1970s and only truck drivers, whose legendary obesity has them blacklisted by the WHO, will tolerate such a dreadful diet on a daily basis.

At the beginning of the day it's complex carbohydrates you want, not a stomach full of fat and salt. Slow-release carbs keep you going till lunchtime, don't put your gall bladder on action stations and contain negligible fat. Ask for a big bowl of **porridge**, ideally cooked with milk and a little salt and if you do go fried, keep off offal-packed sausages, hope the bacon and tomatoes are grilled not fried, and throw fried bread and black pudding back into the kitchen. (Black pudding is a sausage of oats soaked in blood, in case you didn't know, and a constituent of a 'Full *Yorkshire* breakfast').

Remember, too, to plan ahead: at least four of the stages in this book are devoid of eateries or shops so read ahead about the next day's walk to make sure you never go hungry.

## Cream teas
Never miss a chance to avail yourself of the treats on offer in the tearooms and farmhouses of Cumbria and Yorkshire. Nothing relaxes and revives like a decent pot of tea, and the opportunity to accompany it with a scone served with jam and cream, or a cake or two, is one that should not be passed up.

## Evening meals
If your B&B doesn't do an evening meal you may find that in many villages, the pub is the only place to eat out. **Pubs** are as much a feature of this walk as moorland, churches and views, and in some cases the pub is a tourist attraction as much as the finest ruined abbey. Most of them have become highly attuned to the needs of walkers and offer both lunch and evening meals (with often a few regional dishes and usually a couple of vegetarian options), some locally brewed beers, a garden to relax in on hot days and a roaring fire to huddle around on cold ones. The standard of the food varies widely, though portions are usually large, which is often just about all walkers care about at the end of a long day.

That other great British culinary tradition and a favourite of Wainwright's in the bigger towns is the **fish 'n' chip shop** which will deep fry your dinner and then slather it in a layer of mushy peas and brown sauce. Larger towns also have Chinese and Indian **takeaways**; a welcome change from too much pub food and usually the only places still serving food late in the evenings, staying open until at least 11pm.

## Catering for yourself
The list of village shops (often combined with a post office) along the route grows sadly shorter with each edition but those that manage to remain in busi-

ness have a pretty good selection of foods and your diet will depend on what you can find there. A couple of these small stores sell camping gas stove cartridges (which you can also pick up in the bigger towns such as Grasmere, Kirkby Stephen and Richmond). Part 4 goes into greater detail about what can be found where.

The Patterdale Village Store & Post Office is the perfect example of a well run business that serves not only the needs of the community but those of serious walkers and campers. You'll find everything from a pork rib sandwich to a new pair of hiking socks here.

## Drinking water
There may be plenty of ways of perishing on the Coast to Coast trail but thirst won't be one of them. Be careful, though, for on a hot day in some of the remoter parts of the Lake District after a steep climb or two you'll quickly dehydrate, which is at best highly unpleasant. Always carry some

water with you and in hot weather aim to drink **three or four litres** per day, supplemented by rehydration tablets such as Nuun.

Out of the hills, don't be tempted by the water in the streams you come across in lowland areas where the chemicals from the pesticides and fertilisers used on the farms may become concentrated. It's a lot safer to fill up from taps or high mountain pools and becks. Remember, what makes you ill can't be seen by the naked eye so filling up from a peat-stained tarn or fellside beck will probably be much less polluted than a dribbling brook in somewhere like the intensively farmed Vale of Mowbray.

## MONEY

**Banks** are very few and far between on the Coast to Coast path. There's one in Shap open just a few hours a week, a couple in Kirkby Stephen, and Richmond has branches of all the major banks, but apart from in these places there's nothing. **Post offices**, however, provide a very useful service. You can get cash (by debit card) for free at any post office counter if you bank with most banks or building societies. For a full list see 💻 www.postoffice.co.uk/branch-banking-services. Some post offices also play host to the village **cashpoint/ATM**. Usually you can withdraw cash for free but some may still be privately operated and charge £1.25-1.75 per withdrawal.

Another way of getting cash is to use the **cashback** system: find a store that will accept a debit card and ask them to advance cash against the card. A number of the local village stores as well as some pubs will do this, though you'll usually have to spend a minimum of £5 with them first. It pays to ask.

As not all local stores, pubs or B&Bs accept credit/debit cards, it's essential to carry plenty of cash (reckon on £200 per person). A **chequebook** could prove useful as a back-up.

## INTERNET ACCESS

Most places to stay offer **wi-fi** free to visitors, or in the case of some hotels, for a small fee. Some B&Bs and hotels provide an internet-enabled **computer** in the guest lounge free of charge while the bigger youth hostels do so for around £4 an hour. Otherwise, where present and open, the local **library** is the place to find internet access.

## OTHER SERVICES

Most small villages have a **post office** that doubles as the local store and bank (see Money, above), and nearby you'll usually find a **phone box**, though be warned, to combat vandalism some only accept cards, taking a £1 connection fee which is charged whether you get an answer or not. Otherwise 60p is the minimum fee to make a cash call; no change is given.

There are **outdoor equipment shops** and **pharmacies** in the larger towns of Grasmere, Kirkby Stephen and Richmond and **tourist information centres** at Kirkby Stephen, Ullswater (near Patterdale), Reeth and Richmond.

## WALKING COMPANIES

It's possible to turn up with your boots and backpack at St Bees and just start walking without planning much other than your accommodation (about which, see the box on p21). The following companies, however, are in the business of making your holiday as stress-free and enjoyable as possible.

### Baggage carriers

There are several baggage-carrying companies serving the Coast to Coast route. With all these services you can usually book up to around 8pm the previous evening, though it can be cheaper if you book in advance. Most stipulate a maximum weight per bag of around 20kg. The cost is around £7.25-8 to take your bag to your next destination. All baggage forwarders will give an estimated latest time by which you can expect your bags to be delivered, usually 4.30pm. These companies also offer **self-guided holidays** (see opposite), long-term car parking and passenger bus services using their baggage vans along the Coast to Coast route.

These last two services have two important consequences for trekkers. Firstly, it means that, should you want to skip a walking stage, you can ride with your luggage on their **passenger bus service** to the next stage. Secondly, you can use Kirkby Stephen (Coast to Coast Packhorse), Richmond (Sherpa Van) or Kirkby Malham (Brigantes) as your base, getting a lift in their van to St Bees, and another back to their base at the end of the walk back from Robin Hood's Bay. However, note that seating is often limited so you must book well in advance.

You can leave your car at the **secure parking** at their base, which is better than the alternative of leaving it in St Bees and travelling all the way back from the east coast to pick it up again. Or you can buy a return train ticket from your home to one place which may be cheaper and quicker than having to buy one ticket to St Bees, and another from Robin Hood's Bay.

● **Sherpa Van** (baggage line ☎ 01748 826917, 🖳 www.sherpavan.com, also see Sherpa Expeditions on p30 & p31), based at 29 The Green, Richmond, is a national organisation that runs a baggage-delivery service from April to mid-October for many of Britain's other walking and cycling trails as well as the Coast to Coast. They charge from £7.75 a bag and will transfer (or effectively, store) your excess baggage left at St Bees and deliver it to Robin Hood's Bay for £25.

They also operate two daily **passenger bus services**: in the mornings between Richmond (leaving at 7.30am), Kirkby Stephen and St Bees (arriving 10am); and in the afternoon from Robin Hoods Bay (leaving at 4pm) to Richmond (arriving at 5.45pm). They have secure **parking** in Richmond (£3 per day) and can also arrange parking in St Bees and Kirkby Stephen.

● **Coast to Coast Packhorse** (☎ 017683 71777, 🖳 www.c2cpackhorse.co.uk; see also p30; early Apr-Sep) based near Kirkby Stephen receives regular recommendations from our readers and also shifts the baggage for many other Coast to Coast operators. Having paid for baggage transfers – from £7.25 per stage – Packhorse customers are welcome to ride on the minibus with their bags, at no extra cost, should the need arise. Non-baggage customers are also welcome to hop on and off as the Packhorse passes through, paying only the appropriate fee for the distance on this **daily westbound bus service** along the route.

One van departs Kirkby Stephen at 8.30am, arriving at St Bees around 10.15am, before travelling via the pick-up points back to Kirkby Stephen. A second bus also leaves Kirkby Stephen at 8.30am, stopping at the drop-off points before reaching Robin Hood's Bay at 3.30pm, departing at 4pm for the direct trip back to Kirkby Stephen, arriving around 6.15pm. In other words, the buses stop at the various drop-off points only when travelling from west to east. The cost of travelling directly from Kirkby Stephen to St Bees or Robin Hood's Bay to Kirkby Stephen is £27 per person.

They also have a **secure parking** lot in Kirkby Stephen, where you can leave a car for the duration of the walk for £3.67 per day.

● **Brigantes Walking Holidays** (☎ 01756 770402, 🖥 www.brigantesenglish walks.com; see also below; early Apr-Sep) run a family operated baggage courier service with 16 vehicles which support trails across the north of England.

For baggage transfer they charge £7.50 per bag per stage. If there's room in the van you can also travel with your baggage to the next stage. At the end of your walk, they can take you by minibus to an agreed railway/bus terminal, or to their free car park, in Kirkby Malham.

### Self-guided holidays

Self-guided means that the company will organise accommodation, baggage transfer (some contracting out the work to other companies), transport to and from the walk and various maps and advice, but leave you on your own to actually walk the path and cover lunch and dinner. In addition to these, don't forget the specialist Coast to Coast websites (see box p48) that can also book accommodation and provide details of the walk.

● **Absolute Escapes** (☎ 0131 240 1210, 🖥 www.absoluteescapes.com)  This Edinburgh-based company offers the full walk as well as shorter walks covering half the route.

● **Alpine Exploratory** (☎ 01729 823197, 🖥 www.alpineexploratory.com)  A small and flexible Settle-based company. Offers basic trail (14 days) but can tailor-make walks and offers both Coast to Coast West (6 days) and Coast to Coast East (8 days).

● **AMS Outdoors** (☎ 0845 680 8246, 🖥 www.ams-outdoors.com) also offers the Coast to Coast walk in full and in two parts.

● **Brigantes Walking Holidays** (☎ 01756 770402, 🖥 www.brigantesenglish walks.com)  Based near Skipton, North Yorkshire, this is primarily a baggage-transfer and accommodation-booking service but they also offer walks west to east and east to west, for 14 days and can tailor make as required. An innovative budget option involves a trailer tent/camping package or caravan for two people, moved across the country as you walk; further details on the website.

● **British and Irish Walks** (☎ 01242 254353, 🖥 www.britishandirishwalks .com)  Based in Cheltenham, Gloucestershire. This walks specialist offers the complete trail in 14-18 days, west to east.

● **Coast to Coast Packhorse** (☎ 017683 71777, 🖳 www.c2cpackhorse.co.uk)
Coast to Coast specialist Packhorse offers a tailor-made approach to scheduling
your trip depending on your own preferences. Any number of nights can be
accommodated, ranging from short sections to full trips and at whatever pace
suits you.

● **Contours Walking Holidays** (☎ 01629 821900, 🖳 www.contours.co.uk)
Based in Wirksworth, Derbyshire, they offer seven itineraries covering the Coast
to Coast from the strenuous to the easy over 12 to 18 days. Also offer either western or eastern sections only and can tailor-make walks.

● **Discovery Travel** (☎ 01904 632226, 🖳 www.discoverytravel.co.uk)
Operating from York, they offer a standard 14-day Coast to Coast walk, as well
as the walk from east to west. Can tailor-make walks.

● **Explore Britain** (☎ 01740 650900, 🖳 www.explorebritain.com)  Based in
Ferryhill, north of Richmond, County Durham, Explore Britain lays on treks of
14, 17 or 18 days along the entire path, as well as dividing the walk into two,
with a seven-day walk from St Bees to Kirkby Stephen, and an eight-day walk
from Kirkby Stephen to Robin Hood's Bay. Offer walks in both directions and
can tailor-make walks.

● **Footpath Holidays** (☎ 01985 840049, 🖳 www.footpath-holidays.com)
Offers inn-to-inn walks for the whole of the path or in part.

● **Freedom Walking Holidays** (☎ 07733 885390, 🖳 www.freedomwalking
holidays.co.uk) Based in Goring-on-Thames, Berkshire. Offer 5-14 nights along
part or the whole trail, west to east. Can tailor-make walks.

● **Load Off Your Back** (🖳 www.loadoffyourback.co.uk)  Part of Ramblers
Worldwide Holidays. Offers four itineraries from 6-7 days walking along half
the path and 14-17 days for the complete path, west to east.

● **Macs Adventure** (☎ 0141 530 8886, 🖳 www.macsadventure.com)   A
Glasgow-based company that offers the full trail in 12-16 days, and also two
parts, the western section and the eastern section in 6-8 days each. The walks are
west to east and can be tailor-made.

● **Mickledore** (☎ 017687 72335, 🖳 www.mickledore.co.uk)  Offers the complete trail in 12-17 days, and both halves in 5-9 days. Walks are west to east and
can be tailor-made.

● **Northwestwalks** (☎ 01257 424889, 🖳 www.northwestwalks.co.uk)  A family run business, Wigan-based Northwestwalks has an excellent reputation and
organises 7- to 11-day walks along half of the path, or 12-20 days for the complete trail. Walks are west to east and can be tailor-made.

● **Peak Outdoor Training** (☎ 01663 743278, 🖳  www.peakoutdoortraining.co
.uk)  Offers self-guided walks along the whole path and can tailor make as
required.

● **Sherpa Expeditions** (☎ 020 8577 2717, 🖳 www.sherpa-walking-holidays.co
.uk)  Sherpa offers itineraries of 8 days for half the walk and 15 or 18 days for
the full walk, starting on any day you choose (Apr-Oct). They can extend the 15
day itinerary if required.

● **The Walking Holiday Company** (☎ 01600-713008; 🖳 www.thewalkingholi daycompany.co.uk; Monmouth) Offers from 6 to 19 nights and everything in between. Will tailor make itineraries to suits all needs.

● **Wandering Aengus Treks** (☎ 016974 78443, 🖳 www.watreks.com) Based in Fellside, Cumbria. Offer easy to book 'off the peg' holidays on the complete trail in 12-17 days, or in two sections of 5-7 days for the western part and 7-9 days for the eastern part. Also offer tailor-made walks of any duration east to west.

### Group/guided walking tours

If you don't trust your navigational skills or simply prefer the company of other walkers as well as an experienced guide, the following companies will be of interest. Packages nearly always include all meals, accommodation, transport arrangements, minibus back-up and baggage transfer.

Look very carefully at each company's website before booking as each has its own speciality and it's important to choose one that's suitable for you.

● **Alpine Exploratory** (see p29) Offers private guided trips.

● **Cumbria Tourist Guides** (☎ 01228 562096 or 07557 915855, 🖳 www.cum briatouristguides.org) Has fully qualified Blue Badge Guides who lead walks along the path. Can arrange a personalised itinerary for individuals travelling on their own or groups of any size.

● **Footpath Holidays** (see opposite) Runs guided walking tours along the trail in three 4- to 6-day sections from individual bases (one in the Lake District, one in the Yorkshire Dales, and one in the North York Moors) so avoiding the hassle of daily packing. Guests can book one section or all three to complete the whole trail. Can tailor-make walks if required.

● **HF Holidays** HF Holidays (☎ 020 8732 1250, 🖳 www.hfholidays.co.uk) A reliable and frequently recommended Hertfordshire and Cumbria-based company that runs 15-day Coast to Coast treks.

● **Northwestwalks** (see opposite) operate eight 15-day guided holidays, and one 19-day guided holiday a year. Also operate guided holidays along half the route. Also operate tailor-made guided holidays for private groups.

● **Peak Outdoor Training** (see opposite) Offers the complete path or can tailor-make a walking holiday to suit.

● **Ramblers Countrywide Holidays** (☎ 01707 386800, 🖳 www.ramblerscoun trywide.co.uk) This walking specialist offers the western part of the Coast to Coast from St Bees to Kirkby Stephen (7 days) and the eastern part from Kirkby Stephen to Robin Hood's Bay (8 days), as well as packages to Grasmere and the Lakes and a Highlights of Wainwright walk.

● **Sherpa Expeditions** (see opposite) Runs five 15-day Coast to Coast treks a year.

## WALKING WITH A DOG                                   (see also p257)

The Coast to Coast is a dog-friendly path, though it's extremely important that dog owners behave in a responsible manner. Dogs should always be kept on leads while on the footpath to avoid disturbing wildlife, livestock and other walkers. Dog excrement should be cleaned up and not left to decorate the boots of others; take a pooper scooper or plastic bag if you're walking with a dog.

It's particularly important to **keep your dog on a lead** when crossing fields with livestock in them, especially around calving or lambing time which can be as early as February or as late as the end of May. Most farmers would prefer it if you did not bring your dog at all at this time.

In addition, in certain areas on the Coast to Coast trail (particularly around Sunbiggin Tarn, east of Shap) there are notices ordering owners to keep their dogs on a lead to protect endangered ground-nesting birds between March and July; dogs can frighten them off and possibly cause them to desert their nests.

Remember when planning and booking your accommodation that you'll need to check if your dog will be welcome. Youth hostels do not permit them unless they're for assistance. Places that accept dogs in the accommodation are identified in the route guide by the symbol 🐾 : some charge an extra £5-10 for a dog.

Note, too, that your dog needs to be extremely fit to complete the Coast to Coast path. You may not believe it when you watch it haring around the fields, but they do have a finite amount of energy (the hyperactive collies of some walkers we met finally went lame around Osmotherley), so make sure your dog is up to the task of walking for 10-20 miles a day.

For general information about long-distance walking with a dog see p257.

# Budgeting

England is not a cheap place to go travelling and, while the north may be one of the less expensive regions, the towns and villages in the Lakes especially can get all the business they can handle and charge accordingly. You may think before you set out that you're going to keep your budget to a minimum by camping every night and cooking your own food, but it's a rare trekker who sticks to this. Besides, the B&Bs and pubs on the route are amongst the Coast to Coast's major attractions and it would be a pity not to sample their hospitality from time to time.

If the only expenses of this walk were accommodation and food, budgeting would be a piece of cake. Unfortunately, in addition to these there are all the little **extras** that push up the cost of your trip: for example beer, cream teas, internet use, buses or taxis, baggage carriers, laundry, souvenirs. It's surprising how much these add up!

## CAMPING

You can survive on less than £15 per person per day if you use the cheapest campsites, don't visit a pub, avoid all the museums and tourist attractions in the towns, forage for or cook all your own food from staple ingredients ... and generally have a pretty miserable time of it. Even then, unforeseen expenses will probably nudge your daily budget up. Include the occasional pint, and perhaps a pub meal every now and then, and the figure will be nearer £20 per day.

## HOSTELS, BUNKHOUSES AND CAMPING BARNS

The charge for staying in a **hostel** is £17-27 per night. Whack on another £6 for breakfast and £9-12 for an evening meal, though you can use their self-catering facilities for both, and there's also lunch (packed lunches about £5.50) to consider. This means that, overall, it will cost £30-40 per day, or £45-50 to live in a little more comfort, enjoy the odd beer and go out for the occasional meal.

There are a few basic **camping barns** along the Coast to Coast. They vary in quality and price (expect to pay around £10).

## B&BS, GUESTHOUSES AND HOTELS

B&B prices start at around £30 per person per night but can be up to twice this. Add on the cost of food for lunch and dinner and you should reckon on about £50 minimum per day. Staying in a guesthouse or hotel will cost more. Remember that there is often a supplement of £10-20 for single occupancy of a double or twin room and you may even have to pay the full price of the room.

# Itineraries

Most people tackle the Coast to Coast from west to east, mainly because this allows them to walk 'with the weather at their back' (most of the time the winds blow off the Atlantic from the south-west). It's also usual for people to attempt the walk in one go, though there's much to be said for breaking it up and not crawling into Robin Hood's Bay in an Ibuprofen-induced daze.

Part 4 of this book has been written from west to east, but there is of course nothing to stop you from tackling it in the opposite direction (see p34). To help plan your walk look at the **planning maps** (see opposite inside back cover) and the **table of village/town facilities** (on pp36-7), which gives a run-down on the essential information you'll need regarding accommodation possibilities and services at the time of writing. You could follow one of the **suggested itineraries** (see boxes pp34-5) which are based on preferred type of accommodation and walking speeds. There's also a list of recommended linear **day and weekend walks** on pp38-9 which cover the best of the Coast to Coast path, all of which are well served by public transport or the Packhorse/Sherpa van. The services table is on pp52-5 and **public transport map** on p52.

Once you have an idea of your approach turn to Part 4 for detailed information on accommodation, places to eat and other services in each village and town on the route. Also in Part 4 you will find summaries of the route to accompany the detailed trail maps.

## WHICH DIRECTION?

There are a number of advantages in tackling the path in a west to east direction, not least the fact that the prevailing winds will, more often than not, be behind you. If you are walking alone but wouldn't mind some company now and again you'll find that most of the other Coast to Coast walkers are heading in your direction, too. However, there is also something to be said for leaving the Lake District – many people's favourite part of the British Isles, let alone the path – until the end of the walk.

## SUGGESTED ITINERARIES

The itineraries in the boxes on these pages are based on different accommodation types – camping (not including wild camping which opens your options right out), hostels/bunkhouses/camping barns, and B&Bs – with each one divided into three alternatives depending on your walking speed (relaxed, medium and fast). They are only suggestions so feel free to adapt them. Don't forget to **add your travelling time** before and after the walk.

PLANNING YOUR WALK

### STAYING IN HOSTELS/CAMPING BARNS/BUNKHOUSES

| | Relaxed pace | | Medium pace | | Fast pace | |
|---|---|---|---|---|---|---|
| Night | Place | Approx Distance miles/km | Place | Approx Distance miles/km | Place | Approx Distance miles/km |
| 0 | St Bees | | St Bees | | St Bees | |
| 1 | Sandwith | 3/5 | Sandwith | 3/5 | Ennerdale | 20/32 |
| 2 | Ennerdale Br* | 12/19.5 | Ennerdale | 15.5/25 | Grasmere | 20.5/33 |
| 3 | Black Sail YH | 8.5/13.5 | Borrowdale§ | 10.5/17 | Shap | 23.5/38 |
| 4 | Borrowdale§ | 5.5/9 | Grasmere | 10/16 | K. Stephen | 20.5/33 |
| 5 | Grasmere | 10/16 | Patterdale | 10/16 | Reeth [Dales] | 29/47 |
| 6 | Patterdale | 10/16 | Shap | 15.5/25 | East Applegarth | 10/16 |
| 7 | Shap | 15.5/25 | K. Stephen | 20.5/33 | Osmotherley | 28.5/46 |
| 8 | Orton* | 8/13 | Keld | 13/21 | Blakey Ridge* | 20.5/33 |
| 9 | K. Stephen | 13/21 | Reeth [Grinton] | 12.5/20 | Grosmont* | 13.5/22 |
| 10 | Keld | 13/21 | East Applegarth | 9.5/15 | R. Hood's Bay | 15.5/25 |
| 11 | Reeth [Dales] | 12.5/20 | Danby Wiske* | 16.5/26.5 | | |
| 12 | East Applegarth | 10/16 | Osmotherley | 12/19.5 | | |
| 13 | Danby Wiske* | 16.5/26.5 | Clay Bank Top†* | 11/18 | | |
| 14 | Osmotherley | 12/19.5 | Glaisdale* | 19/30.5 | | |
| 15 | Clay Bank Top†* | 11/18 | R. Hood's Bay | 19/30.5 | | |
| 16 | Blakey Ridge* | 9/14.5 | | | | |
| 17 | Glaisdale* | 10/16 | | | | |
| 18 | Littlebeck* | 7/11.5 | | | | |
| 19 | R. Hood's Bay | 12/19.5 | | | | |

\* *No camping barns, bunkhouses or hostels but alternative accommodation is available*
§ *Borrowdale = Longthwaite, Rosthwaite & Stonethwaite*
† *Clay Bank Top = Urra, Chop Gate & Gt Broughton*

Note: some of the above are seasonal so check in advance

## CAMPING (Note: campsites may be seasonal)

| Night | Relaxed pace Place | Approx Distance miles/km | Medium pace Place | Approx Distance miles/km | Fast pace Place | Approx Distance miles/km |
|---|---|---|---|---|---|---|
| 0 | St Bees | | St Bees | | St Bees | |
| 1 | Cleator* | 11/18 | Ennerdale Br* | 14/22.5 | Ennerdale Br* | 14/22.5 |
| 2 | Ennerdale Br* | 7/11 | Borrowdale§ | 15/24 | Borrowdale§ | 15/24 |
| 3 | Seatoller | 13/21 | Grasmere* | 9/14.5 | Patterdale | 16/26 |
| 4 | Grasmere* | 11/18 | Patterdale | 8.5/13.5 | Shap | 15.5/25 |
| 5 | Patterdale | 7.5/12 | Shap | 15.5/25 | K. Stephen | 20.5/33 |
| 6 | Shap | 15.5/25 | Kirkby Stephen | 20.5/33 | Reeth | 28/45 |
| 7 | Orton | 8/13 | Keld | 13/21 | Colburn | 17/27 |
| 8 | Kirkby Stephen | 13/21 | Reeth | 11/18 | Ingleby Cross | 20/32 |
| 9 | Keld | 13/21 | East Applegarth | 8/13 | Blakey Ridge | 20.5/33 |
| 10 | Reeth | 11/18 | Danby Wiske* | 17.5/28 | Grosmont | 13.5/22 |
| 11 | East Applegarth | 8/13 | Osmotherley | 12/19.5 | R. Hood's Bay | 15.5/25 |
| 12 | Brompton-o-S | 8.5/13.5 | Blakey Ridge | 20.5/33 | | |
| 13 | Danby Wiske* | 8.5/13.5 | Grosmont | 13.5/22 | | |
| 14 | Ingleby Cross | 9/14.5 | R. Hood's Bay | 15.5/25 | | |
| 15 | Clay Bank Top†* | 11.5/17.5 | | | | |
| 16 | Blakey Ridge | 9/14.5 | | | | |
| 17 | Grosmont | 14/22.5 | | | | |
| 18 | High Hawsker | 10/16 | | | | |
| 19 | R. Hood's Bay | 5.5/9 | | | | |

*No campsite, alternative accommodation available*
§ *Borrowdale = Longthwaite, Rosthwaite & Stonethwaite*
† *Clay Bank Top = Urra, Chop Gate & Gt Broughton*

## STAYING IN B&Bs

| Night | Relaxed pace Place | Approx Distance miles/km | Medium pace Place | Approx Distance miles/km | Fast pace Place | Approx Distance miles/km |
|---|---|---|---|---|---|---|
| 0 | St Bees | | St Bees | | St Bees | |
| 1 | Cleator | 11/18 | Ennerdale Br | 14/22.5 | Ennerdale Br | 14/22.5 |
| 2 | Ennerdale Br | 5/8 | Borrowdale§ | 15/24 | Borrowdale§ | 15/24 |
| 3 | Seatoller | 14/22.5 | Grasmere | 9/14.5 | Patterdale | 17/27 |
| 4 | Grasmere | 10.5/17 | Patterdale | 8.5/13.5 | Shap | 15.5/25 |
| 5 | Patterdale | 7.5/12 | Shap | 15.5/25 | K. Stephen | 20.5/33 |
| 6 | Shap | 15.5/25 | K. Stephen | 20.5/33 | Reeth | 28/45 |
| 7 | Orton | 8/13 | Keld | 13/21 | Colburn | 17/27 |
| 8 | K. Stephen | 13/21 | Reeth | 11/18 | Ingleby Cross | 20/32 |
| 9 | Keld | 13/21 | Richmond | 10.5/17 | Blakey Ridge | 20.5/33 |
| 10 | Reeth | 11/18 | Danby Wiske | 14/22.5 | Littlebeck | 17.5/28 |
| 11 | Richmond | 10.5/17 | Osmotherley | 12/19.5 | R. Hood's Bay | 12/19.5 |
| 12 | Danby Wiske | 14/22.5 | Clay Bank Top† | 11/18 | | |
| 13 | Ingleby Cross | 9/14.5 | Blakey Ridge | 8.5/13.5 | | |
| 14 | Clay Bank Top† | 12/19.5 | Grosmont | 13.5/22 | | |
| 15 | Blakey Ridge | 8.5/13.5 | R. Hood's Bay | 15.5/25 | | |
| 16 | Glaisdale | 10/16 | | | | |
| 17 | Littlebeck | 7/11.5 | | | §/† *See **notes** above* | |
| 18 | R. Hood's Bay | 12/19.5 | | | | |

PLANNING YOUR WALK

**VILLAGE AND**

| Place name (Places in brackets are a short walk off the Coast to Coast path) | Distance from previous place approx miles/km | Cash Machine/ ATM | Post Office | Tourist Information Centre/Point (TIC/TIP) |
|---|---|---|---|---|
| **St Bees** | | ✔ | ✔ | TIP |
| **Sandwith** | 4.5/7.2 | | | |
| **Moor Row** | 3.5/5.6 | | | |
| **Cleator** | 1/1.6 | | | |
| **Ennerdale Bridge** | 6/9.6 (via Dent) | | | |
| **Seatoller** | 14/22.5 | | | |
| **Borrowdale** | 2/3.2 (to Rosthwaite) | | | |
| (Longthwaite, Rosthwaite, Stonethwaite) | | | | |
| **Grasmere** | 9/14.5 (from Rosthwaite) | ✔ | ✔ | |
| **Patterdale** | 7.5/12 (not Helvellyn routes) | ✔** | ✔ | TIC (at Glenridding) |
| **Shap** | 15.5/25 | ✔** | ✔ | |
| **(Orton)** | 8/12.9 | | ✔ | |
| **Kirkby Stephen** | 20.5/33 (from Shap) | ✔ | ✔ | TIC |
| **Keld** | 13/21 (not Green route) | | | |
| **(Thwaite)** | 2/3.2 (from Keld) | | | |
| **(Muker)** | 3.5/5.6 (from Keld) | | | |
| **(Gunnerside)** | 2.5/4 (from Muker) | | | |
| **Reeth** | 4/6.4 (from Gunnerside) | ✔ | ✔ | TIC/NPC* |
| | 11/18 (from Keld on high route) | | | |
| **Marrick** | 3.5/5.6 | | | |
| **Richmond** | 10.5/16.9 | ✔ | ✔ | TIC |
| **Colburn** | 3/4.8 | | | |
| **Catterick Bridge** | 2/3.2 | | | |
| **(Brompton-on-Swale)** | 0.5/0.8 | | | |
| **Danby Wiske** | 7.5/12.1 | | | |
| **Oaktree Hill** | 2.5/4 | | | |
| **Ingleby Cross/Arncliffe** | 8/12.9 | | ✔ | |
| **(Osmotherley)** | 3/4.8 (from Ingleby Cross) | | ✔ | |
| **Clay Bank Top†** | 12/19.3 | | | |
| **Blakey Ridge** | 8.5/13.7 | | | |
| **Glaisdale** | 10/16.1 | | ✔ | |
| **Egton Bridge** | 2/3.2 | | | |
| **Grosmont** | 2/3.2 | ✔** | ✔ | NPC* |
| **Littlebeck** | 3.5/5.6 | | | |
| **High Hawsker** | 7.5/12 | | | |
| **Robin Hood's Bay** | 4.5/7.2 | ✔** | ✔ | |

**TOTAL DISTANCE** 189.5 miles (305km) – see p18
\* NPC = National Park Centre       \*\* cashback available (no ATM)

## TOWN FACILITIES

| Eating Place ✔=one; ✔✔=two; ✔✔✔=three+ | Food Store | Campsite (approx miles off the path) | Hostels Y (YHA) H-B (IndHostel or Bunkhouse) B (Barn) | B&B-style accommodation ✔=one; ✔✔=two; ✔✔✔=three+ | Place name (Places in brackets are a short walk off the Coast to Coast path) |
|---|---|---|---|---|---|
| ✔✔✔ | ✔ | ✔ | | ✔✔✔ | **St Bees** |
| | | | B | | **Sandwith** |
| ✔ | | | | ✔ | **Moor Row** |
| ✔ | ✔ | | | ✔✔✔ | **Cleator** |
| ✔✔ | | ✔(1.5) | B(5)/H-B(1.5)/ Y(5) | ✔✔✔ | **Ennerdale Bridge** |
| ✔ | | ✔ | Y(1.5) | ✔✔ | **Seatoller** |
| ✔✔✔ | ✔ | ✔ | Y/B | ✔✔✔ | **Borrowdale** |
| | (basics) | | | | (Longthwaite, Rosthwaite, Stonethwaite) |
| ✔✔✔ | ✔ | | Y/H-B | ✔✔✔ | **Grasmere** |
| ✔✔ | ✔ | ✔ | Y/H-B | ✔✔✔ | **Patterdale** |
| ✔✔✔ | ✔ | ✔ | H-B | ✔✔✔ | **Shap** |
| ✔ | ✔ | ✔ | | ✔✔✔ | (Orton) |
| ✔✔✔ | ✔ | ✔ | H-B | ✔✔✔ | **Kirkby Stephen** |
| ✔✔ | | ✔ | H-B | ✔✔✔ | **Keld** |
| ✔ | | | | ✔ | (Thwaite) |
| ✔ | ✔ | | | ✔✔✔ | (Muker) |
| ✔✔ | | | | ✔ | (Gunnerside) |
| ✔✔✔ | ✔ | ✔ | Y/H-B | ✔✔✔ | **Reeth** |
| | | ✔ | | ✔ | **Marrick** |
| ✔✔✔ | ✔ | ✔(3) | H-B(3) | ✔✔✔ | **Richmond** |
| ✔ | | ✔ | | ✔ | **Colburn** |
| ✔ | | ✔ | | ✔ | **Catterick Bridge** |
| | | ✔ | B | | (Brompton-on-Swale) |
| ✔ | | ✔ | | ✔✔✔ | **Danby Wiske** |
| | | ✔ | H-B | ✔ | **Oaktree Hill** |
| ✔ | | ✔ | | ✔✔✔ | **Ingleby Cross/Arncliffe** |
| ✔✔✔ | ✔ | ✔ | Y | ✔✔✔ | (Osmotherley) |
| ✔ | | ✔(3.5) | | ✔✔✔ | †**Clay Bank Top** |
| ✔ | | ✔ | | ✔✔ | **Blakey Ridge** |
| ✔ | ✔ | | | ✔✔✔ | **Glaisdale** |
| ✔✔✔ | | | | ✔✔✔ | **Egton Bridge** |
| ✔✔ | ✔ | ✔ | | ✔✔✔ | **Grosmont** |
| | | ✔ | | ✔ | **Littlebeck** |
| ✔ | | ✔ | | | **High Hawsker** |
| ✔✔✔ | ✔ | ✔ | Y | ✔✔✔ | **Robin Hood's Bay** |

PLANNING YOUR WALK

**DISTANCE** Distances are between places directly on the Coast to Coast path
† Clay Bank Top This refers to Urra, Chop Gate & Great Broughton

## ❏ DAY WALKS

### The best day loops and weekend walks on the Coast to Coast

The following suggested trails are for those who don't want to tackle the entire path in one go or just want to get a flavour of the challenge before committing themselves.

You won't go thirsty on the Esk Valley Glaisdale to Grosmont day walk.
© Jim Manthorpe

In our opinion they include the best parts of the Coast to Coast path, and are all described in more detail in Part 4.

Day walks bring you back to your starting point, either along other routes not mapped in this book or in some cases it is possible to use public transport.

There is good public transport (see pp52-5) to the start and end points on the suggested weekend walk but no direct service between Reeth and Kirkby Stephen. However, if there are two of you, you can shuttle with two cars, or a car and bike as many walkers do.

### St Bees to Sandwith                                  5 miles/8km (pp93-8)
Get a flavour of setting out from St Bees and striking off along the red rock sea cliffs – even if you're back in St Bees that night on the bus or by walking from Sandwith.

### Around Ennerdale Water                        11 miles/18km (pp104-13)
The first truly gorgeous stretch of the Coast to Coast passes along the south shore of Ennerdale Water to the River Liza. You can carry on to Black Sail along an easy track, then take a walk back along the northern access track.

### Borrowdale to Grasmere and back           15 miles/24km (pp119-29)
Grasmere for lunch? In good weather it's a great training walk and you'll be able to pin down the Greenup Edge crossing to boot. Warm yourself up on the long climb to the Edge and we recommend you take the regular valley route down to Grasmere. Rest up, revive yourself in the fleece-wearing capital of the UK, and then take the haul back with the sun to Borrowdale. We don't recommend the high route via Helm Crag unless you're really on form.

### Grasmere to Grasmere                          m 8 miles/13km (pp122-9)
A very popular day trip for the more active visitor to Grasmere. It's up to you which direction you take; probably reversing the Coast to Coast by tackling the acute climb up to Helm Crag is best. At the junction at the top of Easedale (Wpt 30, p122) you come down the valley. A great day out but tougher than you think.

### Grasmere to Patterdale and back          16$^{1}$/2 miles/26.5km (pp129-39)
A pretty hefty proposition and another great training walk through the heart of the Lakes. The walk takes you up to Helvellyn summit and along Striding Edge, lunch at the pub and then back either up the valley or along St Sunday Crag (same distance but more climbing on the latter) and back down the other side of Tongue Gill. With very little overlapping, it's easily one of the best days out in the Lakes.

### Patterdale to Kidsty Pike and back                13 miles/21km (pp137-42)

Take a 6¹/₂ mile walk to the 784-metre (2572ft) summit of Kidsty Pike on the eastern edge of the Lakes and the highest point on the original Coast to Coast route (though Helvellyn and St Sunday are much higher).

Have a sandwich and a look around then walk right back down again to Patterdale for a slap-up meal in the pub. It's a stiff old climb up to Angle Tarn but from there on the gradients just blend in with the surroundings and the views all the way up and down are well worth the effort. Another Lakeland classic that will have you fired up for the real thing.

### Kirkby Stephen to Nine Standards and back       12 miles/19.5km (pp160-9)

An easy climb to the mysterious stone cones atop Nine Standards Rigg. From the top you might try a southward link towards Rigg Beck and the Green Route back to town, adding a mile or two, but that can involve some messy bog-trotting.

### Keld to Reeth                                       12¹/₂ miles/20km (pp176-90)

Whether you take the high route via a string of evocative mine ruins between breezy moors, or the lowland amble past the hamlets of Upper Swaledale, you're sure to find something you like. If you want to return to Keld you can either take a bus or, with a bit of forward planning, can cycle-shuttle back to the car.

### Lord Stones Café to Clay Bank Top and back      7¹/₂ miles/12km (pp224-7)

On some days a rather too popular run with Teeside dog walkers but the gradients will all be good training for the big day.

### The Esk Valley: Glaisdale to Grosmont          4 miles/6.5km (see pp238-43)

Not so much a trek as an easy pub crawl, this path takes you along the Esk Valley following the course of the river through woodland and along country tracks, via pretty Egton Bridge. Grosmont, at the end of the trail, has steam trains to Pickering or Whitby or buses and regular trains to Scarborough, Whitby, and even the beginning of the trail. There are also buses back to Glaisdale.

### Little Beck Wood excursion                         4¹/₂ miles/7km (pp244-7)

 A shady afternoon's round trip to Falling Foss waterfall and the adjacent tea room through the lovely Little Beck Wood.

### Whitby to Robin Hood's Bay                         7 miles/11.5km (pp250-5)

Not on the Coast to Coast until the last few miles but a stirring cliff-top tramp nonetheless, ending at the hallowed slipway below the Bay Hotel. You won't be the first to pretend you've just finished the entire Coast to Coast, but no one need know. Take the regular bus service back to Whitby, which is a fun place too.

### ❑ WEEKEND WALKS

In addition to the walk described below, any number of the day walks can be combined into a two-day trek, particularly in the Lake District.

### Kirkby Stephen to Reeth                            28 miles/45km (pp160-90)

Anyone who manages to scramble over the Pennines and negotiate the boggy ground down to the old mining village of Keld deserves a reward of some sort, and picturesque Swaledale is just that. As an encore, take Wainwright's high route over the moors to Reeth or the less demanding stroll down the dale, passing through or near the villages of Muker, Gunnerside and Thwaite to end up in Reeth.

PLANNING YOUR WALK

❏ **Next time I do the C2C...**

Next time we do the coast to coast we will make sure that we have booked into B&Bs that have baths! It's incredible how hard it is to stand up in a shower after a day's walking and also it is good to soak your muscles.

Parts of the walk are very remote and it is therefore important to make sure you have plenty of cash and/or your cheque book. Very few places accept cash cards and it is easy to get caught out. Likewise we would suggest that you take plenty of Compeed plasters for your possible blisters and pain killers as they are hard to get hold of once you get going on the walk and if you have a similar experience to ours then you'll go through plenty!

Be prepared for all weathers no matter what time of year you are walking. We experienced five days of horrendous weather in the Lakes at the end of July. A pair of gloves and a woolly hat are essential, along with a trusty compass for the top of mountains when you can't see beyond your arm!

Walking poles are a must for all ages – they saved our knees. In our experience they worked for us for a number of reasons from taking some of the weight off our feet, to clearing pathways, supporting our leaps across fast flowing streams and warning off angry looking cattle! Invest in a camel pack (at least two litres). By having easy access to water it means that you don't get dehydrated. Take innersoles to cushion feet as they came into their own, especially on the middle section of the walk when it is very flat and your feet take a pounding.

Birkdale Farm B&B in Keld is a find. It is the best accommodation we had the pleasure of staying in en route and if we knew this prior to our walk, we may well have stayed there for more than one night. The accommodation is a converted barn and completely self sufficient with a great open fire and a whole stash of logs!

**Noelle Cox and Chris Foster**

---

❏ **Next time ...**

I'll have to go east to west\*; with the promise of the Lake District always ahead of me and the mid-day rush of fellow C2C-ers to meet coming from the west. I will happily take the gamble of walking into the weather when I know that ascending to Helvellyn will be so much easier from Patterdale than it is at the end of a long, tiring day from Rosthwaite. The east to west route also means that you meet different people in the pub every evening and you can swap information on the path conditions ahead.

I will also discipline myself to take more time on the trail and to savour the experience of the walking. The metronomic, almost trance-like state that can occur when all you need to do is put one foot in front of the other is rarely achieved when you're focussing on getting to the end. Too often I arrived at my destination by 3pm or even 2pm and although this means more time relaxing in the pub it also means I could have taken more time on the hills, perhaps sitting quietly enjoying a view or taking time to divert from the path to explore the landscape.

I will of course use Brookfield House in Shap again, as I have on my two previous crossings. The welcome you receive from Margaret when you knock on the door here is second to none. I will also make sure I book early because her reputation means the place is always in demand. **Stuart Greig**

\* **NOTE**: In 2011 Stuart did it. See 🖥 www.lonewalker.walkingplaces.co.uk for an account of the Coast to Coast trip from east to west.

## SIDE TRIPS

The Coast to Coast path is long enough and few walkers will be tempted to make side trips. However, Wainwright's series of guides to Lakeland fells describes other walks around the Lake District in further detail and it may be worth making time for an ascent of some of the hills in the area as they give an entirely different perspective of the Lakeland landscape. Old favourites include Great Gable, Striding Edge on Helvellyn, High Street and England's highest mountain Scafell Pike (3209ft/978m).

# What to take

Not ending up schlepping over the fells like an overloaded mule with a migraine takes experience and some measure of discipline. **Taking too much** is a mistake made by first-time travellers of all types, an understandable response to not knowing what to expect and not wanting to be caught short. The village store in Patterdale even has a special counter for Coast to Coasters sending stuff home.

By UK standards the Coast to Coast is a long walk but it's not an expedition into the unknown. Experienced independent hill walkers trim their gear down to the essentials because they've learned that an unnecessarily heavy pack can exacerbate injuries and put excess strain on the already hard-pressed feet. Note that if you need to buy all the gear listed, keep an eye out for the ever-more frequent online **sales** at outdoor gear shops; time it right and you could get it all half price.

## TRAVELLING LIGHT

Organised tours apart, baggage-forwarding services tempt walkers to partially miss the point of long-distance walking: the satisfaction of striding away from one coast knowing that you're carrying everything you need to get to the other. But if you've chosen to carry it all you must be ruthless in your packing choices.

## HOW TO CARRY IT

Today's rucksacks are hi-tech affairs that make load-carrying as tolerable as can be expected. Don't get hung up on anti-sweat features; unless you use a wheelbarrow your back will always sweat a bit. It's better to ensure there is thick padding and a **good range of adjustment**. In addition to hip belts (allied with some sort of stiff back frame/plate), use an unelasticated **cross-chest strap** to keep the pack snug; it makes a real difference.

If camping you'll need a pack of at least 60-litres' capacity. Staying in hostels 40 litres should be ample, and for those eating out and staying in B&Bs a 20- to 30-litre pack should suffice; you could even get away with a daypack.

Few backpacks these days claim to be waterproof, use a waterproof **liner** or the elasticated backpack cover like a shower cap that comes with some packs.

It's also handy to **compartmentalise** the contents into smaller bags so you know what is where. Take a few (degradable) **plastic bags** for wet things, rubbish etc; they're always useful. Finally, pack intelligently with the most frequently used things readily accessible.

## FOOTWEAR

### Boots

A good pair of boots is vital. Scrimp on other gear if you must – you'll only use waterproofs some days but you'll be walking every mile on every day. Expect to spend up to £150 on quality, three-season items which are light, breathable and waterproof, and have ankle support as well as flexible but thick **soles** to insulate your own pulverised soles. Don't buy by looks or price and avoid buying online until you've been to a shop and tried on an identical pair (and even this can backfire on you). Go to a big outdoor shop on a quiet weekday and spend an hour trying on everything they have in stock that appeals to you.

With modern fabric **breaking in** boots is a thing of the past (traditional one-piece leather Meindels are not so accommodating, as one updater found to his cost...), but arriving in St Bees with an untried pair of boots is courting disaster. You must try them out beforehand, first round the house or office, and

PLANNING YOUR WALK

---

❏ **Next time...**

Take our time. It's a holiday. Forget about the keen types who set off before 8am – let them go. Plan most days at 10-14 miles, that gives plenty of time.

Expect to feel tired, especially on days 2-4. It isn't Pennine Way-tough, but it isn't an easy stroll either.

Stay in B&Bs, especially farms. Last time, except for the terrific Langstrath, the pubs and hotels were a bit disappointing while the B&Bs were all good to great.

See the eagle in Riggindale again. We saw it for a few seconds last time, fabulous.

Do the high routes, weather permitting – Helm Crag and St Sunday Crag are fantastic on clear days. Helvellyn next time?

If we've time, have a rest day in Kirkby Stephen as well as in Richmond. It's welcome after the Lakes. (And there's a launderette!).

Take the Swale route from Keld to Reeth. The mines are interesting but bleak; everyone said the river is beautiful ... but then, lots of them wished they'd done the high-level route.

Spend longer in the Swaledale Museum in Reeth, and stay overnight in their lovely quirky cottage. Then stock up in the Reeth Bakery.

Take a lightweight camera, binoculars, a notebook. Make notes at least every evening – it's easy to forget the details, the days merge into one another. Take more notice of the small things: wild flowers, how the dry-stone walls change, curlews. The big things are dramatic, but the small ones are fascinating.

Make sure boots are 100% waterproof. A tiny damp spot on a Sunday stroll in Cheshire is trench foot on Nine Standards Rigg.

Think about going east to west. The Lakes are the highlight but they're hard work at the start. They'd be a great climax starting from the east, when we're more walking-fit. As for the rain-in-your-face argument ... what rain?!

**David Bull**

then on a full day's walk or two. An old and trusted pair of boots can be resoled and transformed with shock-absorbing after-market **insoles**. Some of these can be thermally moulded to your foot in the shop, but the less expensive examples are also well worth the investment, even if the need for replacement by the end of the walk is likely. Some walkers wisely carry old trusted boots in their luggage in case their new footwear turns on them. Blisters are possible even with a much-loved boot if you walk long and hard enough; refer to p83 for blister-avoidance strategies.

Boots might be considered over the top for the Coast to Coast; much of the walking is on easy paths and some experienced walkers have turned to trail shoes. They won't last as long as boots, be as tough or crucially, have the height to keep your socks dry in the bogs and streams, but the rewards of nimbleness and greater comfort can transform your walk, just as bad footwear can cast a shadow over it.

### Socks

As with all outdoor gear, the humble sock has not escaped the technological revolution (with prices to match) so invest in two non-cotton pairs designed for walking. Although cushioning is desirable, avoid anything too thick which will reduce stability. A correctly sized boot with an anatomically shaped insole gives a sure-footed feel. As well as the obvious olfactory benefits, frequent washing will maintain the socks' springiness.

### CLOTHES

### Tops

The proven system of **layering** is a good principle to follow. A quick-drying synthetic, or a less odiferous merino wool, **base layer** transports sweat away from your skin; the mid-layer, typically a **fleece** or woollen jumper, keeps you warm; and when needed, an outer 'shell' or **jacket** protects you from the wind and rain.

Maintaining a comfortable temperature in all conditions is the key, and this means not **overheating** just as much as the more obvious effects of **wind chill**. Both can prematurely tire you. Trudging out of Patterdale on a warm day will soon have you down to your base layer, but any exposed and prolonged descent, or rest on an unsheltered summit like Kidsty Pike, with a strong wind will soon chill you. Although tedious, the smart hiker is forever fiddling with zips and managing their layers and headwear to maintain an optimal level of comfort.

Avoid cotton; as well as being slow to dry, when soaked it saps away body heat but not the moisture – and you'll often be wet from sweat if not rain. Take a change of **base layers** (including underwear), a **fleece** suited to the season, and the best **breathable waterproof** you can afford. **Soft shells** are an alternative to walking in rustling nylon waterproofs when it's windy but not raining.

It's useful to have a **spare set of clothing** so you're able to get changed should you arrive chilled at your destination, but choose **quick-drying clothes** as washing them reduces your payload. Once indoors your body heat will quickly dry out a synthetic fleece and nylon leggings. However, always make sure you have a **dry base layer** in case you or someone you're with goes down with hypothermia. This is why a quality waterproof is important.

PLANNING YOUR WALK

## Leg wear

Your legs are doing all the work and don't generally get cold so your trousers can be light which will also mean quick-drying. Although they lack useful pockets, many walkers find leg-hugging cycling polyester **leggings** very comfortable (eg Ron Hill Tracksters). Poly-cotton or microfibre trousers are excellent. Denim jeans are cotton and a disaster when wet.

If the weather's good, **shorts** are very agreeable to walk in, leaving a light pair of trousers clean for the evenings. It also means your lower legs get muddy and not the trousers. On the other hand **waterproof trousers** would only suit people who really feel the cold; most others will find them unnecessary and awkward to put on and wear; quick drying or minimal legwear is better. For Lakeland stream crossings and Pennine peat bogs, **gaiters** are a great idea; they also stop irritating pebbles dropping into your footwear. You don't have to wear them all the time.

## Headwear and other clothing

Your head is both exposed to the sun and loses most of your body heat so, for warmth, carry a woolly beany that won't blow away and for UV protection a peaked cap; a bandana or microfibre buff makes a good back-up or sweat band too. Between them they'll conserve body heat or reduce the chances of dehydration. **Gloves** are a good idea in wintry conditions (carry a spare pair in winter).

## TOILETRIES

Besides **toothpaste**/brush, **liquid soap** can also be used for shaving and washing clothes, although a ziplock bag of **detergent** is better if you're laundering regularly. Carry **toilet paper** and a lightweight **trowel** to bury the results out on the fells (see pp78-9). Less obvious items include **ear plugs**, **sun screen**, **moisturiser**; **insect repellent** if camping and possibly a means of **water purification**.

## FIRST-AID KIT

Apart from aching limbs your most likely ailments will be blisters so a first-aid kit can be minimal. **Ibuprofen** and **paracetamol** help numb pain although rest of course is the only real cure. '**Compeed**', or '**Second Skin**' all treat blisters. An **elastic knee support** is a good precaution for a weak knee as are walking poles (see box p40). A tube of Nuun tablets can flavour water and restore lost minerals on the march, and a few sachets of Dioralyte or Rehydrat powders will quickly remedy more serious dehydration. Other items worth considering are: **plasters** for minor cuts; a small selection of different-sized **sterile dressings** for wounds; **porous adhesive tape**; **antiseptic wipes**; **antiseptic cream**; **safety pins**; **tweezers**; and **scissors**.

## GENERAL ITEMS

### Essential

Carry a **compass**, **whistle** and **mobile phone** as well as at least a one-litre **water bottle** or bag; an LED **headtorch**; **emergency snacks**, a **penknife** and a **watch**.

## Useful

If you're not carrying a proper bivvy bag or tent, a compact foil **space blanket** is a good idea in the cooler seasons. Many people take a **camera**, **batteries** and **sunglasses**. A **book** is a good way to pass the evenings, especially in mid-summer wild camps. A **vacuum flask**, for hot drinks or soup, is recommended if walking in a cooler season. Studies have shown that nothing improves a hilltop view on a chilly day like a hot cup of tea or soup.

## SLEEPING BAG & CAMPING GEAR

If you're camping or planning to stay in camping barns you'll need a sleeping bag. Many bunkhouses now offer bedding, some at a nominal cost. All youth hostels provide bedding and insist you use it.

A **two-season bag** will do for indoor use, but if you can afford it or anticipate outdoor use, go warmer. The choice over a **synthetic** or **down** filling is a debate without end. Year by year less expensive synthetic-filled bags (typically under £100) approach down's enviable qualities of good compressibility while expanding or 'lofting' fully once unpacked to create maximum warmth. But get a down bag wet (always a risk in the UK) and it clogs up and loses all its thermal qualities; and drying down bags takes half a day at the launderette.

If committed to the exposure of wild camping you'll need a **tent** you can rely on; light but able to withstand the rain and wind. In campsites you may just get away with a cheap tent. Otherwise, a good one-man tent suited to the wilds can cost under £120 and weigh just 1.5kg, with a sub-2kg two-man example costing around £250. An inflatable **sleeping mat** is worth many times its weight.

As for **cooking**, is it really worth the bother on the Coast to Coast? The extra weight and hassle in buying provisions is only viable when shared by a group of three or more; otherwise get down the pub and help support the local economy.

## MONEY

**Cash machines** (ATMs) are infrequent along the Coast to Coast path, with none east of Richmond (but you can get cashback in Grosmont and Robin Hood's Bay), though their numbers are growing as post offices and shops along the trail install them or turn to the simpler **cashback** (see p27) system. Banks are even rarer, with only Shap, Kirkby Stephen and Richmond boasting any. Not everybody accepts **debit** or **credit cards** as payment either – though many B&Bs and restaurants now do. As a result, you should always carry plenty of cash with you, just to be on the safe side. A **cheque book** from a British bank is useful in those places where credit cards are not accepted. See also the table of village and town facilities on pp36-7. Crime on the trail is thankfully rare but it's always a good idea to carry your money in a **moneybelt**.

## MAPS

The much-improved hand-drawn maps in this edition cover the trail at a scale of just under 1:20,000: one mile equals $3^{1}/_{8}$ths of an inch (1km = 5cm). At this

PLANNING YOUR WALK

generous scale, combined with the notes and tips written on the maps, and the waypoints, they should be enough to stop you losing your way as long as you don't stray too far off the route. That said, a supplementary map of the region – ie one with contours – can prove invaluable should you need to abandon the path and find the quickest route off high ground in bad weather. They also help you to identify local features and landmarks and devise possible side trips.

Unfortunately, the two Outdoor Leisure strip maps produced by the **Ordnance Survey** (☎ 08456 050505, 🖳 www.ordnancesurvey.co.uk) that covered the entire trail at a scale of 1:27,777 went out of print in 2002, and although it may still be possible to get second-hand copies these are increasingly rare; look for sheets OL33 covering the trail from St Bees to Keld and OL34 cover-

**PLANNING YOUR WALK**

### ❏ Digital mapping

There are a number of software packages available on the market today that provide Ordnance Survey maps for a PC or smartphone. The two most well known are Memory Map and Anquet, but more suppliers join the list every year. Maps are supplied not in traditional paper format, but electronically, on DVD or USB media, or by direct download over the Internet. The maps are then loaded into an application, also available by download, from where you can view them, print them and create routes on them.

Digital maps are normally purchased for an area such as a National Park, but the Coast to Coast walk is available as a distinct product from some vendors. When compared to the eight OS Explorer maps that are needed to cover the walk, they are very competitively priced. Once you own the electronic version of the map you can print any section of the map you like, as many times as you like.

The real value of the digital maps though, is the ability to draw a route directly onto the map from your computer or smartphone. The map, or the appropriate sections of it, can then be printed with the route marked on it, so you no longer need the full versions of the OS maps. Additionally, the route can be viewed directly on the smartphone or uploaded to a GPS device, providing you with the whole C2C route in your hand at all times while walking. If your smartphone has a GPS chip, you will be able to see your position overlaid onto the digital map on your phone.

Many websites now have free routes you can download for the more popular digital mapping products. Anything from day walks around the Lakes to complete Long Distance Paths like the Coast to Coast. It is important to ensure any digital mapping software on your smartphone uses pre-downloaded maps, stored on your device and doesn't need to download them on-the-fly, as this will be impossible in the hills.

Taking OS quality maps with you on the hills has never been so easy. Most modern smartphones have a GPS receiver built in to them and almost every device with built-in GPS functionality now has some mapping software available for it. One of the most popular manufacturers of dedicated handheld GPS devices is Garmin, who have an extensive range of map-on-screen devices. Prices vary from around £100 to £600.

Smartphones and GPS devices should complement, not replace, the traditional method of navigation (a map and compass) as any electronic device is susceptible to failure and if nothing else, battery failure. Remember that battery life will be significantly reduced, compared to normal usage, when you are using the built-in GPS and running the screen for long periods.

**Stuart Greig**

ing it from Keld to Robin Hood's Bay. The good news is that electronic copies are available online and could of course be printed off. Have a look at 🖳 www.walkingplaces.co.uk/c2c/osmaps.htm.

In their place the Ordnance Survey now have the Explorer series of maps at a scale of 1:25,000 but in order to cover the whole trail you will need eight maps. The trouble here, of course, is one of weight and expense and also, **they don't always show the path** and are sometimes out of date with details like plantations (Dent Hill and Ennerdale on the OL4 were good examples in 2009). The details are: 303 (for St Bees); Outdoor Leisure (OL) 4 for the western Lake District; OL5 for the eastern Lake District; OL19 for the upper Eden Valley (Kirkby Stephen); OL30 for Swaledale; Explorer Series 304 for Richmond and the Vale of Mowbray; OL26 for the western North York Moors; and OL27 for the eastern half to Robin Hood's Bay. While it may be extravagant to buy all of these maps, members of Ramblers (see box p48) can borrow up to 10 maps for free from their library, paying only for return postage.

We say again that with a bit of nous many readers manage with the maps in this book, but if any two of the above OS maps are worth getting they are the **OL4 and OL5** covering the Lake District where the weather can be bad, the waymarking is worse and the consequences of losing the path vexing in the extreme. By a stroke of luck both these double-side sheets can be neatly cut in half while still retaining the full extent of the path from west to east. The alternatives to OS are the strip maps produced by either **Footprint** (🖳 www.stirling-surveys.co.uk) or **Harvey Maps** (🖳 www.harveymaps.co.uk), both of which cover the trail over two maps at a scale of around 1:50,000 and 1:40,000 respectively. The problem is that, like our maps, they only cover a narrow strip either side of the trail and consequently give limited opportunities for exploring further afield. Weighing 45g each, Footprint's maps are waterproof, have a useful cumulative mile count and cost around £6.95; Harvey's waterproof maps are £12.95 each and weigh 60g.

## RECOMMENDED READING

Most of the following books can be found in the tourist information centres; the centre at Richmond has a particularly good supply of books about the path and the places en route. As well as stocking many of the titles listed below, the tourist offices also have a number of books about the towns and villages en route, usually printed by small, local publishers.

### Guidebooks, travelogues and DVD

We have to mention here Wainwright's original *A Coast to Coast Walk (Wainwright Pictorial Guides*, 2010), a veritable work of art and now reprinted by local publisher, Frances Lincoln. For the coffee table *Coast to Coast with Wainwright* (also Frances Lincoln, 2009) marries Wainwright's original text with photos by Derry Brabbs; it makes a great souvenir of the walk. *Ancient Feet* (Matador, 2008) by Alan Nolan, is a humourous tale of five friends in their sixties tackling the path. Returning with the Wainwright theme, Hunter

## ❏ SOURCES OF FURTHER INFORMATION

### Online trail information

💻 **www.coast2coast.co.uk** Run by Sherpa Van, this site is crammed full of information and has an online shop for books and maps as well as a popular accommodation-booking and luggage-transfer service (see p28). They also have a busy Coast to Coast forum, where trekkers share their experiences and others post questions, although it does suffer from a level of flippancy by the 'seen-it-all' regulars who dominate the board. Scrutinise at length before enquiring; it's probably been asked before.

💻 **www.coasttocoastguides.co.uk** Richmond-based organisation and another excellent website with books and maps for sale and a thorough accommodation guide based on Doreen Whitehead's booklet (see opposite).

💻 **www.walkingplaces.co.uk/c2c** An extensive and cleanly designed website that's not trying too hard to do everything or sell you something. Run by a Coast to Coast enthusiast, there are some excellent resources here that you won't find anywhere else, as well as a tolerant and supportive Coast to Coast forum. The site also hosts blogs (many with lots of photos) by recent walkers, that make interesting reading.

💻 **www.wainwright.org.uk** The website of the Wainwright Society, dedicated to 'keeping alive the fellwalking traditions promoted by AW', has a section on the trail.

### Tourist information organisations

● **Tourist information centres (TICs)** TICs are based in towns throughout Britain and provide all manner of locally specific information and an accommodation-booking service. There are four centres relevant to the Coast to Coast path: **Ullswater/Glenridding** (near Patterdale, p139), **Kirkby Stephen** (p162), **Reeth** (p188) and **Richmond** (p198).

● **Yorkshire Tourist Board** (💻 www.yorkshire.com) The tourist board oversees all the local tourist information centres in the county. It's a good place to find general information about the county as well as on outdoor activities and local events. They can also help with arranging holidays and accommodation.

● **Cumbria Tourist Board** (💻 www.cumbria-the-lake-district.co.uk) Performing much the same role as the Yorkshire board above but, of course, for the county encompassing the Lake District.

### Organisations for walkers

● **Backpackers' Club** (💻 www.backpackersclub.co.uk) A club aimed at people who are involved or interested in lightweight camping through walking, cycling, skiing and canoeing. They produce a quarterly magazine, provide members with a comprehensive advisory and information service on all aspects of backpacking, organise weekend trips and also publish a farm-pitch directory. Membership is £12/15/7 per year for an individual/family/anyone under 18 or over 65.

● **The Long Distance Walkers' Association** (💻 www.ldwa.org.uk) Membership includes a journal (*Strider*) three times per year with details of challenge events and local group walks as well as articles on the subject. Information on over 730 paths is presented in their *UK Trailwalkers' Handbook*, published by Cicerone. Membership is £13 a year.

● **Ramblers** (💻 www.ramblers.org.uk) A charity that looks after the interests of walkers throughout Britain and promotes walking for health. Membership costs £32/43 individual/joint and includes their quarterly *Walk* magazine (£3.60 to non-members).

Davies's *Wainwright: The Biography* (Orion Press) is an absorbing account of this complex man.

Towards the end of each year Doreen Whitehead produces the latest edition of her long-running publication *Coast to Coast Bed & Breakfast Accommodation Guide*. For ordering details see 🖥 www.coasttocoastguides.co.uk.

It's possible you saw *Coast to Coast with Julia Bradbury* (DVD; Acorn Media, 2009, 165 mins), the five-part BBC show broadcast twice in 2009 and part of a 'Wainwright Walks' series. Julia Bradbury makes an engaging presenter and approaches the task with gusto, interviewing characters along the way (including writer Alan Nolan, see *Ancient Feet* above). Unfortunately, the production hit terrible weather in the Lakes which dampened the impression of that part of the walk; many of the aerial shots were filmed in much better conditions. Rumours circulated on the web and along the trail about body doubles standing in on long shots while she got choppered to the summits looking fresh as a daisy, and whether she walked the entire route. The reality of television as well as of filming outdoors makes the former likely (though she may well have done the walk on another occasion) and watching the parts in quick succession you can't help thinking that it's more fun to walk than to watch. Nevertheless, to have the Coast to Coast featured on mainstream TV at all is something of a coup for British long-distance paths and has further enshrined the popularity of the trail. The DVD contains no 'special features' of any significance.

If you're a seasoned long-distance walker, or even new to the game and like what you see, check out the other titles in the Trailblazer series; see p268.

### Flora and fauna field guides

Collins *Bird Guide* with its beautiful illustrations of British and European birds continues to be the favourite field guide of both ornithologists and laymen alike. For a guide to the flora you'll encounter on the Coast to Coast path, *The Wild Flower Key* (Warne) by Francis Rose and Clare O'Reilly, is arranged to make it easy to identify unfamiliar flowers. Another in the Collins Gem series, *Wild Flowers*, is more pocket-sized and thus more suitable for walkers.

There are also several field guide apps for smart phones and tablets, including those that can aid in identifying birds by their song as well as by their appearance.

# Getting to and from the Coast to Coast path

Both St Bees and Robin Hood's Bay are quite difficult to reach on public transport. For this reason, many people who are using the baggage carrier companies (see pp28-9) opt to start and finish at their bases (Kirkby Stephen, Richmond or Kirkby Malham) where they have car parking facilities and offer their own transport links to St Bees and Robin Hood's Bay

If you want to make your own way to **St Bees**, it's best to take a train to Carlisle or Barrow-in-Furness, and then take the train to St Bees. Alternatively take a bus from Carlisle to Whitehaven (Stagecoach No 300, 301 & No 600; see box p55) and then walk, bus or train the 4$^1/_2$ miles south from Whitehaven.

For **Robin Hood's Bay**, Arriva's No 93 Middlesbrough to Scarborough bus service operates daily (see box p55); all these towns are well connected by rail.

## NATIONAL TRANSPORT

All train **timetable and fare information** can be found at National Rail Enquiries (☎ 08457 484950, 24hrs; 🖳 www.nationalrail.co.uk). Alternatively, and to book tickets, you can look on the websites of the train companies concerned: **Virgin Trains** (🖳 www.virgintrains.co.uk), **East Coast** (🖳 www.eastcoast.co.uk),

---

❏ **GETTING TO BRITAIN**

● **By air** Manchester Airport (🖳 www.manchesterairport.co.uk) is the nearest major international airport to St Bees but for most foreign visitors one of the London airports is likely to be their entry point to the country. Nevertheless, if you've no business in London do check out flights to Manchester. Trans-Pennine Express (see p51) operates services from the airport to Barrow-in-Furness and Northern Rail (see p51) from there to St Bees.

Leeds Bradford Airport (🖳 www.leedsbradfordairport.co.uk) is convenient for Kirkby Stephen and has flights to many European destinations. Durham Tees Valley Airport (www.durhamteesvalleyairport.com) is 7 miles/11km outside Darlington and useful for Richmond; it's also the nearest airport to Robin Hood's Bay but is served mainly by domestic flights.

A number of **budget airlines** (easyJet 🖳 www.easyjet.com, jet2 🖳 www.jet2 .com and Ryanair 🖳 www.ryanair.com) fly from many of Europe's major cities to Manchester and the London terminals (Stansted, Luton, Gatwick and Heathrow). See p51 & p56 for details about Getting to St Bees, Kirkby Stephen or Robin Hood's Bay from London.

● **From Europe by train** Eurostar (🖳 www.eurostar.com) operates a high-speed passenger service via the Channel Tunnel between Paris, Brussels (and some other cities) and London St Pancras International – convenient for both the trains for Carlisle (which leave from nearby Euston) and to the north-east coast (which leave from neighbouring King's Cross). For more information about rail services from Europe contact your national rail operator, or Railteam (🖳 www.railteam.eu).

● **From Europe by coach** Eurolines (🖳 www.eurolines.com) have a huge network of long-distance coach services connecting over 500 cities in 25 European countries to London. Check carefully, however: once such expenses as food for the journey are taken into consideration, it often does not work out that much cheaper than taking a flight, particularly when compared to the prices of some of the budget airlines.

● **From Europe by ferry (with or without a car)** Numerous ferry companies operate routes between the major North Sea and Channel ports of mainland Europe and the ports on Britain's eastern and southern coasts as well as from Ireland to ports in both Wales and England. For further information see websites like 🖳 www.directferries.com.

● **From Europe by car** Eurotunnel (🖳 www.eurotunnel.com) operates the shuttle train service for vehicles via the Channel Tunnel between Calais and Folkestone taking one hour between the motorway in France and the motorway in Britain.

---

**Northern Rail** (🖥 www.northernrail.org) and **Trans-Pennine Express** (🖥 www.tpexpress.co.uk). Timetables and tickets are also available on 🖥 www.thetrainline.com and 🖥 www.qjump.co.uk. You are advised to book in advance. Bought at Darlington at the end of the walk, a ticket to London will cost over £100; if booked ahead it could cost from £35, depending on the day and time you travel. If your journey involves changes, it's worth checking which train company operates each leg of the journey – you may find you can save money by buying separate tickets for each train company rather than one through ticket for your whole journey.

Coach travel is generally cheaper (though with the excellent advance-purchase train fares that is not always true) but takes longer. The principal coach (long-distance bus) operator in Britain is **National Express** (☎ 08717 818178, 24 hrs, 🖥 www.nationalexpress.com). **Megabus** (🖥 www.uk.megabus.com) has a more limited service though may be cheaper.

### Getting to St Bees

● **Train** Carlisle and Barrow-in-Furness are the main access points for St Bees. Virgin's London Euston to Glasgow service calls at Carlisle; trains operate approximately hourly during the day and the journey takes $3^1/_4$-4 hours. Virgin's Birmingham New St to Edinburgh/Glasgow service stops in Carlisle hourly.

Trans-Pennine Express operates a service from Manchester Airport/Manchester Piccadilly to Barrow-in-Furness (Mon-Sat 10/day, Sun 4/day). They also operate a service from Manchester Airport/Piccadilly to Glasgow/Edinburgh via Carlisle (Mon-Sat 11/day, Sun 8/day).

Northern Rail (see above) operates a service from Carlisle to Barrow-in-Furness via St Bees (Mon-Sat 7-9/day). On Sunday the service only goes from Carlisle to Whitehaven (3-5/day). However, Whitehaven is just over four miles up the road from St Bees and the X6 bus service runs between the two on Sunday.

● **Coach/bus** Whitehaven is the closest place to St Bees that National Express services operate to; stops on the once daily NX571 London to Whitehaven service include Grasmere, and Kendal for bus services to Kirkby Stephen. From there trekkers can either take a No 26 bus to St Bees or, a No X6 on a Sunday (see box p54).

Alternatively, National Express has services to Carlisle from several towns and cities in Britain. Services that stop at least once a day in Carlisle include: NX590/592 London to Aberdeen; NX920 London to Stranraer; NX538 Coventry to Inverness; NX539 Bournemouth to Edinburgh and NX336 Plymouth to Edinburgh.

From Carlisle take a train (see above) to St Bees, or a bus to Whitehaven (Stagecoach No 300, 301 & No 600; see box p54). See above for details of how to get to St Bees from Whitehaven.

● **Car** You can of course drive to St Bees and leave your car (for a fee) at a B&B there. The nearest motorway is the M6 to Carlisle which joins the M1 just outside Coventry. From the south, leave the M1 at junction 36 (the Southern Lakes turn-off), then take the A590 till it meets the A5092; this then meets the A595 (to Whitehaven) and turn off just before Egremont. (*cont'd on p56*)

PLANNING YOUR WALK

## ☐ LOCAL PUBLIC TRANSPORT SERVICES

Public transport is limited along the Coast to Coast path. While most places do have some sort of bus service, these services may be irregular and often just two or three times per day (although this didn't stop one Coaster we met doing the walk by taking a bus back to his car every night!). Usually the choice of destination is limited too, often the nearest big town.

To check the current bus timetables, contact **traveline** (☎ 0871 200 2233; ☐ www.traveline.info), which has public transport information for the whole of the UK. This is usually easier than contacting the operator directly as many bus services are run by more than one operator. From the Cumbria County Council website (☐ www.cumbria.gov.uk/buses) you can download or request a postal copy of *Go Cumbria*, which gives details of buses, trains and ferries in the county. For information about services in North Yorkshire visit ☐ www.dalesbus.org or ☐ www.northyorks.gov.uk.

### Notes

● Service details were as accurate as possible at the time of writing but it is essential to check before travel
● Services on Bank Holiday Mondays are usually the same as Sunday services; services that operate Monday to Saturday generally don't operate on Bank Holiday Mondays
● Services generally operate at the same frequency in both directions
● Be aware that where routes are serviced by more than one operator (usually during the peak season), the different operators may not accept each other's tickets.
● In rural areas where there are no fixed bus stops it is usually possible to 'hail and ride' a passing bus though it is important to stand where visibility is good and also somewhere where it would be safe for the driver to stop
● See pp28-9 for details of **Packhorse**'s and **Sherpa Van**'s services along this route.

### RAIL SERVICES & OPERATORS

**Northern Rail Ltd** (☎ 0845 000 0125 Mon-Sat 8am-8pm, Sun 9am-5pm, ☐ www.northernrail.org)
See p51 & p56 for details of the services to Carlisle for St Bees, to Whitby (for Robin Hood's Bay) and to Kirkby Stephen
● Middlesbrough to Whitby (Esk Valley Railway) via Glaisdale, Egton & Grosmont, Mon-Sun 4/day May-Sep, Sun 1/day Oct-Apr

**North York Moors Railway** (enquiries ☎ 01751 472508, option 1 for talking timetable, ☐ www.nymr.co.uk)
● Grosmont to Pickering/Whitby via Goathland, Newtondale Halt & Levisham, daily Mar-Oct plus in holiday periods such as Christmas/New Year and February half-term, weekends only at other times; 6-9/day depending on the time of year.

See pp54-5 for BUS SERVICES

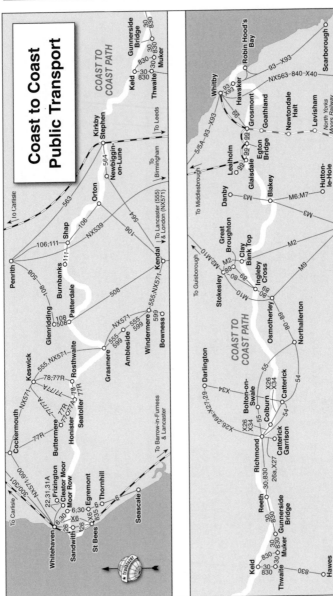

## Coast to Coast Public Transport

PLANNING YOUR WALK

## BUS SERVICES & OPERATORS – CUMBRIA

SEE p53 FOR MAP

| Route No | From | To | Via | Frequency | Operator |
|---|---|---|---|---|---|
| 6 | Whitehaven | Seascale | Moor Row & Egremont | Mon-Sat 4-5/day | Stagecoach, 3D Travel |
| X6 | Whitehaven | Millom | St Bees & Egremont | Sun 4/day | Stagecoach, 3D Travel |
| 22 | Whitehaven | Frizington | Cleator Moor | Mon-Sat from 8pm 2-3/day, Sun 5/day | Stagecoach |
| 26 | Whitehaven | Egremont | Sandwith & St Bees | Mon-Sat 4-6/day | Stagecoach, Sim's Travel |
| 30 | Whitehaven | Thornhill | Egremont | Mon-Sat 1-2/hr, Sun 1/hr | Stagecoach |
| 31/31A | Whitehaven | Frizington | Cleator Moor | Mon-Sat 1-2/hr to 7pm | Stagecoach |
| 32 | Whitehaven | Cleator | Cleator Moor | Mon-Sat 1/hr to 6pm | Stagecoach |
| 77/77A | Keswick | Keswick | Circular route via Buttermere, Honister slate mine & Seatoller | Apr-Oct 4/day | Honister Rambler, Stagecoach |
| 77R | Cockermouth | Keswick | B'mere, Honister, Seatoller, Rosthwaite | late Jul-early Sep daily 2/day | Reays Coaches |
| 78 | Keswick | Seatoller | Rosthwaite | Apr-Oct, Mon-Sat 1-2/hr, Sun 8/day | Borrowdale Rambler, Stagecoach |
| 106 | Penrith | Kendal | Shap & Orton | Mon-Sat 6-9/day | Kirkby Lonsdale, Reays Coaches |
| 108/508 | Penrith | Patterdale Hotel | Glenridding | Apr-Oct daily 4-5/day | Stagecoach |
| 111 | Penrith | Burnbanks Village | Shap | Tue only 1/day | Haweswater Rambler, Alba Travel |
| 300/301 | Whitehaven | Carlisle | | Mon-Sat hourly, Sun 5/day | Stagecoach |
| 555 | Keswick | Lancaster | Grasmere, Ambleside, Windermere & Kendal | Mon-Sat 8/day, Sun 5-9/day | Stagecoach, Reays Coaches |
| 563 | Penrith | Kirkby Stephen | | Mon-Sat 5-6/day | Grand Prix Coaches |
| 564 | K'by Stephen | Kendal | Newbiggin-on-Lune | Mon-Sat 4-5/day | Grand Prix Coaches |
| 599 | Grasmere | Bowness | Ambleside & Windermere | Apr-Oct daily 2/hr, Nov-Mar Mon-Sat 1/hr | Open-top Lakeland Experience, Stagecoach |
| 600 | Carlisle | Whitehaven | Cockermouth | Mon-Fri 3/day, Sat 5/day | Stagecoach |
| 835 | St Bees | Egremont | | Mon-Sat 4/day | Brownriggs |

CONTACTS Alba Travel (☎ 01768 870219 Mon-Fri 9am-5pm, ⌨ www.albatravelcumbria.co.uk); Brownriggs (☎ 01946 820205, ⌨ www.sjbrownrigg.co.uk); Grand Prix Coaches (☎ 017683 41328 Mon-Fri 9am-5pm, ⌨ www.grandprixservices.co.uk); Kirkby Lonsdale Coach Hire (☎ 01524 733831, ⌨ www.kirkbylonsdalecoachhire.co.uk or ⌨ www.dalesbus.org); Reays Coaches (☎ 016973 49999, ⌨ www.reays.co.uk); Sim's Travel (☎ 019467 23227 ext 0199, ⌨ www.simstravel.co.uk); Stagecoach (Traveline ☎ 0871 200 2233, ⌨ www.stagecoachbus.com); 3D Travel (☎ 01946 812828 Mon-Fri 9am-5pm)

## BUS SERVICES & OPERATORS – NORTH YORKSHIRE

SEE p53 FOR MAP

| Route No | From | To | Via | Frequency | Operator |
|---|---|---|---|---|---|
| M2 | Helmsley | Guisborough | Clay Bank Top & Stokesley | Apr-Oct Sun/Bank Hols 4/day | Moorsbus |
| M3 | Helmsley | Danby | Blakey Lion Inn | Apr-Oct Sun/Bank Hols 5/day | Moorsbus |
| M6/M7 | Blakey | Hutton le Hole | | Apr-Oct Sun/Bank Hols 2/day | Moorsbus |
| M9 | Osmotherley | Helmsley | | Apr-Oct Sun/Bank Hols 3/day | Moorsbus |
| M10 | Osmotherley | Guisborough | Stokesley | Apr-Oct Sun/Bank Hols 1/day | Moorsbus |
| 5/5A | Whitby | Middlesbrough | | Mon-Sat 1-2/hr, Sun 1/hr | Arriva North East |
| X26 | Catterick Village | Darlington | Richmond | Mon-Sat 2/hr, Sun 1/hr | Arriva North East |
| X27/26a | Catterick Garrison | Darlington | Richmond | Mon-Sat 2/hr, Sun 1/hr | Arriva North East |
| 29 | Darlington | Richmond | | Mon-Sat 6/day | Dales & District |
| 30 | Keld | Richmond | Thwaite, Muker, Gunnerside Bridge & Reeth | Mon-Sat 2-3/day | Dales & District |
| 30 | Reeth | Richmond | | Mon-Sat 6/day | Dales & District |
| X34 | Richmond | Darlington | Brompton-on-Swale & Catterick | Mon-Sat 4-6/day | Dales & District |
| 54 | Richmond | Northallerton | Catterick Bridge | Mon-Sat 3/day | Dales & District |
| 55 | Richmond | Northallerton | Brompton-on-Swale & Bolton-on-Swale | Mon-Sat 4-5/day | Dales & District |
| 80 | Stokesley | Northallerton | Ingleby Cross & Osmotherley | Mon-Sat 5-7/day | G Abbott |
| 89 | Stokesley | Northallerton | Great Broughton, Ingleby Cross & Osmotherley | Mon-Sat 5/day | G Abbott |
| 93/X93 | Scarborough | M'brough | Robin Hood's Bay, Hawsker Village & Whitby | daily 1-2/hr | Arriva North East |
| 99 | Whitby | Lealholm | Grosmont, Egton Bdge, Glaisdale | Mon-Sat 4-5/day | M&D Minicoaches |
| 830 | Hawes | Richmond | Thwaite, Keld, Muker, Gunnerside & Reeth | mid May-mid Oct Sun 1/day | Northern Dalesman, Kirkby Lonsdale |
| 840/X40 | Leeds | Whitby | York | Mon-Sat 6/day, Sun 1-2/day | Yorkshire Coastliner |

CONTACTS  G Abbott (☎ 01677 422858);  Arriva North East (☎ 01677 422858);  Dales & District (☎ 01677 425203, ▢ www.arrivabus.co.uk);  Arriva North East (☎ 01947 895418);  Moorsbus (☎ 01845 597000, ▢ www.northyorkmoors.org.uk/moors www.procterscoaches.com);  M&D Minicoaches (☎ 01947 895418);  Moorsbus (☎ 01845 597000, ▢ www.northyorkmoors.org.uk/moors bus);  Stagecoach (Traveline ☎ 0871 200 2233, ▢ www.stagecoachbus.com) Yorkshire Coastliner (☎ 01653 692556, ▢ www.yorkbus.co.uk)

## NATIONAL TRANSPORT (cont'd from p51)

### Getting to Robin Hood's Bay

● **Train** Robin Hood's Bay is, if anything, even harder to reach than St Bees. The nearest rail station is at Whitby: East Coast's London King's Cross to Newcastle/Edinburgh/Glasgow service calls at Darlington, change here for Middlesbrough (Northern Rail service), then change at Middlesborough for a train to Whitby (see box p52). From London to Whitby takes 5-6 hours. From Whitby Arriva's No 93 (see box p55) bus takes 20 minutes to Robin Hood's Bay.

A better way, involving only one change of train, is to get off the East Coast train at York and take one of TransPennine Express's trains to Scarborough and then take Arriva's No 93 (see box p55) bus to the Bay. The bus journey is longer (approximately 40 minutes) but the train journey is only around three hours in total.

● **Coach/bus** National Express operates one direct service (NX563) a day to Whitby (leaving London Victoria at 12.30pm, arriving in Whitby at 8.25pm). Arriva's No 93 service (Scarborough to Middlesbrough) calls in at Whitby and Robin Hood's Bay and it should be possible to get a bus to Robin Hood's Bay on the same day but this would mean arriving very late.

● **Car** It's not entirely straightforward to get to Robin Hood's Bay by car either, though compared to public transport it is at least the simplest. From London head up to Doncaster on the M1/A1(M), then the M18/A19 to York. From there you can head north-east to Scarborough on the A64, then follow the A171 heading towards Whitby, turning off on the B1447 for Robin Hood's Bay. Coming from Manchester take the M62 north-east to Leeds, then the A64 all the way to Scarborough, from where you pick up the A171 as outlined above.

### Getting to Kirkby Stephen

● **Train** Kirkby Stephen is a stop on the Carlisle to Settle line. Coming from London (Kings Cross) either take an East Coast train from King's Cross to Leeds ($2^{1}/_{4}$ hours) and then catch a Northern Rail train to Kirkby Stephen (Mon-Sat 6-8/day, Sun 3/day; $1^{3}/_{4}$ hours), or take a Virgin train to Carlisle ($3^{1}/_{4}$ hours) from London Euston and then a Northern rail train to Kirkby Stephen (Mon-Sat 6-8/day, Sun 3/day; 50 mins).

● **Coach/bus** National Express coach services run to Kendal and Grasmere (both stops on the NX570 service). Grand Prix Coaches' No 564 operates from Kendal to Kirkby Stephen and Stagecoach's No 555 from Kendal to Grasmere.

National Express also runs to Penrith (NX545/539 London to Glasgow via Birmingham), from where you can get Grand Prix Coaches' No 563 service to Kirkby Stephen (see box p54).

● **Car** The A685 runs through the town and the trans-Pennine A66 (which shadows the Coast to Coast path to the north) crosses the A685 just four miles north of the town. The nearest motorway, the M6, is 22 miles west of the A66 interchange. See pp28-9 for information about longstay parking facilities operated by the baggage carrier companies.

# THE ENVIRONMENT & NATURE

## Conserving the Coast to Coast path

With a population of over 62 million Britain is an overcrowded island, and England is the most densely populated part of it. As such, the English countryside has suffered a great deal of pressure from both over-population and the activities of an ever more industrialised world. Thankfully, there is some enlightened legislation to protect the surviving pockets of forest and heathland.

Apart from these, it is interesting to note just how much man has altered the land that he lives on. Whilst the aesthetic costs of such intrusions are open to debate, what is certain is the loss of biodiversity that has resulted. The last wild boar was shot near the Coast to Coast trail a few centuries ago; add to that the extinction of bear and wolf as well as, far more recently, a number of other species lost or severely depleted over the decades and you get an idea of just how much of an influence man has over the land, and how that influence is all too often used negatively.

There is good news, however. In these enlightened times when environmental issues are quite rightly given more precedence, many endangered species, such as the otter, have increased in number thanks to the active work of voluntary conservation bodies. There are other reasons to be optimistic. The environment is no longer the least important issue in party politics and this reflects the opinions of everyday people who are concerned about issues such as conservation on both a global and local scale.

### GOVERNMENT AGENCIES AND SCHEMES

#### Natural England
Natural England is responsible for enhancing biodiversity, landscape and wildlife in rural, urban, coastal and marine areas; promoting access, recreation and public well-being; and contributing to the way natural resources are managed. One of its roles is to identify, establish and manage: national trails, national parks, areas of outstanding natural beauty (AONBs), national nature reserves (NNRs), sites of special scientific interest (SSSIs), and special areas of conservation (SACs) and to enforce regulations relating to these sites.

The highest level of landscape protection is the designation of land as a **national park** which recognises the national importance of an area in terms of landscape, biodiversity and as a recreational resource. At the time of writing there were nine national parks in England (plus the Norfolk and Suffolk Broads which enjoy equivalent status and protection). Three of these are bisected by the Coast to Coast path (Lake District and Yorkshire Dales national parks, both awaiting a decision about expansion of their borders at the time of research, and the North York Moors national park). This designation does not signify national ownership and these are not uninhabited wildernesses, making conservation a knife-edged balance between protecting the environment and the rights and livelihoods of those living in the parks.

The second level of protection is **area of outstanding natural beauty** (AONB). The only AONB passed on the Coast to Coast trail covers the very southern extremity of the North Pennines as you pass Nine Standards Rigg and before you enter the Yorkshire Dales. The primary objective for an AONB is conservation of the natural beauty of a landscape. As there is no statutory administrative framework for their management, this is the responsibility of the local authority within whose boundaries they fall. Some AONBs, including the North Pennines, have also been designated **geoparks** (🖳 www.europeangeo parks.org), a European Union initiative originally set up as a socio-economic project to help the development and management of deprived areas which nevertheless benefited from a rich geological heritage, defined as both unique and important. The concept has since moved on, with today's geoparks designed to raise awareness of an area and to educate the general public.

**National nature reserves** (NNRs) are places where the priority is protection of the wildlife habitats and geological formations. There are over 200 (including Smardale in Cumbria) in England and they are either owned or managed by Natural England or by approved organisations such as wildlife trusts.

**Local nature reserves** (LNRs) are places with wildlife or geological features that are of special interest to local inhabitants; there are nine in Cumbria and 17 in North Yorkshire.

**Sites of Special Scientific Interest** (SSSIs) range in size from little pockets protecting wild flower meadows, important nesting sites or special geological features, to vast swathes of upland, moorland and wetland. SSSIs, of which there are over 4100 in England, are a particularly important designation as they have some legal standing. They are managed in partnership with the owners and occupiers of the land who must give written notice before initiating any operations likely to damage the site and who cannot proceed without consent from Natural England. Many SSSIs are also either a NNR or a LNR.

**Special Area of Conservation** (SAC) is an international designation which came into being as a result of the 1992 Earth Summit in Rio de Janeiro, Brazil. This European-wide network of sites is designed to promote the conservation of habitats, wild animals and plants, both on land and at sea. Every land SAC is also an SSSI.

❑ **Government agencies and other bodies**
● **Department for Environment, Food and Rural Affairs** (🖳 www.gov.uk/defra)
Government ministry responsible for sustainable development in the countryside.
● **Natural England** (🖳 www.naturalengland.org.uk)  See p57.
● **English Heritage** (🖳 www.english-heritage.org.uk)  Organisation with a central aim
of ensuring that the historic environment of England is properly maintained. It is offi-
cially known as the Historic Buildings and Monuments Commission for England.
● **Forestry Commission** (🖳 www.forestry.gov.uk)  Government department for
establishing and managing forests for a variety of uses.
● **National Association of Areas of Outstanding Natural Beauty** (🖳 www.land
scapesforlife.org.uk); for further information on the North Pennines AONB visit 🖳
www.northpennines.org.uk.
● **Lake District National Park Authority** (🖳 www.lakedistrict.gov.uk); **Yorkshire
Dales National Park Authority** (🖳 www.yorkshiredales.org.uk); **North York
Moors National Park Authority** (🖳 www.northyorkmoors.org.uk). The government
authorities charged with managing the respective areas. None of these has much in
the way of specific Coast to Coast trail information on their websites, though they
might be worth contacting to find out the latest developments to the path.

## CAMPAIGNING AND CONSERVATION ORGANISATIONS

These voluntary organisations started the conservation movement in the mid-
19th century and are still at the forefront of developments. Independent of government but reliant on public support, they can concentrate their resources either
on acquiring land which can then be managed purely for conservation purposes,
or on influencing political decision-makers by lobbying and campaigning.

Managers and owners of land include well-known bodies such as the RSPB,
the NT and the CPRE. The **Royal Society for the Protection of Birds** (RSPB;
🖳 www.rspb.org.uk), has over 150 nature reserves and more than a million
members. There are two reserves on the Coast to Coast path, both of great significance. St Bees Head, at the very start of the trail, is the largest seabird colony
in north-west England, home in spring and summer to guillemots, kittiwakes,
fulmars and razorbills; while Haweswater, at the eastern end of the Lake
District, is England's only golden eagle territory.

The **National Trust** (NT; 🖳 www.nationaltrust.org.uk) is a charity with
over three million members which aims to protect, through ownership, threat-
ened coastline, countryside, historic houses, castles and gardens, and archaeological remains for everyone to enjoy. On the Coast to Coast trail, the NT's
properties are concentrated in the Lakes where they look after such beauty spots
as Ennerdale, supposedly England's wildest valley; parts of Ullswater; and
4925 hectares (12,170 acres) of Grasmere and Great Langdale including, curiously, the bed of Grasmere Lake, Johnny Wood (see p117) and Bay Ness (see
Map 93, p250).

The **Campaign to Protect Rural England** (CPRE; 🖳 www.cpre.org.uk)
exists to promote the beauty and diversity of rural England by encouraging the

THE ENVIRONMENT AND NATURE

❏ **Campaigning and conservation organisations**
● **Royal Society for the Protection of Birds** (RSPB; 🖥 www.rspb.org.uk)  See p60.
● **National Trust** (NT; 🖥 www.nationaltrust.org.uk)  See p60.
● **Campaign to Protect Rural England** (CPRE; 🖥 www.cpre.org.uk)  See p60.
● The umbrella organisation for the 47 wildlife trusts in the UK is **The Wildlife Trusts** (🖥 www.wildlifetrusts.org). Two relevant to the Coast to Coast path are **Cumbria Wildlife Trust** (🖥 www.cumbriawildlifetrust.org.uk) and **Yorkshire Wildlife Trust** (🖥 www.ywt.org.uk).
● **Woodland Trust** (🖥 www.woodlandtrust.org.uk)  Restores woodland throughout Britain for its amenity, wildlife and landscape value.

sustainable use of land and other natural resources in both town and country.

A huge increase in public interest and support of these and many other conservation/campaigning groups since the 1980s indicates that people are more conscious of environmental issues and believe that it cannot be left to our political representatives to take care of them for us without our voice. We are becoming the most powerful lobbying group of all, an informed electorate.

## BEYOND CONSERVATION

Pressures on the countryside grow year on year. Western society, whether directly or indirectly, makes constant demands for more oil, more roads, more houses, more cars. At the same time awareness of environmental issues increases, as does the knowledge that our unsustainable approach to life cannot continue. Some governments appear more willing to adopt sustainable ideals, others less so.

Yet even the most environmentally progressive of governments are some way off perfect. It's all very positive to classify parts of the countryside as national parks and Areas of Outstanding Natural Beauty but it will be of little use if we continue to pollute the wider environment, the seas and skies. For a brighter future we need to adopt that sustainable approach to life. It would not be difficult and the rewards would be great.

The individual can play his or her part. Walkers in particular appreciate the value of wild areas and should take this attitude back home with them. This is not just about recycling the odd green bottle or two and walking to the corner shop rather than driving, but about lobbying for more environmentally sensitive policies in local and national government.

The first step to a sustainable way of living is in appreciating and respecting this beautiful, complex world we live in and realising that every one of us plays an important role within the great web. The natural world is not a separate entity. We are all part of it and should strive to safeguard it rather than work against it. So many of us live in a way that seems far removed from the real world, cocooned in centrally heated houses and upholstered cars. Rediscovering our place within the natural world is both uplifting on a personal level and important regarding our outlook and approach to life.

THE ENVIRONMENT AND NATURE

# Flora and fauna

The beauty of walking from one side of England to the other is that on the way you pass through just about every kind of habitat this country has to offer. From woodland and grassland to heathland, bog and beach, the variety of habitats is surpassed only by the number of species of flower, tree and animal that each supports.

The following is not in any way a comprehensive guide – if it were, you would not have room for anything else in your rucksack – but merely a brief guide to the more commonly seen flora and fauna of the trail, together with some of the rarer and more spectacular species.

## MAMMALS

The Coast to Coast path is alive with all manner of native species and the wide variety of habitats encountered on the way means that the wildlife is varied too. Unfortunately, most of these creatures are shy and many are nocturnal, and walkers can consider themselves extremely lucky if during their trek they see more than three or four species.

One creature that you will see everywhere along the walk, from the cliffs at St Bees to the fields outside Robin Hood's Bay, is the **rabbit** (*Oryctolagus cuniculus*). Timid by nature, most of the time you'll have to make do with nothing more than a brief and distant glimpse of their white tails as they stampede for the nearest warren at the first sound of your footfall. Because they are so numerous, however, the laws of probability dictate that you will at some stage get close enough to observe them without being spotted; trying to take a decent photo of one of them, however, is a different matter.

If you're lucky you may also come across **hares**, often mistaken for rabbits but much larger, more elongated and with longer back legs and ears.

Rabbits used to form one of the main elements in the diet of the **fox** (*Vulpes vulpes*), one of the more adaptable of Britain's native species. Famous as the scourge of chicken coops, their reputation as indiscriminate killers is actually unjustified: though they will if left undisturbed kill all the chickens in a coop in what appears to be a mindless and frenzied attack, foxes will actually eat all their victims, carrying off and storing the carcasses in underground burrows for them and their families to eat at a later date. These days, however, you are far more likely to see foxes in towns, where they survive mostly on the scraps and left-overs of the human population, rather than in the country. While generally considered nocturnal, it's not unusual to encounter a fox during the day too, often lounging in the sun near its den.

One creature that is strictly nocturnal, however, is the **bat**, of which there are 17 species in Britain, all protected by law. Your best chance of spotting one is just after dusk while there's still enough light in the sky to make out their flitting forms as they fly along hedgerows, over rivers and streams and around street lamps in their quest for moths and insects. The most common species in Britain is the pipistrelle (*Pipistrellus pipistrellus*).

The Lakes offer one of the few chances in England to see the rare **red squirrel** (*Sciurus vulgaris*), particularly around Grasmere. While elsewhere in the country these small, tufty-eared natives have been usurped by their larger cousins from North America, the **grey squirrel** (*Sciurus carolinensis*), in the Lakes the red squirrel maintains a precarious foothold.

© Bryn Thomas

Patterdale offers walkers on the Coast to Coast their best chance of seeing the **badger** (*Meles meles*). Relatively common throughout the British Isles, these nocturnal mammals with their distinctive black-and-white-striped muzzle are sociable animals that live in large underground burrows called setts, appearing after sunset to root for worms and slugs.

One creature which you almost certainly won't encounter, though they are said to exist in the Lakes, is the **pine marten** (*Martes martes*). Extremely rare in England since being virtually wiped out during the 19th century for their pelts and their reputation as vermin, there are said to be a few in the valley of Ennerdale. In addition to the above, keep a look out for other fairly common but little-seen species such as the carnivorous **stoat** (*Mustela erminea*), its smaller cousin the **weasel** (*Mustela nivalis*), the **hedgehog** (*Erinaceus europaeus*) – these days, alas, most commonly seen as roadkill – and a number of species of **voles**, **mice** and **shrews**.

One of Britain's rarest creatures, the **otter** (*Lutra lutra*), is enjoying something of a renaissance thanks to concerted conservation efforts. Though more common in the south-west, otters are still present in the north of England. At home both in salt and freshwater, they are a good indicator of a healthy unpolluted environment. Don't come to the north expecting otter sightings every day though. If you see one at all you should consider yourself *extremely* fortunate, for they remain rare and very elusive. There are said to be some in Swaledale.

A surprisingly large number of trekkers encounter deer on their walk. Mostly this will be the **roe deer** (*Capreolus capreolus*), a small native species that likes to inhabit woodland, though some can also be seen grazing in fields. As with most creatures, your best chance of seeing one is very early in the morning, with sightings particularly common in Ennerdale, the upper end of Swaledale and the Vale of Mowbray.

Britain's largest native land mammal, the **red deer** (*Cervus elaphus*), is rarely seen on the walk though it does exist in small pockets around the Lakes.

## BIRDS

The Coast to Coast is without doubt an ornithologist's dream. The seaside cliffs, woods, moorland and hedgerows encountered on the path provide homes for a wealth of different species including the golden eagle, Britain's rarest and most

THE ENVIRONMENT AND NATURE

**GUILLEMOT**
L: 450mm/18"

majestic bird, and even a flock of parrots.

The red sandstone cliffs above St Bees (see p94) have been owned by the RSPB since 1973 and dotted along the trail are viewpoints where you can gaze down at the nesting seabirds. This is in fact the only colony of cliff-nesting seabirds in north-west England to which birds return year after year to lay their eggs and hatch chicks.

The most common of the seabirds is the **guillemot** (*Uria aalge*), with an estimated minimum of 5000 crowding onto the cliff's open ledges, including the rare **black guillemot** (*Cepphus grylle*); indeed, the cliffs are believed to be the only place where this rare sub-species nests in England.

**Razorbills** (*Alca torda*), a close relative of the guillemot, are also present, as are **puffins** (*Fratercula arctica*), though their numbers seldom rise above two dozen or so.

**Kittiwakes** (*Rissa tridactyla*), **fulmars** (*Fulmarus glacialis*) and **gulls** (family *Larus*) may be seen, while a little further inland **ravens** (*Corvus corax*) and **peregrine falcons** (*Falco peregrinus*) nest.

**BLACK GUILLEMOT**
L: 350mm/13.5"

Away from the coast, the rarest species in England is the **golden eagle** (*Aquila chrysaetos*), a pair of which had set up an eyrie near the Coast to Coast trail, on the way down to Haweswater Reservoir from Kidsty Pike (see p141). Enthusiastic twitchers could be seen peering up the valley most hours of the day, and there was also a 24hr guard keeping watch to protect it from the predations of the egg collectors. This was the only pair of breeding golden eagles in England. However, since the female has disappeared it is hoped another one can be attracted down from Scotland for the lone male.

**GOLDEN EAGLE**
L: 910mm/36"

The first wild **ospreys** (*Pandion haliaetus*) to breed in England for centuries are also present in the Lakes, though not near the trail. Other birds of prey include **kestrel** (*Falco tinnunculus*), **buzzard** (*Buteo buteo*), **barn owl** (*Tyto alba*) and **short-eared owl** (*Asio flammeus*).

One of the most common birds seen on the path, particularly in the latter half of the walk, is the **pheasant** (*Phasianus colchicus*). Ubiquitous on the moors, the male is distinctive thanks to his beautiful long, barred tail feathers, brown body and glossy green-black head with red head-sides, while the female is a dull brown. Another way to distinguish them is by the distinctive strangulated hacking sound they make, together with the loud flapping of wings as they fly off.

THE ENVIRONMENT AND NATURE

**LAPWING/PEEWIT**
L: 320MM/12.5"

Another reasonably common sight on the moors of Yorkshire is the **lapwing** (*Vanellus vanellus*), also known as the peewit. Black and white with iridescent green upper parts and approximately the size of a pigeon or tern, the lapwing's most distinctive characteristic is the male's tumbling, diving, swooping flight pattern when disturbed, believed to be either a display to attract a female or an attempt to distract predators from its nest, which is built on the ground.

Less common but still seen by most walkers is the **curlew** (*Numenius arquata*), another bird that, like the lapwing, is associated with coastal and open fields, moors and bogs. With feathers uniformly streaked grey and brown, the easiest way to identify this bird is by its thin elongated, downward curling beak. Both the lapwing and the curlew are actually wading birds that nest on the moors in the spring, but which winter by the coast.

Other birds that make their nest on open moorland and in fields include the **redshank** (*Tringa totanus*), **golden plover** (*Pluvialis apricaria*), **snipe** (*Gallinago gallinago*), **dunlin** (*Calidris alpina*) and **ring ouzel** (*Turdus torquatus*).

**CURLEW**
L: 600MM/24"

Somewhat ironically, these birds have benefited from the careful management of the moors which is mainly done to protect the populations of game birds such as **black grouse** (*Tetrao tetrix*).

In the deciduous woodland areas on the trail, look out for **treecreepers** (*Certhia familiaris*), **tits** (family *Paridae*, including blue, coal and great), **nuthatches** (*Sitta europaea*), **pied flycatchers** (*Ficedula hypoleuca*) and **redstarts** (*Phoenicurus phoenicurus*), while in the conifers watch out for **crossbills** (*Loxia curvirostra*) and **siskins** (*Carduelis spinus*).

Finally, for something completely different, in Kirkby Stephen there are ten or so '**homing parrots**': macaws let out by their owner to fly around the town during the day, before returning home each night.

**BLACK GROUSE**
L: 580MM/23"

## REPTILES

The **adder** is the only common snake in the north of England, and the only poisonous one of the three species in Britain. They pose very little risk to walkers – indeed, you should consider yourself extremely lucky to see one, providing you're a safe distance away. They only bite if provoked, preferring to hide instead. The venom is designed to kill small mammals such as mice, voles and shrews, so deaths in humans are very rare, but a bite can be extremely unpleasant and occasionally dangerous to children or the elderly. You are most likely to encounter them in spring when they come out of hibernation and during the summer when pregnant females warm themselves in the sun. They are easily identified by the striking zigzag pattern on their back. Should you be lucky enough to encounter one, enjoy it but leave it undisturbed.

## FLOWERS

Spring is the time to come and see the spectacular displays of colour on the Coast to Coast path. Alternatively, arrive in August and you'll see the heathers carpeting the moors in a blaze of purple flowers.

### The coastal meadows

The coastline is a harsh environment subjected to strong, salt-laced winds. One plant that does survive in such conditions, and which will probably be the first you'll encounter on the path, is **gorse** (*Ulex europaeus*) with its sharp-thorned bright yellow, heavily perfumed flowers. Accompanying it are such cliff-top specialists as the pink-flowering **thrift** (*Armeria maritima*) and white **sea campion** (*Silene maritima*) and **fennel** (*Foeniculum vulgare*), a member of the carrot family which grows to over a metre high.

Gorse
*Ulex europaeus*

### Woodland and hedgerows

From March to May **bluebells** (*Hyacinthoides non-scripta*) proliferate in the woods along the Coast to Coast, providing a wonderful spectacle. Little Beck (see p244) and Clain (see p222) woods are particularly notable for these displays. The white **wood anemone** (*Anemone nemorosa*) and the yellow **primrose** (*Primula vulgaris*) also flower early in spring. **Red campion** (*Silene dioica*), which flowers from late April, can be found in hedgebanks along with **rosebay willowherb** (*Epilobium angustifolium*) which also has the name fireweed due to its habit of colonising burnt areas.

In scrubland and on woodland edges you'll find **bramble** (*Rubus fruticosus*), a common vigorous shrub,

Thrift (Sea Pink)
*Armeria maritima*

Sea Campion
*Silene maritima*

THE ENVIRONMENT AND NATURE

Dog Rose
*Rosa canina*

Forget-me-not
*Myosotis arvensis*

Heather (Ling)
*Calluna vulgaris*

responsible for many a ripped jacket thanks to its sharp thorns and prickles. **Blackberry** fruits ripen from late summer into autumn. Fairly common in scrubland and on woodland edges is the **dog rose** (*Rosa canina*) which has a large pink flower, the fruits of which are used to make rose-hip syrup.

Other flowering plants common in wooded areas and in hedgerows include the tall **foxglove** (*Digitalis purpurea*) with its trumpet-like flowers, **forget-me-not** (*Myosotis arvensis*) with tiny, delicate blue flowers and **cow parsley** (*Anthriscus sylvestris*), a tall member of the carrot family with a large globe of white flowers which often covers roadside verges and hedgebanks.

## Heathland and scrubland

There are three species of heather. The most dominant one is **ling** (*Calluna vulgaris*), with tiny flowers on delicate upright stems. The other two species are **bell heather** (*Erica cinerea*), with deep purple bell-shaped flowers, and **cross-leaved heath** (*Erica tetralix*) with similarly shaped flowers of a lighter pink, almost white colour. Cross-leaved heath prefers wet and boggy ground. As a result, it usually grows away from bell heather which prefers well-drained soils.

Heather is an incredibly versatile plant which is put to many uses. It provides fodder for livestock, fuel for fires, an orange dye and material for bedding, thatching, basketwork and brooms. It is still sometimes used in place of hops to flavour beer, and the flower heads can be brewed to make good tea. It is also incredibly hardy and thrives on the denuded hills, preventing other species from flourishing. Indeed, at times, highland cat-

Bell Heather
*Erica cinerea*

Foxglove
*Digitalis purpurea*

Bluebell
*Hyacinthoides non-scripta*

Common Dog Violet
*Viola riviniana*

Heartsease (Wild Pansy)
*Viola tricolor*

Common Vetch
*Vicia sativa*

Lousewort
*Pedicularis sylvatica*

Primrose
*Primula vulgaris*

Ox-eye Daisy
*Leucanthemum vulgare*

Rowan (tree)
*Sorbus aucuparia*

Common Hawthorn
*Crataegus monogyna*

Red Campion
*Silene dioica*

Rosebay Willowherb
*Epilobium angustifolium*

Yarrow
*Achillea millefolium*

Hogweed
*Heracleum sphondylium*

THE ENVIRONMENT AND NATURE

Bird's-foot trefoil
*Lotus corniculatus*

Germander Speedwell
*Veronica chamaedrys*

Tormentil
*Potentilla erecta*

Early Purple Orchid
*Orchis mascula*

tle are brought to certain areas of the moors to graze on the heather, allowing other species a chance to grow.

Not a flower but worthy of mention is the less attractive species, **bracken** (*Pteridium aquilinum*), a vigorous non-native fern that has invaded many heathland areas to the detriment of native species.

## Grassland

There is much overlap between the hedge/woodland-edge habitat and that of pastures and meadows. You will come across **common bird's-foot trefoil** (*Lotus corniculatus*), **Germander speedwell** (*Veronica chamaedrys*), **tufted** and **bush vetch** (*Vicia cracca* and *V. sepium*) and **meadow vetchling** (*Lathyrus pratensis*) in both.

Often the only species you will see in heavily grazed pastures are the most resilient. Of the thistles, the three most common species are **creeping thistle**, **spear thistle** and **marsh thistle** (*Cirsium arvense, C. vulgare* and *C. palustre*). Among them you may find **common ragwort** (*Senecio jacobaea*), **yarrow** (*Achillea millefolium*), **sheep's** and **common sorrel** (*Rumex acetosella* and *R. acetosa*), and **white** and **red clover** (*Trifolium repens* and *T. pratense*).

Other widespread grassland species include **harebell** (*Campanula rotundifolia*), delicate yellow **tormentil** (*Potentilla erecta*) which will often spread up onto the lower slopes of mountains along with **devil's-bit scabious** (*Succisa pratensis*). Also keep an eye out for orchids such as the **fragrant orchid** (*Gymnaadenia conopsea*) and **early purple orchid** (*Orchis mascula*).

## TREES

It seems incredible that, before man and his axe got to work, most of the bleak, empty moors and windswept Lakeland fells were actually covered by trees. These days, the biggest and most ubiquitous areas of tree cover are the ghastly pine plantations of Ennerdale and other places in the Lakes. But the overgrazing of land by sheep and, to a lesser extent, deer, which eat the young shoots of trees, has ensured that the ancient forests have never returned. Yet there are still small patches of indigenous woodland on the Coast to Coast path. Perhaps the most interesting are the Atlantic Oakwoods at Borrowdale, including Johnny Wood (see map p117) on the way to Longthwaite. The woods are owned and

Ramsons (Wild Garlic)
*Allium ursinum*

Meadow Buttercup
*Ranunculis acris*

Marsh Marigold (Kingcup)
*Caltha palustris*

Meadow Cranesbill
*Geranium pratense*

Water Avens
*Geum rivale*

Scarlet Pimpernel
*Anagallis arvensis*

Harebell
*Campanula rotundifolia*

Herb-Robert
*Geranium robertianum*

Cotton Grass
*Eriophorum angustifolium*

Common Ragwort
*Senecio jacobaea*

Hemp-nettle
*Galeopsis speciosa*

Cowslip
*Primula veris*

THE ENVIRONMENT AND NATURE

cared for by the National Trust and are actually correctly known as temperate rainforest, the moist Atlantic climate creating a landscape of boulders covered by liverworts and ferns, under **oaks** (*Quercus petraea*) dripping in moss and lichen.

There are other areas of woodland in the Lakes, including Easedale Woods on the way into Grasmere and Glenamara Park, just before Patterdale, which has some truly spectacular mature trees. One interesting thing about oak trees is that they support more kinds of insects than any other tree in Britain and some of these insects affect the oak in interesting ways. The eggs of the gall-fly, for example, cause growths on the leaves, known, appropriately enough, as galls. Each of these contains a single insect. Other kinds of gall-flies lay eggs in stalks or flowers, leading to flower galls – growths the size of currants.

Oak woodland is a diverse habitat and not exclusively made up of oak. Other trees that flourish in oak woodland include **downy birch** (*Betula pubescens*), its relative the **silver birch** (*Betula pendula*), **holly** (*Ilex aquifolium*), and **hazel** (*Corylus avellana*) which has traditionally been used for coppicing (where small trees are grown for periodic cutting). Further east there are some examples of limestone woodland. **Ash** (*Fraxinus excelsior*) and oak dominate, along with **wych elm** (*Ulmus glabra*), **sycamore** (*Acer*) and **yew** (*Taxus*).

The **hawthorn** (*Crataegus monogyna*) also grows on the path, usually in isolated pockets on pasture. These species are known as pioneer species and play a vital role in the ecosystem by improving the soil. It is these pioneers, particularly the **rowan** (*Sorbus aucuparia*) and hawthorn, that you will see growing all alone on inaccessible crags and ravines. Without interference from man, these pioneers would eventually be succeeded by longer-living species such as the oak. In wet, marshy areas and along rivers and streams you are more likely to find **alder** (*Alnus glutinosa*).

### Colour photos (following pages)

● **Opposite Top**: Approaching Fleswick Bay on the first day (© CS). **Bottom**: Parts of the church at St Bees including the Great West Door date back to Norman times (© HS).

● **pp72-3 Left**: Local sculptor Colin Telfer's 'Coast to Coast' figure stands at the seven-mile mark (**top** © JM). Wordsworth's Dove Cottage (**middle**, see p128) in Grasmere. (© HS). Walkers on High Stile, with Red Pike behind, on the high level route between Ennerdale Bridge and Borrowdale (**bottom** © JM). **Main picture**: Angle Tarn (© CS, see p141). **Bottom right**: Seatoller, Borrowdale. (© JM).

● **pp74-5 Top left**: The Hermitage (see p244). **Main picture**: Climb Richmond castle's keep for a great view of the marketplace (see p203). **Centre left**: Try to catch a performance at Richmond's Theatre Royal, the most complete Georgian theatre in the country, which dates back to 1788 (see p203). **Bottom**: The mysterious Nine Standards (see p169) mark the boggy transit of the Pennines. (© BT).

# MINIMUM IMPACT & OUTDOOR SAFETY

## Minimum impact walking

In this world in which people live their lives at an increasingly frenetic pace, many of us living in overcrowded cities and working in jobs that offer little free time, the great outdoors is becoming an essential means of escape. Walking in the countryside is a wonderful means of relaxation and gives people the time to think. However, as the popularity of the countryside increases so do the problems that this pressure brings. It is important for visitors to remember that the countryside is the home and workplace of many others.

By following a few simple guidelines while walking the Coast to Coast path you can have a positive impact, not just on your own well-being but also on local communities and the environment, thereby becoming part of the solution.

### ENVIRONMENTAL IMPACT

A walking holiday in itself is an environmentally friendly approach to tourism. The following are some ideas on how you can go a few steps further in helping to minimise your impact on the environment while walking the Coast to Coast path.

### Use public transport whenever possible
Public transport along the Coast to Coast trail is not bad (though it can be a little infrequent at times), with just about everywhere served by at least one bus or train a day. Public transport is always preferable to using private cars as it benefits everyone: visitors, locals and the environment.

### Never leave litter
'Pack it in, pack it out'. Leaving litter is antisocial so carry a degradable plastic bag for all your rubbish, organic or otherwise and even other people's too, and pop it in a bin in the next village. Or better still, reduce the amount of litter you take with you by getting rid of packaging in advance.

---

(**Opposite**) **Top**: Looking down Greenup, on the trail between Borrowdale and Grasmere; Skiddaw in the distance. (© HS)

Support local businesses
© Bryn Thomas

● **Is it OK if it's biodegradable?** Not really. Apple cores, banana skins, orange peel and the like are unsightly, encourage flies, ants and wasps, and ruin a picnic spot for others; they can also take months to decompose. In high-use areas such as the Coast to Coast path either bury them or take them away with you.

### Buy local

Look and ask for local produce to buy and eat. Not only does this cut down on the amount of pollution and congestion that the transportation of food creates, so-called 'food miles', it also ensures that you are supporting local farmers and producers.

### Erosion

● **Stay on the main trail** The effect of your footsteps may seem minuscule but when they're multiplied by several thousand walkers each year they become rather more significant. Avoid taking shortcuts, widening the trail or taking more than one path, especially across hay meadows and ploughed fields. This is particularly true on parts of the Coast to Coast with the boggy Pennine stage now divided into three trails to be used for four months a year (see p166), so reducing erosion on any one trail.

● **Consider walking out of season** Maximum disturbance by walkers coincides with the time of year when nature wants to do most of its growth and repair. In high-use areas, like that along much of the Coast to Coast path, the trail is often prevented from recovering.

Walking at less busy times eases this pressure while also generating year-round income for the local economy. Not only that, but it may make the walk a more relaxing experience with fewer people on the path and less competition for accommodation.

### Respect all flora and fauna

Care for all wildlife you come across along the path; it has as much right to be there as you. Tempting as it may be to pick wild flowers, leave them so the next people who pass can enjoy them too. Don't break branches off trees.

If you come across wildlife keep your distance and don't watch for too long. Your presence can cause considerable stress, particularly if the adults are with young, or in winter when the weather is harsh and food is scarce. Young animals are rarely abandoned. If you come across young birds keep away so that their mother can return.

### The code of the outdoor loo

'Going' in the outdoors is a lost art worth reclaiming, for your sake and everyone else's. As more and more people discover the joys of the outdoors this is becoming an important issue. In some parts of the world where visitor pressure is higher than in Britain, walkers and climbers are required to pack out their excrement. This might one day be necessary here. Human excrement is not only offensive to our senses but, more importantly, can infect water sources.

● **Where to go**  Wherever possible **use a toilet**. Public toilets are marked on the trail maps in this guide and you'll also find facilities in pubs, cafés and campsites along the path. If you do have to go outdoors, avoid ruins which can otherwise be welcome shelter for other walkers, as well as sites of historic or archaeological interest, and choose a place that is at least **30 metres away from running water**. Use a stick or trowel to **dig a small hole** about 15cm (6") deep to bury your excrement. It decomposes quicker when in contact with the top layer of soil or leaf mould. Stirring loose soil into your deposit speeds up decomposition. Do not squash it under rocks as this slows down the composting process. If you have to use rocks to cover it make sure they are not in contact with your faeces.

● **Toilet paper and tampons**  Toilet paper takes a long time to decompose whether buried or not. It is easily dug up by animals and may then blow into water sources or onto the path.

The best method for dealing with it is to **pack it out**. Put the used paper inside a paper bag which you then place inside a plastic bag. Then simply empty the contents of the paper bag at the next toilet you come across and throw the bag away. If this is too much bother, light your used toilet paper and watch it burn until the flames are out, you don't want to start a wild fire. Pack out **tampons** and **sanitary towels**; they take years to decompose and may also be dug up and scattered about by animals.

## Wild camping

Wild camping is not encouraged within the national parks which make up the majority of the walk. This is a shame since wild camping is much more fulfilling than camping on a designated site. Living in the outdoors without any facilities provides a valuable lesson in simple, sustainable living where the results of all your actions, from going to the loo to washing your plates, can be seen.

If you do wild camp always ask the landowner for permission. In most cases this is, of course, completely impractical so don't camp on farmland at all, but out on the uncultivated moors or in forests, and follow these suggestions:

● **Be discreet**  Camp alone or in small groups, spend only one night in each place, pitch your tent late and leave early.
● **Never light a fire**  Accidental fire is a great fear for farmers and foresters. Never make a camp fire; take matches and cigarette butts out with you to dispose of safely. The deep burn caused by camp fires, no matter how small, damages turf which can take years to recover. Cook on a camp stove instead.
● **Don't use soap or detergent**  There is no need to use soap; even biodegradable soaps and detergents pollute streams. You won't be away from a shower for more than a couple of days. Wash up without detergent; use a plastic or metal scourer, or failing that, a handful of fine pebbles or some bracken or grass.
● **Leave no trace**  Endeavour to leave no sign of having been there: no moved boulders, ripped up vegetation or dug drainage ditches. Make a final check of your campsite before departing; pick up any litter leaving the place in the same state you found it in, or better.

MINIMUM IMPACT & OUTDOOR SAFETY

## ACCESS

Britain is a crowded island with few places where you can wander as you please. Most of the land is a patchwork of fields and agricultural land and the terrain through which the Coast to Coast path marches is no different. However, there are countless public rights of way, in addition to the Coast to Coast path, that criss-cross the land.

This is fine, but what happens if you feel a little more adventurous and want to explore the moorland, woodland and hills that can also be found near the walk?

### Right to roam

The Countryside & Rights of Way Act 2000 (CRoW), or 'Right to Roam' as dubbed by walkers, came into effect in 2005 after a long campaign to allow greater public access to areas of countryside in England and Wales deemed to be uncultivated open country; this essentially means moorland, heathland, downland and upland areas. Some land is covered by restrictions (ie high-impact activities such as driving a vehicle, cycling, horse-riding are not permitted) and some land is excluded (such as gardens, parks and cultivated land). Full details are given on 🖳 www.naturalengland.org.uk.

With more freedom in the countryside comes a need for more responsibility from the walker. Remember that wild open country is still the workplace of farmers and home to all sorts of wildlife. Have respect for both and avoid disturbing domestic and wild animals.

### The Countryside Code

The Countryside Code seems like common sense but sadly some people still appear to have no understanding of how to treat the countryside they walk in. The Countryside Code is revised from time to time (a major revision took place after the CRoW Act (see above). The following is an expanded version, launched under the logo 'Respect, Protect and Enjoy':

● **Be safe** The Coast to Coast path is pretty much hazard free but you're responsible for your own safety so follow the simple guidelines outlined on pp82-5.

● **Leave all gates as you found them** Normally a farmer leaves gates closed to keep livestock in but may sometimes leave them open to allow livestock access to food or water. Leave them as you find them and if there is a sign, follow the instructions.

● **Leave livestock, crops and machinery alone** Help farmers by not interfering with their means of livelihood.

---

❏ **The Countryside Code**

**Respect other people**
● Consider the local community and other people enjoying the outdoors
● Leave gates and property as you find them and follow paths unless wider access is available

**Protect the natural environment**
● Leave no trace of your visit and take your litter home
● Keep dogs under effective control

**Enjoy the outdoors**
● Plan ahead and be prepared
● Follow advice and local signs

There's more on each point at
🖳 www.naturalengland.org.uk/
ourwork/enjoying/countrysidecode

● **Take your litter home**

● **Keep your dog under control** See pp31-2. During lambing time they should not be taken with you at all.

● **Enjoy the countryside and respect its life and work** Access to the countryside depends on being sensitive to the needs and wishes of those who live and work there.

Being courteous and friendly to those you meet will ensure a healthy future for all based on partnership and co-operation.

> ❏ **Lambing**
> Lambing takes place from mid-March to mid-May when dogs should not be taken along the path. Even a dog secured on a lead can disturb a pregnant ewe.
> If you see a lamb or ewe that appears to be in distress contact the nearest farmer.
> Also, be aware of cows with calves.

● **Keep to paths across farmland** Stick to the official path across arable or pasture land. Minimise erosion by not cutting corners or widening the path.

● **Use gates and stiles to cross fences, hedges and walls** The Coast to Coast path is well supplied with stiles where it crosses field boundaries. On some of the side trips you may find the paths less accommodating. If you have to climb over a gate because you can't open it always do so at the hinged end.

● **Guard against all risk of fire** See p79.

● **Help keep all water clean** Leaving litter and going to the toilet near a water source can pollute people's water supplies. See p78-9 for more guidelines.

● **Take special care on country roads** Drivers often drive dangerously fast on narrow winding lanes. To be safe, walk on the right facing the oncoming traffic and carry a torch or wear highly visible clothing when it's getting dark.

● **Protect wildlife, plants and trees** Care for and respect all wildlife you come across along the Coast to Coast path. Don't pick plants, break trees or scare wild animals. If you come across young birds that appear to have been abandoned leave them alone.

● **Make no unnecessary noise** Enjoy the peace and solitude of the outdoors by staying in small groups and acting unobtrusively.

# Outdoor safety

## AVOIDANCE OF HAZARDS

With good planning and preparation most hazards can be avoided. This information is just as important for those out on a day walk as for those walking the entire Coast to Coast path. Always make sure you have suitable **clothing** (see pp43-5) to keep warm and dry, whatever the conditions, and a change of inner clothes. Carrying plenty of food and water is vital too.

The **emergency signal** is six blasts on the whistle or six flashes with a torch, best done when you think someone might see or hear them.

MINIMUM IMPACT & OUTDOOR SAFETY

## Safety on the Coast to Coast path

Sadly every year people are injured while walking the Coast to Coast path. The most dangerous section is the Lake District, where the visitor numbers, elevation, lack of signage and the sometimes extreme weather all combine to imperil walkers. Locally based mountain-rescue teams are staffed by volunteers who are ready 24 hours a day 365 days of the year.

© Bryn Thomas

In an emergency phone ☎ 999 and the police will activate the service. Rescue teams rely on donations (the Patterdale's running costs are estimated to be £40,000 a year), and are called out on average about 60 times a year. There is another rescue team based at Kirkby Stephen.

All rescue teams should be treated as very much the last resort, however, and it's vital you take every precaution to ensure your own safety:

● Avoid walking on your own if possible, particularly on the Lakeland fells.
● Make sure that somebody knows your plans for every day that you're on the trail. This could be a friend or relative whom you have promised to call every night, or the place you plan to stay in at the end of each day's walk. That way, if you fail to turn up or call that evening, they can raise the alarm.
● If the weather closes in suddenly and mist descends while you're on the trail, particularly on the moors or fells, and you become uncertain of the correct trail, do not be tempted to continue. Just wait where you are and you'll find that mist often clears, at least for long enough to allow you to get your bearings. If you're still uncertain, and the weather does not look like improving, return the way you came to the nearest point of civilisation.
● Fill up with water at every opportunity and carry some high-energy snacks.
● Always carry a torch, compass, map, whistle, mobile phone and wet-weather gear with you.
● Wear sturdy boots or shoes, not trainers.
● Be extra vigilant if walking with children.

### Dealing with an accident

● Use basic first aid to treat the injury to the best of your ability.
● Work out exactly where you are. If possible leave someone with the casualty while others go to get help. If there are only two people, you have a dilemma. If you decide to get help leave all spare clothing and food with the casualty.
● In an emergency dial ☎ 999 (or the EU standard number ☎ 112). Don't assume your mobile won't work up on the fells. In 2009 a rescue was called in this way on Greenup Edge, out of Borrowdale.

## WEATHER FORECASTS

The Coast to Coast suffers from enormously unpredictable weather so it's wise to try to find out what the weather is going to be like before you set off for the day, especially if heading for high routes in the Lakes. Many hostels and tourist information centres will have pinned up somewhere a summary of the weather forecast.

The **Mountain Weather Information Service** (🖥 www.mwis.org.uk) gives detailed online forecasts for the upland regions of Britain including the Lake District and Yorkshire Dales. Online weather forecasts are also available at 🖥 www.bbc.co.uk/weather or 🖥 www .metoffice.gov.uk/public/weather/forecast.

© Chris Scott

Pay close attention to the forecast and consider altering your plans accordingly. That said, even if a fine sunny day is forecast, always assume the worst and pack some wet-weather gear.

## BLISTERS

It's essential to try out new boots before embarking on your long trek. Make sure they're comfortable and once on the move try to avoid getting them wet on the inside and remove small stones or twigs that get in the boot. Air and massage your feet at lunchtime, keep them clean, and change your socks regularly. As soon as you start to feel any hot spots developing, stop and apply a few strips of low-friction zinc oxide tape. Leave it on until the foot is pain free or the tape starts to come off. As you're walking continuously the chances are it won't get better, but it won't get worse so quickly. If you know you have problems apply the tape pre-emptively. If you've left it too late and a blister has developed you should apply a plaster such as Compeed (or the slightly cheaper clone now made by Boots). Many walkers have Compeed to thank for enabling them to complete their walk; they can last for up to two days even when wet and work with a combination of good adhesive, a gel pad and a slippery outer surface. Popping a blister reduces the pressure but can lead to infection. If the skin is broken keep the area clean with antiseptic and cover with a non-adhesive dressing material held in place with tape.

Blister-avoiding strategies include rubbing the prone area with Vaseline or wearing a thin and a thick sock as well as adjusting the tension of your laces. All are ways of reducing rubbing and foot movement against the inside of the boot.

## HYPOTHERMIA

Also known as exposure, hypothermia occurs when the body can't generate enough heat to maintain its normal temperature, usually as a result of being wet, cold, unprotected from the wind, tired and hungry. It's usually more of a problem in upland areas such as in the Lakes and on the moors.

Hypothermia is easily avoided by wearing suitable clothing, carrying and consuming enough food and drink, being aware of the weather conditions and checking the morale of your companions. Early signs to watch for are feeling cold and tired with involuntary shivering. Find some shelter as soon as possible and warm the victim up with a hot drink and some chocolate or other high-energy food. If possible give them another warm layer of clothing and allow them to rest until feeling better.

If allowed to worsen, erratic behaviour, slurring of speech and poor co-ordination will become apparent and the victim can very soon progress into unconsciousness, followed by coma and death. Quickly get the victim out of wind and rain, improvising a shelter if necessary.

Rapid restoration of bodily warmth is essential and best achieved by bare-skin contact: someone should get into the same sleeping bag as the patient, both having stripped to the bare essentials, placing any spare clothing under or over them to build up heat. Send or call urgently for help.

## HYPERTHERMIA

Not an ailment that you would normally associate with the north of England, hyperthermia (heat exhaustion and heatstroke) is a serious problem nonetheless.

Symptoms of **heat exhaustion** include thirst, fatigue, giddiness, a rapid pulse, raised body temperature, low urine output and, if not treated, delirium and finally a coma. The best cure is to drink plenty of water.

**Heatstroke** is another matter altogether, and even more serious. A high body temperature and an absence of sweating are early indications, followed by symptoms similar to hypothermia (see above) such as a lack of co-ordination, convulsions and coma.

Death will follow if treatment is not given instantly. Sponge the victim down, wrap them in wet towels, fan them, and get help immediately.

## SUNBURN

It can happen, even in northern England and even on overcast days. The only surefire way to avoid it is to stay wrapped up or smother yourself in sunscreen (with a minimum factor of 15) and apply it regularly throughout the day. Don't forget your lips, nose and the back of your neck.

## COLLAPSE OF MORALE

This is not something that can be quickly treated with medication, but is probably the biggest cause of abandoned attempts on the Coast to Coast walk. Weather and injury which add up to exhaustion might be presumed to be the most common culprit, but as we know plenty manage the walk in monsoonal conditions and hobble into Robin Hood's Bay with a great experience behind them. Others though, can suddenly think: 'what's the point, I'm not enjoying this'.

One morning we met a teenager tramping along the road to Kirkby. He had all the right gear but we could tell he'd had enough that day if not altogether. A morning's rain in the patchy bogs west of Ravenseat had weakened his resolve to tackle the notorious Nine Standards (he was heading Lakeward). He'd done a long-distance path before, but in company, and at that age he'd had much more fun. He was merely lonely, but for others it's the wrong company that leads to resentment and thus a no less miserable experience.

What it all boils down to is this: knowing your limitations and addressing your motivation; matching expectations with your companions; avoiding putting yourself under stress and being flexible rather than insisting on hammering out every last mile without repetition, hesitation or deviation. You can add having good equipment to that list too.

Above all, settle on a **realistic schedule** with at least one, if not two, rest day(s) over the full trek. Even then, it's amazing how sore muscles and feet can recover overnight, especially if you can at least start the day in sunshine. Don't assume a rest day has to be in a town like Kirkby or Richmond. A big room in a lone moorland farmhouse or even two nights in a holiday cottage with a telly or a fat book may suit those who find the bigger towns an intrusion on the spirit of the walk.

A paradox of the Coast to Coast's popularity is the need to book accommodation or baggage-carrying services, so erasing all spontaneity in the adventure. How nice it would be to be able to walk as far as you feel on any given day; on most stages there's certainly enough accommodation to do so, but unfortunately, to paraphrase Jack Nicholson, 22 million people live within 100 miles of the trail and usually some have got there before you. And so every day for the next fortnight is rigidly mapped out, but how can you predict at what point your knee or festering blisters will make walking intolerable? The only alternative is to put up with camping or plan an unbooked accommodated schedule out of the high season and which furthermore avoids weekends in busy spots. Or swallow your pride and skip a stage if you can't face it, catching a lift with the Packhorse/Sherpa van (see pp28-9) or public transport to keep on schedule with your B&Bs or hostels.

© Henry Stedman

It's not fashionable to admit it, but not every day on the Coast to Coast will necessarily be a winner. It's one reason why many people go on to do the walk again and again; the first time is often looked back on as an eye-opening reconnaissance (see the boxes on p40 & p42).

Perhaps the best way to avoid the risk of getting fed up is not to tackle the full 200 miles in one go. Wainwright certainly didn't (but then he was in his sixties). Thirteen days non-stop on the trail, come rain or shine, really is a bit much for most people (a schedule which at first glance the thirteen stages of this book may seem to encourage). Some days end up as nothing more than forced marches or gritty lessons in pain management because, for many, our prized vacation time is treated as an extension of our busy work life where we must make the most of every minute, 24/7. Here at Trailblazer we propose: turn on, tune in and slow down.

# 4 ROUTE GUIDE & MAPS

## Using the guide

The route is described from west to east and divided into 13 stages. Though each of these roughly corresponds to a day's walk between centres of accommodation, it's not necessarily the best way to structure *your* trek. There are enough places to stay – barring a couple of stretches – for you to pretty much divide the walk up however you want. This is even more true if you're prepared to camp, in which case you can pitch your tent virtually anywhere, as long as you follow the guidelines on p79.

On pp34-5 are tables to help you plan an itinerary. To provide further help, practical information is presented on the trail maps, including waypoints (WPT) and walking times, places to stay, camp and eat, as well as shops from which to buy provisions. Further service details are given in the text under the entry for each settlement. See box pp91-3 for navigation trouble spots.

### TRAIL MAPS [for map key see inside back cover]
### Scale and walking times
The trail maps are to a scale of 1:20,000 (1cm = 200m; $3^1/_8$ inches = one mile). Each full size map covers about two miles but that's a very rough estimate owing to variety of terrain.

Walking times are given along the side of each map; the arrow shows the direction to which the time refers. Black triangles indicate the points between which the times have been taken. These times are merely a tool to help you plan and are not there to judge your walking ability. After a couple of days you'll know how fast you walk compared with the time bars and can plan your days more accurately as a result. **See note on walking times in the box p87**.

### Up or down?
The trail is shown as a dashed line. An arrow across the trail indicates the gradient; two arrows show that it's steep. Note that the *arrow points uphill*, the opposite of what OS maps use on steep roads. A good way to remember our style is: '**front-pointing on crampons up** a steep slope' and 'open arms – Julie Andrews-style – **spreading out** to unfold the view **down** below'.

### GPS waypoints
The numbered GPS waypoints refer to the list on pp259-63.

___

❑ **Important note – walking times**
Unless otherwise specified, **all times in this book refer only to the time spent walk-ing**. You will need to add 20-30% to allow for rests, photography, checking the map, drinking water etc. When planning the day's hike count on 5-7 hours' actual walking.

___

### Other features
Features are marked on the map when they are pertinent to navigation. To avoid clutter, not all features have been marked each time they occur.

### Accommodation
Accommodation marked on the map is either on or within easy reach of the path. Many B&B proprietors based a mile or two off the trail will offer to collect walkers from the nearest point on the trail and take them back next morning.

Details of each place are given in the accompanying text. The number of **rooms** of each type is given at the beginning of each entry, ie: **S** = Single, **T** = Twin room, **D** = Double room, **Tr** = Triple room and **Qd** = Quad. Note that many of the triple/quad rooms have a double bed and one/two single beds thus in a group of three or four, two people would have to share the double bed but it also means the room can be used as a double or twin.

**Rates** quoted for B&B-style accommodation are **per person (pp)** based on two people sharing a room for a one-night stay; rates are usually discounted for longer stays. Where a single room **(sgl)** is available the rate for that is quoted if different from the rate per person. The rate for single occupancy **(sgl occ)** of a double/twin may be higher, and the per person rate for three/four sharing a triple/quad may be lower. At some places the only option is a **room rate**; this will be the same whether one or two people (or more if permissible) use the room. See p24 for more information on rates.

The text also mentions whether the bedrooms have a **private bathroom** (usually en suite but it may be just outside the room) or a shared bathroom. Most of these have only a shower. In the text ☛ signifies that at least one room has a bathroom with a **bath**, or access to a bath, for those who prefer a relaxed soak at the end of the day. Also noted is whether the premises have WI-FI (WI-FI), if **dogs** (🐾 – see also p31 & p257) are welcome, if packed lunches (Ⓛ) are available and the associated charges.

# The route guide

## ST BEES                    see map p89
The settlements along the Cumbrian coast are not all jewels, but situated close to the county's westernmost point, the ancient vil-lage of St Bees makes a fine starting point to your walk, with just enough facilities and services to set you on your way.

The village is agricultural in origin; many of the buildings along the main street were once farms dating back to the 17th century and, on Outrigg, there's even an ancient **pinfold** – a circular, stone-walled enclosure once used to house stray live-stock recovered from the surrounding hills.

The livestock would remain in the pinfold until the farmer could afford to pay a fine to retrieve them.

The town's main sight is its distinctive red sandstone **Priory Church**, once part of a thriving 12th-century Benedictine priory dedicated to the saints Bega (see box below) and Mary. Original Norman features include the impressively elaborate Great West Door and, standing opposite, the curious carved Dragon Stone, a door lintel also from the 12th century. The church is believed to stand on a site that had been holy to Christians for centuries prior to the monastery's foundation and has seen over eight hundred years of unbroken worship since then. Not even the dissolution of the monasteries ordered by Henry VIII in 1538, which led to the closure of this and every other priory you'll come across on the Coast to Coast path, could stop the site from being used by the villagers as their main centre of worship even though Henry's commissioners had removed the lead from the roof and for much of the 16th century the whole building was left open to the elements. Restoration began in the early 17th century, with a major overhaul of the building taking place in the 19th. Thankfully, however, the architects preserved much of the church's sturdy Norman character.

As with quite a few of the larger churches on the route, there's a table just inside the door with various pamphlets on the history of both the church and the village. Don't miss the glass case in the southern aisle displaying a shroud and a lock of woman's hair unearthed in the excavation of a 14th-century grave; and the graveyard to the north of the church, where you'll find the shaft of a stone cross from the 10th century (in other words, older than every other part of the church), with its Celtic decorations still visible.

Incidentally, **St Bees School** across the road from the church is one of the most venerable in Cumbria, having been founded by **Edmund Grindal** on his deathbed in 1583. Grindal rose to become Archbishop of Canterbury during the reign of Elizabeth I and his birthplace, on the junction of Finkle St and Cross St, is the oldest surviving house in St Bees.

### Services

There's a well-stocked **post office** and **shop** (☎ 01946 822343, ☐ www.stbees-post office.co.uk; post office Mon-Fri 9am-5.30pm, Sat 9am-12.30pm, shop Mon-Sat 6am-8pm, Sun 7.30am-8pm) with a decent selection of groceries, including delicious hot pies, wine and beer, Coast to Coast maps, T-shirts (£4.99) and souvenirs. It's also the home of the local Link **cash machine** (£1.75 fee); the last on the trail before Grasmere. There's a **tourist infor-**

---

### ❑ Who was St Bees?

St Bees is actually a corruption of St Bega, an Irish princess who fled her native country sometime between the 6th and 9th centuries to avoid an arranged marriage with a Norwegian prince. Landing on England's north-west coast, so the story goes, St Bega lived as a hermit and became renowned for the good deeds she carried out. And that's about it really, or at least it would be, if it wasn't for the legends that have grown up over the centuries. In the most famous of these, St Bega approached the local landlord, Lord Egremont, for some land for a convent she wished to found.

The statue of **St Bega** on Station Rd.

Egremont promised St Bega all the land covered by snow the next day; which, as it was to be midsummer's day, was not as generous an offer as it first appeared. Miraculously, however, snow did fall that day and St Bega was able to build her convent, around which the village was founded.

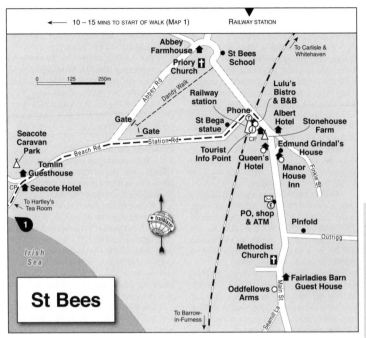

← 10 – 15 MINS TO START OF WALK (MAP 1)   RAILWAY STATION

Abbey Farmhouse
Priory Church
St Bees School
To Carlisle & Whitehaven
Railway station
Lulu's Bistro & B&B
Albert Hotel
Stonehouse Farm
Abbey Rd
Dandy Walk
Phone
Gate
Gate
St Bega statue
Station Rd
Edmund Grindal's House
Beach Rd
Seacote Caravan Park
Tomlin Guesthouse
Seacote Hotel
To Hartley's Tea Room
Tourist Info Point
Queen's Hotel
Manor House Inn
Finkle St
trailblaze
PO, shop & ATM
Pinfold
Outrigg
Irish Sea
Methodist Church
St Bees
Fairladies Barn Guest House
Oddfellows Arms
Main St
Seamill Brow
To Barrow-in-Furness

0  125  250m

ROUTE GUIDE AND MAPS

mation point** by the train station but it has limited information; a better bet is St Bees' website (🖳 www.stbees.org.uk). There's also a **public phone**.

Two things the town lacks are an outdoor shop and a pharmacy, but a 10-minute train ride north to Whitehaven will deliver you alongside a huge Tesco as well as both a Millets and a Boots on King St, ten minutes' walk into town. Alternatively you have to wait until you reach Grasmere.

### Where to stay

On the front behind the RNLI lifeboat station and owned by the adjacent hotel (see p90) are the serried cabins of *Seacote Caravan Park* (Map 1, p95; ☎ 01946 822777, 🖳 www.seacote.com; 🐾£3 ; WI-FI free but only available in the hotel). You can camp for £10-18 depending on the size of your tent. They recommend booking in peak season though they will try to accommodate

Coast to Coast walkers. **Camping** (£5pp) is also available in the back garden of the central *Stonehouse Farm* (☎ 01946 822224, 🖳 www.stonehousefarm.net; 1S/3D/1T/4Tr; all en suite; 🛏; 🐾£5; Ⓛ £6; WI-FI), where you can fall asleep to the hooting of the barn owl. A long-established and reliable **B&B**, Stonehouse is situated just 30 metres from the station and is the only working farm within St Bees. Stonehouse's en suite rooms are located in its Georgian farmhouse, while the dairy next door has been converted into a spacious family cottage. On the other side of the farmhouse is an even older cottage (dating back to 1660) where the character of the building more than compensates for the lack of en suite facilities. B&B costs £35pp (£40/45 for a single/single occupancy). They accept most credit cards. Breakfast is available for campers (around £7). **Long-term parking** (£2 per night) is also available.

*Abbey Farmhouse* (☎ 01946 823534; ☐ www.abbeyfarm-stbees.co.uk; 1S/2D/1T; en suite or private facilities; ☞; WI-FI; Ⓛ £6) is a comfortable place just around the corner from the church. B&B is from £40pp and they also have long-stay parking facilities for £2 a night, donated to charity. They offer a free bottle of wine to guests who have just finished the Coast-to-Coast.

Recommended by readers for its cosy rooms, good breakfast and welcoming staff is *Lulu's Bistro & Wine Bar* (☎ 01946 822600, ☐ www.lulusbistro.co.uk; 3D; en suite; ☞; WI-FI; Ⓛ £6.50). B&B costs from £35pp (sgl occ £55); £30pp (sgl occ £50) with a continental breakfast.

Further up Main St the 17th-century *Queen's Hotel* (☎ 01946 822287; ☐ www.marstonspubs.co.uk/queenshotelcumbria; 3S/4D/3D or T/2T/1Qd; all en suite; ☞; WI-FI currently only in public areas) charges £35-55 for a single, £27.50-35pp for two sharing or £80 for the quad room.

*Manor House Inn* (☎ 01946 820587, ☐ www.manorhousestbees.co.uk; 1S/3D/3T/1Tr; all en suite; ☞; 🐾£5; WI-FI) is another impressive-looking hotel in St Bees with B&B from £35pp (sgl/sgl occ £50; £85 for three in the triple room).

*Albert Hotel* (☎ 01946 822345, ☐ www.alberthotel-stbees.co.uk; 1 Finkle St; 2S/2D/3T; some en suite; others share facilities; Ⓛ £4) has B&B for £32-40pp. There are great views from some of the rooms. They have laundry and drying facilities and also have a bar and a beer garden.

Up the top of Main St, *Fairladies Barn Guest House* (☎ 01946 822718, ☐ www.fairladiesbarn.co.uk; 1S/3D/2T/2Tr; all en suite; WI-FI; Ⓛ £6.50) is a cut above the rest; a large, restored 17th-century sandstone barn with varied and charming rooms. The most popular is the unusually shaped studio room under the roof at the end of the barn; this is used as a triple. They also have a small **bar** (daily in the evenings). B&B costs £22.50-32.50pp, single occupancy is £45.

*Tomlin Guest House* (☎ 01946 822284, ☐ iwhitehead44@yahoo.co.uk; 1D/2D or T/1Tr; one en suite, others share facilities; 🐾; WI-FI; Ⓛ £5.50) is on Beach Rd, a short walk from Mile Zero (see Map 1, p95) and is a friendly little place charging £20-30pp, single occupancy £40. Off-street parking is £1.50 per night.

The massive complex by the beach car park is *Seacote Hotel* (☎ 01946 822300, ☐ www.seacote.com/Hotel/; 7S/28D/24T/4Qd; all en suite; ☞; WI-FI). B&B costs £30-37.50pp, £50/60 for a single/single occupancy and £105 for four in a quad room; breakfast is £8.50pp.

## Where to eat and drink

If it's just a snack you want, the pies in the **village shop** are excellent. You can buy provisions here and also in Hartley's Beach Shop & Tea Room (see below).

*Manor House Inn* (see Where to stay; food served Mon-Sat noon-9pm, Sun noon-3pm & 5-8.30pm) is a reliable place with a comprehensive menu and a Sunday carvery lunch from £7.95. The restaurant was being renovated at the time of research but should now be open. They also have the *Coast to Coast* bar (daily noon to around 1am) so how can you resist a swift pint here?

The waiting room at the railway station has been reborn as *Lulu's Bistro & Wine Bar* (see Where to stay; Tue-Sat 6pm to late; in the main season if the weather is good they may be open all day). Sharing platters (seafood, charcuterie, nachos or oriental) range from £11 to £26 for 2-4 people. Other interesting choices include Thai beef salad (£13.95), moules frites (£13.95) and barbary duck with sloe gin (£17.25).

*Queen's Hotel* (see Where to stay; food served Easter to Oct daily noon-2pm & 5-9pm, Nov to Easter Sun-Thur 5-9pm, Fri-Sun noon-2pm & 5-9pm) has a good-value menu and a bar known for its real ales (such as the Jennings Bitter) and malt whiskies. Most main dishes are under the £10 mark and include curries, fish pie and giant Yorkshire pudding.

Up the hill at 92 Main St, you'll get pub grub from under £7 at *Oddfellows Arms* (☎ 01946 822317; food served Thur-Sat 6.30-9pm & Sun noon-4pm).

For sea views, cream teas and excellent ice-cream made on the premises, call in at *Hartley's Beach Shop & Tea Room*

(Map 1, p95; ☎ 01946 820175; daily summer 8am-8pm, winter to 5pm) on the foreshore, just a short walk before Mile Zero. They also sell provisions, books and maps. At nearby *Seacote Hotel* (see Where to stay) there's a bar serving pub grub noon-8.30pm.

**Transport**      **(see also pp52-5)**
**Trains** (Mon-Sat) from St Bees go north to Carlisle and south to Barrow-in-Furness; see p51.

The No 26 **bus** (Mon-Sat) runs to Sandwith and Whitehaven; on Sunday the X6 service goes to Whitehaven.

## ❑ HOW NOT TO LOSE YOUR WAY

Although it improves incrementally, the Coast to Coast path is the least well signposted of Britain's popular long-distance trails. Principally this is because it's not been officially designated a 'National Trail' with all the funding benefits that involves, such as consistent and effective signage or slabs over bogs that the less used Pennine Way got years ago. The trail also passes through the Lake District where the national park authorities have elected not to sully the upland trails with signposts. All this, combined with occasions of low visibility, may in places give problems with navigation. The minute you step out of the Lake District National Park signage by local authorities, local landowners or well-wishers, improves in places, all the way across the Pennines into Yorkshire. Here, among other signs, the North Yorkshire County Council's yellow waymark discs are used towards the North Yorkshire Moors and the North Sea. Elsewhere, wooden 'Coast to Coast' fingerposts point the way, though not always accurately.

In 2012 the Wainwright Society announced agreements had been made to mark fingerposts at public road crossings with a special C2C logo featuring Wainwright's 'AW' monogram. In late 2013 we spotted very few of these so the value seems more promotional than navigational, to celebrate the fortieth anniversary of the original guidebook's publication.

Consistency aside, what is actually needed are *additional* marker posts and directional waymarks across the trouble spots listed below, as well as a few other places. In many places supportive farmers have taken it upon themselves to fulfill this task.

### A few tips
Our advice is to **study the book's maps closely** and read through the entire day's stage before you start it, making a note of possible tricky spots. Once on the move it's easy to get distracted, be it blindly following others who may be on some other walk, or simply following the obvious trail while engrossed in a natter, and so miss an obscure but crucial turn off. It's a nuisance, but the C2C being what it is, you'll have to consult the book frequently to keep on track.

**Keep this book readily accessible** come rain or shine; at times you'll be referring to it several times an hour. A large pocket will do in the dry, but overall a waterproof **map case** on a neck string works best. In pelting rain you tend to get your head down and press on, but the book's maps may still need frequent attention.

This guidebook's maps depict only a narrow strip along the trail. Depending on your experience in reading maps as well as the location of the accommodation you may use, getting the **Ordnance Survey sheets OL4, OL5 and OL19** covering the Lake District and the Pennines might be worthwhile. Even then, a **compass** helps on the occasions when you're not sure the path you're following is heading in the same direction as the one you think you're on according to the book.   *(cont'd overleaf)*

ROUTE GUIDE AND MAPS

## ❏ HOW NOT TO LOSE YOUR WAY (cont'd from p91)

### Trailblazer tracklog and GPS waypoints

The absolute bombproof way of not getting lost on the Coast to Coast is to refer to a **GPS tracklog**, displayed as a continuous line on either a GPS unit or a smartphone running GPS. Ground-based mobile location signals aren't the same and anyway, don't cover remote areas or even some lakeland valleys. The C2C requires a GPS satellite signal which on a smartphone eats battery power. Clearly you won't depend on a tracklog every step of the way, so save the batteries on either unit by merely activating them when in need. To download the GPS tracklog on which this edition's maps are based, see the Trailblazer website. In addition, **GPS waypoints** are listed on pp259-63 and are also downloadable from the website. They can be imported into a device or simply manually keyed from the back of the book into a GPS or plotted on an OS map to pin down a location.

### Common navigational trouble spots

These are the well-known trouble spots on the Coast to Coast path. The list may well be rendered obsolete by improvements in waymarking and signage, and in some cases, drainage – or by simply making use of the book's GPS data. On our maps we've also highlighted the places where people frequently get lost with a **warning triangle** to emphasise the need for vigilance; note them well. That's not to say that you won't get lost elsewhere, but we think in most places you'll recognise your error within less than a mile.

● **Stanley Pond** (Maps 3 & 4)  Just after the rail tunnel the route is often waterlogged, causing walkers to detour to the south, get disoriented and so take the wrong route into the woods. At the woods (Wᴘᴛ 004) head north-east up the field to the tunnel, as the map suggests.

● **Dent Hill** (Maps 5 & 6)  Forestry clearance only evident on aerial imagery (and not on OS maps), as well as a key sign that used to point the other way can all add up to a fractious experience. On one occasion in bad visibility a compass helped us get from the point where the wall ends on Dent Hill to the stile (Wᴘᴛ 012), but at the key junction down the other side (Wᴘᴛ 013), a sign now points clearly east-north-east to the very tall stile leading to Raven Crag hill. If the weather/visibility are terrible on your Dent Hill day, consider taking the quiet road from Black How Farm to Ennerdale Bridge.

● **Leaving Black Sail Hut** (Wᴘᴛ 021 and 22) (Map 12)  Another common trap; take the less obvious but more northerly path through the drumlin hillocks to the bottom of Loft Beck (Wᴘᴛ 022), not the more obvious path heading southeast to Great Gable.

● **Top of Loft Beck** (Map 12)  Clear as a bell in good conditions, in poor visibility some lose their way here and OS maps aren't much help. If you miss the massive, beck-top cairn (Wᴘᴛ 022) and arrive at the fence in the bogs, just follow it east and south to the stile (Wᴘᴛ 023), then carry on towards Grey Knotts (Map 13).

● **Greenup Edge** (Map 16) The 'edge' is actually a broad col preceded by bogs crossed by an indistinct path marked by hard-to-see cairns on low outcrops. Even in perfect visibility hitting the right fence post and nearby twin cairns (Wᴘᴛ 029) takes some luck as other, more prominent fenceposts along the col's rim can lure you astray. Aim resolutely for the southern side of the col at a point where a track begins to ascend to Low White Stones to the south. Or, do as many do and hit the Edge early to avoid the mired cairned path, then follow it southeast to Wᴘᴛ 029. Having located the twin cairns, the route down to the next key junction at the top of Easedale is clearer.

● **Boredale Hause** (Map 25)  Several converging paths can make this grassy junction confusing; take the most used one heading south-east then south to Angle Tarn.

● **High Street** (Map 27)  From Angle Tarn to The Knott is these days a single, clear path and short of a white-out, it's hard to think what the problem is at High Street other than simply missing the flattened trackside cairn before the col. It marks another clear track running north-east to Kidsty Pike, the route's high point.

● **South of Oddendale** (Map 36)  Some experience a brief route-finding wobble here even though there are poles and good landmarks. Leave the main track for WPT 061 at the southern corner of the strip plantation, then head up to the wall-like rim of limestone and use the 'two trees' landmark (WPT 062).

● **Sunbiggin Tarn** (Maps 39 & 40)  Locate the clear path off the road curving south of the tarn and over a footbridge (WPT 067), then at the southern edge of a walled pen aim uphill for the reservoir head on a hilltop, just over a minor road.

● **Nine Standards routes** (Maps 45, 46 & 47)  In very thick mist seeing the mysterious cairns (WPT 082) before they see you can be tricky, as can continuing from there south past the trig point to the key Red and Blue route junction (WPT 085, half a mile away) while avoiding bogs on the way. If you get to this junction, the Blue route has posts leading to Whitsundalebeck valley, the Red route has less frequent landmarks. This ruined section is in dire need of Pennine-Way-like paving. The lower Green route is easier to follow and much less of a mire.

● **Graystone Hills** (Maps 91 & 92)  Even in clear weather, when crossing this final stretch of moorland one marker pole doesn't quite seem to lead to the next and others distract you, even though you can see the cars on the nearby A171. Then once off the moor, getting the 500m from WPT 147 to the start of the rocky ditch may take some intuition. Watch your orientation closely or use GPS.

## STAGE 1: ST BEES TO ENNERDALE BRIDGE  MAPS 1-7

### Introduction

There is a lot of variety in this **14-mile (22.5km, 6¼hr)** stage, beginning with a cliff-top walk along the Irish Sea and ending (weather permitting) with a high-level view from Dent Hill across to the brooding western fells of the Lake District.

Most will find this first day a bit of a struggle, particularly the haul up and over Dent Hill into Ennerdale Bridge (where there are few places to stay). If you think this may include you, pace yourself while you have a choice and consider stopping near Cleator or Egremont, both a mile or two off the path, before continuing on the second day to the youth hostels at High Gillerthwaite or even Black Sail. In a couple of days you may be glad you did.

## The route

As far as we and most other walkers are concerned, '**Mile Zero**' (WPT 001) on the path is at the Coast to Coast monument by the RNLI hut facing the Irish Sea. To get to Mile Zero follow Beach Rd to the shore, baptise your boots in the surf and take a photo by the sign with its new steel adornment showing the entire C2C elevation profile. Some walkers even collect a small pebble as a keepsake to drop into the North Sea at the end of the walk. Suitably initiated, turn north-west, steel yourself for the adventure about to unfold, and climb up the steep path to the clifftop. You're now on the Coast to Coast path, with a fence on one side and what becomes a 300ft (90m) drop on the other.

The cliffs themselves are made of red St Bees sandstone, used in the construction of many of the buildings in the vicinity since medieval times and part of a broad sedimentary bed which you'll encounter again in the Vale of Eden on the far side of the Lakes.

The first notable landmark is the cleft of **Fleswick Bay** (Map 2) composed of a secluded pebble beach surrounded by red sandstone cliffs with some unusually weathered boulders on the shore, if you can be bothered to make the short detour. This bay marks the dividing line between the constituent parts of St Bees Head: **South Head**, which you've been on up to now, and **North Head** (Map 2), which you now climb up to from the bay. Two features distinguish this latter part of St Bees Head: the three **RSPB observation points**, to the left of the path, which allow you to safely peer over the cliffs and observe the seabirds nesting there (including puffins, terns and England's only colony of black guillemots); and **St Bees Lighthouse**, a little way inland from the path but clearly visible since South Head.

If you're already puffed out, ***Tarn Flatt Hall*** (Map 2; ☎ 01946 692162, 🖳 www.lakelandcampingbarns.co.uk), a basic **camping barn**, is best reached by turning off the path here towards the lighthouse and continuing east for quarter of a mile/400m. It sleeps 12 and costs £9.50pp. The barn comes with electric lighting (no power sockets), a slab to put your camping stove on and a wood-burning fire, with wood available from the farm. Showers cost 50p. Booking is recommended and should be done through the website; however, if you have queries you can phone. Parking (long- and short-stay) is also available.

After the lighthouse the path continues to the tip of **North Head** before curving east along the coast and eventually turning inland after **Birkham's Quarry**.

Fifteen minutes later you arrive in the village of **Sandwith** (pronounced 'Sanith'). This is the first settlement of note on the trail; it's almost five miles/8km along the path from St Bees (though only two miles/3km as the crow flies!). ***Grovewood House B&B*** (Map 3; ☎ 01946 63482; 🖳 www.grovewood house.com; 1D or T en suite with whirlpool bath 👅; WI-FI; continental breakfast; £45-47.50pp, £60-65 sgl occ) offers self-contained accommodation with a kitchenette. The owners are happy to meet people at St Bees station and take their luggage which means you can arrive in St Bees and then set off on the walk unencumbered for the first stage. The village pub, the ***Dog and Partridge*** (☎ 01946 592177) is now open daily and also does **food**. If you've had enough

# MAP 1

SOUTH HEAD

START OF WALK AT THE SIGN ON THE SEA WALL. CROSS BRIDGE OVER ROTTINGTON BECK THEN CLIMB UP CLIFFS ON STEPS WITH FENCE ON RIGHT

ROTTINGTON BECK

SIGNPOST: ROBIN HOOD'S BAY 191 MILES

FENCE AROUND LANDSLIP

ALTERNATIVE PATH

BENCH

FENCE

AFTER GATE, FENCE BETWEEN YOU & CLIFF EDGE

ALTERNATIVE PATH ON OTHER SIDE OF FENCE

RUINED COASTGUARD STATION. CAN SEE SELLAFIELD TO SOUTH, LIGHTHOUSE TO NORTH AND ISLE OF MAN ACROSS THE WATER

'MILE ZERO COAST SIGN' TO COAST SIGN

001

BENCHES

IRISH SEA

SEACOTE CARAVAN PARK

SEACOTE CARAVAN PARK

RNLI

TOILET

PHONE

CP

Tomlin Guesthouse

Seacote Hotel

Hartley's Tea Room

BEACH ROAD

TO ST BEES

¼ mile

500m

0    APPROX SCALE    0

2

40 MINS TO FLESWICK BAY (MAP 2)

START OF COAST TO COAST PATH

already, a **bus** (No 20/26, Mon-Sat) passes through en route between St Bees and Whitehaven; see pp52-5 for further details. Some readers have found going back to St Bees for a second night and catching the bus back to Sandwith next morning is a gentle way to break themselves into the trek. Others arrive in St Bees by train mid-afternoon from just about anywhere in the country and make it to Cleator in three hours.

Taking the road past the pub, the path crosses Byerstead Rd and, just over half a mile (0.8km) later, the B5345 linking Whitehaven to St Bees. From the tunnel beneath the railway line (Map 3) at the foot of the hill, the trail crosses waterlogged fields around what was **Stanley Pond** (with possible navigation issues; see box p92) and a small stream (**Scalegill Beck**; Map 4), before passing underneath a disused railway. We, however, advise you to take the steps on your right up the side of the tunnel onto the disused railway track; take a left here and follow the 'track' to Moor Row.

### MOOR ROW                     MAP 4, p99

Moor Row lacks the village-green charm of Sandwith but does have a **phone** and *Su Ellen's Baker's Shop* ( ☎ 07749 485492, Tue-Fri 7am-4pm, Sat 8am-noon) which does takeaway pasties, pies and snacks. Just past the war memorial is the *Walkers Pop In Café* (Easter to Nov, daily 10am-6pm, closed Wed), a good spot for a sit down and a cuppa. The owner is very friendly and will tell you, with an encouraging smile, that you are exactly half way to Ennerdale Bridge.

Around the corner, *Jasmine House* (☎ 01946 815795, 🖳 www.jasminehouse

bandb.com; 1S/2D/2D or Tr; all en suite; ☛; WI-FI; Ⓛ £5 if ordered the night before) does B&B from £30pp (sgl £35, three in room £85). The owner, Jean, is very welcoming to Coast to Coasters and offers transport to and back from the nearest pub for an evening meal, making this a great first night if you don't feel quite ready for the long haul over Dent Hill to Ennerdale.

The No 6 **bus** (Mon-Sat) passes through on its route between Whitehaven and Seascale/Muncaster Castle; see pp52-5 for further details.

Following the uncomfortably narrow and busy road south out of Moor Row (signposted to Egremont), you're relieved to soon get off it and head into a field. A series of kissing gates follows as you cross the dismantled railway once more on your way towards Cleator, arriving alongside St Leonard's Church.

### CLEATOR                      MAP 5, p101

As with Moor Row before it, it's clear that Wordsworth's lyrical ballads never reached out to immortalise the grim, pebbledashed, terraces of Cleator. Remnants of 12th-century masonry in the **church** (St Leonard's) attest to the village's venerability, but the abiding impression dates from a 19th-century iron-ore mining boom at which time Irish migrants flooded into the area (as the many Celtic house names suggest). The mining collapsed in the latter half of the 19th century and the nearby settlements followed suit; a familiar story repeated across west Cumbria, ameliorated today by the ongoing decommissioning of

the ageing Sellafield nuclear plant, offering work to the 10,000 who want it.

Note that **Cleator Stores** (☎ 01946 810038; summer Mon-Fri 6am-6.30pm, Sat 8am-2pm, Sun 8.30am-3pm; winter Mon-Fri 6am-6pm, Sat 8am-2pm, Sun 8.30am-12.30pm) is now the **last decent store** until Grasmere, although you can get basics in Borrowdale (see p118). Otherwise, **Cleator Moor**, the regional hub with many grand 19th-century edifices, some once painted by Lowry, is a mile to the north, with an ATM, corner shops and several junk-food outlets. There's also an ATM at Egremont.

(cont'd on p100)

PATH CLOSE TO
CLIFF EDGE.
TAKE CARE

BIRKHAM'S
QUARRY

GAP IN
FENCE

ST BEES
HEAD SIGN

GATE AT END
OF WALL

BENCH

BROKEN
STILE

**3**

PATH IS NARROW -
TAKE CARE HERE
OR GO VIA
SHORTCUT

STONE
BENCH

TWO BOULDERS
SAFER SHORTCUT

PATH BY
CLIFF EDGE

COASTGUARD
STATION

TO TARN FLATT
CAMPING BARN

ST BEES
LIGHTHOUSE

trailblazer

BIRD
OBSERVATION
POINTS

NORTH
HEAD

RSPB
NATURE
RESERVE

FLESWICK BAY

**MAP 2**

AN ISOLATED DELIGHT &
YOUR LAST CHANCE TO DIP
YOUR FEET IN THE IRISH SEA

**1**

0 — ¼ mile
0 — 500m
APPROX SCALE

50 MINS TO SANDWITH (MAP 3)

COASTGUARD STATION

20 MINS

FLESWICK BAY

ROUTE GUIDE AND MAPS

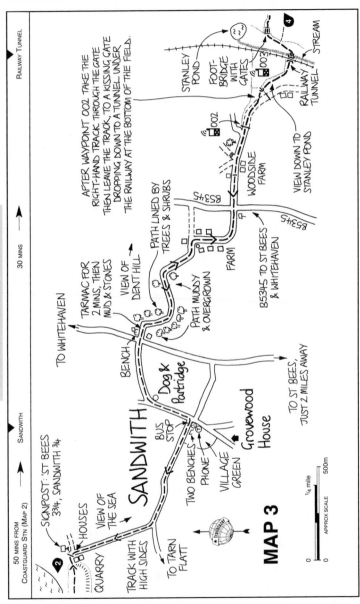

MAP 3

50 MINS FROM COASTGUARD STN (MAP 2) → SANDWITH → 30 MINS → RAILWAY TUNNEL

SIGNPOST: 'ST BEES 3¾, SANDWITH ¾'

HOUSES

VIEW OF THE SEA

QUARRY

TRACK WITH HIGH SIDES

TO TARN FLATT

TO WHITEHAVEN

BENCH

TARMAC FOR 2 MINS, THEN MUD & STONES

VIEW OF DENT HILL

PATH LINED BY TREES & SHRUBS

PATH MUDDY & OVERGROWN

SANDWITH

Dog & Partridge

BUS STOP

TWO BENCHES

PHONE

VILLAGE GREEN

Grovewood House

TO ST BEES, JUST 2 MILES AWAY

FARM

B5345 TO ST BEES & WHITEHAVEN

B5345

B5345

WOODSIDE FARM

VIEW DOWN TO STANLEY POND

002

AFTER WAYPOINT 002 TAKE THE RIGHT-HAND TRACK THROUGH THE GATE THEN LEAVE THE TRACK, TO A KISSING GATE DROPPING DOWN TO A TUNNEL UNDER THE RAILWAY AT THE BOTTOM OF THE FIELD.

STANLEY POND

FOOT-BRIDGE WITH GATES

003

RAILWAY TUNNEL

STREAM

4

2

¼ mile

APPROX SCALE

500m

# MAP 4

**MOOR ROW**

*Jasmine House B&B*

20 MINS TO CLEATOR (KILN BROW) → (MAP 5)

Moor Row

45 MINS FROM RAILWAY TUNNEL (MAP 3)

OVERHEAD ELECTRICITY WIRES

HEAD UPHILL DIAGONALLY THROUGH FIELD TO GATE

SCALEGILL BECK

OLD WALL

SMALL FOREST

WATERLOGGED FIELDS

DON'T ENTER FOREST BUT HEAD NORTH-EAST KEEPING FOREST AND FENCE TO YOUR RIGHT

SUPERIOR ALTERNATIVE ROUTE ON OLD TRACK WITH INTERESTING SCULPTURES EN ROUTE

IMMEDIATELY AFTER PASSING THROUGH TUNNEL YOU'LL SEE A SET OF STEPS ON YOUR RIGHT WHICH LEAD UP TO THE DISUSED RAILWAY. TAKE STEPS FOR PRETTIER, ALTERNATIVE ROUTE

SIGNPOST POINTS TO ALTERNATIVE ROUTE DOWN PATH TO DISUSED RAILWAY

STEPS UP

A595

BUSY ROAD WITH PAVEMENT

COAST TO COAST STATUE

WAR MEMORIAL

SCALEGILL RD

WORKING MEN'S CLUB

SCHOOL

PHONE

Su Ellen's Bakers Shop

BUS STOP

DALZELL ST

HOUSES

TO WHITEHAVEN

CYCLE ROUTE TO PARKSIDE HOTEL, 2 MILES/3KM

Walkers Pop In Café

HOUSE

NARROW, BUSY LANE

KISSING GATE & SIGNPOST, 'PUBLIC FOOTPATH'

KISSING GATES

MILLENNIUM MILEPOST

TWO PILLARS

CRICKET GROUND

KISSING GATE

'WAINWRIGHT PASSAGE'

LOVELY VICARAGE

PHONE

ST LEONARD'S CHURCH

TO EGREMONT

TO EGREMONT FOR BOOKWELL GARTH GH, 1½ MILES/2.5KM

¼ mile
APPROX SCALE
500m
0

★ trailblazer

**CLEATOR** (*cont'd from p96*)   Stage-coach's **bus** No 22 (Mon-Sat) calls in at Cleator and Cleator Moor on its way between Whitehaven and Egremont; the No 32 shuttles between Whitehaven and Cleator, or there's also the No 31/31A which travels between Whitehaven and Frizington via Cleator Moor; see pp52-5 for details.

### Where to stay and eat

Nine miles along the Coast to Coast path from St Bees we still think Cleator can make a better first day of a long, long walk.

Set in the former council offices, *Ennerdale Country House Hotel* (☎ 01946 813907, 🖳 www.oxfordhotelsandinns.com; 2S/14D/8T/4Tr/2 suites; all en suite; 🛏; 🐾 £5; WI-FI; open all year) is pitched at visiting nuclear executives, weddings and conferences, but with online offers from just £27.50pp for B&B at the weekend (£45-65pp during the week; single/single occupancy £50-75; £80-100 for three sharing a room), it could be worth a look as it's closest to the path. Food is served daily (noon-9pm) in both the restaurant and the bar.

Less than half a mile further up the road, *Grove Court Hotel* (☎ 01946 810503, 🖳 www.grovecourthotel.co.uk; 7D/3D or T/1T; all en suite; 🛏; WI-FI in some rooms;

open all year; Ⓛ £4.95) is a slightly classier version of the same, with rooms from £40pp (sgl occ £70). Evening meals are available (7-9pm); booking in advance is recommended.

Two miles north of Cleator along the A5086 is the lonesome *Parkside Hotel* (☎ 01946 811001, 🖳 www.parksidehotelcumbria.co.uk; 1S or T/2T/4Tr or Qd; most en suite; 🛏; 🐾 £2.50; WI-FI; Ⓛ £2.50-4.50). It's well priced at £27.50-34pp, sgl occ £35-45. Meals won't cost the earth and the bar is open daily: we're told John, the proprietor, makes a G&T like a pro. It's a dreary roadside schlep up from Cleator to the Parkside Hotel so it's better to get a bus or follow the quieter cycleway directly from Moor Row (Map 4) north-east for two miles via Cleator Moor to the Inn. Alternatively, if he is not busy John will pick you up/drop you off the next morning.

As an alternative to Cleator, **Egremont** is only 1½ miles/2.5km to the south and has *Bookwell Garth Guest House* (☎ 01946 820271, 16 Bookwell; 5S/6T/1Tr; shared shower facilities; 🐾 £5; Ⓛ £variable); B&B from £28pp. They also have a large car park. Several **bus** services stop in Egremont: No 26 (Mon-Sat), No 30 (daily), No 6 (Mon-Sat) and X6 (Sun); see pp52-5 for details.

From Cleator it's possible to take the road route north and east to Ennerdale Bridge, so avoiding Dent Hill, either off the A5086 or at Black How Farm just before you enter the Dent-side plantation. Either way is said to be not too bad for traffic, though unless the weather is positively treacherous, or you're intent on saving energy, take the high route. It would be a shame to miss the summit of **Dent Hill** (Map 5) and the trickling tranquility of Nannycatch Beck that lies hidden away at its foot. The long and sweaty climb to Dent Hill summit takes about an hour from Cleator. At the top there could be views to the Lakeland fells ahead and the sea behind, with the gigantic plant of Sellafield to the south-west and, on a good day, the silhouette of the Isle of Man and Galloway (Scotland) across the Solway Firth.

After the hilltop the Coast to Coast path signpost points left to the tall stile from where you contour and then descend Raven Crag hill (Map 6). Although very steep, it's become the *de facto* path now, contrary to Wainwright's original instructions. Maybe he had a point as when we say steep we mean it; poles may help and irate readers still write in and complain about the gradient down Raven Crag hill but trust us, it's a lot quicker, good for the quads and more scenic.

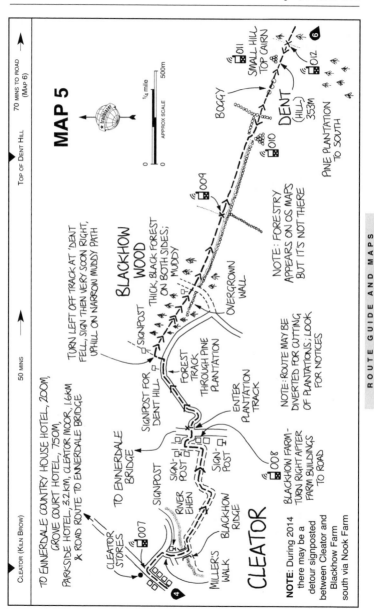

MAP 5

TO ENNERDALE COUNTRY HOUSE HOTEL, 200M, GROVE COURT HOTEL, 750M, PARKSIDE HOTEL, 3.2KM, CLEATOR MOOR, 1.6KM & ROAD ROUTE TO ENNERDALE BRIDGE

CLEATOR STORES

TO ENNERDALE BRIDGE

SIGNPOST

TO ENNERDALE BRIDGE

007

008

CLEATOR

MILLER'S WALK

BLACKHOW RIDGE

RIVER EHEN

SIGN-POST

SIGN-POST

BLACKHOW FARM – TURN RIGHT AFTER FARM BUILDINGS TO ROAD

NOTE: During 2014 there may be a detour signposted between Cleator and Blackhow Farm south via Nook Farm

SIGNPOST FOR DENT HILL

ENTER PLANTATION TRACK

NOTE: ROUTE MAY BE DIVERTED FOR CUTTING OF PLANTATIONS; LOOK FOR NOTICES

FOREST TRACK THROUGH PINE PLANTATION

SIGNPOST

TURN LEFT OFF TRACK AT 'DENT FELL' SIGN THEN VERY SOON RIGHT, UPHILL ON NARROW MUDDY PATH

BLACKHOW WOOD

THICK, BLACK FOREST ON BOTH SIDES; MUDDY

OVERGROWN WALL

NOTE: FORESTRY APPEARS ON OS MAPS BUT IT'S NOT THERE

009

010

BOGGY

DENT (HILL) 353M

PINE PLANTATION TO SOUTH

SMALL HILL TOP CAIRN

011

012

6

1/4 mile
APPROX SCALE
0          500m

From Nannycatch, head due north along the pretty beck, following the course of the water to the road leading into Ennerdale Bridge. Here you'll find *Low Cock How Farm* (Bradley's Riding Centre; Map 6; ☎ 01946 861354, 💻 www.walk-rest-ride.co.uk; 1D or T en suite, 1D/3T; shared shower facilities; 🐾; Ⓛ £5), a riding centre with B&B from £33pp, a well-equipped 10-berth **bunkhouse** for £18pp as well as **camping** for £8pp. There are shower and cooking facilities for campers. Breakfast (for bunkhouse and campers) costs £5 but it must be booked the night before. Evening meals are not available but anyone can order a home delivery; there are three menus to choose from.

MAP 6

❼

Low Cock How Farm
B&B & Campsite △⛺
& BRADLEY'S RIDING CENTRE

JOIN ROAD

GORSE

FLAT FELL

NANNYCATCH BECK
(STREAM) WATCH FOR
BIRDS OF PREY

📱015

★ trailblazer

📱013
AT THE JUNCTION TAKE
THE PATH THAT HEADS
EAST-NORTH-EAST

RUBBLE –
WAS A BIG
CAIRN

FORDS

HEAD OVER THE VERY TALL (DEER
PROOF) LADDER STILE AND CONTOUR
ROUND THE SUMMIT OF RAVEN CRAG
(ACTUALLY A GRASSY HILL)

📱014
GATE

DON'T GO OVER
STILE TO YOUR RIGHT,
BUT KEEP THE WALL
TO YOUR RIGHT AS
YOU FOLLOW IT

50 MINS FROM TOP OF DENT HILL (MAP 5)

TWO OLD
WATER
TANKS

RAVEN
CRAG

❺

NANNYCATCH
GATE

CONTINUE
NORTH-EAST

UPON HITTING VALLEY
FLOOR, WALK ALONGSIDE
STREAM

THIS IS JUST ABOUT THE STEEPEST
PATH ON THE WHOLE TRAIL. MIND
YOUR ANKLES! THIS PATH WAS NOT
ACTUALLY ON THE ORIGINAL C2C,
BUT HAS LONG SINCE BECOME THE
STANDARD PATH

0          ¼ mile
0    APPROX SCALE    500m

ROUTE GUIDE AND MAPS

TO GHYLL FARM 1 MILE/1.6KM
AND THE STORK IN ROWRAH 2 MILES/3.2KM

**ENNERDALE BRIDGE**

Shepherd's Arms
Cloggers
CHURCH
PHONE
Fox & Hounds
Thorntrees
ENNERDALE BRIDGE  016

25 MINS TO WEIR (MAP 8)

ENNERDALE BRIDGE

**ENNERDALE BRIDGE**
SEE MAP ABOVE

SIGN: 'ENNERDALE LAKE, 1 MILE'

016

8

WHITE HUT, GOOD SHELTER

MOOR END

NOW FOOTPATH OFF TO RIGHT

**MAP 7**

PANORAMIC INTERPRETATION PANEL

30 MINS FROM JOINING ROAD (MAP 6)

GOOD VIEWS ACROSS TO ENNERDALE BRIDGE AND LAKE

0        1/4 mile
0    APPROX SCALE    500m

HICKBARLEY FOREST

CATTLE GRID

6

ROUTE GUIDE AND MAPS

## ENNERDALE BRIDGE          MAP 7

Ennerdale Bridge is the first of the self-consciously pretty Lakeland villages, occupying a wonderful location spanning the River Ehen in one of Britain's least-developed valleys.

### Where to stay and eat

The *Fox and Hounds* (☎ 01946 861373, 🖥 www.foxandhoundsinn.org; 2D/1T; all en suite; 🛏; 🐾 £5; WI-FI; Ⓛ £6) is run by the community and we've had several very good reports of the **food** (daily noon-2pm & 5.30-9pm), the service and the beer here. **B&B** is £35-43.50pp (sgl occ £40-60). You can **camp** for £5 per tent; there are no facilities but campers can use the toilet in the pub when it's open. Breakfast for campers is £6.

*Thorntrees B&B* (☎ 01946 862549; 🖥 www.thorntreesennerdale.co.uk; 1D/1T en suite, 1Tr private facilities; 🛏; WI-FI; Ⓛ £6) is on the trail just entering the village. B&B is from £37.50pp. It's a recommended place and they do an excellent breakfast.

*Cloggers* (☎ 01946 862487; 1D/1T; shared bathroom; 🛏) is good value with B&B from £29pp (sgl occ £40). They don't do evening meals or packed lunches but you can get both from the pubs.

In the centre of the village *Shepherd's Arms Hotel* (☎ 01946 861249, 🖥 www.shepherdsarms.com; 2D or T/2T/4D; all with private facilities; 🛏; 🐾; WI-FI; Ⓛ £3.50-6.50) offers B&B for £35-45pp (sgl occ £40-55, £90-105 for three sharing a room. **Food** is available daily Apr-Oct noon-8.45pm, Oct-Apr noon-2pm & 6-9pm. Mains are around £9-12.

A mile away near **Kirkland** is *Ghyll Farm B&B* (☎ 01946 861330, 🖥 www .ghyllfarm.co.uk; 2D or T, 1Tr en suite; WI-FI; Ⓛ £5.50). They pick up Coast to Coasters from either of the pubs in Ennerdale Bridge after a meal at the end of the day's walk and can drop them off back at Ennerdale Bridge in the morning, by prior arrangement. B&B is from £43.50pp, with single occupancy costing £55.

*The Stork Hotel* (☎ 01946 861213, 🖥 www.storkhotel.co.uk; 2S/2D/1T/1Tr; all en suite with good showers; WI-FI; Ⓛ £2.50-4.50) is another mile away in **Rowrah** but they also pick up Coast to Coasters who book in advance. B&B starts at £37.50pp, £40 in a single, £90 for the triple. They do **food** (daily 6.30-9pm, Fri & Sun noon-2pm) with mains from £8 and portions generous.

## STAGE 2: ENNERDALE BRIDGE TO BORROWDALE          MAPS 7-14

### Introduction

As with any day in the Lakes, the enjoyment of this **15-mile (24km, 6½hr** via low route) stage depends largely on the weather. And be warned you are heading towards the spot which records the highest rainfall in England; the wryly named **Sprinkling Tarn** just south of Seathwaite receives an average of 185 inches (a phenomenal 4.7m) of rain a year. In the Lakeland wash-out that was 2009, it was well over 200 inches, helped by no less than 12.4 inches (315mm)

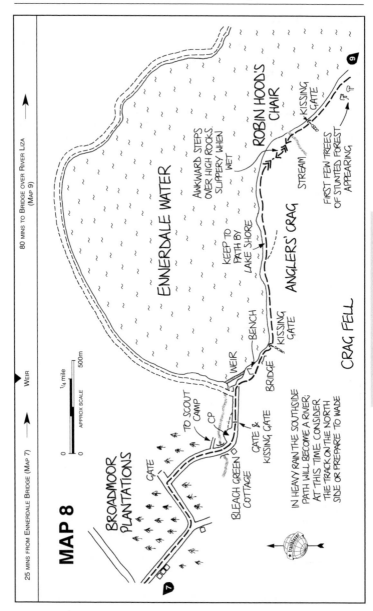

MAP 8

25 MINS FROM ENNERDALE BRIDGE (MAP 7) →   WEIR ▲   80 MINS TO BRIDGE OVER RIVER LIZA (MAP 9)

0   ¼ mile
0   APPROX SCALE   500m

BROADMOOR PLANTATIONS

GATE

TO SCOUT CAMP
CP
BLEACH GREEN COTTAGE
GATE & KISSING GATE

ENNERDALE WATER

WEIR
BENCH
BRIDGE
KISSING GATE

KEEP TO PATH BY LAKE SHORE

AWKWARD STEPS OVER HIGH ROCKS. SLIPPERY WHEN WET

ROBIN HOOD'S CHAIR

KISSING GATE

ANGLERS' CRAG

STREAM

FIRST FEW TREES OF STUNTED FOREST APPEARING

CRAG FELL

IN HEAVY RAIN THE SOUTHSIDE PATH WILL BECOME A RIVER; AT THIS TIME CONSIDER THE TRACK ON THE NORTH SIDE OR PREPARE TO WADE

★ trailblazer

ROUTE GUIDE AND MAPS

falling at Seathwaite Farm in one 24-hour period in late November, a new record for the British Isles since records began nearly 300 years ago. Indeed if it's raining horizontally with waterfalls running off the crags, chances are the path along the **southern edge of Ennerdale Water** will be one long stream with occasional fords rising halfway up your shin. Unless you like splashing about in such weather the access track along the north shore may be preferable.

Beyond the lake's end, in clear conditions even the high route via Red Pike can get busy, but be warned it's a fair old climb and you can still enjoy great views down to Buttermere from the top of Loft Beck or Grey Knotts on the standard route. If the weather is closing in, it would be foolhardy to attempt the fell-top alternative. It's a long walk from Ennerdale Bridge, your first real stage in the Lakes, although you can rearrange this day at any of the four hostels spaced out along the route.

### The route

The stage's first half involves a walk along the southern side of **Ennerdale Water** and though it's not quite the dreamy lakeside stroll you may have imagined, navigation couldn't be simpler. At one point the path rises to clamber over the outcrop of **Robin Hood's Chair** (Map 8; take the easier right route at the top of the crag) to enter mossy light woodland as you near the eastern extremity of the lake. Here it's been reported that the path along the southern banks of the **River Liza**, as shown on Maps 9-11, has been washed away in places; stick to the original route which scenically is no different.

*Low Gillerthwaite Field Centre* (Map 10; ☎ 01946 861229, 🖥 www.lgfc .org.uk; 🐕 but dogs must be kept on a lead) has **camping** for £5pp; **bunkhouse** accommodation (40 beds: 2x4 beds, 1x8, 1x10, 1x14) is available from £14.50pp. There is a kitchen, a drying room and two lounges with open wood fires as well as shower and toilet facilities; campers also have access to shower/ washing facilities and a basic cooking area. Note that if a school group is in residence (which is not unusual) you may not be allowed to stay. Call ahead.

Up the track a bit *YHA Ennerdale* (Map 10; ☎ 0845 371 9116, 🖥 www.yha.org.uk/hostel/ennerdale; 24 beds, 3x4 beds, 2x6 beds; beds £16-21, 4-bed rooms £68-79; Ⓛ £5.50), at High Gillerthwaite is a small hostel that's open from the week before Easter to the end of October. Meals are available, though these should be booked in advance. The hostel is licensed and has a slick self-catering kitchen and cosy lounge, though sharing a tiny, six-bed dorm with five others could require good organisation. The hostel generates its own hydro-powered electricity. The hostel reception opens at 5pm but hot drinks are available all day (pay using the honesty box). Next door, *Ennerdale Camping Barn* (aka *High Gillerthwaite Camping Barn*; bookings ☎ 0800 0191700, arrival ☎ 01946 861237, 🖥 www.yha.org.uk/ barn/high-gillerthwaite-camping-barn; 14 beds) is managed by the YHA. Beds here are £10pp; there's electric lighting but no plug sockets, and a cooking area though no cooking facilities so you'll either need a stove or have to pop next door for a meal.

Just beyond the camping barn is the start of the alternative trail up to Red Pike, High Stile and Hay Stacks (see p109-11 and Maps 10a and 10b).

ROUTE GUIDE AND MAPS

70 MINS FROM WEIR (MAP 8)

BRIDGE OVER RIVER LIZA

APPROX SCALE

0   ¼ mile
0   500m

ENNERDALE WATER

BRIDGE OVER RIVER LIZA

FOREST TRACK

RIVER LIZA

STILE & GATE

BRIDLEWAY

GATE. DON'T GO THROUGH BUT GO ROUND END OF FENCE TO RIVERSIDE PATH. OBSCURE AT FIRST, IT SOON BECOMES CLEAR

EASIEST & MOST STRAIGHTFORWARD PATH

BRIDGE

PATH IS PAVED INTERMITTENTLY FROM HERE

PATH GOES ROUND END OF WALL

WONDERFUL LITTLE MOSSY FOREST RIVEN WITH SMALL STREAMS

GATE IN WALL

BIG STREAM—CROSS ON STONES

THE SIDE
NATIONAL TRUST

MAP 9

25 MINS FROM BRIDGE OVER RIVER LIZA (MAP 9) — TURN-OFF TO RED PIKE ROUTE — 80 MINS TO BLACK SAIL YH (MAP 11) VIA TWO LOW ROUTES

MAP 10

DO NOT TURN EAST TOO EARLY OR YOU COULD FIND YOURSELF ON DANGEROUS SCREE

650M ASCENT TO HIGH STILE

LOOK FOR CAIRNS LEADING THE WAY UP THE HILL

RED PIKE ROUTE

SHEEPFOLD

TREE PLANTATIONS

TO HAY STACKS

019

ORIGINAL ROUTE

OLD SHEEPFOLD

ALTERNATIVE, RIVERSIDE ROUTE

DUCKBOARDS

STREAM

NATIONAL TRUST SIGN: GILLERTHWAITE

Ennerdale Camping Barn

GATE

018

TWO BRIDGES CLOSE TOGETHER

NOTE: THE ALTERNATIVE ROUTE SOUTH OF THE RIVER LIZA CAN BE WASHED AWAY IN PLACES

YHA Ennerdale

RIVER LIZA

MOSS DUB (POND)

MAIN BRIDLEWAY

Low Gillerthwaite Field Centre

1/4 mile

500m

0

APPROX SCALE

0

# MAP 10a

HIGH LEVEL ROUTE VIA RED
PIKE & HIGH STILE

BLEABERRY
TARN

VIEWS TO SAIL
BECK VALLEY

HIGH STILE
807M - HIGHEST
SUMMIT ON
COAST TO
COAST PATH

CHAPEL
CRAGS

FOLLOW
BOUNDARY
POSTS

RED PIKE
755M

FOLLOW
BOUNDARY
POSTS

VIEW TO
CRUMMOCK
WATER

ATTENTION!
FOLLOW THIS INSTRUCTION OR YOU COULD
BE IN DANGER. KEEP ALONG STREAM,
HEADING NORTH; DON'T TURN NORTH-
EAST UNTIL PATH IS OBVIOUS IN THAT
DIRECTION. KEEP FOLLOWING CAIRNS
ACROSS GRASS

STREAM

LOOK FOR LARGE CAIRN TO
WEST OF STREAM. CROSS HERE
AND YOU SHOULD SEE TRAIL OF
CAIRNS LEADING UPHILL

10

¼ mile
0                    500m
0
APPROX SCALE

ROUTE GUIDE AND MAPS

**ROUTE GUIDE AND MAPS**

### The Red Pike, High Stile & Hay Stacks route
#### Maps 10, 10a, 10b & 12

'*All I ask for, at the end, is a last, long resting place by the side of Innominate Tarn, on Haystacks where the water gently laps the gravelly shore and the heather blooms and Pillar and Gable keep unfailing watch. A quiet place, a lonely place. I shall go to it, for the last time, and be carried: someone who knew me in life will take me there and empty me out of a little box and leave me there alone. And if you, dear reader, should get a bit of grit in your boot as you are crossing Haystacks in the years to come, please treat it with respect. It might be me.*  **Alfred Wainwright** *Memoirs of an Ex-Fellwanderer*

In his *Coast to Coast* guide Wainwright describes this route as suitable only for 'very strong and experienced fellwalkers' in clear weather. While we don't think the group of people who can do this walk is quite as exclusive as Wainwright suggests, we certainly agree that the weather needs to be clear, if only because the views possible at the top – in particular across Buttermere to the north and Great Gable and Pillar in the south – benefit from it. (If the weather takes a significant turn for the worse up there, you can drop down from Scarth Gap on steps to the Black Sail hostel; see Map 10b.) There are no technically difficult parts, though there are some steep ascents and particularly descents which will hammer the knees, and route finding on the way up to Red Pike can be tricky. This alternative route should add about **1¹/₂ miles (2.5km, 1³/₄hrs)** to this stage, all in all making it a pretty tough day so early in the walk.

The high-level route takes in a number of summits, including Red Pike (755m), High Stile (807m), High Crag (744m) and Hay Stacks (597m), the lowest but the most interesting. The place where some err from the path is on the initial climb up to Red Pike where it's tempting to branch off eastwards too early: make sure that, having crossed the stream, you continue north-east (following cairns) until you're firmly on the grassy upper reaches of Red Pike (Map 10a). There are *just* enough cairns to show the way, though if in doubt, your motto should be: head up the slope rather than along it.

Having gained the ridge the path becomes clear and you'll find yourself ticking off one peak after another as you make your way to **Innominate Tarn** (Map 12). From there, Wainwright recommends ignoring the obvious path that continues in an easterly direction to the north of **Blackbeck Tarn**, instead continuing in a south-easterly direction to an unmarked reunion with the low route near the top of **Loft Beck**. Though you'll struggle to follow any clear path in the ground, this trail is marked on Map 12. However, it's said that few trekkers actually manage to successfully rejoin the low route and instead forge their own path to **Honister Quarries**. If you wish to try, the best tactic from Innominate Tarn is to aim for the **Brandreth Fence** to the south and continue along it until you come to a reunion with the regular route at the stile in the fence (WPT 023). Otherwise, the easiest solution is to continue on the clear trail to Blackbeck, from where you can follow the wide track down to Honister (see p116). Just make sure you don't start to descend to Buttermere.

Continuing on the low route up the valley, just over 90 minutes after joining the forest track you emerge at the head of Ennerdale and the isolated bothy that is now *YHA Black Sail* (Maps 11/12; ☎ 0845 371 9680, 🖳 www.yha.org.uk/hostel/black-sail; 16 beds: 2x4 beds, 1x8 beds; beds £19.50-23pp, rooms from £45;

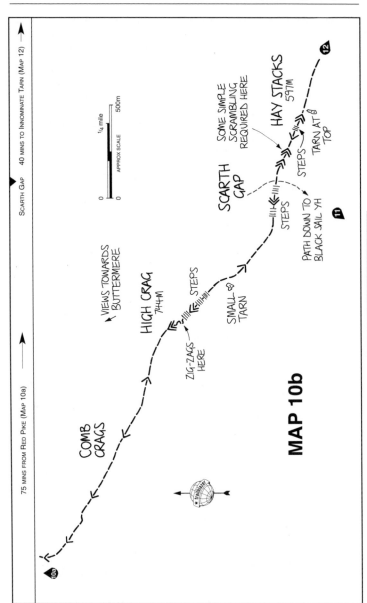

**MAP 10b**

SCARTH GAP  40 MINS TO INNOMINATE TARN (MAP 12)

75 MINS FROM RED PIKE (MAP 10a)

COMB CRAGS

HIGH CRAG 744M

VIEWS TOWARDS BUTTERMERE

ZIG-ZAGS HERE

STEPS

SMALL TARN

¼ mile
APPROX SCALE
500m

SCARTH GAP

SOME SIMPLE SCRAMBLING REQUIRED HERE

HAY STACKS 597M

STEPS

TARN AT TOP

STEPS

PATH DOWN TO BLACK SAIL YH

10a

11

12

★ trailblazer

fully open Mar-Oct). Recently renovated, who could not wish to wake up here one sunny morning? Breakfast, packed lunches and evening meals are served (these need to be booked in advance) and the hostel is licensed; credit cards aren't accepted. Having a torch is recommended. The hostel is left open during the day, providing welcome shelter from rain and the chance to make a cup of tea in the kitchen. Note that Black Sail is beyond the reach of the baggage carriers. Incidentally, if the weather clears, just before the hostel are some steps leading up to Scarth Gap (Map 10b) on the high route (see p110).

From the hostel things can get a little tricky. You need to follow the correct path east to meet the climb up the side of **Loft Beck** and from there the path to Grey Knotts from where the long descent to Honister Hause and Borrowdale begins. Armed with this advice, in fine weather the way is crystal clear, but unfortunately such conditions are infrequent in these parts, particularly in the afternoon when most attempt the climb. At the top of Loft Beck follow Map 12 carefully to negotiate this section and have a compass or GPS at hand. At worst, at the top of the Beck blunder north over the boggy saddle to the Brandreth Fence and follow it east (right) to the stile at WPT 023.

From the stile at **Brandreth Fence**, an initially indistinct path rises to contour around the western face of Brandreth and **Grey Knotts** (Map 13), with occasional cairns along the way. The working Hopper Quarry can be seen in the distance to the north. The path soon joins the larger track (WPT 025) coming

---

### ❏ Honister Slate Mine

The story of mining at Honister began 400 million years ago when volcanic ash, combined with water and subsequent compression, formed the fine-grained rock now called slate. When the glaciers of the last Ice Age retreated up Gatesgarthdale they exposed three parallel veins of slate along the steep sides of the valley and sporadic mining may have taken place before the Roman era. Certainly by the early 1700s slate was being quarried here on an industrial scale and, as well as the disused tramway you walk down, there were roads and aerial ropeways to take the slate to the road. The workers who split and finished the slate lived in barracks in Honister during the week; the adjacent youth hostel is a former quarry workers' building. After closing in the 1980s, the mine (along with the nearby quarry) re-opened in 1997 and has since developed into a slick, tourist-oriented facility backed by small-scale mining operations.

The **Visitors' Centre** (☎ 01768 777230, 🖥 www.honister.com; daily 9am-5pm) is well worth a look. There are guided tours into the mine daily at 10.30am, 12.30pm and 3.30pm for £12.50. For those with energy to spare they've also set up a *via ferrata*. Common in the Dolomites of northern Italy, a via ferrata, or 'iron way', is essentially a series of fixed iron ropes, ladders and other climbing aids to help non-climbers reach places that would otherwise be inaccessible. The one at Honister, for which a guide is compulsory, takes climbers through the quarry up to Fleetwith Pike on what they claim is the old miners' route to work. The cost is from £35, including equipment hire. Book via the website. The **shop** is full of slate-based souvenirs, from great slabs that have been fashioned into coffee tables, to smaller chippings sold by the bagful. Some of the stuff is lovely but think twice before leaving with a full-size slate coffee table on your back; it's still a long way to Robin Hood's Bay. Something small such as a Coast to Coast coaster may be more appropriate.

BLACK SAIL YH

90 MINS FROM TURN-OFF TO RED PIKE (MAP 10) VIA TWO LOW ROUTES

YHA Black Sail

UP TO SCARTH GAP

OLD GATE

FORD

END OF FOREST

THE MAIN TRACK BENDS SOUTH

RIVER LIZA

STILL WALKING THROUGH THE FOREST PLANTATION; STILL HOT, STILL TEDIOUS

PILLAR

MAP 11

¼ mile
500m
APPROX SCALE

down from Brandreth and Great Gable and drops gently to the **Drum House**, now little more than a massive pile of stones and slate. The path's arrow-straight course betrays its previous incarnation as a quarry tramway; the Drum House's original purpose was to house the cable that operated the tramway that ran to the cutting sheds. At the bottom of the steep tramway track is **Honister Hause**, and the hullabaloo surrounding **Honister Slate Mine Visitor Centre** (see p112) at the crest of the notoriously steep Honister Pass road which many a caravanner has regretted tackling. *YHA Honister Hause* (Map 13; ☎ 0845 371 9522, 💻 www.yha.org.uk/hostel/honister-hause; 24 beds: 2x2 beds, 5x4 beds; beds £21.50-23, rooms £47-69; fully open Mar-Oct) is next door, serves meals and is licensed. Credit cards are accepted. Stagecoach's No 77 **bus** runs from here to Seatoller (8 minutes) and to Keswick (40 minutes) and the 77A goes via Buttermere to Keswick (60 mins); see pp52-5 for details.

From Honister the Coast to Coast path parallels the B5289 to Little Gatesgarthdale. Down in the valley the path loops back on itself to join the road at **Seatoller**, although for a nifty short cut avoiding this village and saving you half a mile, see Map 14.

## SEATOLLER    MAP 14, p117

The National Trust village of Seatoller has a couple of B&Bs, an outdoor activity centre, a public phone, post box and bus stop.

Stagecoach's 77/77A and 78 **bus** services call here between Easter & Sep/Oct; see pp52-5 for details.

### Where to stay and eat

You're now well and truly among the valleybound Lakeland honeypots with prices which can suddenly make hostelling seem not such a bad idea after all. In the village centre *Seatoller House* (☎ 01768 777218, 💻 www.seatollerhouse.co.uk; 1D/3T/4Tr/2Qd; all with private facilities; ♥; 🐾; WI-FI; ⓛ £5-6; Mar-Nov) is a 300-year-old building that's been a guesthouse for over a century. The rate is £45-49pp (sgl occ £51-55) for B&B, or £68-72pp (sgl occ £74-78) with a four-course dinner (fixed menu) served at 7pm every day except Tuesday.

Right opposite, *Seatoller Farm* (☎ 01768 777232, 💻 www.seatollerfarm .co.uk; 2D/1T; all en suite; ♥; ⓛ from £3; mid Jan to mid Dec) is a working National

Trust hill farm that charges £30-37pp (sgl occ £50-60). They also allow **camping** (£6pp including use of a shower; late Mar-Oct). Breakfast may be available for campers by prior arrangement for £6.

Just outside the village, *Glaramara House* (017687 77222, www.glaramara house.co.uk; 22S/18T or D; WI-FI; 🐾 £5; ⓛ £6) is a hotel and outdoor activity centre. Despite the slightly institutional atmosphere it's a great place to stay with good food and it's well set up for walkers and there are lots of single rooms. Facilities include a spacious residents' lounge with log fires, bar, and drying room. Prices start at £39 per person for B&B with an additional £6 en-suite premium charge. Ten of the twin rooms are en suite. Home made **food** is good value at £19 for a three course meal, using local and seasonal ingredients. Non-residents can use the **tearoom** during the day which is convenient following the closure of the Yew Tree tearoom in the centre of the village but locals will fill you in on the gossip.

From Seatoller the trail wends its way through **Johnny Wood** (see p68), joining the short cut mentioned above and passing the YHA hostel into Borrowdale (Map 14, p117).

'HIGH' ROUTE: INNOMINATE TARN → 35 MINS JUNCTION OF TWO ROUTES 60 MINS TO HONISTER SLATE MINE (MAP 13)

THIS IS EXTREMELY BOGGY IN PLACES AND THERE IS NO PATH. INSTEAD, KEEP TO THE FENCE, MOVING AWAY TO AVOID THE BOGGY SECTIONS, IGNORING THE STILES UNTIL THE CORRECT ONE IS FOUND, WITH CAIRN-LINED PATHS LEADING AWAY ON BOTH SIDES

MAIN PATH GOING DOWN TO BLACKBECK TARN. PATH ALSO LEADS TO HOPPER QUARRY- A USEFUL, SIMPLER PATH TO THE 'ORIGINAL' C2C ROUTE

MAP 12

ATTENTION! AT BOGGY SADDLE (WPT 22) TURN EAST AND CLIMB PATH MARKED BY CAIRNS TO A STILE IN FENCE

INNOMINATE TARN

10b

BRANDRETH FENCE

RED PIKE ALTERNATIVE

BLACKBECK TARN

JUNCTION NOT OBVIOUS

VIEWS TO BUTTERMERE

024

13

STILE IN FENCE

PATHS JOINING FROM RIGHT

YHA Black Sail

THIN BUT DEFINITE PATH

022

023

CAIRNS MARK THE WAY HERE

11

021

LOFT BECK

DRUMLINS (HILLOCKS)

LOW LEVEL ROUTE

STEPS FOLLOWING STREAM UP STEEP HILL

BRANDRETH FENCE

ATTENTION! PATH GOES OFF EASTISH FROM YH - DO NOT TAKE MORE OBVIOUS PATH HEADING SOUTH-EAST

STEEP PATH IS CORRECT ROUTE

0          1/4 mile

0    APPROX SCALE    500m

OFFICIAL 'LOW' ROUTE: 40 MINS FROM BLACK SAIL YH (MAP 11) → TOP OF LOFT BECK 60 MINS TO HONISTER SLATE MINE (MAP 13) →

ROUTE GUIDE AND MAPS

ROUTE GUIDE AND MAPS

60 MINS FROM TOP OF LOFT BECK (MAP 12) ⟶     HONISTER SLATE MINE ⟶     60 MINS TO SEATOLLER (MAP 14) ⟶

MAP 13

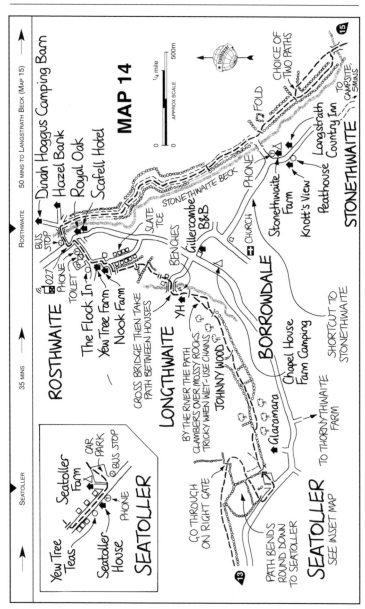

SEATOLLER — 35 MINS — ROSTHWAITE — 50 MINS TO LANGSTRATH BECK (MAP 15)

**MAP 14**

¼ mile 500m
0
0
APPROX SCALE

**ROSTHWAITE**

Dinah Hoggus Camping Barn
Hazel Bank
Royal Oak
Scafell Hotel

BUS STOP
027 PHONE
TOILET
The Flock In
Yew Tree Farm
Nook Farm

SLATE TCE

STONETHWAITE BECK

CROSS BRIDGE THEN TAKE PATH BETWEEN HOUSES

BENCHES

Gillercombe B&B

CHURCH

PHONE

**LONGTHWAITE**

YH

**BORROWDALE**

Stonethwaite Farm
Knott's View
Langstrath Country Inn
Peathouse

**STONETHWAITE**

FOLD

CHOICE OF TWO PATHS

TO CAMPSITE, 5 MINS

SHORTCUT TO STONETHWAITE

BY THE RIVER THE PATH CLAMBERS OVER MOSSY ROCKS. TRICKY WHEN WET - USE CHAINS

JOHNNY WOOD

Glaramara

Chapel House Farm Camping

TO THORNYTHWAITE FARM

GO THROUGH ON RIGHT GATE

PATH BENDS ROUND DOWN TO SEATOLLER

**SEATOLLER**
SEE INSET MAP

Yew Tree Teas
Seatoller Farm
CAR PARK
BUS STOP
PHONE
Seatoller House

**SEATOLLER**

## BORROWDALE          MAP 14, p117

Borrowdale is made up of three separate settlements: Longthwaite, Rosthwaite and Stonethwaite. Small, picturesque and composed largely of slate-roofed, whitewashed stone farm cottages, these are the iconic Lake District hamlets that tourists from around the world flock to see.

Stagecoach's No 78 (Easter/Apr-Oct) **bus**, known as the Borrowdale Rambler, runs between Seatoller and Keswick (from where buses run to other destinations in Cumbria) via Rosthwaite; see pp52-5 for details.

### Longthwaite

The first building you come to in Borrowdale is *YHA Borrowdale* (☎ 0845 371 9624, ☐ www.yha.org.uk/hostel/borrowdale; 86 beds in 2-, 3-, 4-, 6-bedded rooms; beds £17.50-21, 4-bed rooms £64-84; WI-FI), a spacious and well-run lodge with an alcohol licence and spirited catering well worth crossing the fells for; it also has a laundry and drying room. Some accommodation is in pods outside. Credit cards are accepted and you can also **camp** here.

Longthwaite also plays host to *Gillercombe B&B* (☎ 01768 777602; 1S/1D/2T; shared facilities; ☞; ⓛ £5; Mar-Oct). The friendly owner, Rachel Dunckley, is a mine of useful local information and local gossip, and her B&B offers a comfortable and convenient place to stay right in the heart of Borrowdale. B&B rates are £35pp. However, it is essential to book well in advance to stay here.

A hop and a skip down the road is *Chapel House Farm Campsite* (☎ 01768 777256, ☐ www.chapelhousefarmcampsite.co.uk; dogs; Mar-Oct; ⓛ £4) where you can pitch in a roadside field for £6pp. Facilities are basic with a rough and ready toilet and shower block (50p for a shower). They recommend booking – particularly if you are having luggage delivered.

### Rosthwaite

The biggest settlement of the three is Rosthwaite to the north. Stagecoach's No 78 bus calls here. On the way into town there are two National Trust farms offering B&B. The first is *Nook Farm* (☎ 01768 777677, ☐ www.nookfarmborrowdale.co.uk; 1D with en suite shower/1Tr with private bathroom; ☞; WI-FI; ⓛ £5; Feb-Nov), a 16th-century farmhouse with lovely open fires – the perfect treat after a rainy day's walk. B&B costs £33-35pp (sgl occ £50-70).

Round the corner *Yew Tree Farm* (☎ 01768 777675, ☐ www.borrowdaleherdwick.co.uk; 2D/1T; all en suite; ☞; WI-FI; ⓛ £5-7; Feb-mid Nov) charges from £40pp (sgl occ £60). As well as selling their own produce, they also run a tearoom *The Flock In* (Feb-mid Nov daily 10am-5pm, less in winter), opposite, where the tea is served in pints or half pints. Most of their dishes are home made, many using produce from the farm though presumably not the chewy Ewe's Poo Cookies (£1.50)! Particularly recommended is the Herdwick Stew served with a brown bun (£6.95) and you can try Borrowdale teabread and cheese (£2.95) here, too.

*The Royal Oak Hotel* (☎ 01768 777214, ☐ www.royaloakhotel.co.uk; 2S/2T/3D/4Tr/1Qd; all with private facilities; ☞; ☜; WI-FI; Feb-Nov), is a fine family-run place which once hosted the poet William Wordsworth. They normally accept bookings only on a dinner, bed and breakfast basis; rates are £62-70pp; single/single occupancy is £62-70/£74 by prior arrangement. In peak season at weekends there may be a two-night minimum stay. The majority of rooms are in the main hotel but some are in a converted barn across the farmyard. The owner is a keen walker and walkers get a warm welcome.

Next door is *Scafell Hotel* (☎ 01768 777208, ☐ www.scafell.co.uk; 3S/10D/7T/2Tr; all en suite; ☞; ☜£6-10; WI-FI downstairs only area), a large place which has served as a coaching inn since 1850, with some rooms furnished with antiques. B&B costs £50-85pp and dinner B&B is £65-110pp. The menu is extensive and the **food** good. The restaurant is open daily 6.30-9pm but booking is essential; the set menu costs £34.95. Their *Riverside Bar* (generally open daily noon-9pm) has cheaper bar meals (£8-15.95) including burgers, steak and local trout.

On the Coast to Coast path leading over the river out of the village, *Hazel*

*Bank Country House* (☎ 017687 77248, 🖳 www.hazelbankhotel.co.uk; 7D or T; all with private facilities; ●; WI-FI; Feb-Nov), is a very comfortable hotel set in extensive grounds. B&B is £60-70pp; single occupancy is £80-90. Dinner, B&B is £79-89pp. In peak season there may be a two-night minimum stay.

Nearby is *Dinah Hoggus Camping Barn* (☎ 01768 777689, 🖳 www.lakelandcampingbarns.co.uk; shower available) is a very simple but attractively rustic place sleeping 12 people. They charge £9.50pp (bring your own sleeping bag; mattresses provided); booking is essential.

### Stonethwaite

Just under a mile (about 1.6km) to the south and away from the relative clamour of Rosthwaite, Stonethwaite nestles in its own little world at the end of a road running parallel to the beck that shares its name. Although frequently rained upon, it's among the prettiest of the Lakeland hamlets with an attractive little church.

As for lodgings, as you enter the village *Stonethwaite Farm* (☎ 01768 777234, 🖳 www.stonethwaitefarm.co.uk; 1S/2D/1T; one en suite, others share facilities; Ⓛ £5; Feb-Oct) comes highly recommended. B&B rates are £27.50-32.50pp (sgl £35). They

also offer **camping** (60 pitches; Mar-Oct; £5pp; toilets and cold running water) in a field half a mile up the valley (see Map 15).

*Knotts View* (☎ 01768 777604, 2D/1T/1D or T; shared facilities; Ⓛ £5.75) charges from £35pp (sgl occ £38) for B&B. The building is 450 years old and, with its low ceilings, it feels like it. Under the same ownership is the *Peathouse Tea & Coffee Shop* (Easter-Nov; flexible opening hours) next door. Incidentally, if you're not familiar with the nature of peat, by the time you get to Greenup Edge tomorrow you'll be an expert.

Best of all is *The Langstrath Country Inn* (☎ 01768 777239, 🖳 www.the-langstrath.com; 3D/5D or T; all en suite; ●; Mar-Nov Tue-Sun, mid Nov to Dec Fri-Sun; WI-FI) whose reputation for fine **food** (Mar-Nov Tue-Sun noon-2.30pm & 6-9pm; bar Tue-Sun noon-10.30pm; winter hours may vary) extends well beyond Borrowdale and includes such locally sourced dishes as slow-roasted Rosthwaite Herdwick lamb. Mains cost £12.95-17.95. The rooms are just as worthy of praise. B&B costs £50-64pp (sgl occ £70-84) but in general they don't accept advance bookings for single-night stays on a Friday or Saturday. All in all, you want to run down from Honister to make the most of this place.

## STAGE 3: BORROWDALE TO GRASMERE  MAPS 14-18

### Introduction

In good weather this **9-mile (14.5km, 4-5½hr high route)** stage is a Lakeland classic, a straightforward climb up past Lining Crag to Greenup Edge, followed by the high-level ridge walk we recommend (see p123) or a less adventurous and slightly shorter plod down the valley to the edge of Grasmere. Wainwright combines this stage with the next one to Patterdale, adding up to at least a 17-mile (27.5km) hike, and a few walkers do just that. Sticking to the valley routes as Wainwright did, it's not too demanding. If doing so, we recommend you take at least one of the high-level options on either stage; this is the Lake District after all. Taking on the high routes in one long day – not least via Helvelyn and Striding Edge which will add **two miles and up to two hours** – may leave you a little drained for the 15½-miler from Patterdale to Shap which follows and along which there are no easy gradients.

### The route
The stage begins with a level amble through the fields alongside **Stonethwaite Beck** (Maps 14 and 15), with **Eagle Crag** a looming presence across the water. It looks massive but by the time you get to Greenup Edge you'll be looking *down* on Eagle Crag.

At Stonethwaite you join **Greenup Gill** (Map 15), one long torrent of white water and waterfalls when we came through, with views back down to Borrowdale growing more impressive with every upward step. The path's gradient picks up a notch past Eagle Crag, drops into a chummy basin of drumlins

ROUTE GUIDE AND MAPS

50 MINS FROM ROSTHWAITE (MAP 14) → LANGSTRATH BECK → 70 MINS TO LINING CRAG (MAP 16) →

**14**

CROSS STREAM ON STONES

Stonethwaite Farm Campsite

BRIDGE TO RIGHT OF PATH TO FOOT OF EAGLE CRAG WHICH LOOMS ABOVE

★ trailblazer

SHEEP FOLDS

**MAP 15**

START OF STEPS AGAIN. FORD STREAM ON STONES

GO THROUGH GAP IN WALL

LANGSTRATH BECK

WATERFALL

CAIRN

TWIN WATERFALLS

AFTER RAIN STONETHWAITE BECK IS ONE CONTINUOUS TORRENT OF WHITE WATER WITH OCCASIONAL WATERFALLS

0          ¼ mile

0     APPROX SCALE     500m

EAGLE CRAG c 525M

WATER-FALL

GREENUP GILL  **16**

MAP 16

15 BIG STREAMS

70 MINS FROM LANGSTRATH BECK (MAP 15)

LINING CRAG

50 MINS TO FENCEPOSTS (WAYPOINT 36) (MAP 17)

TOP OF FIRST CLIMB; NOW LOOKING OVER DRUMLIN BASIN; FOLLOW PATH TO LINING CRAG

028

LINING CRAG
GREAT VIEWS OF SCAFELL AND BACK TO THE COAST

CAIRN

CAIRNS NOT CLEAR EVEN IN BROAD DAYLIGHT

CAIRN ON BOULDER

ALT ROUTE AVOIDS BOGS

FENCEPOSTS ON TOP OF OUTCROP ON GREENUP EDGE

GREENUP EDGE PASS

TWIN CAIRNS 029

WYTHBURN VALLEY DO NOT GO NORTH-EAST DOWN VALLEY!

17

FENCEPOSTS AT SOUTH END OF COL

LOOK FOR TWIN CAIRNS JUST AFTER FENCEPOST AS THEY WILL SHOW START OF PATH HEADING CLEARLY DOWNHILL

0    ¼ mile
0    APPROX SCALE    500m

⚠ ATTENTION! APPROACHING THE PASS IS BOGGY AND THE PATH FREQUENTLY DISAPPEARS. LOOK FOR THE CAIRNS AND CRAGTOP

ROUTE GUIDE AND MAPS

(mounds created by glacial action) and a stepped climb up onto the top of **Lining Crag** (Map 16) from where, weather permitting, views reach over towards Scafell Pike, England's highest summit at 3210ft (978m).

Look to the south and you'll also make out the beginning of the path to the broad col of **Greenup Edge**. This next section is where some lose their way, the boggy ground and indistinct cairns obscuring the correct direction even in ideal conditions. As you near the col look out for the old fence posts which once stretched up and over to Low White Stones, the hill south of the col; see box p92. If you see one on an outcrop, aim to the south of it to a less conspicuous fence post at ground level and, a few metres further on, the key twin **cairns** (WPT 029) from where the descent from the Edge commences across the head of **Wythburn Valley**. You cross the upper basin of **Wythburn** on clearer tracks to the 'gateposts' on Map 17 (WPT 030) marking its neighbour, **Far Easedale**. From here you choose the valley route or the more demanding high route which most hikers take these days, along with casually clad day trippers out of Grasmere who commonly combine both into a loop.

HIGH ROUTE:    FENCEPOSTS WHERE PATHS DIVIDE          75 MINS TO HELM CRAG (MAP 18)

LOOK FOR THREE FENCE POSTS & ONE CAIRN CLOSE TOGETHER AS IF GATEPOSTS. RIDGE WALK TRAIL AND LOW VALLEY ROUTE DIVERGE HERE

030

CALF CRAG
538M

MOMENT CRAG

RIDGE WALK

STILL BOGGY IN PLACES

FAR EASEDALE

PIKE OF CARRS

VALLEY WALK

BREATHTAKING VIEWS DOWN TO GRASMERE

GIBSON KNOTT

VIEW OF EASEDALE TARN (OFF MAP)

18

18

EASEDALE BECK

MAP 17

WYTH BURN

EASIER BUT POSSIBLY WATERLOGGED TRAIL DOWN VALLEY STARTS A FEW METRES TO RIGHT OF 'GATEPOSTS'

CROSS WYTH BURN THREE TIMES. LAST RUNNING WATER BEFORE HIGH ROUTE TO GRASMERE

16

¼ mile
APPROX SCALE
0        500m

LOW ROUTE:    FENCEPOSTS WHERE PATHS DIVIDE          100 MINS TO A591 (MAP 18)

## The ridge-walk alternative to Grasmere via Helm Crag
### Map 17 & Map 18

The high-level route takes in **Calf Crag**, **Gibson Knott** and **Helm Crag** amongst others. The ground is often saturated but the climbs up to the various summits take only a few minutes and give some great viewpoints down to Easedale Gill and Easedale Tarn glistening below. It's a long hard walk with rocky steps and bogs; allow at least 90 minutes from the 'gateposts' to Lancrigg Woods. That is the price of surveying Castle, Lang and Silver Hows (hills) behind you to the south-west, and Helvellyn and Great Rigg beyond. By the time you've reached Helm Crag overlooking the following stage, the steep descent to the north-western outskirts of Grasmere may well finish you off!

ROUTE GUIDE AND MAPS

Whichever route you take, when you reach the bottom and Easedale it's worth a diversion through **Lancrigg Woods** along the **Poet's Walk** (Map 18), a tranquil delight that may soothe sore feet. It comes as no surprise to find that the Lakeland poets enjoyed it; indeed, they planted many of the trees that grow in the woods. Along the way is an inscription, in Latin, describing how Wordsworth's sister Dorothy would sit at this spot while her brother walked up and down composing verses. The path crosses the croquet lawn of Lancrigg Hotel (see below) and a minute later, Thorney How Hostel. Here at the road the trail continues north-east for the climb over to Patterdale. To the south a 20-minute walk leads to Grasmere, the Lake District's busiest tourist village.

## EASEDALE                    MAP 18

Picturesque Easedale has a few places to stay and eat right on the path if you aren't diverting into Grasmere.

### Where to stay and eat

Right on the route, *Thorney How Independent Hostel* (Map 18; ☎ 015394 35597, 🖳 www.thorneyhow.co.uk; 7x4-bed rooms, 2x6, 1x2; shared shower facilities; dorm bed £16.50-24, private double £52.80-68.40 inc breakfast; 🐾£5 in kennel; WI-FI) offers **hostel-style accommodation** and a camping barn. There's a *café* and *bar* (open daily around 1-11pm) and they offer dinner, B&B deals. If you make it clear you are walking the Coast to Coast they will allow single-night stays at weekends and in peak periods. Their **camping barn** sleeps eight (£8.50-11.50pp).

On the A591 north of Grasmere near where the path crosses it, there's the plush *Grasmere Independent Hostel* (☎ 015394 35055, 🖳 grasmereindependenthostel.co .uk; 24 beds – 1Tr, 1Qd, 1x5 beds, 2x6 beds; internet access & WI-FI) complete with kitchen, laundry room, lounge and even a Nordic sauna (£4). Each room has its own shower facilities and contains no more than six beds; £20.50-21.50pp. However, since the hostel focuses on groups, individuals cannot book more than six weeks in advance and a minimum 2-night stay is required at the weekend.

*Oak Lodge* (☎ 015394 35527, 🖳 www.oaklodge.homecall.co.uk; 2D/1D or T; all en suite; 🍷; Ⓛ from £3) is on Easedale Rd. It's a very smart little establishment in a wonderful location next to tranquil Easedale Forest. B&B is from £35pp (sgl occ £45-70).

If you stick to the path via Poet's Walk you'll walk right past *Lancrigg Vegetarian Country House Hotel* (☎ 015394 35317, 🖳 www.lancrigg.co.uk; 10D/2T/1 suite; all en suite; 🍷; 🐾£15; WI-FI; Ⓛ £7.50), a large country house with parts dating back to the 17th century. The ambience is rather more conventional 'genteel' than 'vegetarian' in any alternative sense, but in Grasmere £95-140pp (sgl occ £114-168) for DB&B (£75-120pp, sgl occ £90-144 for B&B) is actually not so bad. Like so many fancy Grasmere hotels it's not really a walkers' place but we have no reservations about the food: dinner or breakfast, if what you eat here doesn't get your palate dancing the cancan across the croquet lawn well, nothing will. The vegetarian restaurant (daily 1-3pm & 6.30-8.30pm, to 7.30pm in winter) is open to non residents. If your budget doesn't stretch quite this far, a 5-to 10-minute walk away is *Kitty Crag* (phone details as for Lancrigg, 🖳 www.kittycrag.com; 2D/1D or T; all en suite; 🍷; WI-FI), a vegetarian B&B which charges £60pp (sgl occ £72); guests need to go to the hotel for meals.

On the A591 not far from the Grasmere Hostel, is a pub, the *Traveller's Rest Inn* (☎ 015394 35604, 🖳 www.lakedistrictinns.co.uk/travellers_wel come.cfm; 7D/2T; all en suite; 🐾£15). B&B ranges from £25pp to £60pp. Food is served Feb-Oct daily all day in the main season, other times noon-2pm & 5-9.30pm) and includes hearty portions of mainly local dishes – game of the day is £12.95.

## GRASMERE                    see map p127

Wordsworth called this valley 'the fairest place on earth' and his association with Grasmere has done so much to popularise the place that on some days you might wish you'd not paused here in your wandering o'er the hills and vales. Fleece-clad hordes stream in all summer to mill about or grab a lunch, but looking out to the glorious hills surrounding the village, you can see why. And with facilities and services that include discount hiking outlets, a cash machine, internet access and more than one shop, it can all add up to a worthwhile stopover.

All together now: '*I wandered lonely as a cloud...*' Though Wordsworth lived in Grasmere for only nine years, the period was a productive one and he wrote many of his best-known works here. His cottage is the main sight in the village and his grave is in the grounds of St Oswald's Church (see p129), one of the more peaceful spots in Grasmere's often overcrowded centre.

More spacious than the preceding valley settlements, to the west the large farmhouses and grand homes share the undulating land with forests of mature deciduous trees and flocks of dozy sheep and through the busy jumble of buildings in the centre flows the River Rothay, a tranquil haven for ducks and other waterfowl; to the south lies brooding Grasmere Lake, flanked by steep, forested hills.

### Services

The **cash machine** should now be operational at the **Co-op** (Mon-Sun 7am-10pm), which also provides a cashback service and is the best place to stock up on provisions.

Although there's a chance it may have been forced to close by the time you read this, the **post office** (Mon-Wed & Fri 9am-5pm, Thur & Sat 9am-12.30pm) also has a **cash machine** but with a £1.85 withdrawal charge. However, unless yours is one of the few banks that does not have an agreement with the post office (see p27) you can withdraw cash from the counter at no charge.

Grasmere has an excellent bookshop, **Sam Read Bookseller** (☎ 015394 35374, 🖳 www.samreadbooks.co.uk; open daily 9am-6pm or 5pm in winter; closed some

weeks in Jan) that has been trading since 1887. There's a surprisingly wide range of books in this tardis of a shop and when you've found something to read you can pick up a coffee from the shop next door.

Close to the Co-op is a **pharmacy** (Mon-Fri 9am-5.30pm, Sat 9am-1pm) if your Compeed supply is in peril. There are numerous **outdoors (trekking) shops** dotted around the town centre.

### Where to stay

This is our selection of places to stay in Grasmere; you'll find plenty more on somewhere like 🖳 www.grasmere.com. Being Grasmere, with all the tourist business it can handle, B&Bs will be very reluctant to accept a one-night-only booking on summer weekends. Either stay for two nights or try to avoid the high-season weekends. Single occupancy may well mean paying the full room rate.

**Hostels** The surviving *YHA Grasmere Butharlyp Howe* (☎ 0845 371 9319, 🖳 www.yha.org.uk/hostel/grasmere-butharlyp-howe; 80 beds, 2-/4-/6-bed rooms; beds £16.50-21, 4-bed rooms £50-79; WI-FI; open all year) is in the most central location and has internet access, an alcohol licence, a smart self-catering kitchen and attractive grounds. The meals are good here too. Credit cards are accepted; 24hr access is possible once you've checked in and there is a drying room, laundry facilities and a shop. However, because it's also the largest of the hostels in the area it tends to attract school groups, making the independent hostels far more preferable on these days.

**B&Bs** *Silver Lea* (☎ 015394 35657, 🖳 www.silverlea.com; 2T or D/2D; all en suite; ➤; WI-FI; ⓛ £6; Feb-Nov), on Easedale Rd, is a charming ivy-clad slate cottage, surprisingly bright inside. B&B for a one-night stay is from £50pp (sgl occ £80); this must be paid at the time of booking.

Nearby, *Glenthorne* (☎ 015394 35389, 🖳 www.glenthorne.org; 7S/14T/5D; most en suite, other rooms share facilities; ➤; WI-FI; ⓛ £5; Feb-Nov) is a Victorian, Quaker country house (though folk of any creed can stay) next to another of Wordsworth's old houses, Allan Bank. Though the place feels like a hostel when you first walk in – perhaps owing to the wonderfully informal atmosphere – the rooms are fine. Overriding everything, however, is the hospitality here, with trays of cakes and tea laid out for guests at 4.30pm. Evening meals (7pm) must be booked in advance; all they ask is a few seconds silence before eating. There is a voluntary 15-minute prayer meeting in the mornings. B&B/DB&B is £46.50-52.50/£63-69pp for a one-night stay and yes, they do offer porridge for breakfast – presumably Quaker Oats – though it may be necessary to request it in summer.

*Heidi's Grasmere Lodge* (☎ 015394 35248, 🖥 www.heidisgrasmerelodge.co .uk; 6D; all en suite; ✉; Ⓛ), above Heidi's of Grasmere (see Where to eat) is right in the middle of town. It's very clean and as quaint as a doll's house. B&B here is from £39.50pp (sgl occ £71) but at weekends in high season they often insist on a two-night minimum stay if booking in advance.

*Beck Allans* (☎ 015394 35563, 🖥 www.beckallans.com; 4D/1D or T; all en suite; ✉; WI-FI) is a guesthouse overlooking the Rothay. B&B rates are £43-50pp (sgl occ £60-85). They can dry wet clothes or boots and will make packed lunches but you may prefer to assemble your own from the shops in the village. Note that they have a minimum 2- to 3-night stay policy at (bank holiday) weekends and they may not take one-night bookings during the week unless they have a gap.

*Lake View Country House* (☎ 015394 35384, 🖥 www.lakeview-grasmere.com; 2D/1D or Tr/1T or Tr; all en suite; ✉; 🐕 £6; WI-FI) is, as its name suggests, one of the few places to stay from where you can actually see the lake (from the first floor). It's a lovely place near the centre of Grasmere but quietly tucked away at the end of a lane. B&B costs £48-59.50pp (sgl occ £96-119 with discount for cost of breakfast, three in Tr £36pp). Packed lunches are available. If booking in advance stays of two nights are likely to be required except in winter. There's direct access to

the lakeshore which could be useful for people with dogs; though if your dog is a terrier you might need to keep it on a short leash as there's a badger sett in the garden!

If you can't get a bed in town, try the B&Bs on Keswick Rd, the best of which is *Chestnut Villa* (☎ 015394 35218, 🖥 www.chestnutvilla.com; 2T/8D; all en suite; ✉; WI-FI; Ⓛ £6) charging £37.50-42.50p for B&B (sgl occ £55). Some rooms are in Ivy Dean next door.

South of Grasmere, 150m beyond Dove Cottage is *How Foot Lodge* (☎ 015394 35366, 🖥 howfootlodge.co.uk; 4D/2T all en suite; ✉, 🐕) where B&B starts from £37.50pp.

**Hotels** *Moss Grove Organic* (☎ 015394 35251, 🖥 www.mossgrove.com; 10D/1D or T; all en suite; ✉; 🐕£20; WI-FI) is a smashing place whose strict green ethos extends beyond the kitchen to their accommodation, with some of the beds made from reclaimed timber sitting atop oak floors from sustainable forests. All this, and yet the building still retains its original Victorian charm. The prices, however, do reflect the quality, with B&B costing from £57pp (Sun-Thur in the winter and in the cheaper executive rooms) up to £127.50pp on a Friday or Saturday (sgl occ £42-112.50). One reader wrote saying it was worth it for the luxurious bed alone (they stayed in Room 5). Breakfast is organic; there is no restaurant or bar though it is possible to buy bottles of organic wine. If booking in advance stays of two nights are likely to be required .

*Red Lion Hotel* (☎ 015394 35456, 🖥 www.bw-grasmereredlion.co.uk; 5S/44D or T; all en suite; ✉; 🐕£20; WI-FI) *is* the centre of town; it's been recommended by some readers and it's enough though lacks a little of the charm of some of the other places around here. B&B costs around £49-87pp (sgl £55-70) but special packages are sometimes available. Rates are lowest if booked in advance.

*Dale Lodge Hotel* (☎ 015394 35300, 🖥 www.dalelodgehotel.co.uk; 1T/15D; all en suite; ✉; 🐕£25 per stay; WI-FI) is a huge, rambling place. An old-fashioned-looking pile on the outside, inside it is all polished floorboards and original tilework and really rather chic, with each bedroom individually decorated. The three acres of sprawling gardens are another attraction, as is its location in the heart of town. The attached bar, Tweedies (see Where to eat), is also recommended. B&B costs £40-70pp (sgl occ £80-100).

*The Wordsworth Hotel* (☎ 015394 35592, ☐ www.thewordsworthhotel.co.uk; 2S/33D or T/4 suites; all en suite; ✷; 🐾 £20; WI-FI) was formerly the smartest address in the centre of town, a large attractive hotel with facilities including gym, pool, sauna, Jacuzzi and cocktail bar. B&B/ dinner B&B costs £69-169/89-240pp, £70 for a single. Advance bookings for a one-night

stay on a Saturday may not be accepted.

*Bridge House Hotel* (☎ 015394 35425, ☐ www.bridgehousegrasmere.co .uk; 9D/9D or T; all en suite; ✷; WI-FI in most areas; mid Jan-Nov) is another large place near the river, with two acres of gorgeous grounds. Rates for dinner B&B are £46-79.50pp (sgl occ from £67). Unfortunately, they accept one-night bookings only if it's quiet which, in summer, is unlikely.

## Where to eat and drink

As you'd expect for a major tourist centre like Grasmere, cafés and restaurants are plentiful throughout the village.

For excellent Fair Trade coffee there's *Lucia's Takeaway Coffee Shop* (Fri-Wed

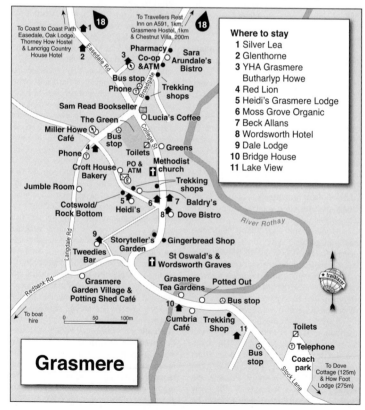

### Where to stay

1 Silver Lea
2 Glenthorne
3 YHA Grasmere Butharlyp Howe
4 Red Lion
5 Heidi's Grasmere Lodge
6 Moss Grove Organic
7 Beck Allans
8 Wordsworth Hotel
9 Dale Lodge
10 Bridge House
11 Lake View

Grasmere

ROUTE GUIDE AND MAPS

9am-4.30pm), beside the bookshop. They also do filled baguettes (£2.60). For sandwiches there's *Croft House Bakery* (Mon-Sat 9am-4pm, Sun 9.30am-4pm), next to the post office; it also does a nice line in pasties, baguettes and butties as well as something to warm you up on a cold day, such as beef stew with a roll (£3.50).

*Heidi's* (daily 10am-6pm) does a good cream tea as well as light lunches. *Baldry's*, across the road, is another genteel tearoom, open daily from 10am to '4.30-ish'.

A number of other cafés vie for position near the bridge, including *Grasmere Tea Gardens* (☎ 015394 35590; daily 9.30am-5pm), overlooking the river, and the contemporary *Potted Out* (☎ 015394 35572; 🖳 www.grasmeregardens.com; daily 11am-8.30pm), an Italian bistro with pizzas from £8.50, and the *Cumbria Café* (daily 9am-5pm, Tue-Sun 6-9pm).

At the Grasmere Garden Village there's the *Potting Shed Café* (Mon-Sat 9.30am-5.30pm; Sun 11am-4.45pm). Related to Potted Out (above) it has a cheaper, more traditional menu, eg fish & chips (£9.95).

At *The Dove Bistro* (Mon-Sat noon-2pm & 6-9pm, Sun noon-9pm), part of Wordsworth Hotel (see Where to stay) you can try a Wordsworth burger in rustic ciabatta or Wordsworth chicken and leek pie and finish with Wordsworth sticky toffee pudding. On the same street is *Greens* (daily 9.30am to 4.30pm), a contemporary eatery specialising in good traditional food. The shepherd's pie is £8.50.

*Miller Howe Café* (daily 9am-5pm) has a long menu with some imaginative dishes – eg boozy beef pot (£8.95) and oven baked ham toasted muffin for £8.45.

On Broadgate, *Sara Arundale's Bistro* (☎ 015394 35266; May-Nov Tue-Sun 10.30am-4pm & 6-9pm; days/hours vary at other times) has also been recommended.

There's a fancy menu at *Tweedies Bar* (daily noon-11pm or midnight; food served Mon-Sat noon-3pm & 6-9pm, Sun noon-3.45om & 6.30-9pm) in Dale Lodge Hotel (see Where to stay). Try local smoked gammon for £15.50. On most Fridays and Saturdays there is live music. The same menu is also available in *Lodge Restaurant*

(Mon-Sat 6-9pm, Sun 6.30-9pm) though in a more formal setting.

Best of all is *The Jumble Room* (☎ 015394 35188, 🖳 www.thejumbleroom .co.uk; Wed-Sun 5.30-10pm but check in advance particularly in Dec-Jan; booking advisable) on Langdale Rd. The decor looks less of a jumble with each passing year but this quirky little place still gets rave reviews. The menu changes frequently and includes dishes from all four corners of the globe with a few extra corners you never knew about. South African Dithoise Chicken, stuffed with pumpkin and sunflower seeds and honey (£17.95) was on the menu when we were there.

## What to see
**Dove Cottage** William Wordsworth lived for less than ten years in beautiful Dove Cottage (☎ 015394 35544, 🖳 www.words worth.org.uk; Mar-Oct daily 9.30am-5pm, Nov-late Dec & Feb 9.30am-4pm; £7.75, children £4.50; student/YHA member discounts available; about 500m walk southeast from The Green, just off the A591, yet its importance in both his development as a poet and his life was enormous. Many of his best-loved and most-powerful works were written here and this was his first home with his wife Mary Hutchinson and where three of his children were born.

Today all but the first room is furnished entirely with items owned by the poet, though some have come from other Wordsworth properties. Guides show visitors around the cottage, pointing out such items as Wordsworth's famous **suitcase** (where he's carefully sewn his name inside but didn't leave enough room for the final 'h' tucked up in the corner); a letter of introduction – a precursor to the modern-day passport – penned by the French authorities, and which has been stamped on the back by the border guards of a host of European countries; and the **Royal Warrant** of 1843 in which he was bestowed with the honour of being Queen Victoria's poet laureate. It was an honour he accepted grudgingly, having already turned down the position twice, and one that he never truly fulfilled; indeed, from his acceptance of the post to his death in 1850,

Wordsworth wrote precisely no official poems as poet laureate, the first (and so far only) poet laureate to do so.

The cottage is, by the standards of the Lake District, relatively large, containing eight rooms rather than the more typical three or four, thus betraying its origins as a 17th-century pub. One of Wordsworth's frequent visitors at the cottage was that other well-known literary figure (and opium fiend) Thomas de Quincey. De Quincey declared the house to be a fortuitous one for writers and when the Wordsworths vacated it in 1808 the de Quinceys moved in, thus continuing the literary connections of the place.

The **museum** next door contains original manuscripts by both Wordsworth and de Quincey and stages frequent special exhibitions.

**Other sights**  Before you leave, you may like to pay a visit to **Wordsworth's family grave** around the back of **St Oswald's**, a 13th-century church named after the 7th-century king of Northumbria who preached on this site. Wordsworth's prayer-book is on display in the church.

Standing by the side entrance to the church grounds is the 150-year-old **Gingerbread Shop** (☎ 015394 35428, 🖥 www.grasmeregingerbread.co.uk), a tiny 'factory' that, incredibly, used to be the local school. It is said that Wordsworth taught here occasionally.

Opposite is the **Storyteller's Garden** (🖥 www.taffythomas.co.uk) which hosts several events throughout the year – see the website for details.

Around the village centre are a number of **galleries** displaying works by local artists.

Make sure, too, that you check out Lancrigg Woods and the Poet's Walk (Map 18, p123), the start of which you walked past on your way into Grasmere.

**Transport**          (see also pp52-5)
From Easter to October Stagecoach's open-top No 599 **bus** service travels regularly via Ambleside (15 mins) and the train station and Bowness Pier at Windermere (25 mins), from where in the evening a few buses go on to Kendal. Their No 555 goes from Keswick to Lancaster via Ambleside, Windermere and Kendal (Grasmere to Lancaster takes 1hr 50mins). Buses leave from The Green.

For other destinations, Grasmere **Taxis** can be reached on ☎ 015394 35506

ROUTE GUIDE AND MAPS

## STAGE 4: GRASMERE TO PATTERDALE                    MAPS 18-25

### Introduction
Ignoring the alternative routes for the moment, this is the shortest of our stages. Short, but no less sweet for it's another classic hike along which walkers can enjoy some great views back to Grasmere and, once over the pass, down across Grisedale to Patterdale, another gorgeous valley with the lake of Ullswater twinkling away to the north.

The most direct routes avoiding Striding Edge are a mere **8½ miles (13.5km, 3-4hrs)** and deliver a simple walk up to **Grisedale Pass (Hause)** and either down the valley or more satisfyingly, up along the ridge of St Sunday Crag. The longer route ascends the 950-metre bulk of Helvellyn, returning to the valley via

❏ **Important note – walking times**
Unless otherwise specified, **all times in this book refer only to time spent walking**. You will need to add 20-30% to allow for rests, photography, checking the map, drinking water etc. When planning the day's hike count on 5-7 hours' actual walking.

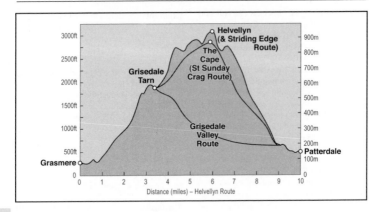

the stirringly named Striding Edge ridge walk; an additional distance of around **two miles** and a considerable amount of climbing and at times, exposure. Both the high routes are described on pp133-6. You can delay your choice on which path to take until Grisedale Tarn, where the three paths go their separate ways.

### The route

First of all you need to reach the heights of Grisedale Tarn, which involves a climb up a bridleway running off the A591 (Map 18, p123) reached by walking up the A591 to the bridleway from Grasmere or, as we've mapped it, picking up the original Coast to Coast path near Thorney How Youth Hostel.

At a footbridge or ford the bridleway divides at the foot of **Great Tongue** (Map 19) into a steeper route alongside **Little Tongue Gill** or a mildly steadier gradient to the east of Great Tongue along Tongue Gill which is slabbed for part of its length. Of course you're still climbing to the same elevation where the two paths rejoin.

Soon you arrive at the pretty mountain lake of **Grisedale Tarn** (Map 20) with the trail zigzagging up **Dollywaggon Pike** towards Helvellyn. Keeping to the easier path down Grisedale valley, the descent is as uncomplicated as the ascent, with the **Brothers' Parting Stone** just below the tarn (so-called because it's said that here in 1800 Wordsworth last met with his brother John, who died at sea a few years later). Just under a mile further on by Ruthwaite Beck, **Ruthwaite Lodge**, a climbers' hut, is usually locked up.

The path continues down the valley and briefly joins a tarmac road (Map 24) where the Helvellyn route comes in. You then leave the road to the right to enter the National Trust's **Glenamara Park** (and where the St Sunday Crag route converges), with some wonderful views over Patterdale and beyond to Ullswater (Norse for 'Water with a Bend'). All being well, you'll drop onto the road just below Patterdale post office and pub about two hours after leaving Grisedale Tarn.

ROUTE GUIDE AND MAPS

**MAP 19**

GRISEDALE HAUSE

20

SHATTERED ROCK

STONE WALL AT TOP OF CLIMB

📱 036

CAIRNS

LARGE BOULDERS TO LEFT OF PATH

CAIRNS

STREAM

PATHS CONVERGE

RIGHT TURN BEHIND ROCKY FACE – FLATTER NOW

WATERFALL

PATH IS GRASSY AND A LITTLE INDISTINCT – JUST KEEP GOING UP

LITTLE TONGUE GILL

GREAT TONGUE

CAIRN BY OUTCROP

KEEP RIGHT HERE

STREAM

TONGUE GILL

CROSS GILL ON BRIDGE OR STEPPING STONES

📱 035

STREAM

OLD RESERVOIR

SHEEPFOLD

PATH TO GRASMERE HOSTEL

0    ¼ mile

0                     500m
APPROX SCALE

18

TOP OF CLIMB

↑ 50 MINS

FOOT OF GREAT TONGUE

↑ 25 MINS FROM A591 (MAP 18)

ROUTE GUIDE AND MAPS

**MAP 20**

0    1/4 mile

APPROX SCALE

0    500m

*trailblazer*

HELVELLYN ROUTE: 3HRS 15 MINS FROM GRISEDALE TARN TO GATE OFF ROAD (MAP 24)

**NETHERMOST PIKE**
CAIRNS EVERY 10M OR
SO ON THIS STRETCH

**HELVELLYN ROUTE**

**HIGH CRAG**

**DOLLYWAGGON PIKE**

METAL
POST

IT CAN BE CHILLY ON THE
PASS AS THE WIND BLOWS
ACROSS THE TARN; NEVER-
THELESS, SOME CAMPERS
PITCH THEIR TENTS HERE

**GRISEDALE TARN**

NOTE THE PATH UP
DOLLYWAGGON PIKE
ZIG-ZAGGING UP
THE HILLSIDE

RUTHWAITE LODGE
(USUALLY LOCKED)

RUTHWAITE BECK

**GRISEDALE VALLEY ROUTE**

ROCKFALL

BROTHERS' PARTING
STONE WHERE
WORDSWORTH SAID
GOODBYE TO
HIS BROTHER

TURN OFF LEFT
TO DOLLYWAGGON
PIKE

Grisedale Beck

**ST SUNDAY ROUTE**

INDISTINCT PATH TO
ST SUNDAY CRAG
BRANCHES OFF SOON
AFTER OLD WALL OR PICK
IT UP WHERE THE TARN
SPILLS OUT

OLD WALL
AT TOP

22

21

21

19

30 MINS TO TREE PLANTATION (MAP 21)

RUTHWAITE LODGE ◀

40 MINS

LOW ROUTE (GRISEDALE VALLEY) TIMES:

TOP OF CLIMB ◀

**The high-level options: Helvellyn & Striding Edge; St Sunday Crag**
If weather conditions allow, one of these two high-level routes should be seriously considered. After all, it would be a shame on this, the penultimate stage in the Lake District, if you didn't try to climb as many peaks as possible.

**Helvellyn & Striding Edge**            **Map 20, Maps 22-24 pp134-5**
Of the two high-level options, **Helvellyn**, at 950m (3113ft) the third highest peak in England after Scafell Pike and Scafell, is understandably the more

WALLED ENCLOSURE OF TREES - THE CROSSING PLANTATION

TREE PLANTATION

BOARDS ACROSS STREAMS

GRISEDALE VALLEY ROUTE

VIEWS TOWARDS ULLSWATER - THE BEST PANORAMA ON THE C2C?

ATTENTION! LEAVE THE CAPE TO THE NORTH, NOT NORTH-EAST

30 MINS FROM RUTHWAITE LODGE (MAP 20)

DO CROSS THIS BRIDGE HOWEVER!

DON'T BE TEMPTED BY THE PRETTY BRIDGE JUST TO YOUR LEFT- KEEP STRAIGHT ON!

LOOK FOR CAIRNS TO SHOW YOU THE PATH FROM THE TOP OF THE CAPE

038

GRISEDALE BECK

LOW ROUTE (GRISEDALE VALLEY):

THE CAPE 841M 037

CAIRNS

ST SUNDAY ROUTE - FROM GRISEDALE TARN (MAP 20) TO GLENAMARA PARK (MAP 24), 2HRS 45MINS

ST SUNDAY CRAG

PATH CLIMBS UP TO COL ON RIDGE

NOW ON RIDGE. NOT NARROW LIKE STRIDING EDGE, BUT IT IS OFTEN VERY, VERY WINDY

trailblaze

**MAP 21**

JOIN MAIN RIDGE PATH AT DEEPDALE HAUSE

RIDGE PATH FROM FAIRFIELD SUMMIT

0        1/4 mile

0     APPROX SCALE     500m

ROUTE GUIDE AND MAPS

ROUTE GUIDE AND MAPS

HELVELLYN ROUTE: 3HRS 15 MINS FROM GRISEDALE TARN (MAP 20) TO GATE OFF ROAD (MAP 24) →

RED TARN

BLEABERRY CRAG

**23**

HELVELLYN 950M

STRIDING EDGE

LOW SPYING HOW

SHELTER

HIGH SPYING HOW

GOUGH MONUMENT

TAKE CARE – CRUMBLING PATH DOWN TO STRIDING EDGE

DIXON MEMORIAL

BIG CAIRN

**20**

LOW PATH GOES TO THE SOUTH OF THE 'EDGE' AT FIRST THEN CROSSES TO THE NORTH. OR, OF COURSE, YOU CAN JUST SCRAMBLE ALONG THE CREST

★ trailblazer

**MAP 22**

0        ¼ mile
0    APPROX SCALE    500m

HELVELLYN ROUTE: 3HRS 15 MINS FROM GRISEDALE TARN (MAP 20) TO GATE OFF ROAD (MAP 24) →

HELVELLYN ROUTE

**24**

GATE IN FENCE

STILE IN WALL

**MAP 23**

LOVELY BRIDGE

**24**

**22**

FARMHOUSE

★ trailblazer

FARM BUILDING

BARN

GRISEDALE VALLEY ROUTE

**21**

PINE FOREST ELMHOW PLANTATION

0        ¼ mile
0    APPROX SCALE    500m

LOW ROUTE (GRISEDALE VALLEY): 40 MINS FROM TREE PLANTATION (MAP 21) TO GATE OFF ROAD (MAP 24)

popular. The climb is arduous and, having reached the top, you then face a nerve-tingling drop on a crumbing slope above Red Tarn, followed by a knife-edge walk along Striding Edge ridge to reach the trail dropping to Patterdale. A memorial plaque to Robert Dixon who was killed here in 1858 whilst following his fox hounds during a hunt does little to calm the nerves but with a steady head and light winds the sense of achievement is ample reward for your efforts.

Wainwright waxes lyrical about this side trip, describing the notorious Striding Edge as the 'best quarter mile between St Bees and Robin Hood's Bay'. He visited Helvellyn on his first trip to the Lakes in 1930, and it was this trip that inspired his passion for the Lakes. He approached the peak from the opposite direction to that given here and he edged along it 'in agonies of apprehension'.

This route takes about 3hrs 15mins from Grisedale Tarn to Patterdale, though that assumes you take the lower path just below the knife-edge crest of Striding Edge which can be traversed in as little as 20 minutes. However, with

HELVELLYN ROUTE: 3HRS 15 MINS FROM GRISEDALE TARN (MAP 20)   GATE OFF ROAD →

TO GLENRIDDING

**23**

HELVELLYN ROUTE

TURN RIGHT THROUGH GATE, OFF ROAD FROM HERE

Braesteads Farm

TARMAC

**25**

040

HEAD SOUTH-EAST FROM OAK TREES

GRISEDALE VALLEY ROUTE

CROSS STREAM ON STEPPING STONES

**23**

HARRISON CRAG

GLENAMARA PARK

**MAP 24**

039
PATH JOINS WALL

trailblazer

0        ¼ mile
0   APPROX SCALE   500m

**21**

ST SUNDAY CRAG ROUTE

LOW LEVEL (GRISEDALE) ROUTE:   40 MINS FROM TREE PLANTATION (MAP 21)   GATE OFF ROAD →

ROUTE GUIDE AND MAPS

the inevitable waiting that needs to be done to let people coming the other way go by (at least at weekends), expect it all to add up to four hours from the tarn. You won't regret the extra time – it is truly exhilarating.

## St Sunday Crag          Maps 20-21 pp132-3, Maps 22-24 pp134-5

It's said that better views, if fewer thrills, lie in wait on the south side of the valley along St Sunday Crag. Indeed, for many people these are the best views on the entire route. What's more, the effort required to climb up to St Sunday Crag is, by the standards of the lakes, fairly negligible, a steady plod away from the Tarn followed by a reasonably steady descent, at least until the sudden drop into Glenamara Park.

Soon after leaving Grisedale Tarn, you'll see a trail rising away from the lake, presently joined by the usual path from the tarn's mouth. You join the ridge at Deepdale Hause, where the path from Fairfield summit feeds in from the right, and soon arrive at the high point known as **The Cape** (841m/2759ft). All along you've fine views of the next stage; a ramp rising steadily past briefly glimpsed Angle Tarn to Kidsty Pike and the unseen depths of Haweswater beyond.

From The Cape make sure you walk briefly north and not east for Gavel Pike. Then at a cairn (WPT 038) the path continues north-east before dropping off the ridge and tumbling down to Glenamara Park, where you meet up with the low-level route and enter Patterdale.

## PATTERDALE          MAP 25, p137

Patterdale is little more than a meandering collection of houses strung along the A592. Normally valleys this beautiful would be full of souvenir shops and tearooms. But Patterdale, while not exactly undiscovered, is mercifully free of the 'Lakeland Babylon' found in Grasmere. The valley is also something of a **wildlife** haven, including a population of red squirrels – some of the last remaining in England.

The **fountain of St Patrick** (Patterdale is a corruption of St Patrick's Dale) is an ornate Victorian construction set in a bank by the side of the road just outside Glenridding, and is said to mark the spot where the saint baptised the locals.

All your needs will be comprehensively met at **Patterdale Village Store** (summer daily 8.30am-6pm, winter to 5.30pm and to noon on Wed & Sun; 🖳 www.patterdalevillagestore.co.uk). Gillian and Tom run one of the best-provisioned village stores along the route and one which, unlike so many others, doesn't look as if it'll be closing down anytime soon.

The shop includes a **post office** (Mon 8.30am-5.30pm, Tue 8.30am-3.30pm, Wed & Thur 8.30am to noon), a large variety of hot and cold sandwiches including bacon rolls fit to choke a hog, delicious BBQ pork rib sandwiches as well as a lavish array of groceries for those camping, staying in the hostel or just unable to resist temptation. There are also hats, gloves, knee supports, maps and Coast to Coast path souvenirs and even copies of this book.

Both the shop and the post office have **cashback** facilities and outside is a walkers' **message board** plus reams of information on local lodgings, bus times, phone numbers and so on.

And finally there's **Crookabeck** (☎ 017684 82742, 🖳 www.crookabeck.co.uk; visits by appointment only), a farm selling products made from the wool sheared from their sheep and Angora goats, as well as knitkits. (See p139 to stay here).

You'll be lucky to get a mobile signal in Patterdale.

### Where to stay and eat

There's a range of **accommodation** in Patterdale, though this being the Lakes, booking ahead is vital if you don't want to end up sleeping in a ditch with a red squirrel

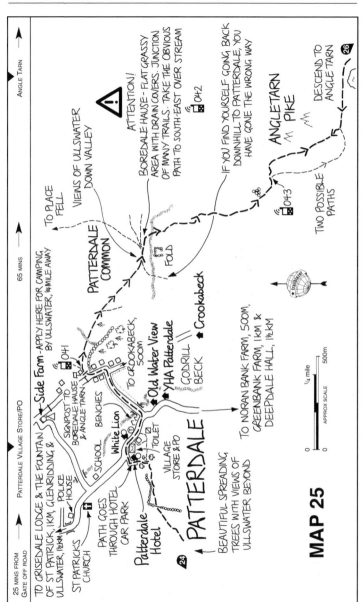

25 MINS FROM GATE OFF ROAD ← PATTERDALE VILLAGE STORE/PO ← 65 MINS → ANGLE TARN →

TO GRISEDALE LODGE & THE FOUNTAIN, 1KM, OF ST PATRICK, 1KM, GLENRIDDING & ULLSWATER, 1½KM

Side Farm - APPLY HERE FOR CAMPING, BY ULLSWATER, ½ MILE AWAY

TO PLACE FELL

VIEWS OF ULLSWATER DOWN VALLEY

ATTENTION!
BOREDALE HAUSE - FLAT GRASSY AREA WITH DRAIN COVERS. JUNCTION OF MANY TRAILS. TAKE THE OBVIOUS PATH TO SOUTH-EAST OVER STREAM

SIGNPOST TO BOREDALE HAUSE & ANGLE TARN

PATTERDALE COMMON

FOLD

IF YOU FIND YOURSELF GOING BACK DOWNHILL TO PATTERDALE, YOU HAVE GONE THE WRONG WAY

POLICE HOUSE

ST PATRICK'S CHURCH

SCHOOL

BENCHES

White Lion

TO CROOKABECK, 500m

Old Water View

YHA Patterdale

GOLDRILL BECK

Crookabeck

ANGLETARN PIKE

DESCEND TO ANGLE TARN

26

TWO POSSIBLE PATHS

VILLAGE STORE & PO

TOILET

TO NORAN BANK FARM, 500m, GREENBANK FARM, 1KM & DEEPDALE HALL, 1½KM

PATTERDALE

Patterdale Hotel

24

PATH GOES THROUGH HOTEL CAR PARK

BEAUTIFUL SPREADING TREES WITH VIEWS OF ULLSWATER BEYOND

MAP 25

0   ¼ mile
0   500m
APPROX SCALE

for a duvet. Remember, the next stage to Shap is commonly agreed to be the toughest on the Coast to Coast walk, so you'll want to be on form. If you run out of luck in Patterdale, there's more accommodation in Glenridding (see box opposite); it's listed on the **community website** ▫ www.patter dale.org, or outside the shop.

For **campers**, across Goldrill Beck is *Side Farm* (☎ 017684 82337, ☎ 07796 128897; ▫ www.patterdale.org/ Side%20Farm.htm; £8pp; dogs if kept on lead; Easter to Oct). Genuine Coast to Coast walkers will always be accepted (sometimes even if the sign says they're full) but in general they do not take advance bookings. The site has toilets, hot showers and laundry facilities. It actually lies a little way beyond the farm on the edge of the lake but they insist you check in at the farm first. However, considering they have a **tea-room** (Easter to Oct, school holidays daily 10.30am-5pm; hours vary at other times), it's a great place to recuperate before pitching your tent. And just in case you thought you'd heard the last of him, it's said our old friend Wordsworth was a regular visitor to Side Farm.

At the other end of the village, *YHA Patterdale* (☎ 0845 371 9337, ▫ www.yha .org.uk/hostel/patterdale; 84 beds, 1x single, 2-/4-/6-/8-/ and 2x10-bed rooms; beds £15-21, 4-bed rooms £60-68) is on the main road. The 1970s' building may not win any design awards, but inside has been refitted comfortably and, unusually, the building is open all day. Meals and packed lunches are available, the hostel is licensed and there is a drying room and laundry facilities. Credit cards are accepted.

At Noran Bank Farm (see p139) you'll find *Shepherd's Crook Bunkhouse* (☎ 01768 482327, ▫ www.patterdale.org/ Noranbank.htm; 🐾£4; Ⓛ £6) with two rooms; one has a double bunk bed and en suite shower, the other sleeps six and has separate shower facilities. It's open all year and is a very reasonable £14-19pp, £5 supplement for single occupancy of the double bunk bed room. There is a fully equipped kitchen and a DIY breakfast costs £6.

Just before the YHA hostel, *Old Water View Country Inn* (☎ 01768 482175, ▫ www.oldwaterview.co.uk; 2D/3Tr/1Qd; all with private facilities; ▼; WI-FI; Ⓛ) is a wonderful place and a favourite of Wainwright's. The current owner is a mine of information and is the guy to speak to about shortcuts along High St to Shap. There's comfortable accommodation and good food here: several readers have recommended it for both. B&B costs £35-42pp (sgl occ £35-52) but accommodation is usually on a dinner, B&B basis (meals from £10.95). Food is available all day 8am-11pm and the bar which serves the local brew, Tirril, on draft is also open those times. There's a beer garden and you can also get essentials such as plasters as well as components for a packed lunch;

Very close to the path and the focus of the village is the 19th-century *White Lion* pub (☎ 01768 482214, ▫ www.pat terdale.org/Whitelion.htm; 1S/1S or D/ 2D/3T; all with private facilities; 🐾£2.85; Ⓛ £4.95). B&B starts at £37pp (sgl occ 42.50) and they do bar meals (daily noon-9pm) too. The extensive menu includes steaks, curry and fish & chips; whatever dish you choose, it will be big! They also do breakfasts (Apr-Sep from 9am; £7.15) for non-residents as long as they have requested this the night before.

The smartest and most expensive lodgings in the village are at *Patterdale Hotel* (☎ 0844 811 5585, ▫ www.patterdale hotel.co.uk; 4S/10T/39D/4Qd; all en suite; ▼; WI-FI; Feb-Nov). Part of a chain, it's an enormous establishment and their reluctance to accept bookings for anything less than two-night stays may deter C2Cers; however, they are happy to take one-night bookings if there is a vacancy near the time. Unravelling the tariff takes a degree in metaphysics, but during the week expect to pay £162-206pp for dinner B&B for two nights (£95-123pp for two nights at weekends). **Food** is served daily 10am-8.30pm; the bar serves hot food and snacks daily noon-5pm & 6.30-8.30pm and the restaurant is open daily 6.30-8.30pm.

There are other B&Bs further south along the road beyond the YHA hostel.

Less than a mile south of the path, *Noran Bank Farm* (see Shepherd's Crook Bunkhouse p138; 1Tr with private bathroom; ☞; ☈£4; Ⓛ £6; Mar-Oct) is a whitewashed 16th-century farmhouse. Rates are £30pp (sgl occ £35). A minimum stay of two nights is required on bank holiday weekends.

Nearby is another old farmhouse, *Greenbank Farm* (☎ 017684 82292, 🖳 www.coast2coast.co.uk/greenbankfarm; 1S/1D/1Qd; shared shower facilities; WI-FI; Ⓛ £5; Mar-Oct) a working sheep farm charging £24pp and £13 for an evening meal (book in advance). They also have a static caravan where up to four people can sleep for £19pp including breakfast.

Just after Greenbank Farm is *Deepdale Hall* (☎ 01768 482369, 🖳 www.deepdalehall.co.uk; 1D/1Tr; both with private facilities; ☞; WI-FI; Ⓛ about £8; Mar-Nov) with B&B from £40pp (sgl occ £65).

*Grisedale Lodge* (☎ 01768 482155, 🖳 www.grisedalelodge.co.uk; 1D/2D or T; all with private facilities; ☞; WI-FI; Ⓛ from £6) is set halfway between Patterdale and Glenridding villages, close to the shores of Ullswater. It's a lovely location and by all accounts a lovely B&B too, with swish rooms and large breakfasts. B&B costs £39pp (sgl occ £45-78).

*Crookabeck B&B* (☎ 07747 587635, 🖳 www.crookabeck.com; 1Tr; en suite; WI-FI; Ⓛ) offers self-contained accommodation with superb views and a fridge (no cooking facilities). A cooked breakfast is brought up to the room. B&B costs from £45pp (sgl occ and triple rates negotiable).

**Transport** (see also pp52-5)
Stagecoach's **bus** No 108 (Patterdale Bus) travels to Penrith railway station and operates Mon-Fri year-round outside the school summer holidays. During the holidays and on Saturday, Sunday and Public Holidays the service is the 508 which travels between Penrith and Bowness.

## ❏ Ullswater and Glenridding

*I wandered lonely as a cloud,*
*That floats on high o'er vales and hills,*
*When all at once I saw a crowd,*
*A host of golden daffodils,*
*Beside the lake, beneath the trees,*
*Fluttering and dancing in the breeze.*
**William Wordsworth**, *Daffodils*

It is said that Wordsworth was inspired to write these words after a trip to Ullswater. Certainly it's a beautiful lake and unlike neighbouring Grasmere and Haweswater there's plenty to do *on* the water too.

There is a **tourist information centre** (☎ 017684 82414, 🖳 ullswater tic@lake-district.gov.uk) in the main car park in Glenridding; it is open daily 9.30am-5.30pm March until the end of October and at weekends only (roughly 9.30am-3.30pm, though phone first to check) the rest of the year. On the board outside they put up a list of B&Bs with vacancies that evening, which could prove invaluable.

**Boats** (motorboats) can be hired from the café at the lake's southern corner. These boats are fine, though don't try to emulate Donald Campbell, who broke the 200mph water speed record on Ullswater in 1955.

For something more sedate, hire a rowing boat, or you can take a cruise on a **steamer** (☎ 017684 82229; 🖳 www.ullswater-steamers.co.uk). There have been steamers on the lake since 1859 and two of the five boats currently in service, *Lady of the Lake* and *Raven*, have been operating since the late 19th century. Services operate year-round, 3-9/day) to Howton, Pooley Bridge and back.

For further details of accommodation, activities and events around Ullswater see 🖳 www.ullswater.co.uk.

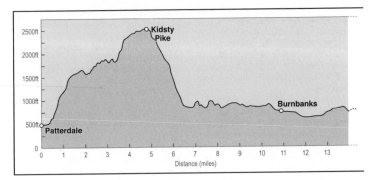

## STAGE 5: PATTERDALE TO SHAP                    MAPS 25-34

### Introduction

Today is the day you leave the Lake District but the crags, knotts, pikes and fells that have been your high-level chums for the past few days won't let you go without a struggle. Be prepared to feel quite tired at the end of this **15½-mile (25km, 6½hr)** stage from Patterdale to Shap. The long climb up to Kidsty Pike, the gnarly descent down to Haweswater (see box below) and the undulating stage above the lake's shore add up to well over **1300 metres** (4400ft) of ascent. Together it all conspires to make the seemingly harmless spin down over field and farmland to Shap enough to curse the very name of Wainwright.

With no accommodation directly on the route nor, indeed, any shops, tea-rooms or pubs, you have little choice but to grit your teeth and knuckle down. To shorten the day, a few walkers now take a 1¼ mile (2km) detour to Bampton (see p144). Otherwise, consider camping at Angle Tarn having come over from

---

**❏ Haweswater Reservoir**

What is now one of Cumbria's largest bodies of water was once a small and fairly unassuming lake stuck on the eastern edge of the national park. In 1929, however, a bill was passed authorising the use of Haweswater as a reservoir to serve the needs of the population of Manchester. A concrete dam, 470m wide and 35m high, was constructed at the northern edge of the lake, raising the depth of the lake by over 30m and increasing the surface area to four miles long by half a mile wide (6km by 1km).

This project was not without its opponents, many protested at the loss of the settlements such as Mardale Green on Haweswater's eastern shore (near the pier). Before the village was flooded, coffins were removed from the graveyard and buried elsewhere and the 18th-century Holy Trinity Church was pulled down. Some of the windows from this church are now in the reservoir tower. Even today, during times of drought when the water level is low, the walls of Mardale emerge from the reservoir.

Despite man's interference the lake is still something of a wildlife haven. Swimming in the waters are wild brown trout, char, gwyniad and perch, while **Riggindale** is an RSPB haven, with wheatear, raven, ring ouzel and peregrine.

Grasmere and stocked up at the Patterdale village store. You won't find many more truly wild places like this in the days to come and at all other times the baggage van can carry the camping gear.

## The route

You'll have spotted the ramp rising up from the far side of Patterdale. After much huffing and puffing it drops you to the grassy platform known as **Boredale Hause** where the right way is actually the most obvious continuing south-east, by one trail or another, to the scalloped shoreline of Angle Tarn. The gradient levels off for a while until another haul leads up around The Knott and soon the hard-to-miss turn-off that brings you with rather less effort than you might expect to **Kidsty Pike**, at a modest 784m (2572ft) the high point on the original Coast to Coast route.

From the top, looking west, you can see the Pillar looking down onto Ennerdale Water from all those days ago, Scafell Pike, Helvellyn and St Sunday from the previous stage. To the south lie unknown lands including the deep cleft of Riggindale in whose crags is said to be the eyrie of England's last **golden eagle**.

The biggest descent on the walk now follows – at times you'll need your hands – to the very shores of Haweswater reservoir, but a lakeside amble while

ROUTE GUIDE AND MAPS

40 MINS FROM GAP IN WALL WITH STREAM (MAP 26)    THE KNOTT    60 MINS TO BRIDGE OVER STREAM BY HAWESWATER (MAP 28)

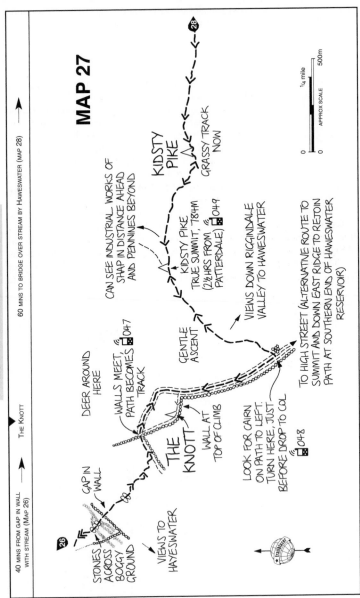

MAP 27

STONES ACROSS BOGGY GROUND

26

GAP IN WALL

VIEWS TO HAYESWATER

DEER AROUND HERE

WALLS MEET, PATH BECOMES TRACK

047

THE KNOTT

WALL AT TOP OF CLIMB

048

LOOK FOR CAIRN ON PATH TO LEFT. TURN HERE, JUST BEFORE DROP TO COL

CAN SEE INDUSTRIAL WORKS OF SHAP IN DISTANCE AHEAD AND PENNINES BEYOND

GENTLE ASCENT

KIDSTY PIKE

KIDSTY PIKE TRUE SUMMIT, 784M (2½ HRS FROM PATTERDALE) 049

VIEWS DOWN RIGGINDALE VALLEY TO HAWESWATER

GRASSY TRACK NOW

28

TO HIGH STREET (ALTERNATIVE ROUTE TO SUMMIT AND DOWN EAST RIDGE TO REJOIN PATH AT SOUTHERN END OF HAWESWATER RESERVOIR)

¼ mile
500m

0        0
APPROX SCALE

spinning your dainty parasol is sadly not on the cards. Instead you're soon panting like a hippo on a treadmill high above the shore, measuring each streaming gill until the dammed waters terminate at the wooded glade along Haweswater Beck.

The 'model' village of **Burnbanks** (Map 30) at the head of the reservoir has a slightly sinister ambience along with an infrequent (Tue & Sat only) bus service (NBM Hire No 111) to Bampton, Penrith, and the outside world (see public transport map and services pp52-5). You can **camp** at *Aragon* (☎ 01931 713629, 🖳 chizzer@homecall.co.uk) for £7pp (showers £1). Booking appreciated. Head along the trail from Burnbanks for five minutes and then turn left where the path crosses the lane at Naddle Bridge. It's a quiet riverside spot with beautiful woodland all around. Look out for red squirrels.

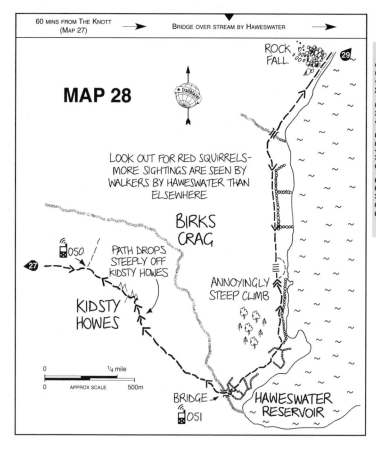

60 MINS FROM THE KNOTT (MAP 27) →

BRIDGE OVER STREAM BY HAWESWATER →

**MAP 28**

ROCK FALL

29

LOOK OUT FOR RED SQUIRRELS- MORE SIGHTINGS ARE SEEN BY WALKERS BY HAWESWATER THAN ELSEWHERE

BIRKS CRAG

27

050

PATH DROPS STEEPLY OFF KIDSTY HOWES

ANNOYINGLY STEEP CLIMB

KIDSTY HOWES

0    ¼ mile

0    APPROX SCALE    500m

BRIDGE

051

HAWESWATER RESERVOIR

ROUTE GUIDE AND MAPS

ROUTE GUIDE AND MAPS

75 MINS FROM BRIDGE OVER STREAM BY HAWESWATER (MAP 28) → BRIDGE →

**MAP 29**

MEASAND FORCES

VERY TALL GATE

BOULDERS BY STREAM CROSSING

HAWESWATER

ROCK FALL

28

30

trailblazer

0          ¼ mile

0          APPROX SCALE          500m

**BAMPTON          OFF MAP 30, p145**

Bampton offers two excellent accommodation possibilities including *The Mardale Inn* (☎ 01931 713244, 🖥 www.mardale inn.co.uk; 4D or T, all with private facilities; 🍷; 🐾; WI-FI), which charges from £40pp (sgl occ £50). **Food** is served Monday to Saturday noon-2pm & 6-9pm, Sunday noon-6pm. The 1987 cult film *Withnail & I* was filmed in the area and the telephone box from which Withnail calls his agent in London is actually a stone's throw from the Inn, in which one would be right to expect nothing less than the finest wines available to humanity. (Incidentally, the famously decrepit cottage of 'Crow Crag' is actually a derelict farmhouse called Sleddale Hall, situated by a reservoir three miles south-west of Shap – off Map 34).

For a B&B that seems to supply your every need, there's *Bampton Village Store* (☎ 01931-713351, 🖥 www.bvs-bandb .co.uk; 1T/1F sleeps 4, both en suite; 🍷; WI-FI). B&B is from £40pp (£47.50 sgl occ). Their **tearoom** does sandwiches and home-made cakes. The **store** is open Mon & Thur 8am-1pm, Tue, Wed, Fri & Sat 8am-5pm, Sun 9am-4pm. There's **internet access** (£1/15mins) plus a **post office** (Mon 9am-1pm, Tue & Wed 9am-noon).

In **Bampton Grange**, about 10 minutes' walk east of Bampton, the equally recommended *Crown and Mitre* (☎ 01931 713225; 🖥 www.crownandmitre.com; 2S/4D/2T; all en suite; 🍷; 🐾£2.50; WI-FI; Ⓛ £variable) charges £42.50-47.50pp (sgl occ £45) for B&B. **Food** is available Sunday noon-2.30pm and daily 6-9pm.

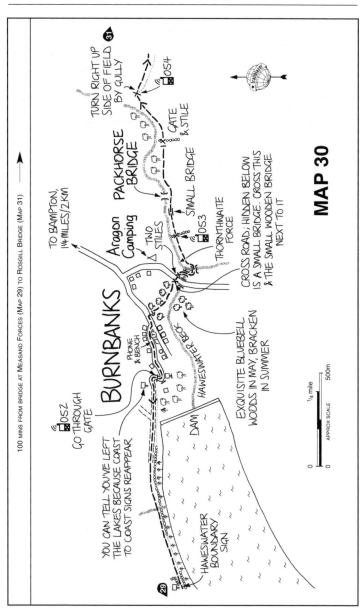

100 MINS FROM BRIDGE AT MEASAND FORCES (MAP 29) TO ROSGILL BRIDGE (MAP 31) →

31

1054

TURN RIGHT UP
SIDE OF FIELD
BY GULLY

GATE & STILE

PACKHORSE
BRIDGE

SMALL BRIDGE

1053

THORNTHWAITE
FORCE

CROSS ROAD; HIDDEN BELOW
IS A SMALL BRIDGE. CROSS THIS
& THE SMALL WOODEN BRIDGE
NEXT TO IT

MAP 30

Aragon
Camping

TWO
STILES

TO BAMPTON,
1¼ MILES/2 KM

BURNBANKS

PHONE
& BENCH

HAWESWATER BECK

EXQUISITE BLUEBELL
WOODS IN MAY, BRACKEN
IN SUMMER

1052
GO THROUGH
GATE

YOU CAN TELL YOU'VE LEFT
THE LAKES BECAUSE COAST
TO COAST SIGNS REAPPEAR

DAM

HAWESWATER BOUNDARY
SIGN

29

¼ mile

0                    500m
0
APPROX SCALE

ROUTE GUIDE AND MAPS

Back on the trail it now feels a relief to be walking on the level, soft grass for miles at a time and, free of the national park's edicts; helpful 'Coast to Coast' signposts reappear too. Wall follows stile follows field follows stile until, towards the end of the stage, you descend on **Shap Abbey** (see box below and Map 32), an atmospheric ruin set in a peaceful spot by the River Lowther. It's just regrettable that, by the time you get there, you'll probably be somewhat of a ruin yourself, your thoughts having long ago turned from holy orders to hors d'oeuvres following a hot bath. From the abbey, all that remains is to tick off the road or parallel paths presaging your triumphant entry into **Shap**.

❑ **Shap Abbey**
Shap Abbey (see Map 32) has the distinction of being the last abbey to be founded in England, in 1199. It was built by the French Premonstratensian order founded by St Norbert at Prémontré in Northern France, who were also known as the White Canons after the colour of their habits.

The abbey was also the last to be dissolved by Henry VIII, in 1540. Presumably Henry's henchmen would have had plenty of practice in plundering monasteries by this time, which is perhaps why the abbey is today in such a ruinous state. The best-preserved section is the **western belltower**, built around 1500.

Since its demise, the abbey has had to suffer the commonplace indignity of having some of its best carved stonework purloined by the locals for use in their own buildings. The cottage by the abbey clearly used a couple of remnants in its construction, albeit to good effect, while Shap's 17th-century market hall, just by the NatWest Bank, is built largely from abbey stone. Even some of the local stone walls contain abbey stones.

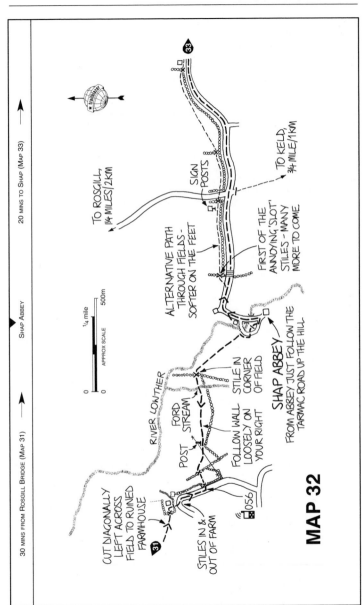

30 MINS FROM ROSGILL BRIDGE (MAP 31) — SHAP ABBEY — 20 MINS TO SHAP (MAP 33)

MAP 32

TO ROSGILL, 1¼ MILES/2KM

TO KELD, ¾ MILE/1KM

SIGN POSTS

ALTERNATIVE PATH THROUGH FIELDS - SOFTER ON THE FEET

FIRST OF THE ANNOYING 'SLOT' STILES - MANY MORE TO COME

¼ mile
500m
APPROX SCALE

RIVER LOWTHER

FORD STREAM

POST

STILE IN CORNER OF FIELD

FOLLOW WALL LOOSELY ON YOUR RIGHT

SHAP ABBEY
FROM ABBEY JUST FOLLOW THE TARMAC ROAD UP THE HILL

CUT DIAGONALLY LEFT ACROSS FIELD TO RUINED FARMHOUSE

STILES IN & OUT OF FARM

056

ROUTE GUIDE AND MAPS

## SHAP                    MAP 33

Shap is a long, narrow village lining a wide street, the former A6, once the north-west's main route to Scotland and still the highest main road in the country as it passes over the Howgill Fells. The road used to supply Shap's traders with enough passing trade to make a living and the village prospered. But then they built the M6 and, like the motel in *Psycho*, things have been pretty quiet since, bar the presence of a couple of quarries and cement factories.

There are some attractive features in town, including a 17th-century **market hall** built with masonry from the **abbey** (see box p146), but overall the place is not exactly Las Vegas on New Year's Eve. However, now you're out of the Lakes you don't have to fight over the great accommodation, plus there's a chippy, a Co-op,

three pubs, a post office and even an outdoor heated (seasonal) **swimming pool**.

By the **post office** (Mon-Thur 9am-12.30pm & 1.30-5.30pm; Fri 9am-12.30pm; Sat 9am-noon) is a decent-sized **Co-op** (daily 8am-10pm) but the ATM here was stolen in 2013 and by early 2014 had still not been replaced. They do cashback at the till, though. The NatWest **bank** (no ATM, Wed only 10am-2pm) is opposite the school and there's a **newsagent** (Mon-Fri 5am-5.30pm, Sat 5.30am-7pm, Sun 8am-noon) at the southern end of town. The **library** (Mon 11am-2pm, Tue 2-5pm, Fri 2-7pm, Sat 10am-2pm) in the Old Courthouse has **internet access**. The village has its own website (🖥 www.shapcumbria.co.uk).

### Where to stay

Being out of the Lakes, many B&B owners need to make more of an effort to attract custom, and with most of their guests being Coast to Coasters, it's something that is appreciated by many of our readers. There's none of that 'two nights minimum stay at weekends' malarkey or overpricing you've put up with on previous days.

As you come into town *The Hermitage* (☎ 01931 716671; 🖥 www.coast2coast.co.uk/thehermitage; 2T/1D/1Tr; mostly en suite; 🛏; WI-FI; ⓛ from £3.50) is on your right and has been recommended by readers. The beautiful house itself is over 300 years old but the rooms come with all mod cons. B&B costs £39pp; evening meals available by prior arrangement.

Over the road *New Ing Lodge* (☎ 01931 716719, 🖥 www.newinglodge.co.uk; 1S/2D/2T/1Tr/1Qd; some en suite with 🛏; most rooms share showers; 🐾£5; WI-FI; ⓛ £6) offers a variety of accommodation. **B&B** costs £27.50-35pp (sgl £28). Under the same roof there are also two notably spacious mixed **dorms** (six in one room, eight in the other) for £15pp plus £2 for bedding. There is **camping** space for up to 24 people (£7pp) in the small back garden under the washing lines. Evening **meals** (two courses for about £12) and breakfast (£4-8) are available if requested in advance; there is also a very basic 'kitchen' which can be used by people

SHAP    30 MINS TO SIGNPOST TO ODDENDALE
                (MAP 34)    →

32

New Ing Lodge

The Hermitage    057

Phone    ⓞ Bus stop
PO ⊠    Co-op

O Shap
Chippy

Abbey
Coffee
Fire    Shop
station

Market
Square

Market    Bus stop
Hall
            School    Swimming
NatWest ⓔ         pool
            ⊠ Toilets
Crown Inn

Library & ⓣ
internet    Newsagent

To Kings Arms, 50m,
Greyhound, 500m,
& Brookfield, 1km        34

## MAP 33 Shap

staying in a dorm. The eggs from the free-roaming chickens taste like something you'd imagine from a Roald Dahl fairy tale (that means delicious, by the way).

Right at the southern end of town, few begrudge the walk to **Brookfield House** (Map 34; ☎ 01931 716397, 🖥 www.brook fieldshap.co.uk; 1S/3D or T/1S or D; all with private facilities; ☛; WI-FI; Ⓛ £6; Mar-Nov) which has become a legend among Coast to Coasters and is frequently cited as the best stay on the entire walk. Nothing is too much trouble for Margaret, who charges £30-39pp (sgl £35). They have a bar, lounge and drying facilities and will do a wash for a small charge; the breakfasts and packed lunches are the talk of the walk.

Refurbished and reopened by new owners in 2013, **The Greyhound Hotel** (Map 34; ☎ 01931 716474, 🖥 www.grey houndshap.co.uk; 2S/7D or T/2D/1Qd; all en suite; ☛; 🐾; WI-FI) dates back to 1680. B&B costs £45-60pp.

**The King's Arms** (Map 34; ☎ 01931 716277, 🖥 www.kingsarmsatshap.co.uk; 1D/2T/3Tr/1Qd, all with private facilities; ☛; WI-FI; Ⓛ £4.95) charges £37.50pp (sgl occ £45, £30-40pp for 3/4 people in a room).

**Where to eat and drink**
The **Greyhound Hotel** (see Where to stay; daily noon-9pm) is reputed to cook the best grub in town. The menu consists of mainly local dishes including steak and ale pie (£10.95), Lakeland lamb Henry (£14.95) or a stilton burger (£9.95). Unfortunately, the Greyhound's location is over a mile from The Hermitage or New Ing Lodge at the top end of town.

The **King's Arms** (see Where to stay; food served Easter to Oct Mon-Sat noon-3pm, Sun noon-2pm, daily 5-8.30pm; Nov to Easter Sat noon-3pm, Sun noon-2pm, Sat & Sun 5-8.30pm) keeps things simple by charging £6.95 for any main meal. **The Crown Inn** also does pub grub. Bar meals are served all day for around £8-10.

The revamped **Shap Chippy** (☎ 01931 716060; 🖥 www.shapchippy.co.uk; Tue-Sat noon-1.30pm, daily 4.30-8pm) does excellent fish and chips either to take away or eat in, in their restaurant here.

A little further south is **Abbey Coffee Shop** (☎ 01931 716238, Tue-Sat 8.30am-4.30pm) which is good for cakes and sandwiches but usually closed by the time Coast to Coasters hobble into town.

**Transport**                      **(see also pp52-5)**
Bus No 106 calls here en route between Kendal and Penrith. The buses leave from Shap's Market Square and take 30 minutes to reach Penrith, 12 minutes to Orton (see p152) and 45 minutes to Kendal.

## STAGE 6: SHAP TO KIRKBY STEPHEN                 MAPS 34-43

### Introduction

Those who struggled over the previous stages may be less than delighted to learn that, at **20½ miles (33km, 7hrs)**, today's hike across the **Westmoreland plateau** is even longer. But the good news is that prolonged gradients and rocky sole-mashing trails have been replaced by grassy strolls across the well-drained limestone bedrock, making it something of a 'recovery day' and, with your fitness now improving, rather satisfying in its own right. Before you unrolls a steady, undulating transit over field and moorland as you flank the enigmatic Howgill Fells to the south and approach the peat-sodden ridge they call the Pennines.

If you're not convinced a fine day's walk lies ahead, there's a chance to break it in two by taking the short diversion into Orton, only eight miles from Shap. It's coming across 'lost' villages like Orton that is part of the appeal of the Coast to Coast walk. Stranded far from well-established tourist trails or national parks, they're simply what they are; places where people live but in a manner and locale that for most of us is long past. It's then that it dawns on you that, away from the coach-tour honeypots, the forgotten corners of rural England are full of these charming places, scraping by with a shop, a pub, a church and maybe even a bus.

This stage is also replete with **prehistoric sites**, though it's fair to say that none of them will make your jaw drop in amazement; unforewarned you'd probably pass by none the wiser but still cheered by a surprisingly great day aboard the Coast to Coast path.

### The route
With over 20 miles to cover, you leave Shap to cross first the railway then the motorway which funnel through north-west England. They are soon forgotten as you skirt the hidden, walled village of **Oddendale** (Map 35) where, just a few minutes off the path to the west lie two **concentric stone circles** dating back nearly 6000 years. Continue south to cut past a strip of plantation and head over limestone pavements and down into Lyvennet Beck. Now you turn north-east, passing **Robin Hood's Grave** (Map 37), a large cairn in a shallow

ROUTE GUIDE AND MAPS

30 MINS FROM SHAP (MAP 33) ⟶                    SIGNPOST TO ODDENDALE ⟶

33  BRIDGE OVER RAILWAY

0 ———— ¼ mile

0   APPROX SCALE   500m

**MAP 34**

SIGNPOSTS

OVERHEAD CABLES

TO JCT 40 FOR PENRITH

M6 MOTORWAY

Kings Arms

**SHAP**

STEPS OVER WALL

HARD TO SEE SHAP, KENDAL MOTORWAY SIGN

THE WEDGE OF KIDSTY PIKE IS VISIBLE 7 MILES TO THE WEST

MUDDY FIELD WITH RABBITS

GATE & STEPS

LOW CRAG

Greyhound

A6

AFTER PASSING BY WALL, HEAD DIAGONALLY LEFT 📱058

HAWTHORN TREES, HORSEFIELD

FARM

SIGN TO ODDEN-DALE

Brookfield House

OVERHEAD CABLES

TO JCT 39 FOR SHAP 📱059

35

TO KENDAL, 15 MILES/26KM

CEMENT WORKS

CONTOURING ROUND HILL WITH OCCASIONAL TREE LEFT & RIGHT

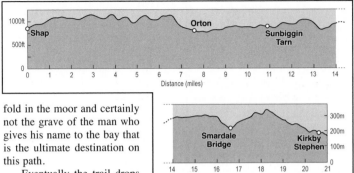

fold in the moor and certainly not the grave of the man who gives his name to the bay that is the ultimate destination on this path.

Eventually the trail drops down to a road, and follows it south to the B6260, soon leaving it to the left to drop down again past a well-preserved **limekiln** above Broadfell Farm. Those bound for Orton, whose white churchtower has been clearly visible since the brow of the hill, should continue down through the farm from here; the rest march resolutely on to join the farm's driveway and continue east round Orton Scar.

ROUTE GUIDE AND MAPS

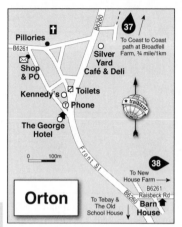

Orton

## ORTON

Orton is typical of the quaint 'unknown' villages in which the Coast to Coast specialises, but one with a couple of surprises in store for walkers. For one thing there's the **church** dating back to 1293 below which are the remains of some **pillories** or stocks once used to punish wrongdoers. Perhaps they were spending too much time round the back of **Kennedy's chocolate factory** (see p154). Popping in here you may think you've been transported to a chocolaterie in some upmarket Parisian suburb but no, this is Orton, east Cumbria, and that is a fantasy of cocoa-based delicacies you see before you.

The well-stocked **village shop** (Mon-Sat 8am-6pm; **post office** hours Mon, Tues & Fri 9am-1pm, 2-5pm, Wed & Sat 9am-noon, closed Thur) is nearby, in rude health we're pleased to report and with enough provisions to restock your travelling larder. Stagecoach's/Apollo 8's **Bus** No 106 (Kendal to Penrith and vice versa) stops in the village; see pp52-5 for details.

### Where to stay and eat

Recommended time and again by Coast to Coasters, *Barn House* (☎ 015396 24259, 🖳 www.thebarnhouseorton.co.uk; 1D/2T; all en suite; ✎; Ⓛ £6; WI-FI) on the south-

ern side of the village on Raisbeck Rd has just three rooms but each is supremely comfortable, with Lillian or David serving cakes on arrival. B&B starts at £38pp (£48 for sgl occ).

*The George Hotel* (☎ 015396 26046, 🖳 www.thegeorgehotelorton.co.uk; 1S/3D/3T/1Qd; most en suite, others share bathroom; ✎; Ⓛ £varies) is in the centre of town. B&B costs £35-40pp (sgl £35, sgl occ £35-50). They have a drying room but also provide a laundry service (£5). They now offer **camping** space (£5 per pitch) for 4-5 tents in part of the beer garden.

*New House Farm* (off Map 38; ☎ 015396 24324) offers **camping** (£7pp; £1 for a shower; ✖) with very basic facilities – perhaps they've now upgraded their showers. Campers can order a cooked breakfast (£8). They also have a caravan (1Tr; £35pp) which can be booked on a **B&B** basis. The farm is best reached from Knott Lane (Map 38). Follow Knott Lane south to the T Junction. Turn left and continue for five minutes. It's on the right.

About three miles south of Orton, in **Tebay** there's the commodious *Old School House* (☎ 01539 624286, 🖳 theoldschooltebay.co.uk; 8 rooms: five rooms sleep three or more people; most en suite, two share a bathroom; ✎; dogs £5; WI-FI; Ⓛ £5) charges £30pp for B&B. Since they are a little way out they are happy to pick walkers up if arranged at the time of booking. Also if requested in advance they can provide an evening meal (£15) and do laundry & ironing for a small charge. They also have a *tea room* (Wed-Sun 10.30am-5pm).

*Silver Yard Café Deli* (☎ 015396 24421; 🖳 www.silveryard.co.uk; daily 10am-4.30pm in summer; WI-FI) is a bright new place on the edge of the village. You can sit inside or out and they serve gourmet sandwiches, pies, stews and hot filled buns all made from locally-sourced ingredients. You could make yourself an excellent picnic from the deli.

For pub grub there's *The George Hotel* (see above; daily noon-2.30pm & 6-9pm; winter Mon & Tue 6-9pm, Wed-Sun noon-2.30pm & 6-9pm). There are pizzas from £7.50. You can't leave Orton without

MAP 36

TWO ISOLATED TREES 100M TO THE NORTH

REMAINS OF FOLD BUILT ON LIMESTONE

C2C POST

🏠 062

POSTS

LIMESTONE PAVEMENTS

OLD WALLS

BIG ISOLATED BOULDER

LYVENNET BECK

BOGGY

POSTS

GROUSE BUTT

🏠 061

POST

🗻 35

ATTENTION! LEAVE THE MAIN SOUTHBOUND TRACK AND DESCEND TO THE CORNER OF THE PINE PLANTATION. THEN FOLLOW POSTS PAST TWO ISOLATED TREES

LOOKS LIKE WALL WHEN COMING FROM WAYPOINT 054

KEEP YOUR DOG ON A LEAD HERE AS THERE ARE A NUMBER OF GROUND-NESTING BIRDS

CROSBY RAVENSWORTH FELL

SHEEP FIELD WALL

POST

🏠 063

WALK TO THE CORNER OF THE WALL THEN FOLLOW IT EASTWARDS

🗻 37

60 MINS TO BROADFELL FARM (MAP 37)

LYVENNET BECK

ROUTE GUIDE AND MAPS

¼ mile

APPROX SCALE

500m

0

0

30 MINS FROM TURN-OFF TO STONE CIRCLE (MAP 35)

LYVENNET BECK

sampling the chocolate at **Kennedy's** (💻 www.kennedyschocolates.co.uk; Mon-Sat 9am-5pm; Sun 11am-5pm; café shuts 30 mins earlier) in their attached coffee house and ice-cream parlour. For a chocoholic overdose, their chocolate cake washed down with a hot chocolate (made with pure chocolate) and topped with grated chocolate ought to hit the mark – with a Coast to Coast souvenir chocolate bar (£4.95), of course.

ROUTE GUIDE AND MAPS

LIMESTONE PAVEMENT

POSTS SHOWING WAY

TO CROSBY RAVENSWORTH, 3 MILES/5.5KM

QUARRY

TO APPLEBY-IN-WESTMORLAND 10 MILES/15KM

36

CARRY ON IN A STRAIGHT LINE AS PATH VEERS OFF LEFT

SIGNPOST (OFF THE PATH) TO ORTON

SOME GO EAST OF PLANTATION BUT ROAD IS QUIET ENOUGH

ROBIN HOOD'S GRAVE

B6260

**MAP 37**

0    ¼ mile
0    APPROX SCALE    500m

B6260

CATTLE GRID

PATH LEADS OFF TO LEFT, SIGNPOSTED TO ORTON

LIME KILN

THREE GATES

BROADFELL FARM

SCARSIDE FARM

CATTLE GRIDS

FALL FLATT

FRIAR BIGGINS FARM

STREAM

TO ORTON, ¾ MILE/1KM

TO ORTON, 1¼ MILES/2KM

38

60 MINS FROM LYVENNET BECK (MAP 36) ⟶ BROADFELL FARM   40 MINS TO ACRES (MAP 38) ⟶

MAP 38

ORTON SCAR

SUNBIGGIN

STONY HEAD

SIGNPOST

39

37

FRIAR BIGGINS FARM

FARM

GATE & SIGN POST TO KNOTT LA.

STICK CLOSE TO FENCE TO YOUR LEFT THROUGH THIS FIELD

KNOTT LANE

SIGN POST

CAN SEE STONE CIRCLE FROM THIS STILE

DOORWAY OF RUINED BUILDING

STONE CIRCLE

TO ORTON

TO NEW HOUSE FARM

B6261

RAISBECK ROAD

ROAD TO ORTON, 1 MILE/1.5KM

BARNS

ACRES

SIGNPOST - LEFT FOR GREAT ARBY, RIGHT TO TARN MOOR

GREAT VIEWS TO HOWGILL FELLS

TO RAISBECK, ½ MILE/1KM

APPROX SCALE

0 ... ¼ mile

0 ... 500m

ROUTE GUIDE AND MAPS

There's a second and more impressive **stone circle** (Map 38) a mile to the east of Orton on the Coast to Coast path. It can be reached, for those who didn't take the Orton detour, via a driveable track running east from Broadfell Farm (Map 37). (Those who *did* visit Orton can rejoin this track at the stone circle by taking the Raisbeck road east and heading up Knott Lane).

After this, the trail continues east across walled fields and on to **Tarn Moor** (Map 39). All being well you'll emerge from the moor on a backroad alongside **Sunbiggin Tarn**, an important bird sanctuary. Here you turn briefly south and then cut directly east across the heather-clad moor; you'll have seen the sign boards indicating the course. You reach another lane on the far side of the moor. (For the accommodation options at Newbiggin-on-Lune follow this lane south).

### NEWBIGGIN-ON-LUNE OFF MAP 40

About a mile and a quarter south of the point where the path crosses a lane after Ravenstonedale Moor you'll find this little village nestling at the foot of Howgill fells.

Well established *Tranna Hill* (☎ 01539 623227, 🖥 www.trannahill.co.uk; 2D/1T; WI-FI; Ⓛ £6) has a cosy lounge with a woodburning stove. B&B starts at £32pp (£40 sgl occ).

To the north of the village is *Brownber Hall Country House* (☎ 015396 23208, 🖥 www.brownberhall.co.uk; 3S/5D/1T/1Tr; all en suite or with private facilities; 🐾£5; WI-FI) where B&B is from £35 per person. They don't provide evening meals but can arrange lifts to somewhere that does, by prior arrangement. However, they are licensed.

To continue on the Coast to Coast don't follow the lane but cross it and head past the underground reservoir and continue east. Tracking a thread of dry-stone

ROUTE GUIDE AND MAPS

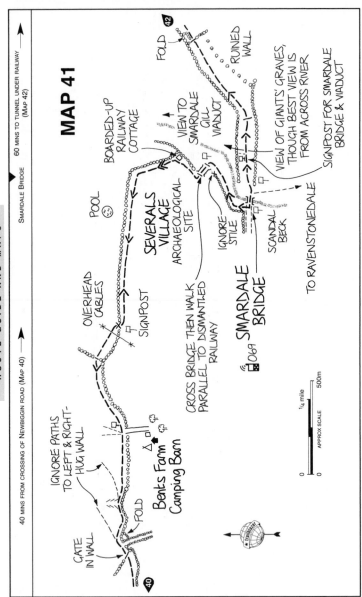

40 MINS FROM CROSSING OF NEWBIGGIN ROAD (MAP 40) ──▶    SMARDALE BRIDGE    ◀── 60 MINS TO TUNNEL UNDER RAILWAY (MAP 42)

MAP 41

FOLD

42

RUINED WALL

VIEW TO SMARDALE GILL VIADUCT

BOARDED-UP RAILWAY COTTAGE

VIEW OF GIANTS' GRAVES, THOUGH BEST VIEW IS FROM ACROSS RIVER

SIGNPOST FOR SMARDALE BRIDGE & VIADUCT

POOL

SEVERALS VILLAGE ARCHAEOLOGICAL SITE

IGNORE STILE

SCANDAL BECK

TO RAVENSTONEDALE

OVERHEAD CABLES

SIGNPOST

CROSS BRIDGE THEN WALK PARALLEL TO DISMANTLED RAILWAY

SMARDALE BRIDGE

069

IGNORE PATHS TO LEFT & RIGHT- HUG WALL

GATE IN WALL

FOLD

Bents Farm Camping Barn

40

¼ mile

500m

0

0

APPROX SCALE

60 MINS FROM SMARDALE BRIDGE (MAP 41)

TUNNEL UNDER RAILWAY

VIEWS NORTH TO WHITE TELECOMS DOME ON GREAT SHUNNER FELL AND CROSS FELL – THE HIGHEST POINT ON THE PENNINE WAY (893M)

CUT DIAGONALLY ACROSS FIELD TOWARDS GULLY

NOW FOLLOW THE GULLY AS THE PATH CURVES LEFT

TUNNEL UNDER RAILWAY

SITE OF ANCIENT SETTLEMENTS UNDER HAWTHORN TREES

KIRKBY STEPHEN RAILWAY STATION

LOOK FOR SIGNPOST POINTING RIGHT OFF ROAD

C2C SIGNPOST

TAKE FIRST LEFT

THROUGH GATE TO ROAD

SMARDALE FELL

HILL TOP

FIRST VIEWS OF KIRKBY STEPHEN & NINE STANDARDS RIGG

SIGNPOST TO SMARDALE BRIDGE, A685 & C2C

STILL ON GRASSY TRACK. WALLS ON LEFT

MAP 42

¼ mile

APPROX SCALE

500m

ROUTE GUIDE AND MAPS

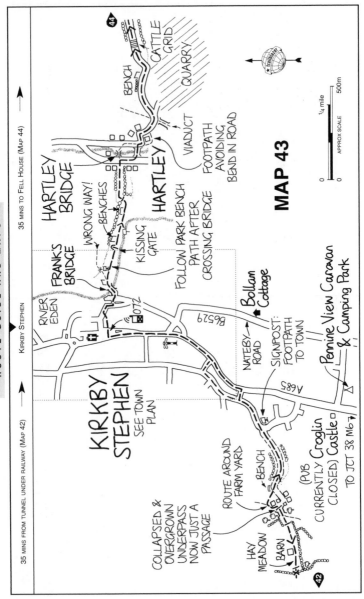

35 MINS FROM TUNNEL UNDER RAILWAY (MAP 42)   Kirkby Stephen   35 MINS TO FELL HOUSE (MAP 44)

MAP 43

APPROX SCALE
0 ──────── ¼ mile
0 ──────── 500m

44

CATTLE GRID

QUARRY

BENCH

VIADUCT

FOOTPATH AVOIDING BEND IN ROAD

HARTLEY BRIDGE

HARTLEY

WRONG WAY!

BENCHES

KISSING GATE

FOLLOW PARK BENCH PATH AFTER CROSSING BRIDGE

FRANK'S BRIDGE

RIVER EDEN

loo

Bollam Cottage

NATEBY ROAD

B6259

SIGNPOST: FOOTPATH TO TOWN

Pennine View Caravan & Camping Park

A685

KIRKBY STEPHEN

SEE TOWN PLAN

COLLAPSED & OVERGROWN UNDERPASS NOW JUST A PASSAGE

ROUTE AROUND FARM YARD

BENCH

(PUB CURRENTLY CLOSED) Croglin Castle

TO JCT 38 M6

HAY MEADOW

BARN

42

walls (see box p191) below Great Ewe Fell will bring you past ***Bents Farm*** (Map 41; bookings ☎ 01768 774301, information ☎ 01768 371760, 🖳 www.bentscampingbarn.com; toilets but no showers; open all year) with a **camping barn** which sleeps 12-14 (bed £9.50pp) and **camping** from £4pp. Booking is recommended as occasionally groups take over the whole barn, which has a well-equipped kitchen. There is a coin meter (£1) for electricity and sleeping bags can be hired if necessary.

The next prehistoric site lies a short way past the farm where, having crossed a stile, a signpost urges you to stick to the recognised path so as not to disturb the archaeological site. This'll probably come as something of a surprise because, no matter how hard you look, there seems to be nothing remarkable. Satellite imagery reveals that what you're actually looking at is the **Severals Village settlement**, said to be one of the most important prehistoric sites in Britain. The fact that it remains unexcavated does nothing to quell the archaeologists' enthusiasm for the place. Without leaving the path, look for irregular or unnatural depressions and bumps in the land here; it's these undulations that have so excited the archaeologists. On the opposite side of Scandal Beck lies the final ancient site on this stage.

The so-called **Giants' Graves** (called 'pillow mounds' on 25k OS maps) are a series of long narrow mounds which, some say, may have been prehistoric rabbit enclosures.

Dropping down to the bridge across Scandal Beck, more recent archeological evidence can be spied in the form of the distant **Smardale Gill viaduct** along a former railway that once joined Kirkby Stephen to what is now the M6 corridor. Climbing to the crest of Smardale Fell, on a clear day the Pennines rise before you like a standing wave with the cairns on Nine Standards Rigg just visible beyond the quarry west of Kirkby Stephen. Looking north across the Eden valley, with less difficulty you may also spot the white dome of the radio station atop Great Shunner Fell and to the left, Cross Fell, at 893m (2930ft), the highest point on the Pennine Way, a great walk for another day.

By now, those nearing Kirkby Stephen will not be mindful of such distant prospects, as slowly the town's churches and then other buildings rise from the wooded vale below.

## KIRKBY STEPHEN    See map p163

Kirkby Stephen (pronounced 'Kirby' Stephen) vies with Richmond as the biggest town on the route, though don't let that fool you into thinking that this place is a metropolis. In fact, Kirkby Stephen is a pleasant and prosperous market town built along the A685 with a population of around 1900, a figure that's swollen considerably during the summer months by walkers, runners, cyclists and other outdoor *bon viveurs*. If you're due a rest after the Lakeland stages, a day off in town is the tonic to numerous woes.

There've been **markets** in Kirkby Stephen since at least 1361 when it was granted a market charter. Note the cobbled outline on the market square's floor; it marks the outer limits of a former bull-baiting area, a popular pastime in the town until 1820 when a bull broke free and ran amok, killing a number of bystanders.

The principal tourist attraction in Kirkby Stephen is the 13th-century **church** (see box p164). Other sites of note include the old and much-photographed **signpost** at the southern end of town, where the

ROUTE GUIDE AND MAPS

distances are given in miles and furlongs; and the curious but attractive **stone seats** in the form of sheep, that stand by the door of the visitor centre. Carved by artist Keith Alexander, they're reputed to increase the fertility of any who sit upon them, ovine or otherwise. **Frank's Bridge** is a pretty double-arched stone footbridge, a quiet place to sit by the grassy riverbank and feed the ducks. It's thought to be named after a local brewer, Frank Birkbeck, who lived here in the 19th century.

One other item of note is the flock of **parrots** that fly around town during the day before returning home to their owner, a local resident, at dusk.

## Services

Kirkby Stephen has become the spiritual (if not *quite* the geographical) heart of the Coast to Coast path. Packhorse (see p28) operate out of the town, and those who opt to take advantage of their 'taxi' service will spend the night in Kirkby Stephen before being shuttled to St Bees the next morning. If you've left your car here, the Packhorse van arrives back in town from Robin Hood's Bay at around 6.30pm.

The **visitor centre** (☎ 017683 71199; 🖳 www.kirkby-stephen.com; Easter to Oct daily 10am-5pm, Nov to Easter Mon, Wed, Fri & Sat 11am-3pm) is crammed with brochures and leaflets and the staff seem knowledgeable. Nearby is the **bookshop**, open Mon/Wed/Fri/Sat, 10am-1pm and 2-5pm. By the church is the **library** (☎ 017683 71775; Mon & Fri 10am-12.30pm & 1.30-5pm, Wed 10am-12.30pm & 1.30-6pm, Sat 10am-1pm) with **internet** connection (£1 for 30 mins). There are two **banks** with **cash machines** while on the other side of the road the **post office** (Mon-Fri 9am-5.30pm, Sat 9am-12.30pm) is at the back of Emporium Deli.

The best **supermarket** in the town centre is the Co-op (Mon-Sun 7am-10pm). There's also a Spar (Mon-Sat 8am-10.30pm, Sun 9am-10.30pm) at the southern end of town closer to the campsite and a bigger Co-op at the northern end of town past the chippy. There's a **launderette** down the lane between the Emporium/post office and a chip shop.

**Eden Outdoors** (☎ 017683 72431; Mon-Sat 9am-5pm) is very well stocked with outdoor gear, maps and books. They also offer out-of-hours emergency help with kit via mobile numbers posted on the shop door. Blister kits and other medications are on sale at Green Tree **pharmacy** (Mon-Fri 9am-5.30pm, Sat 9am-1pm).

## Where to stay

*The Pennine View Caravan and Camping Park* (Map 43; ☎ 017683 71717; dogs; Mar-Oct) is a secure, no-nonsense spot just outside town near Croglin Castle pub, with a laundry room and a clean ablutions block. Camping costs £8.25-8.72pp with a large, flat grassy area set aside for tents away from the motorhomes and caravans. Use of the shower facilities is included in the charge. Long-term parking (£3.55 per car per day) is available.

*Kirkby Stephen Hostel* (☎ 017683 71793 or ☎ 07812 558525, 🖳 www.kirkbystephenhostel.co.uk; 38 beds, 2T/2Qd/3 x 6 beds, 1 x 8 beds; one twin en suite, others share shower facilities; 🐾; WI-FI; Ⓛ) is an independent hostel grandly housed in a former Methodist chapel in the centre of town and run by the welcoming Denise. Rates are from £20pp including a continental breakfast; a cooked breakfast is available for £6pp. Evening meals can also be provided subject to prior arrangement. However, there are self-catering facilities.

Of the B&Bs on the walk, we've received many recommendations for the *Old Croft House* (☎ 017683 71638, 🖳 www.theoldcrofthouse.com; 1S/2D/1T; all with private facilities; 🛏; WI-FI; Ⓛ £5). It's a lovely old Georgian townhouse with a warm, oak-panelled interior full of books, made all the better by the warmth and generosity of the owners who know what Coasters want, welcoming guests with freshly baked cakes and even providing foot spas in the rooms! They also offer meals in the evenings (if booked in advance), with a choice of 2-/3-course menus for around £16/20. B&B costs £37-40pp.

Next to the hostel and a favourite with many readers, with spacious, well-equipped rooms *Fletcher House* (☎ 017683 71013, 🖳 www.fletcherhouse.co.uk; 2D/1T/1Tr;

all en suite; ☕; WI-FI; Ⓛ £2-5) offers B&B for £36pp (sgl occ £50) and internet access (£1/hour). There's also a drying room, guest lounge and a foot spa.

There's tea and cupcakes on arrival at *Castle View* (☎ 07894 066976, 🖳 castleviewbandb.wordpress.com; 3D or T, all en

suite; ☕, WI-FI; Ⓛ £6) at 21 High Street, with rooms from £36 per person (£45 sgl occ). There's also a drying room.

Towards the southern end of town at 63 High St *The Jolly Farmers Guest House* (☎ 017683 71063; 🖳 www.thejollyfarmers.co.uk; 4D/5T; all en suite; ☕;

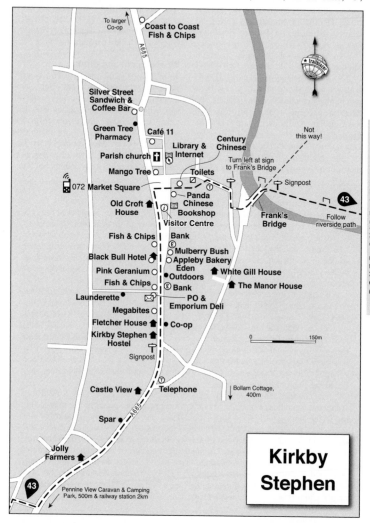

**Kirkby Stephen**

£8; WI-FI; £6) is a converted pub with hydro-spa baths in a couple of the rooms which should help take those aches away, and of course tea and scones on arrival. B&B costs from £36pp (sgl occ £45-55).

*The Black Bull Hotel* (☎ 017683 71237, 🖳 www.blackbullkirkbystephen .co.uk; 1S/5D/3T; all en suite; ✉; 🐾; WI-FI; £6.50), 38 Market Sq, gets good reports and charges £35pp for B&B (sgl £40, sgl occ £40-60).

To the east of the main road on Melbecks *White Gill House* (☎ 017683 72238, 🖳 barbwgh@onetel.com; 1D/1T; both en suite; ✉; WI-FI; £5) has been highly recommended by many readers; the B&B rate is £35pp (sgl occ £70). They also have drying facilities. Nearby is *The Manor House* (☎ 017683 72757, 🖳 Jean_Leeson@hotmail.com; 1D/1Qd; both en suite; 🐾; WI-FI; £5) offering B&B in their plush Georgian townhouse for £35pp

(sgl occ £45). They are happy to do laundry (about £5 a load) and if requested in advance will take people to the station.

A bit further afield down Nateby Rd is lovely *Bollam Cottage* (Map 43; ☎ 017683 72038, 🖳 www.bollamcottage.co.uk; 2T/ 1D; all en suite; ✉; WI-FI; £6; Mar-Oct), with oak beams and a wood burner. B&B costs £37pp (sgl occ £47). They have drying facilities and are happy to do laundry. Guests also have a separate lounge.

## Where to eat and drink

To make up a picnic, call in at *The Appleby Bakery* (Mon-Sat 8am-4pm, Sun 9am-2.30pm) for a mouthwatering range of speciality breads and sandwiches. Excellent value is *Megabite Baguettes* (Mon-Sat 9am-2pm, Sun 10am-2pm), for filled rolls and salad boxes. More upmarket is *The Emporium Deli* (🖳 www.theedenempori um.co.uk; Mon-Fri 9am-5.30pm, Sat 9am-

---

### ❏ Parish church of Kirkby Stephen

The distinctive red sandstone church (part of the same formation found at St Bees) is separated from the market square by the peaceful lawn of the **cloisters**. On entering the main gate, on your right is the **Trupp Stone**, resembling a stone tomb or table, where until 1836 the locals' tithes were collected. Take half an hour or so to wander around inside the church, which is known locally as the Cathedral of the Dales. It is built on the site of a Saxon church, though the earliest feature (the nave) of the present structure dates only to 1220.

Features to look out for include the 17th-century **font**, a great stone lump at the rear of the church, and the nearby **bread shelves**, used for distributing bread to the poor. There's also a **Norman coffin** by the north wall, unearthed in 1980 during restoration work, and a glass display cabinet, also by the north wall, housing 16th- and 17th-century Bibles and, curiously, a **boar's tusk**, said to belong to the last wild boar shot in England. It was killed by the first Sir Richard Musgrave (died 1464), who was buried with the tusk in Hartley Chapel, to the south of the chancel. (The place where Sir Richard shot the boar, by the way, the appropriately named Wild Boar Fell, lies to the south of Kirkby Stephen.)

The church's most interesting feature, however, is the 8th-century **Loki Stone** facing the main door, a metre-high block carved by the Vikings with the horned fig-ure of the Norse god Loki. A bit of a prankster, one of Loki's tricks backfired and resulted in the death of Odin's son, which led to Loki being bound in chains and thrown into a dungeon. When the church was built the locals interpreted the carving as a representation of a demon. The stone was thus placed in the church to remind parishioners of the terrifying creatures that awaited sinners in the afterlife. Indeed, demons still play a big part in the folklore of Kirkby Stephen. At 8pm every day step outside to hear if they are still ringing the **Taggy Bell**, a warning to those who are still on the streets that Taggy, the local demon, now stalks the town looking for prey.

2pm) nearby, with a great selection of the world's finer foodstuffs.

As for tearooms, *Pink Geranium* (☎ 017683 71586; Wed-Sat 9am-4.30pm, Sun 9am-4pm) gives you a great big pot of tea and there's a good range of cakes and light lunches. *The Mulberry Bush* (☎ 017683 71572) is a popular Kirkby Stephen café (Mon-Sat 9am-5pm) that turns itself into a restaurant (Fri-Sat 5-9pm) in the evenings and all day on Sunday (10am-5pm).

*Café 11* at the top end of town is a smart wee place which does a good cup of coffee and light lunches. The *Silver Street Sandwich & Coffee Bar*, on the roundabout at the north end of town, does all that it says it does and is open from 7am.

On the main street there are no fewer than three **chippies** including the *Coast to Coast* (Thur-Sun 11.30am-1.30pm & 4.30-8pm) dating from 1929 and said to be Wainwright's favourite. For Chinese, there's *Panda Chinese Takeaway* (☎ 017683 71283; Sun-Thur 5-11.30pm; Fri & Sat to midnight; closed Tue) and *Century Chinese Restaurant* (☎ 017683 72828; Tue-Sun 5-11pm), next door, both serving the usual array of Oriental fare.

No town is complete without a curry-house and Kirkby Stephen's is one of the best places to eat here. It's right in the mid-dle of town by the market square; most dishes in the *Mango Tree* (☎ 017683 74960) are priced around £9.

Currently the best place to eat in town is *The Black Bull* (see Where to stay; daily noon-9pm, lunch menu till 6pm, evening meal from 6pm; they also serve scones and teacakes in the afternoon. This is where the chef from the much missed Old Forge Restaurant went when it closed in 2013. Duck breast with juniper sausage and bramble sauce is £15 and there's a range of locally-reared steaks (£13.50-20.50). They also do two-/three-course set menus for £16/20.

### Transport                 (see also pp52-5)

Kirkby Stephen is on the Carlisle to Leeds railway line. The **train** station – the only one, apart from St Bees, on the Coast to Coast path – lies over a mile to the south of the town centre.

As for **buses**, Grand Prix Coaches' No 563 runs to Penrith and back from the Market Square Mon-Sat (journey time around an hour), while the No 564 runs from both the Market Square and the railway station to Kendal, a journey of 60-75 minutes.

Finally, for a **taxi** call ☎ 017683, 72557 or 71682.

## STAGE 7: KIRKBY STEPHEN TO KELD                 MAPS 43-50

### Introduction

This **13-mile (21km, 5-6hrs via the high routes)** stage is something of a red-letter day. Not only do you cross the **Pennines** – the so-called backbone of the British Isles across whose flanks the Industrial Revolution gathered pace 200 years ago – but in doing so you cross the **watershed** on the Coast to Coast. From the summit at Nine Standards Rigg all rivers, including the infant headwaters of the Swale which you'll track for the next few days, flow eastwards to drain into the North Sea. In a flush of optimism you could say it's downhill all the way.

You also pass from the county of Cumbria into **Yorkshire**, your home for the rest of the trek and finally, by the end of this stage by our reckoning you're very close to the halfway point, having completed over 90 miles out of our estimated 190-odd total.

Yet in spite of these significant landmarks, the one thing that most walkers remember about the transit of the Pennines is the **peat bogs** they have to negotiate along the way. The maps point out the boggiest sections and on the higher of the **three colour-coded routes** (see pp166-70), it's a good point to don gaiters, if you have them. If you do succumb to the mires, cheer yourself up with the thought that at the end of this stage you'll be spending the night in the gentle pastoral scenery of **Swaledale**, the most northerly of Yorkshire's Dales and some say its loveliest.

**The route**

From Kirkby Stephen you cross the Eden river at Frank's Bridge (Map 43) and continue up to **Hartley** village.

From here follow the lane uphill past the huge quarry – a strenuous start to the day. At the end lies a wide dirt track up Hartley Fell where, five miles from town, the path divides (Map 45, Wᴘᴛ 073): the red and blue routes head east up the hill to the Nine Standards, while the green route parallels a stone wall before striking off over a rising moorland path to the quiet, B6270 Kirkby Stephen–Keld road. The three routes are described in more detail below.

**The three routes over the moors**  Due to severe erosion of the peat by walkers as well as a lack of investment to do something about it, there are **three colour-coded paths** across the Pennines to Keld, the exact route you take depending on the time of year or weather conditions, though most walkers ignore the seasonal guidelines. These three routes are marked on Maps 45a, 46 and 47. They initially diverge at a signpost for Nine Standards (Map 45, Wᴘᴛ 073) at which point boggy episodes set in whichever route you take. Although there are colour-coded signposts at key points, as well as laminated maps showing the three routes nailed to the odd post, you'll see only a few aged colour-coded waymarkers on the blue route.

Furthermore, it has to be said that the junction where the red and blue paths separate really has been ravaged by erosion from your predecessors' footwear and gets worse year by year. If ever there was a part of the Coast to Coast path that needed lining with stone slabs or duckboards, it's here at the southern end of Nine Standards Rigg which looks like a scene from the Somme, circa 1916.

The **blue and red** high routes are about the same length (4 miles from Nine Standards to the point where all three paths converge just west of Ravenseat). The low-level **green route** about half a mile shorter (adding up to 12¹/₂ miles for this stage) and with a couple of miles of road walking saves up to an hour.

The advice seems to be: if you can't see the Nine Standards by the Mile 5 junction (Wᴘᴛ 073) due to low cloud or mist, you'll see even less when you're up there and may even get lost, so take the green route.

It's possible to have your cake and eat it up here. Should you arrive at the Nine Standards and have the weather turn on you, follow a path south for three-quarters of a mile and then head west from the cairns, passing to the west of Rollinson Haggs to pick up Rollinson Gill and so the green route before it reaches the head of Rigg Beck (Wᴘᴛ 075). From there you can follow the road all the way to Keld if you wish.

● **Blue route (Aug-Nov; Maps 45-49; 3hrs 20mins from where the green route separates)** Weather permitting, this is the route to choose to get the full Pennine experience, or should that be immersion? Up to Nine Standards (Wᴘᴛ 082), just 30 minutes from the junction with the green route it matches the red route. Heading south past the **trig point** (662m) and the low ruins to the end of the ridge, at the key junction marked by the mire-bound signpost (Wᴘᴛ 085) this route then takes an eastern course down to Whitsundale Beck. Irregular and ageing posts daubed with forensic traces of light blue paint guide you east

35 MINS FROM KIRKBY STEPHEN (MAP 43) → · FELL HOUSE · 35 MINS TO SIGNPOST (MAP 45) →

ROAD CONTOURS QUARRY

QUARRY

FELL HOUSE

CATTLE GRID

**MAP 44**

BIRKETT HILL

0    1/4 mile

0    APPROX SCALE    500m

SIGNPOST & ACCESS LAND INFO

HAWTHORN & SCRUB

SIGNPOST AS TARMAC ENDS. RIGHT TO LADTHWAITE. WE GO STRAIGHT ON TO 'ROLLINSON HAGGS'

BOARDWALK

ROUGH TRACK

POST WITH WILD BOAR PICTURE

'REST-A-WHILE' CARVED SEAT

ROUTE GUIDE AND MAPS

ROUTE GUIDE AND MAPS

35 MINS FROM FELL HOUSE (MAP 44) → SIGNPOST

BLUE AND RED ROUTES

30 MINS TO NINE STANDARDS RIGG (MAP 46)

44

RUINED BARN & SHEEP PENS

073

SIGNPOST FOR NINE STANDARDS

HARTLEY FELL

SHEEPFOLD

PATH FOLLOWS SOUTHERN BANK OF STREAM

GREEN ROUTE PATH LEAVES WALL HERE

CAIRNS AS PATH BENDS LEFT

RED & BLUE ROUTES

46

BRIDGE

STEPS GETTING WASHED AWAY

HIGH ROUTE TO RUIN IS UNCLEAR. TAKE THE LOWER ROUTE ALONG THE INTAKE WALL

SINK HOLES

GREEN ROUTE

trailblazer

074 PENS

PATH UP TO NINE STANDARDS

RUIN ON RIDGE

60 MINS

STREAM FLOWS THROUGH GAP IN WALL

BOGGY

TO ROLLINSON HAGGS

ROLLINSON GILL

TAILBRIDGE HILL

SINK HOLES

KEEP LEFT, UPHILL

075 HEAD OF RIGG BECK

GREEN ROUTE

LIMESTONE PAVEMENT

SMALL POOL

076

BOGGY

RIGG BECK

SNOW POLES

BIGGER POOL

0    ¼ mile

077

0    APPROX SCALE    500m

B6270

SIGNPOST

PATH CONTINUES ON ROAD

'THE TOWNSHIP OF NATEBY 1856'

NOW IN YORKSHIRE DALES NATIONAL PARK

45a

MAP 45

SIGNPOST

GREEN ROUTE

JOINING ROAD

JUST FOLLOW THE ROAD DOWN

CROOKED SIKE

B6270

SHEEPFOLD

SHEEPFOLD & STONE HUT

BLACK SCAR

0    1/4 mile
0    APPROX SCALE    500m

**MAP 45a**

GREEN ROUTE: 35 MINS FROM JOINING ROAD (MAP 45) TO JUNCTION OF RED AND GREEN ROUTES (MAP 48)

RED & BLUE ROUTES: NINE STANDARDS RIGG →

SINCE THE BRIDGE THE PATH HAS BECOME ERODED AND SPLITS OFF INTO MANY DIFFERENT PATHS. THE GOAL, NINE STANDARDS RIGG, IS CLEAR AHEAD HOWEVER

082

NINE STANDARDS RIGG

VIEWPOINT DIAL

083 TRIG POINT 662M

**ATTENTION!**
LOOK FOR OTHER PILLARS ON RIDGE TO SOUTH OF NINE STANDARDS; PATH FOLLOWS THESE. GROUND GETS BOGGY

**MAP 46**

0    1/4 mile
0    APPROX SCALE    500m

down to the Beck, but if you can't rely on seeing them, a compass bearing of 100° or so will do the same job. Once down in the Beck you follow its winding course south to a reunion with the other two paths, and just 15 minutes from refreshments at Ravenseat Farm (see p170).

● **Red route (May-July; Maps 45-49; 3hrs 35mins from where the green route separates)** In clear conditions this route is straightforward enough. From the boot-ravaged divergence with the blue route (WPT 085; Map 47) things can get a little boggier still and there are no waymarkers as the route rolls south over the barely noticeable crest of **White Mossy Hill**.

From here you should be able to make out a large **pile of stones** (resembling a ruin) to the south; once there you hope to be able to see a tall stone **pillar** (WPT 096) to the south-south-east. At this point you drop south-east over a small bridge and then south down towards the green route where you turn east onto a track and continue on to the farm at **Ravenseat**. Note

ROUTE GUIDE AND MAPS

that on both these higher routes it's well worth taking your time to **avoid the worst bogs** by all means possible: backtracking, taking a running jump, using a pole, using your partner as a plank; whatever works for you. One Trailblazer updater got a bit blasé here and sank down over his knees. Perhaps those tales of calf-swallowing Pennine bogs were not so exaggerated after all.

● **Green route (Dec-Apr; Maps 45, 45a, 48-49; 3hrs 25mins from where the route separates from the red and blue routes)** This is the simplest route and in inclement weather the best one to take, regardless of the season. Note that we found the more used path from the junction post at WPT 073 no longer squelches pointlessly halfway up to Rollinson Haggs only to drop down again (as shown on OS maps).

The more practical route follows the intake wall to the moderately impressive head of Rigg Beck which meanders away down its valley.

After Rigg Beck there follows a rise to a section of weathered limestone pavement before you join the B6270. Note too that later on, the point where the green route *officially* leaves the B6270 (Map 48, WPT 078) at a right-hand bend seems to be another pointless hiding to nothing, this time up a gully on all fours. Instead, continue along the road for another minute or so (Map 48) and turn north up the car track. The official path soon joins it. Shortly you'll pass the bootworn scar of the red route coming down from the pillar to join your track (WPT 079), and soon the track ends by a grouse hut.

From here you follow, and occasionally cross, Ney Gill as it wends its way towards the blue route junction at Whitsundale Beck just out of Ravenseat (WPT 080). All in all, on a rainy day keeping below 1700ft (530m) the green route need not be regarded as a 'consolation prize'. Although it's a shame to miss out the mysterious cairns, it's a fine moorland walk in its own right, getting lost is not too great a risk and the road stage along Birkdale is a fine way to appreciate the peaty wastelands without necessarily sinking into them.

Whichever way you've come over the moors, many readers have confirmed that by the time they get to ***Ravenseat Farm*** (Map 49; ☎ 01748 886387; 🖳 www.ravenseat.com) they're unable to resist a sit down, **walkers' refreshments** and, when Amanda's around to provide them, scones and cream. There's also **camping** (£3.50pp) and for £30pp you can stay (May-Oct) in the delightful **Shepherd's Hut**, a little two-bedded wagon by the river complete with woodburner and breakfast delivered to your door. Evening meals and packed lunches are also available by prior arrangement. There's a separate shower (meter) and toilet 150 yards from the hut.

From Ravenseat the path tracks south alongside the engorged chasm of **Whitsundale Beck**, punctuated with some impressive waterfalls and the finely restored but otherwise unused stone barns or 'laithes' which are a feature of Swaledale. Passing the farmhouse of **Smithy Holme** (Map 50), you can join the B6270 immediately by crossing the bridge, or take the path above the riverside cliff of **Cotterby Scar**. (For once we recommend the road, as it allows you to visit Wainwath Force.) These two paths reunite by the bridge just by ***Park House & Keld Bunk Barn*** (see p175) from where it's a gentle half-mile stroll to what passes for Keld village centre. The tough first half of the Coast to Coast is now behind you; let's just hope your feet are keeping up with the pace.

ROUTE GUIDE AND MAPS

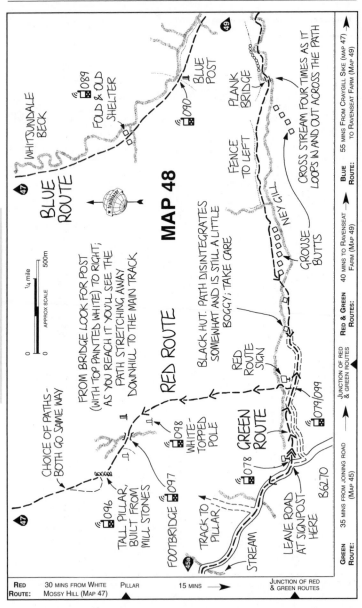

MAP 48

BLUE ROUTE

RED ROUTE

GREEN ROUTE

WHITSUNDALE BECK

🏕089 FOLD & OLD SHELTER

🏕090

BLUE POST

PLANK BRIDGE

55 MINS FROM CRAYGILL SIKE (MAP 47) TO RAVENSEAT FARM (MAP 49)

CROSS STREAM FOUR TIMES AS IT LOOPS IN AND OUT ACROSS THE PATH

BLUE ROUTE:

FENCE TO LEFT

NEY GILL

GROUSE BUTTS

40 MINS TO RAVENSEAT FARM (MAP 49)

RED & GREEN ROUTES:

BLACK HUT: PATH DISINTEGRATES SOMEWHAT AND IS STILL A LITTLE BOGGY; TAKE CARE

RED ROUTE SIGN

🏕079/099

APPROX SCALE

0      ¼ mile
0      500m

CHOICE OF PATHS – BOTH GO SAME WAY

FROM BRIDGE LOOK FOR POST (WITH TOP PAINTED WHITE) TO RIGHT; AS YOU REACH IT YOU'LL SEE THE PATH STRETCHING AWAY DOWNHILL TO THE MAIN TRACK

🏕096 TALL PILLAR, BUILT FROM MILL STONES

FOOTBRIDGE 🏕097

🏕098 WHITE-TOPPED POLE

🏕078

TRACK TO PILLAR

STREAM

LEAVE ROAD AT SIGNPOST HERE

B6270

JUNCTION OF RED & GREEN ROUTES

35 MINS FROM JOINING ROAD (MAP 45)

GREEN ROUTE:

RED ROUTE: 30 MINS FROM WHITE MOSSY HILL (MAP 47)  ▲ PILLAR  15 MINS ⟶  ▲ JUNCTION OF RED & GREEN ROUTES

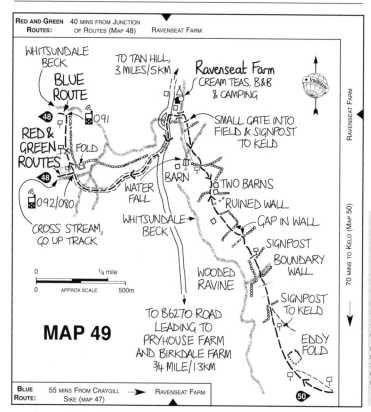

WHITSUNDALE
BECK
BLUE
ROUTE

TO TAN HILL,
3 MILES/5KM

Ravenseat Farm
CREAM TEAS, B&B
& CAMPING

48   091

RED &
GREEN   FOLD
ROUTES
48

SMALL GATE INTO
FIELD & SIGNPOST
TO KELD

092/080

CROSS STREAM,
GO UP TRACK

WATER
FALL

BARN

TWO BARNS

RUINED WALL

GAP IN WALL

WHITSUNDALE
BECK

SIGNPOST

BOUNDARY
WALL

0        ¼ mile

0   APPROX SCALE   500m

WOODED
RAVINE

SIGNPOST
TO KELD

MAP 49

TO B6270 ROAD
LEADING TO
PRYHOUSE FARM
AND BIRKDALE FARM
¾ MILE/1.3KM

EDDY
FOLD

50

RAVENSEAT FARM

70 MINS TO KELD (MAP 50)

ROUTE GUIDE AND MAPS

## KELD                    MAP 50, p174

Keld sits at the head of Swaledale where the Coast to Coast dissects the longer, northbound, Pennine Way. Today it's a tiny hill village huddled against the often inclement weather. However, in common with the rest of Swaledale, in the mid-19th century Keld stood at the heart of a local lead-mining industry. Many of the buildings including the two **Methodist chapels** were constructed at this time, as a quick survey of the construction dates carved on the houses' lintels will confirm.

Another building, the old Literary Institute, has been converted into the unstaffed *Keld Countryside & Heritage Centre* (Apr-Oct 8am-9pm, Nov-Mar 8.30am-5pm) which has displays and photographs of local history and farming heritage. One feature allows you to press buttons to hear the thoughts of local people including a farmer and a historian.

Keld is more about water than lead today. The name means 'spring' in Norse and the **Swale River**, dyed brown by the peat, rushes past the village. Do take the opportunity to visit some of the numerous nearby waterfalls – more accurately called cascades or, locally, **forces** (another Norse word) – including Catrake Force, just above the village, and East Gill Force below it.

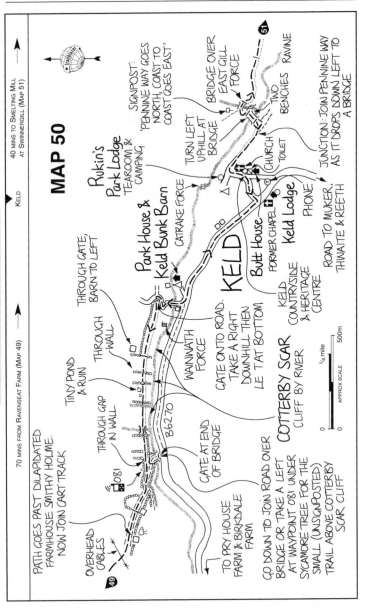

70 MINS FROM RAVENSEAT FARM (MAP 49) ⟶

KELD

40 MINS TO SMELTING MILL AT SWINNERGILL (MAP 51)

MAP 50

PATH GOES PAST DILAPIDATED FARMHOUSE SMITHY HOLME. NOW JOIN CART TRACK

OVERHEAD CABLES

49

TO PRY HOUSE FARM & BIRKDALE FARM

TINY POND & RUIN

THROUGH GAP IN WALL

THROUGH WALL

THROUGH GATE, BARN TO LEFT

B6270

GATE AT END OF BRIDGE

COTTERBY SCAR
CLIFF BY RIVER

GO DOWN TO JOIN ROAD OVER BRIDGE OR TAKE A LEFT AT WAYPOINT 083 UNDER SYCAMORE TREE FOR THE SMALL (UNSIGNPOSTED) TRAIL ABOVE COTTERBY SCAR CLIFF

WAINWATH FORCE

GATE ONTO ROAD. TAKE A RIGHT DOWNHILL THEN LE T AT BOTTOM

CATRAKE FORCE

Park House & Keld Bunk Barn

Rukin's Park Lodge TEAROOM & CAMPING

TURN LEFT UPHILL AT BRIDGE

SIGNPOST: 'PENNINE WAY GOES NORTH, COAST TO COAST GOES EAST'

BRIDGE OVER EAST GILL FORCE

51

TWO BENCHES

RAVINE

CHURCH

TOILET

KELD

Butt House
FORMER CHAPEL

KELD COUNTRYSIDE & HERITAGE CENTRE

Keld Lodge
PHONE

ROAD TO MUKER, THWAITE & REETH

JUNCTION: JOIN PENNINE WAY AS IT DROPS DOWN LEFT TO A BRIDGE

¼ mile

0                    500m
APPROX SCALE

Being a tiny village at the crossroads of two major long-distance paths, let alone situated in the ever-popular Swaledale, accommodation options in Keld can dry up fast if you leave it too late in the high season. Further down the valley the B&Bs in Thwaite and Muker (on the 'low level' route to Reeth) are no less popular. Indeed, such are the charms of Swaledale's rolling scenery, dotted here and there with the distinctive 'laithes' (stone barns for housing hay and livestock) that many hikers forego Wainwright's high route (see p176) via Swinner and Gunnerside gills in favour of the gentle stroll down the Swale valley to Reeth.

The only services in Keld are a **public toilet** and a **phone**. For more details on Keld and the rest of Swaledale visit 🖳 www .swaledale.net.

## Where to stay and eat

The village has at least two **campsites**, although level pitches can be scarce once car-borne weekenders with their giant family tents have spread out.

You'll have walked past *Park House* (*Keld Bunk Barn & Yurts*; ☎ 01748 886549; 🖳 www.keldbunkbarnandyurts .com) on the way into the village. Rates in the **bunk barn** (1D/1Tr/1Qd) are £49 for the double room or £21pp in the triple/quad including bedding, towel and a light breakfast. Readers have praised the bunkhouse which has a kitchen plus a cosy lounge area with a TV. **Camping** is £5pp (Mar-Oct) and they have a big shed with a basic kitchen for campers. They also have genuine Mongolian **yurts** (Mar-Oct) which sleep up to four people (£49 per night for two). Bedding is provided and there is a woodburning stove. The shower available for campers and yurt guests has some kick to it; there are also washing and drying facilities. Hot baguettes and tea or coffee (£3-3.50) can be brought to campers in the morning; evening meals (£6.95; ordered before 6pm) are served and they have an alcohol licence.

*Rukin's Park Lodge* (☎ 01748 886274, 🖳 www.rukins-keld.co.uk) is at the bottom of the village, though their actual **campsites** (Easter to end Oct; from

£5pp) are in two different places: below Butt House and right by the river. There is a block with shower and toilet facilities between these campsites; at present there are no laundry facilities. They don't take bookings but walkers will always be accepted. They also have a lovely little **tea-room** (Easter to end Sep; daily 9am-6pm) in the farmhouse with tables and chairs in the front garden. There are bacon rolls and a limited selection of groceries plus beer and wine; they also serve an extra pot of hot water when you order tea – always a sign of a good tearoom in our opinion.

*Butt House* (☎ 01748 886374, 🖳 www.butthousekeld.co.uk; 1D/2T/1Tr; all en suite; ☛; 🐾 £3.50; WI-FI; Ⓛ £6.50) offers a warm welcome and highly praised food. It's a popular place and B&B starts at £40pp (sgl occ £50) with an à la carte **evening meal** menu from around £3.80 for starters, £9.80 for mains, £4.95 for puddings. The house speciality is curried banana soup. There is also a washing/drying service for £5.50.

Once the village youth hostel, *Keld Lodge* (☎ 01748 886259, 🖳 www.keld lodge.com; 1S/3T/4D/1Tr, all en suite; 2S 'pod rooms' share shower facilities; 🐾 £7.50; WI-FI; Ⓛ) has been adapted into a cosy country lodge with an above-average restaurant. There is a drying room and most bedrooms have wonderful views. Rates are from £50pp (sgl £40-50, three in triple £150). The **restaurant** (open during the day for drinks, food served daily noon-2pm & 6-8pm) is open to non residents. Mains around £12: beef braised in Black Sheep Bitter with puff pastry (£10.50) is good.

Two miles back up the road to Kirkby (or just a mile back west from where the path joins the B6270 at the gated bridge before Cotterby Scar) is *Pry House Farm* (☎ 01748 886845; 🖳 www.pryfarm house.co.uk; 1D en suite/1T private bath; ☛; WI-FI; Ⓛ £5.50) where B&B costs from £37.50pp. They will take you to the pub for an evening meal.

On the same road, past the turn off north to Ravenseat (a useful short cut avoiding backtracking from Keld) and nearly three miles from the village is

*Birkdale Farm* (☎ 01748 886044; 🖳 www.birkdalefarm.com; 1D or T en suite; 1Qd en suite; 🛏; Ⓛ £5; Apr-Oct). The accommodation here is in a spacious barn conversion (Little Birkdale); the self-contained studio upstairs sleeps two and the other downstairs up to four. The food for dinner and breakfast is provided and guests cook or heat it up whenever it suits. Rates (£45pp; sgl occ full room rate) are on a dinner B&B basis. You may find it a real treat to spread out and enjoy this remote locale in Upper Swaledale. With advance notice they'll pick you up and drop you off the next day (although the OS map shows an interesting path from the farm down to the river, over Keld Side and around Kisdon Hill to Muker to pick up the valley route to Reeth).

For further accommodation options in Muker and Gunnerside (on the recommended low-level path) see p185 and p187.

### Transport                    (see also pp52-5)
Dales & District's **bus** No 30 (Mon-Sat) travels to Reeth and Richmond via Thwaite, Muker and all the Swaledale villages. Kirkby Lonsdale Coach Hire's No 830 runs on Sunday (May-Oct) between Hawes and Richmond via Thwaite, Keld, Muker, Gunnerside and Reeth.

### THWAITE                        OFF MAP 50
Two miles down the road from Keld, *Kearton Country Hotel* (☎ 01748 886277, 🖳 www.keartoncountryhotel.co.uk; 1S/6D/4T/1Tr; all en suite; 🛏; WI-FI; Ⓛ about £4.25; Feb-Dec) is a good-looking place. B&B costs from £47.50pp and dinner B&B £59.50pp. Their smart *restaurant* is open to non-residents; dinner is served daily 6.30-7.30pm. The bar is open daily all day and the bar menu is served noon-5pm.

Dales & District's **bus** No 30 (Mon-Sat) stops here on its Keld to Richmond route, as does Kirkby Lonsdale Coach Hire's No 830 on Sundays (May-Oct); see pp52-5.

## STAGE 8: KELD TO REETH                        MAPS 50-56

### Introduction
One might rightly assume the **original high-level route** is the way to go but many walkers who've done both find the **low-level (Swaledale Valley) route** (see p185) most agreeable, and of course a tad less effortful.

The high-level walk as described in Wainwright's book begins at the foot of Keld village – a bit of a pain to those who've spent the night down in Thwaite or Muker (see p185) from where following the valley alternative to Reeth makes sense. But if you wish to take the high-level route you could catch the No 30 bus back up to Keld. There's one morning service a day Monday to Saturday from Muker to Keld via Thwaite. Note that on this high-level route there's nowhere to buy any food or drink so come prepared.

### The high-level route                        Maps 51-56
The wildlife along this **11-mile (18km, 4½hr)** walk can be abundant, so try to set off as early as possible to increase your chances of encountering pheasants and deer. However, as with Stage 6 from Shap to Kirkby Stephen, this route is mainly about archaeology and the evidence of man's industrial enterprise in the far north of England. Today's walk takes you through a part of Yorkshire that has been forever scarred by the activities of lead mining. The first sign of this crops up at **Crackpot Hall** (Map 51), 30 minutes from Keld along a pretty trail high above the Swale. Though there's been a house here since the 16th century, the ruin you see today actually dates from the 18th century and, while not directly

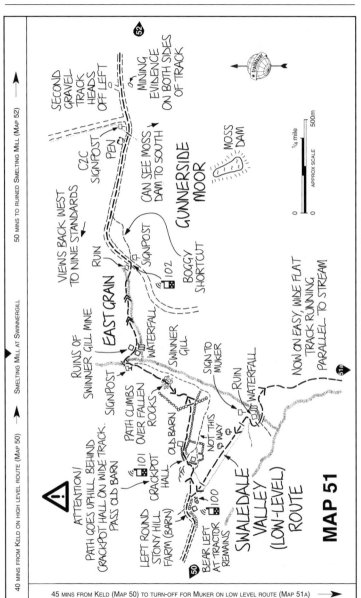

**MAP 51**

52

SECOND GRAVEL TRACK HEADS OFF LEFT

MINING EVIDENCE ON BOTH SIDES OF TRACK

C2C SIGNPOST

PEN

CAN SEE MOSS DAM TO SOUTH

GUNNERSIDE MOOR

MOSS DAM

VIEWS BACK WEST TO NINE STANDARDS

RUIN

SIGNPOST

102

BOGGY SHORTCUT

0     ¼ mile

0     500m

APPROX SCALE

EAST GRAIN

RUINS OF SWINNER GILL MINE

WATERFALL

SWINNER GILL

SIGNPOST

NOW ON EASY, WIDE FLAT TRACK RUNNING PARALLEL TO STREAM

SIGN TO MUKER

RUIN

WATERFALL

51a

⚠ ATTENTION! PATH GOES UPHILL BEHIND CRACKPOT HALL ON WIDE TRACK. PASS OLD BARN

PATH CLIMBS OVER FALLEN ROCKS

101 CRACKPOT HALL

OLD BARN

NOT THIS WAY

LEFT ROUND STONY HILL FARM (BARN)

BEAR LEFT AT TRACTOR REMAINS

50

100

SWALEDALE VALLEY (LOW-LEVEL) ROUTE

connected to the mining industry, the farmhouse was once owned by one of the mine's managers. Quiet and ruined now, the location would be a nice spot for a wild camp were it allowed, as would be many of the mining ruins on this stage. Crackpot', by the way, means 'Deep hole or chasm that is the haunt of crows', and is not a comment on the value of the endeavours of the former residents.

ROUTE GUIDE AND MAPS

❑ **Lead mining in Swaledale**

According to the best estimates, lead has been mined in Swaledale since at least Roman times, and very possibly there was some small-scale mining back in the Bronze Age. A couple of pigs (ingots) of lead, including one discovered in Swaledale with the Roman name 'Hadrian' marked upon it, have been found. A versatile metal which oxidises slowly, lead is used in plumbing (indeed the word 'plumbing' comes from the Latin for lead), ship-building and roofing as well as in the manufacture of glass, pottery and paint. During medieval times lead was much in demand by the great churches and castles that were being built at that time.

The onset of the Industrial Revolution caused mining in Swaledale to become more organised and developed from the end of the 17th century. The innovation of gunpowder blasting, too, led to a sizeable increase in production, and the Yorkshire sites were at the centre of the British lead-mining industry. Indeed, during the mid-19th century Britain was producing over half the world's lead, and the mines in Yorkshire were producing 10 per cent of that.

But while some of the mine-owners grew fabulously wealthy on the proceeds, the workers themselves suffered appalling conditions, often staying for a week or more at the mine and spending every daylight hour inside it. Deaths were common as the mines were rarely built with safety in mind, and as advances in technology drove the mines ever deeper, so conditions became ever more hazardous. Illnesses from the cramped, damp and insanitary conditions were rife. As if to rub salt into the wounds, many of the workers did not even own their own tools, but instead hired them from an agent. The industry continued to prosper throughout much of the 19th century until the opening of mines in South America led to an influx of cheaper imports and a fall in price, sending many British mines into bankruptcy. Many workers drifted away, usually to the coal mines around Durham, or to London and North America, in search of better prospects. By the early 20th century many of the villages were struggling to survive. Indeed, in the words of one resident of Reeth, when the mines closed the village became a 'City of the Dead'. Thankfully, tourism today has gone some way to securing the future of these attractive mining villages, and with the establishment of the Yorkshire Dales National Park, the future looks a lot brighter for the villages of Swaledale.

MAP 52

MELBECKS MOOR

FOLLOW WIDE TRACK WEST ACROSS WASTELAND

THREE RUINED BUILDINGS

WOODEN PEN ROUND SHAFT

JOIN MAIN TRACK 106

POST

RUIN

LESS STEEP GULLY

TO GUNNERSIDE

JOIN PATH FROM GUNNERSIDE 104 BY CAIRN

RUINED PEAT STORE

BLAKETHWAITE RUINS, NICE LUNCH STOP

RUIN

CROSS BECK ON HUGE SLAB BETWEEN SMELT MILL RUINS

RUINED BUILDINGS

DEEP GULLY

CAIRNS

GROUSE BUTTS 103

BEFORE TRACK BENDS RIGHT, TURN OFF LEFT BY CAIRNS ON A CLEAR-IF NARROW- PATH THROUGH THE HEATHER

GUNNERSIDE BECK

105

FOUR-WAY SIGNPOST; TAKE PATH TO YOUR LEFT, SIGNED 'SURRENDER BRIDGE' GOING STEEPLY UP BUNTON HUSH OR THERE'S A LESS STIFF CLIMB A LITTLE FURTHER ON

¼ mile
500m
APPROX SCALE

ROUTE GUIDE AND MAPS

The path bends north now from behind the Hall to pass an 'old house' on the map and after a gate, traverse the narrow gorge of Swinner Gill. Make sure you head uphill to follow the correct trail or you'll eventually find yourself on a lower, parallel but precipitous sheep track barely two boots wide and clinging to the side of the gorge below the correct route – see Map 51. Whichever route you stumble on, before long you arrive at the eerie remains of **Swinner Gill smelting mill** with waterfalls alongside. Again, from here it's possible to follow a tricky path alongside the north bank of **East Grain Beck** instead of the easier way a little higher up the valley side. Once climbing east, after passing the last mill ruin on your left, look for a higher path after the first stream crossing about 250m on. Either way both paths deliver you with a sweaty brow onto the breezy expanse of **Gunnerside Moor**.

Initially climbing and passing **Moss Dam** to the south, on the ensuing descent you leave the track to curve north-east and descend steeply to more picturesque ruins at **Blakethwaite** (Map 52) in the valley of Gunnerside Beck. This is an ideal, if slightly premature, location to enjoy a picnic lunch out of the wind. While sitting on the grassy bank behind the large ruined peat store with its impressive arched windows (peat was used with coal to heat the smelting furnace), look for the flue coming down from the hill, finishing near the kiln on the western banks.

From here the path zig-zags east back up onto **Melbecks Moor**. It's not uncommon to lose your way on the final climb onto the moor; we recommend that at the signpost for 'Surrender Bridge' (Map 52, WPT 105), you either get stuck directly into Bunton Hush gully, or the ascent just to the south which is less of a landslip. Once on the top, cairns or tracks lead to the wooden-penned

ROUTE GUIDE AND MAPS

LEVEL HOUSE BRIDGE          35 MINS TO SURRENDER BRIDGE (MAP 53)

52

LEVEL HOUSE BRIDGE

**MAP 53**

HARD LEVEL GILL

SIGNPOST: 'LEVEL HOUSE BRIDGE'

0          ¼ mile
0     APPROX SCALE     500m

★ trailblaze

HUT

OLD GANG SMELTING MILL

BENCH

54

35 MINS FROM LEVEL HOUSE BRIDGE (MAP 53) ⟶ SURRENDER BRIDGE ⟶ 40 MINS TO THIRNS FARMHOUSE (MAP 55)

**MAP 54**

TO LANGTHWAITE, 2 MILES/3.2KM

AFTER CAIRN CONTINUE AHEAD, UNTIL PATH DROPS STEEPLY TO CRINGLEY BOTTOM

107 CAIRN

BOGGY

STILE IN WALL, NOW HEADING EAST WITH WALL TO RIGHT

BOGGY

RUIN

STEPS TO CRINGLEY BOTTOM. BRIDGE THEN CLIMB UP

MILL RUINS TO RIGHT. VEER LEFT ON SATURATED GROUND AIMING FOR CAIRNS

SIGNPOSTS

GATE ONTO ROAD; CONTINUE ACROSS ROAD AND ONTO FOOTPATH OPPOSITE

SURRENDER BRIDGE

TO FEETHAM, 1¼ MILES/2KM

TO HEALAUGH, 2 MILES/3.2KM

APPROX SCALE

¼ mile

500m

trailblazer

ROUTE GUIDE AND MAPS

ROUTE GUIDE AND MAPS

THIRNS FARMHOUSE ◀            40 MINS TO REETH (MAP 56) →

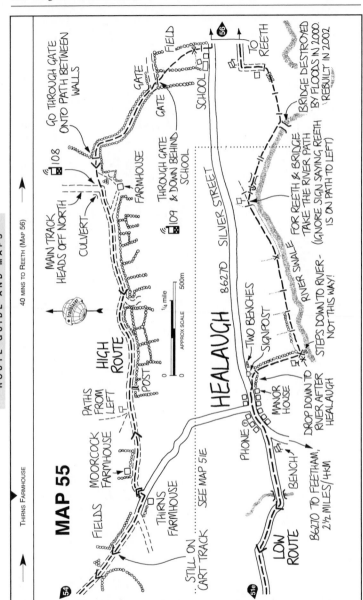

MAP 55

THIRNS FARMHOUSE    SEE MAP 51E

STILL ON CART TRACK

FIELDS

MOORCOCK FARMHOUSE

THIRNS FARMHOUSE

PATHS FROM LEFT

HIGH ROUTE

POST

MAIN TRACK HEADS OFF NORTH (MAP 56)

CULVERT

GO THROUGH GATE ONTO PATH BETWEEN WALLS

📷 108

FARMHOUSE

📷 109

THROUGH GATE & DOWN BEHIND SCHOOL

GATE

GATE

FIELD

GATE

SCHOOL

56

TO REETH

BRIDGE DESTROYED BY FLOODS IN 2000. REBUILT IN 2002.

FOR REETH & BRIDGE TAKE THE RIVER PATH (IGNORE SIGN SAYING REETH IS ON PATH TO LEFT)

RIVER SWALE

SILVER STREET

B6270

HEALAUGH

STEPS DOWN TO RIVER – NOT THIS WAY!

TWO BENCHES

SIGNPOST

MANOR HOUSE

PHONE ☎

DROP DOWN TO RIVER AFTER HEALAUGH

BENCH

B6270 TO FEETHAM, 2½ MILES/4KM

LOW ROUTE

51E

54

APPROX SCALE
0          500m
0       ¼ mile

shaft on the big track (WPT 106), a key point. Up here the landscape can be a bit of a shock. The mining relics encountered thus far have been rather quaint, but you are now faced by an eerie desolation stripped of topsoil by artificially channelled water to expose the minerals underneath. Such gullies, like the one you just clambered up, are known as a *hush*.

At the end of your 'moon walk' lies **Level House Bridge** (Map 53), where you cross **Hard Level Gill** before following it down to the remains of **Old Gang Smelting Mill**, the most extensive ruins yet where warning notices beseech you not to 'ruin the ruins'. Soon you arrive at **Surrender Bridge** (Map 54) where you cross a minor road leading up to obscure Arkengarthdale and continue past another smelt-mill ruin, dropping down to bridge the finely named **Cringley Bottom** to continue with hopefully fine views of Swaledale's iridescent verdure and dry-stone walls (Map 55) as the track tumbles down to Reeth.

**MAP 51a**

0 _____ ¼ mile
0 _____ APPROX SCALE _____ 500m

IVELET WOOD

VERY QUIET AND PEACEFUL WALK ALONG THE BANKS OF THE SWALE ON A CLEAR WIDE TRACK

MAIN TRACK VEERS OFF LEFT 200

RIVER SWALE

SIGNPOST TO GUNNERSIDE

TO MUKER, 10 MINS ON FLAGSTONE PATH THROUGH SERIES OF SMALL BUT GORGEOUS HAY MEADOWS

IGNORE PATH TO MUKER/KELD

BARN

HOUSES

BARN

SIGNPOST: 'PUBLIC FOOTPATH'

★ trailblazer

45 MINS FROM KELD (MAP 50)

TURN-OFF FOR MUKER

40 MINS TO IVELET (MAP 51b)

ROUTE GUIDE AND MAPS

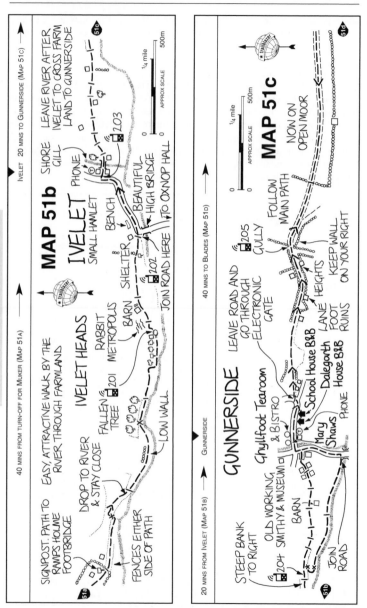

40 MINS FROM TURN-OFF FOR MUKER (MAP 51A) → IVELET  20 MINS TO GUNNERSIDE (MAP 51C)

MAP 51b

SIGNPOST. PATH TO RAMPS HOLME FOOTBRIDGE

EASY, ATTRACTIVE WALK BY THE RIVER THROUGH FARMLAND

LEAVE RIVER AFTER IVELET TO CROSS FARM LAND TO GUNNERSIDE

DROP TO RIVER & STAY CLOSE

FENCES EITHER SIDE OF PATH

LOW WALL

IVELET HEADS

FALLEN TREE  201

RABBIT METROPOLIS

BARN

SHELTER  202

JOIN ROAD HERE

IVELET SMALL HAMLET

BENCH

BEAUTIFUL HIGH BRIDGE  TO OXNOP HALL

SHORE GILL

PHONE  103

¼ mile
APPROX SCALE
0     500m

20 MINS FROM IVELET (MAP 51B) → GUNNERSIDE → 40 MINS TO BLADES (MAP 51D)

MAP 51c

STEEP BANK TO RIGHT

OLD WORKING SMITHY & MUSEUM  204

BARN

JOIN ROAD

GUNNERSIDE

Ghyllfoot Tearoom & Bistro

Mary Shaws

School House B&B

Dalegarth House B&B  PHONE

LEAVE ROAD AND GO THROUGH ELECTRONIC GATE

LANE HEIGHTS

LANE FOOT RUINS

KEEP WALL ON YOUR RIGHT

GULLY  205

FOLLOW MAIN PATH

NOW ON OPEN MOOR

¼ mile
APPROX SCALE
0     500m

## The low-level Swaledale Valley alternative route
### Map 51 p177, Maps 51a-e pp183-7, Map 56 p193

This option adds up to about 4½ **hours** of level walking (11½ **miles, 18.5km**) and you may well end up in Reeth soon after lunch. Some Coasters are tempted to roll it in with the previous stage, making a hefty 23-mile day, but doing so you can expect to hobble into Reeth in a bit of a state. Others in a rush knock out Keld to Richmond in one day; about the same distance and probably with the same consequences. Our advice? Kick back and enjoy the first leisurely stage for a while, stop frequently to admire the valley and commune with nature, take the diversion to Muker. Suppress the urge to press on with a pint or two of Old Peculier while overlooking Reeth's village green. It's a beautiful stroll, particularly in the early morning before the crowds gather. The path is so easy that for once you can fully appreciate your surroundings, looking for riparian wildlife such as herons, ducks and, so it is said, otters. It's not all so rosy down in the valley. One thing you'll remember about Swaledale, all the way to Marrick, is the number of awkwardly **narrow stone stiles** barely a leg wide and often embellished with a tiny, sprung gate. If you're lame, stiff or just lugging a heavy backpack, getting jammed on one of these trekkers' traps really can upset your composure.

The villages passed on the way are a joy. **Muker** (off Map 51a and actually slightly off the route) is a very pleasant little place and one of James Herriot's (see p188) favourites. Pronounced 'Miu-ker', you'll find a **church** with the Ten Commandments written large upon the wall, and the *Farmers Arms* (☎ 01748 886297; 🖳 www.farmersarmsmuker.co.uk; food served daily noon-2.30pm & 6-8.30pm), where 'muddy boots are welcome'. It has also been the home for 30 years of **Swaledale Woollens** (🖳 www.swaledalewoollens.co.uk), their raw material shorn from the hardy Swaledale sheep whose tough wool is considered ideal for carpets. The shop claims that it saved the village following the depression caused by the collapse of the mining industry. Following a meeting in the local pub, a decision was made to set up a local cottage industry producing knitwear, and today over 30 home workers are employed knitting the jumpers, hats and many other items available in the store.

*Muker Village Store and Teashop* (☎ 01748 886409, 🖳 www.mukervillage.co.uk) comprises the **village shop** (Mar/Apr to end Oct daily 10am-5pm, Nov to Mar/Apr Tue, Thur-Sun 9am-noon, a **tearoom** (Mar/Apr to end Oct, Wed-Mon 11am-ish to 'when it goes quiet'; weekends only in winter) and **B&B** (1D or T en suite; Ⓛ £variable; from £32.50pp, in general they don't accept solo walkers).

Accommodation is also available at *Chapel House* (☎ 01748 886822, 🖳 www.mukerchapel.co.uk; 1D en suite; Ⓛ £variable; Easter to Nov), just up from Swaledale Woollens, where B&B is from £40pp (sgl occ £80). The 18th-century *Swale Farm* (☎ 01748 886479, 🖳 www.mukervillage.co.uk/more accomodation.php; 1D/1T, en suite; WI-FI; Ⓛ £4-5; Mar-Oct), near the shop, charges from £30pp, sgl occ £35. They offer transport for Coast to Coasters to/from Keld or back to the path. From Monday to Saturday the No 30 **bus** calls here, and in Gunnerside, and on Sunday Kirkby Lonsdale Coach Hire's No 830 bus stops in both villages; see p52-5 for details.

Between Muker and Gunnerside there's more accommodation at *Oxnop Hall* (☎ 01748 886253, 🖳 www.oxnophall.com; 1S/1T 2D or T, all en suite; ♥; Ⓛ £variable; Easter to Oct), a farm offering B&B from £40pp. They're 800m

ROUTE GUIDE AND MAPS

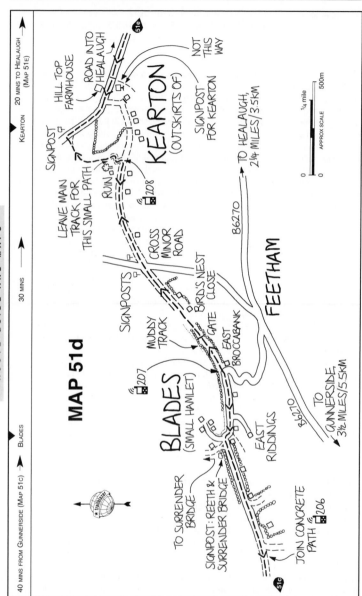

40 MINS FROM GUNNERSIDE (MAP 51c) ➤ BLADES ▲ 30 MINS ▲ KEARTON 20 MINS TO HEALAUGH (MAP 51e)

MAP 51d

BLADES (SMALL HAMLET)

KEARTON (OUTSKIRTS OF)

FEETHAM

HILL TOP FARMHOUSE

ROAD INTO HEALAUGH

NOT THIS WAY

SIGNPOST

SIGNPOST FOR KEARTON

LEAVE MAIN TRACK FOR THIS SMALL PATH

RUIN

2D8

CROSS MINOR ROAD

BIRD'S NEST CLOSE

SIGNPOSTS

MUDDY TRACK

GATE

EAST BROCCABANK

2D7

B6270

TO HEALAUGH, 2¼ MILES/3.5KM

TO GUNNERSIDE, 3½ MILES/5.5KM

EAST RIDDINGS

B6270

TO SURRENDER BRIDGE

SIGNPOST: REETH & SURRENDER BRIDGE

2D6

JOIN CONCRETE PATH

APPROX SCALE

0    ¼ mile

0    500m

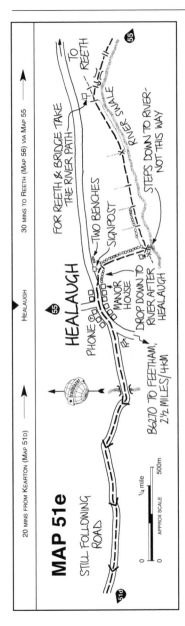

MAP 51e

20 MINS FROM KEARTON (MAP 51d)

STILL FOLLOWING ROAD

¼ mile

APPROX SCALE

0    500m

B6270 TO FEETHAM, 2½ MILES/4KM

HEALAUGH

PHONE

MANOR HOUSE

DROP DOWN TO RIVER AFTER HEALAUGH

TWO BENCHES

SIGNPOST

STEPS DOWN TO RIVER - NOT THIS WAY

RIVER SWALE

FOR REETH & BRIDGE TAKE THE RIVER PATH

TO REETH

30 MINS TO REETH (MAP 56) VIA MAP 55

HEALAUGH

from Ivelet, off Map 51b. From the trail turn right onto the road over the bridge west of Ivelet, then right at the main road and they're about 300m along on the left.

**Gunnerside** (Map 51c; 🖳 www.gunnerside.info) has an old smithy with an attached **museum** (Easter to Oct 11am-5pm, closed Mon; £2.50).

The pub has closed but opposite is the new *Mary Shaws Café* serving hot food including soups and paninis, good coffee and cakes to eat in or take away. The genteel *Ghyllfoot Tearoom & Bistro* (☎ 01748 886239; 🖳 www.ghyllfoot.co.uk; Feb to Oct, 10.30am-5pm, closed Tue) also serves meals on Wed and Sat evenings (7-9pm), a roast at lunchtime (12.30-2pm) on Sunday and takeaway curries on Monday evening. There's a lounge bar upstairs. Their hiker's brunch (£9.25) is popular.

There's accommodation at *Dalegarth House* (☎ 01748 886275, 🖳 dalegarth@btinternet .com; 1T en suite; WI-FI; Ⓛ £vari-able) on the way out of the village towards Reeth. B&B costs £29pp (sgl occ £32). They will run you down to the pub in Muker for supper. The *School House* (01748 886874, 🖳 schoolhousebandb@hotmail.co .uk; 1D en suite/1T & 1Tr both with private bathroom; ☕; WI-FI; Ⓛ £5) offers B&B from £40pp (sgl occ £45).

From Gunnerside the path crosses moor and farmland, even-tually dropping down to **Healaugh** (Map 51e), from where it returns to the river to continue past the suspension bridge to Reeth, which it enters via Quaker Rd.

## REETH
**Map 56 p193**

Reeth, the 'capital' of Swaledale, is the archetypal Yorkshire dales village: flanked to north and south by mine-scarred valleys and ringed by dry-stone walls. At its heart lies a village green surrounded on all sides by several examples of those twin institutions of Yorkshire hospitality: the **tearoom** and the **pub**. As if to underline its Yorkshire credentials still further, it also has a renowned brass band. Hardly surprising, therefore, that the village was used as a location for many episodes of the quintessential 1980s Yorkshire TV saga *All Creatures Great and Small* based on the books of rural vet, James Herriot.

Mentioned in the Domesday survey nine centuries earlier, the village grew on the profits of the 19th-century mining boom, though unlike other nearby villages it could always claim a second string to its bow as the main market town for Swaledale (the market is still held on The Green on Fridays). After the mines closed tourism gave Reeth a new lease of life and today the town hosts a number of B&Bs and hotels, as well as some **gift shops** (Garden House and Dales Centre) and a small museum.

**Swaledale Museum** (☎ 01748 884118, 🖥 www.swaledalemuseum.org; Easter to 30 Sep, Sun-Fri 10am-5pm; £3) is housed in the old 19th-century Methodist school room. It holds some surprisingly intriguing exhibits and is well-worth an hour of your time, particularly if you want to learn more about the local mining and farming industries. The dry-stone wallers' craft (see box p191) is examined, and the museum also looks at the social history of the area in some detail, attempting to show how the locals used to live a hundred or more years ago.

### Services
The **tourist office** and **National Park centre** (☎ 01748 884059, 🖥 www.yorkshire dales.org.uk; Apr-Oct daily 10am-5.30pm, Nov-Mar Sat & Sun 10am-4pm) is to the west of The Green in Hudson House. Tucked round the back of these is Swaledale Outdoors (☎ 01748 880298) full of **outdoor clothing and equipment**.

On the other side of The Green the **general store** (Mon-Sat 8.30am-5.30pm, Sun 10am-4pm) has a **post office** (Mon-Fri 9am-5.30pm, Sat 9am-12.30pm). Otherwise there are **cash machines** or cashback in both the Black Bull or the **village store** (Mon-Fri 7am-7.30pm, Sat 7am-7pm, Sun 8am-4pm; £1) at the bottom of the hill on the way out of town. **Internet access** is available at the tourist office.

### Where to stay
There is no shortage of accommodation in Reeth. The nearest **hostel** is *YHA Grinton Lodge* (off Map 56; ☎ 0845 371 9636, 🖥 www.yha.org.uk/hostel/grinton-lodge; 81 beds, 2-/3-/4-/6-bed rooms; beds £17-19, 4-bed rooms £60-84), a lovely old shooting lodge, but at just over a mile on past Reeth and up a very steep hill, it can be too much to bear. However, it is only half a mile from the path and offers superior lodgings with meals, is licensed and has a TV and a games room. Credit cards are accepted, there are drying facilities and packed lunches can be provided. They also have some camping pods (see 🖥 www.thepod.info).

Just half a mile from Reeth and even closer to the path are the converted stone barns of the *Dales Bike Centre* (Map 56; ☎ 01748 884908, 🖥 www.dalesbikecentre.co .uk; 3T/2F sleep 4; all bunks; showers available; ⓛ £4.50) in **Fremington** village. Welcoming all outdoor enthusiasts, not just cyclists, there is a kitchenette, laundry and drying facilities. Bunk and breakfast (cereals and a bacon sandwich) at the Centre costs £28pp. There's also a *café/lounge* with WI-FI and the *Bridge Inn* (Map 56) is just down the road for a steak and a Martini, shaken, not stirred.

**Campers** pitch up at *The Orchard Caravan Park* (Map 56; ☎ 01748 884475; check-in at the house signed 'Warden Enquiries'; book in advance in peak season; 🐾; WI-FI; Apr-Oct). The enthusiastic owners have transformed the place and, though dominated by caravans, it's still popular with C2Cers. You can camp here for £5pp (shower facilities 20p) and, wonderfully, if it's raining they'll allow you to shelter in one of their old caravans for the same price.

***Springfield House*** (☎ 01748 884634, 🖥 www.springfield-house.co.uk; 1D en suite/1T private bathroom; ✎; WI-FI; Ⓛ from £5; Apr-Oct) is on Quaker Close, reached via Langhorne Drive. B&B is £35pp (sgl occ £60); they offer complimentary refreshments if you arrive between 3.30 and 5pm.

***Hackney House*** (☎ 01748 884302, 1S shared bathroom, 1D/1T/1D or T/1Tr all en suite; ✎; WI-FI; Ⓛ £6), Bridge Terrace, at the bottom of the village, has received commendations from readers; the breakfasts are big and the welcome friendly. B&B costs from £40pp (sgl £42).

***The Laurels*** (☎ 01748 880257, 🖥 www.thelaurelsreeth.com; 2D/1D or Tr; en suite; 🐾£5; WI-FI; Ⓛ) is a very comfortable B&B, opened recently in a restored Georgian house. B&B is £42.50pp (sgl occ

£85) and there may be a minimum stay of two nights at weekends. Another place to try is ***Walpardo*** (☎ 01748 884626, 🖥 walpardoreeth@aol.com; 1S/1T shared bathroom; ✎; Ⓛ £6), just off The Green on Anvil Square, where B&B is just £35pp.

***The Olde Temperance*** (☎ 01748 884401; 1S/1D/1Tr; shared bathroom; ✎; dogs £3) is situated above a Christian bookshop and charges £30pp.

Across The Green and above the tearoom, ***Ivy Cottage*** (☎ 01748 884418, 🖥 www.ivycottagereeth.co.uk; 2D en suite; ✎; WI-FI; Ⓛ from £5) charges £30-40pp (sgl occ £60-80). There may be a minimum two-night stay at weekends.

***The Manse B&B*** (01748 884136, 🖥 www.themanseinreeth.co.uk; 1D/2T; all en suite; WI-FI; Ⓛ £6) is a comfortable B&B charging from £40pp (sgl occ £50). They have a drying room and offer laundry facil-

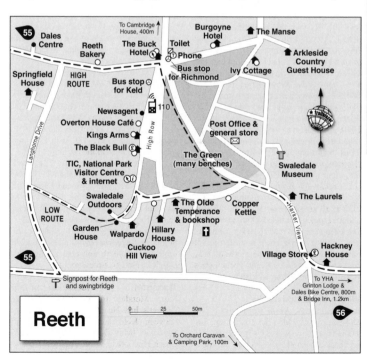

ities (£5 wash and dry). Complementary tea and cakes are served on arrival.

*Arkleside Country Guest House* (☎ 01748 884200, ☐ www.arklesidereeth.co .uk; 3D/2D or T/1T/1Tr; all with private facilities; ✒; WI-FI; Ⓛ £7.50) charges £35-40pp for B&B (£45pp with a packed lunch; sgl occ £65 inc packed lunch). They generally have a minimum two-night stay at weekends Mar-Oct.

Enjoying the views from the top of the village, *Burgoyne Hotel* (☎ 01748 884292, ☐ www.theburgoyne.co.uk; 8D or T; all en suite; ✒; ⛺£10; WI-FI; Ⓛ), is the grandest place to stay here. B&B is from £70pp (sgl occ £122.50).

For pubs there are three options. *The Buck Hotel* (☎ 01748 884210, ☐ www.buckhotel.co.uk; 1S/2D/4D or T/2T/1Qd; all en suite; ✒; ⛺; Ⓛ £variable), which charges £42-44.50pp (sgl £45-49, sgl occ £59-69, £96-109 for three/four in triple/quad); *The Black Bull* (☎ 01748 884213, ☐ www.theblackbullreeth.co.uk; 4D/3T/2Tr; all with private facilities; ✒; ⛺; WI-FI in the bar only; Ⓛ £6) dates back to 1680 and has rooms overlooking The Green and down Swaledale. B&B costs £35-40pp). *The Kings Arms* (☎ 01748 884259, ☐ www.thekingsarms.com; 2T/7D/1Qd; all en suite; ✒; ⛺; WI-FI; Ⓛ £6.95), next door, charges £30-35pp for B&B in their rear bedrooms which we found to be bright and clean and with a spacious bathroom, or £35-40pp for those overlooking The Green (sgl occ is £40-50, three/four in a room £95/110).

*Cambridge House* (☎ 01748 884633, ☐ www.cambridgehousereeth.co.uk; 1S/3D/1T; all en suite; ✒; WI-FI; Ⓛ £5) lies about a quarter of a mile (400m) north from Buck Hotel on the road to Arkengarthdale; you'll find it on the left. It is stuffed full of antiques and curios and the rooms all face south with views over Reeth. For a night's B&B they charge from £41.50pp.

### Where to eat and drink

It's a real shame *Reeth Bakery* (☎ 01748 884735; Apr-Oct Mon-Sat 10am-4pm, Sun 11am-5pm; Nov-Mar days/hours variable so check in advance), on Silver St, opens late and closes early most days. Along with a variety of breads and heavenly cakes, the still-warm filled rolls sure make a change from the plastic-cocooned sandwiches found at most village shops. If you can't squeeze into the tiny **tearoom**, take your purchases out onto one of the The Green's many benches.

*Ivy Cottage* (see Where to stay) has a popular tearoom open daily in the season from noon to 5pm. Toasted teacakes or crumpets with butter are £1.80, or you could try Yorkshire curd tart with cream (£3.20).

The *Copper Kettle* (☎ 01748 884748; Apr-Sep Sat-Thur 10am-7.30pm, Fri 10am-3pm; Mar & Oct 10.30am-5pm; closed Nov-Feb) is a traditional establishment serving Swaledale afternoon tea. They also offer more substantial fare throughout the day, with most dishes, including beef lasagne and lamb moussaka, around £8-9.

*Cuckoo Hill View* (☎ 01748 884929; daily in summer 11.30am-5pm, occasionally up to 8pm, weekends only in winter) is an ice-cream parlour at the foot of The Green serving such flavours as 'rhubarb crumble' and 'chocoholic'.

Next to the Kings Arms the licensed *Overton House Café* (☎ 01748 884045; Tue & Wed 11.30am-2.30pm, Thur 8am-5.30pm, Fri 10am-2pm & 6-10pm, Sat 11am-2pm & 6-10pm) gets great reviews and offers all sorts of coffees and cakes by day and specials (£12-17), such as lemon sole with scallops, in the evening.

Otherwise the pubs like *The Buck Hotel*, *Kings Arms* (daily noon-2.30pm & 6-9pm; see Where to stay) and *Black Bull* (daily noon-2pm & 6-9pm; see Where to stay) put on the usual spreads with the latter known for its homemade pies from £8.25.

If you've something to celebrate the exclusive *Burgoyne Hotel* (see Where to stay) does a superb four-course dinner for £40. Reservations necessary.

### Transport                    (see also pp52-5)

From Monday to Saturday Dales & District's **bus** No 30 stops here en route between Keld and Richmond and on Sundays (May-Oct) Kirkby Lonsdale Coach Hire's No 830 calls here.

## STAGE 9: REETH TO RICHMOND                                    MAPS 56-61

### Introduction
There are a couple of lovely tracts of woodland on this rural, **10½-mile (17km, 4½hr)** stage, a simple walk that should allow you time to explore the sights of Richmond at the end of the day if you set off early enough and don't lose your way. A couple of charming villages are passed en route too, as well as the remains of an old priory. Overall, it's not a spectacular day as you leave the Pennines behind but, if the weather's fine, an exceedingly pleasant one.

### The route
The walk starts out along the B6270 which you've been tracking since Kirkby Stephen, but soon after leaving Reeth and crossing Arkle Beck, you leave the road and are led along a fence corridor through riverside pastures to meet the road again at Grinton Bridge over the meandering Swale. Over the road you briefly continue along the Swale and then, like a startled badger, dart uphill to

---

### ❏ Dry-stone walls

*I am a Dry Stone Waller*
*All day I Dry Stone Wall*
*Of all appalling callings*
*Dry Stone Walling's worst of all*
**Pam Ayres** (British poet), 1978

Along the Coast to Coast path you'll pass hundreds of dry-stone walls out of Britain's estimated 125,000 miles-worth. Beautiful and photogenic, particularly when covered in a layer of velvety green moss, they're probably the most ubiquitous feature of northern England's landscape. That said, few walkers give much thought to who built them, nor have any idea just how much skill and effort goes into making these walls.

Dry-stone walls, so called because they are built without mortar, have been around since Elizabethan times when, as now, they were used to demarcate the boundaries between one farmer's land and another. Many others were built during the Enclosure Acts between 1720 and 1840, when previously large fields shared between a number of farmers were divided into strips of land. A very few of these 18th-century walls are still standing: those nearest to a village tend to be the oldest, as it was this land that was divided and enclosed first. The fact that the walls have lasted so long is largely due to the care that goes into construction.

The first step is to dig some deep, secure foundations. That done, the next step is to build the wall itself, or rather walls, for a typical dry-stone wall is actually made up of two thinner walls built back to back; a design that helps make the wall as sturdy as possible. Every metre or so a through or tie stone is built into the wall to bind the two halves together. It's estimated that one tonne of stone is required for one square yard of wall. Each stone is chosen carefully to fit exactly: a bad choice can upset the pressure loading, leading to an early collapse. Smaller chippings or pebbles are used to fill the gaps and a dry-stone waller we once met in the North Pennines reckoned he could erect just two metres of wall on a good day.

Dry-stone walling has had its heyday; it now faces competition from the wire fence which is a cheaper, simpler and just as effective a way of dividing land, and while the existing dry-stone walls have to be repaired occasionally, more often than not the farmer would rather do it himself than call in a professional. However, the art is certainly not dead; for further information visit the Dry Stone Walling Association's website (🖳 www.dswa.org.uk).

ROUTE GUIDE AND MAPS

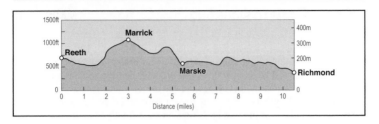

meet and cross a minor road and follow more walled pastures to **Marrick Priory** (Map 57), just 40 minutes from Reeth. Though it's visible from a distance, casual visitors are no longer allowed to visit the adjacent ruins which have been incorporated into an Outdoor Education Centre. Nevertheless, it seems that staff don't mind people walking down the drive to inspect the remains. The abbey was founded by local noble, Roger de Aske, for Benedictine nuns who numbered 17 at the priory's dissolution in 1540. There are a couple of tomb slabs in the grounds, including one by the entrance belonging to a Thomas Peacock who died in 1762 at the grand old age of 102.

Those disappointed at not being able to explore the ruins thoroughly will find some consolation in the walk to Marrick village, a pretty uphill amble through the first of this stage's woods, known as Steps Wood and notable as the first dense shade you may have experienced on the trail for several days. The path you're ascending is known as the **Nuns' Steps**, so-called because the nuns are said to have constructed the 375 steps as a walkway to the abbey. At the top, after a couple of fields, lies the village that gave Marrick Priory its name.

From **Marrick** the trail begins a long north-easterly march up to Marske through farmland punctuated by any number of tiny stiles and gates. If you manage to miss the signs for *Elaine's Farmhouse Kitchen* at *Nun Cote Nook Farm* (Map 57; ☎ 01748 884266; **camping** £6pp; **bed** in a static caravan sleeping up to six £20pp; 🐾) you need to get on to Specsavers fast. She serves **snacks and drinks** (daily 9am to late) overlooking a quiet open field that gives farm camping a good name. They also offer a two-course **evening meal** (with the meat coming from their farm) for campers for just £13. Even if you're not camping here, many Coasters agree Elaine's is well worth a detour for a brew, a snack and a chat about the price of wool.

Nun Cote Nook is just about the last hill farm and so you bid farewell to the Pennines and tramp diagonally across pastures until you join the road to **Marske** and impressive Marske Hall (Map 58) on the right. Continuing up the hill, you pass the crenellated profile of **St Edmund the Martyr**, built on the site

---

❏ **Important note – walking times**
Unless otherwise specified, **all times in this book refer only to the time spent walking.** You will need to add 20-30% to allow for rests, photography, checking the map, drinking water etc. When planning the day's hike count on 5-7 hours' actual walking.

MAP 56

40 MINS TO MARRICK PRIORY (MAP 57)

REETH

FREMINGTON

GRINTON

TO MARSKE, 5 MILES/ 8KM

BARN

📷 114

57

SIGNPOST: MARRICK 1 MILE

CROSS VIA STILE TO THE LEFT, NOT GATE TO RIGHT

📷 113
GATE & TAP

CROSS LANE INTO NEXT FIELD

WALK ALONG RIVERSIDE

Dales Bike Centre

Bridge Inn

TO GRINTON LODGE YHA, 750M

B6270 TO KELD

REETH
SEE TOWN PLAN

📷 110

📷 111
B6270

BENCH

ARKLE BECK

FARM

📷 112

CHURCH

PATH RUNS IN FENCED CORRIDOR ALL THE WAY FROM FARM TO GRINTON BRIDGE

RIVER SWALE

MEDICAL CENTRE

LOW ROUTE ALTERNATIVE

Orchard Caravan & Camping Park

PLAYGROUND

55

¼ mile

APPROX SCALE

0          500m
0

★ trailblazer

ROUTE GUIDE AND MAPS

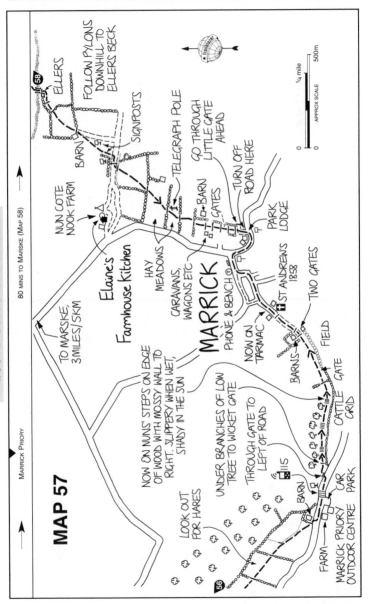

MAP 57

MARRICK PRIORY

80 MINS TO MARSKE (MAP 58)

ELLERS

FOLLOW PYLONS DOWNHILL TO ELLERS BECK

58

SIGNPOSTS

BARN

TELEGRAPH POLE

GO THROUGH LITTLE GATE AHEAD

NUN COTE NOOK FARM

BARN

GATES

TURN OFF ROAD HERE

PARK LODGE

Elaine's Farmhouse kitchen

HAY MEADOWS

TO MARSKE, 3 MILES/5KM

CARAVANS, WAGONS ETC.

MARRICK

PHONE & BENCH

ST ANDREW'S 1858

TWO GATES

NOW ON TARMAC

FIELD

NOW ON NUNS' STEPS ON EDGE OF WOOD WITH MOSSY WALL TO RIGHT. SLIPPERY WHEN WET, SHADY IN THE SUN

BARNS

CATTLE GRID

GATE

LOOK OUT FOR HARES

UNDER BRANCHES OF LOW TREE TO WICKET GATE

THROUGH GATE TO LEFT OF ROAD

BARN

MARRICK PRIORY OUTDOOR CENTRE

FARM

CAR PARK

56

¼ mile          500m

APPROX SCALE

0          0

ROUTE GUIDE AND MAPS

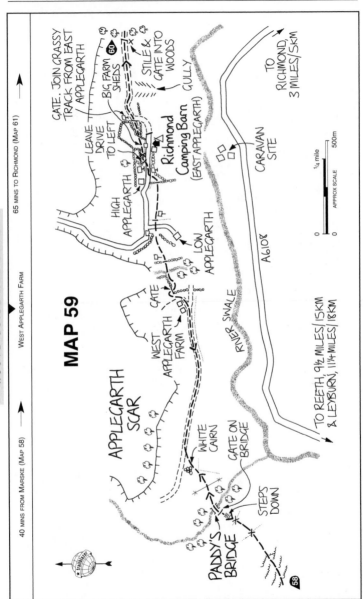

MAP 59

GATE. JOIN GRASSY TRACK FROM EAST APPLEGARTH

BIG FARM SHEDS

60

STILE & GATE INTO WOODS

LEAVE DRIVE TO LEFT

GULLY

Richmond Camping Barn (EAST APPLEGARTH)

HIGH APPLEGARTH

TO RICHMOND, 3 MILES/5KM

CARAVAN SITE

LOW APPLEGARTH

WEST APPLEGARTH FARM

GATE

APPLEGARTH SCAR

RIVER SWALE

A6108

¼ mile
500m
0
APPROX SCALE

WHITE CAIRN

GATE ON BRIDGE

PADDY'S BRIDGE

STEPS DOWN

58

TO REETH, 9½ MILES/15KM & LEYBURN, 11¼ MILES/18KM

65 MINS TO RICHMOND (MAP 61)  ━━▶

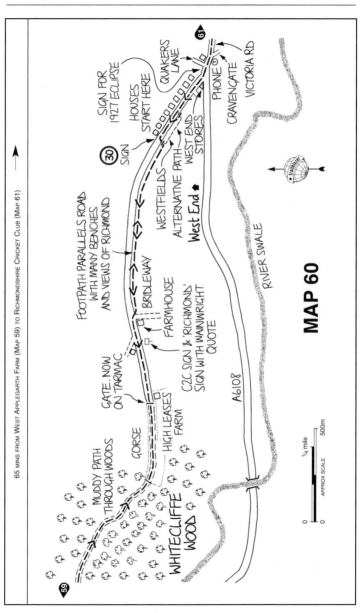

65 MINS FROM WEST APPLEGARTH FARM (MAP 59) TO RICHMONDSHIRE CRICKET CLUB (MAP 61)

SIGN FOR 1927 ECLIPSE

HOUSES START HERE

QUAKERS LANE

PHONE

CRAVENGATE

VICTORIA RD

30 SIGN

FOOTPATH PARALLELS ROAD WITH MANY BENCHES AND VIEWS OF RICHMOND

WESTFIELDS

ALTERNATIVE PATH

WEST END STORES

West End

BRIDLEWAY

FARMHOUSE

GATE, NOW ON TARMAC

C2C SIGN & 'RICHMOND' SIGN WITH WAINWRIGHT QUOTE

A6108

RIVER SWALE

MAP 60

HIGH LEASES FARM

GORSE

MUDDY PATH THROUGH WOODS

WHITECLIFFE WOOD

trailblazer

¼ mile

APPROX SCALE

0        500m
0

ROUTE GUIDE AND MAPS

of an earlier church dating back to 1090 from which the north and south doors and hexagonal supporting pillars survive. St Edmund, incidentally, was a Saxon king put to death by the Danes in AD870. Half a mile out of the village the road is once again forsaken in favour of grassy pasture as the trail unfolds, bending east at the white cairn below **Applegarth Scar** to pick up the farm track to West Applegarth (Map 59).

The farms of Low and High Applegarth are passed before the trail reaches a third farm at **East Applegarth** where, high above the wooded valley, the rustic *Richmond Camping Barn* (Map 59; ☎ 01748 822940; �殺; Mar-Nov) is the nearest cheap accommodation option this side of Richmond, three miles on. However, booking in advance is essential because the barn may be booked for sole occupancy. There's an 8- and a 4-bed **dorm** (from £8.50pp with bedding). Electricity (including the shower but not lighting) is on a meter (£1 coins only). Subject to prior arrangement food can be made available to cook meals using the facilities provided. There's also a grassy patch for **camping** (from £4pp; campers can use the facilities in the barn unless it has been booked for sole occupancy).

The trail continues into sometimes muddy **Whitecliffe Wood**, emerging 15 minutes later at High Leases Farm where the ensuing road walk can actually be paralleled on a footpath behind the fence on the right. Fine views of Richmond soon emerge; terracotta and slate roofs backed by the distant Cleveland Hills until you enter the town's suburbs.

## RICHMOND    MAP 61

*Up above a castle! Down below a stream!*
*Up above a ruin! Down below a dream!*
*Man made the castle, rude, forbidding, bare.*
*God made the river, swift, eternal, fair.*
From the recollections of **Mr M Wise** as recorded in *Richmond Yorkshire in 1830s* (Wenham Publishers 1977).

This is the largest settlement on the Coast to Coast and feels it. Richmond is a busy market town that evolved around the **castle**, built by one Alan the Red in the 11th century.

As the castle fell into disrepair over time its stones were scavenged to build the surrounding houses, giving the entire town the same sombre hue. During the Georgian era, as the town's fortunes waned still further, Richmond discovered a new source of prosperity as a centre for fine cabinet-making. Many of the buildings leading off the main marketplace date back to this era (indeed, the town museum is housed in a former cabinet-maker's workshop) and, following its restoration in 2003, the **Georgian theatre** is now said to be the finest in the land.

At the centre of the town is the large, cobbled **marketplace** off which run numerous winding alleys, known as *wynds*. Most of the town's attractions can be found on or near this marketplace, though a couple of the ruins nearby may also warrant further investigation.

Although it's a very pleasant place, the size and scale of Richmond – to say nothing of the noise, the bustle and the traffic – can come as something of a shock to fell-weathered Coasters used to more rural locales. As with so many provincial English towns, Richmond can get rowdy at weekends, but it does have its advantages in terms of the facilities it provides, as well as enough sights to amuse those who decide to rest here for a day.

### Services
The **tourist office** (☎ 01748 850549, 🖳 www.richmond.org; daily 9.30am-5pm), on the junction of Victoria Rd and Queens Rd, inside Calverts Carpets, is run by volunteers. It stocks all manner of souvenirs (including some very tasteful blue and white

# MAP 61 Richmond

0 — 100m

Arandale Guest House

Pottergate Guesthouse

Pottergate

Frenchgate Guesthouse

Rosedale Guest House

Co-op supermarket

Car park

Library & Internet

La Piazza 2

Dundas St

Frenchgate Restaurant & Hotel

Amantola

Bread Bowl Café

Nornay House

Willance House

Richmondshire Cricket Club

Grey Friars Tower

Queens Rd

St Mary's

60

To West End GH (700m)

Cordilleras House

117

Georgian Theatre Royal

Toilets

TIC

Richmondshire Museum

Station Rd

To Easby Abbey

Hurgill Road

Victoria Rd

From Marske & East Applegarth

Lily's Café

A Taste of Thailand

Ryders Wynd

Pharmacy

King St

Rosemary La

Richmond Fisheries

Tasty Macs

Rustique Restaurant

PO

Taylor's Pies

Kings Head

Newbiggin

Finkle St

Boots

Co-op

The Buck Hotel

Black Lion

Marketplace

Frenchgate Fudge

Yeoman's

Bank

Cobbles Café

Bank

Richmond Grill

Jefferson's

Green Howards Museum

Barkers Fish & Chips

Castle Fisheries

Bank

Cobbles

Cross View Tearoom

New Rd

Bookshop

Tandoori Night

Bargate

Castle House

New Treasure Garden

Richmond Castle

10 MINS

Bridge St

Old Brewery Guesthouse

Castle Walk

To Culloden Tower

Riverside Road

62

Milligate

River Swale

To Colburn & Catterick Bridge

RICHMONDSHIRE CRICKET CLUB

RICHMOND BRIDGE

ROUTE GUIDE AND MAPS

trailblazer

mugs), books and brochures about nearby attractions and has an accommodation-booking service (see Where to stay).

The **library** (Mon, Tue, Thur, Fri 10am-6pm, Wed & Sat 9.30am-1pm; closed Sun) has free wi-fi and offers **internet** access (it has ten terminals) and charges £2 for 30 minutes to temporary members.

The **post office** (Mon-Fri 9am-5.30pm, Sat 9am-noon) does foreign exchange and all the major banks are represented on the main square and have longed-for **cashpoints**. The **outdoors shop**, Yeoman's (Mon-Sat 9am-5.30pm, Sun 10am-4pm), on Finkle St, is worth checking out for replacement equipment. There's a Boots on the main square and a second **pharmacy**, Richmond Pharmacy, by the roundabout on King St.

Castle Hill **Bookshop** (☎ 01748 824243, 🖳 www.castlehillbookshop.co.uk; Mon-Sat 9am-5pm), below the castle, has an excellent range of books and an interesting selection on local history.

For **food shopping** there's a small Co-op (daily 7am-10pm) on the main square, and a larger Co-op superstore (Mon-Sat 6am-10pm, Sun 10am-4pm) to the north of Grey Friars Tower.

### Where to stay

Currently there are no hostels in Richmond and the nearest **cheap accommodation** (camping/camping barn) is either three miles back at East Applegarth (see p198), the *Hildyard Arms* (see p205) in Colburn three miles further along the Coast to Coast path, or the better-appointed *Brompton Camping Barn* (see p205) two miles after Colburn. So if you want to stay in town it's going to have to be a B&B or a hotel. If you haven't pre-booked, your best bet is the free accommodation-booking service at the tourist office, which posts lists of available accommodation in the window. What follows is our selection of the options based on readers' feedback and our own experiences.

Just west of the centre of town, *West End Guesthouse* (Map 60 p197; ☎ 01748 824783, 🖳 www.stayatwestend.co.uk; 2S/1D or T/2D/1T; all with private facilities; WI-

FI; Ⓛ), 45 Reeth Rd, is a comfortable place. For B&B it's £40-42.50pp (sgl £45-50).

At 11 Hurgill Rd, near the cricket club, is *Cordilleras House* (☎ 01748 824628, www.cordillerashouse.co.uk; 1D/1D or T en suite/1Tr, private facilities; 🖤; WI-FI; Ⓛ £5) where walkers are warmly welcomed with a drink and home-made treats. Rooms start from £80 for two sharing (£60 sgl occ) or £105 for three in the family room.

Fellow Coasters recommend *Willance House* (☎ 01748 824467, 🖳 www.willance house.com; 1D/2D or T; all en suite; WI-FI; Ⓛ from £6; Mar-Dec), at 24 Frenchgate, an oak-beamed house (or rather, three houses) dating back to the 17th century. It's named after the first alderman of Richmond. It has a guest lounge; B&B costs from £37pp (sgl occ £55). Almost opposite Willance House is the smart *Frenchgate Restaurant & Hotel* (☎ 01748 822087, 🖳 www.the-frenchgate.co .uk; 2S/D/6D or T/1 suite; all en suite; 🖤; WI-FI; Ⓛ £variable), 59-61 Frenchgate. With marble floors, limestone walls, oak-framed beds and showcasing local artists, it's a classy venue for a relaxing stay with B&B from £59pp for a standard room with plusher options at £79pp and the suite from £125pp. Sadly, the weary solo traveller must hand over at least £88.

Around the corner on Dundas St, walker-friendly *Nornay House* (☎ 01748 826469, 🖳 www.nornayhouse.co.uk; 1F en suite/2D private bathroom; WI-FI; Ⓛ) is good place and excellent value. B&B is from £35pp, but if you've seen enough full English breakfasts by this stage their room-only rate is just £25 per person.

Further away from the marketplace at No 66 is *Frenchgate Guesthouse* (☎ 01748 823421, 🖳 www.66frenchgate.co.uk; 2D/2T/2Tr/1Qd; all en suite; 🖤; WI-FI; Ⓛ £variable), which, like the others, has fine views down across the Swale. B&B costs £37.50-47pp (sgl occ £45-90).

On the square itself and part of the Best Western chain there's *The Kings Head Hotel* (☎ 01748 850220, reservations ☎ 0808 178 7666, 🖳 www.kingsheadrich mond.co.uk; 6S/19D/1T; all en suite; 🖤; 🐾£10; WI-FI; Ⓛ from £4.50), probably the smartest hotel in town. Rates start from

£40pp (sgl £50) for B&B; however, they can also be quite a bit higher.

*The Buck Hotel* (☎ 01748 822259, 🖥 www.thebuckhotelrichmond.co.uk; 1S or D/3D or T/2Tr; all en suite; 🐾£5; WI-FI; Ⓛ £5) on Newbiggin is an unpretentious, friendly place parts of which are currently being renovated now that it's been bought by a former footballer. B&B costs £35-40pp (sgl £50, £100 for three in a room).

To the north on Pottergate is the friendly *Pottergate Guesthouse* (☎ 01748 823826, 🖥 www.pottergateguesthouse.co .uk; 3D/1T/1Tr; all with private facilities; WI-FI; Ⓛ £variable), 4 Pottergate, charging £36pp (sgl occ £50, three in the triple £108) for B&B and £5-8.50 to do your laundry. Also here is *Rosedale Guest House* (☎ 01748 823926 🖥 www.richmondbedandbreakfast .co.uk; 2T/4D/1Tr or Qd; all en suite; WI-FI; Ⓛ £3.50-5.50), where the silver-starred, high-ceilinged Georgian rooms all come with sherry and chocolates on your bedside table and a pleasingly varied breakfast menu. B&B costs £35-44pp (sgl occ from £55, three/four in triple/quad £120/130). They do laundry for £8.

Across the road is *Arandale Guest House* (☎ 01748 821282, 🖥 www.arandaleguesthouse.co.uk; 3D/1D or T; all en suite; 🐾; WI-FI; Ⓛ £variable) which has been recommended, particularly for their hot tub, their comfortable beds and great breakfasts. Rates in this Victorian townhouse are £47.50-55pp (sgl occ £55). The hot tub accommodates up to six people at a time (30-60 mins; swimwear required) and must be booked in advance.

On the small green in the south of the town is *The Old Brewery Guesthouse* (☎ 01748 822460, 🖥 www.oldbreweryguest house.com; 1S/6D/2T; most en suite, others share bathroom; 🐾; 🐾£5; WI-FI; Ⓛ £5), another Grade II Georgian building and the nerve centre for Sherpa Van (see p28). B&B costs £37.50-40pp (sgl/sgl occ from £55).

For a little luxury you could try *Castle House* (☎ 01748 823954; 4D/1Tr; all en suite; 🐾; WI-FI; Ⓛ) a boutique B&B on Castle Hill. Rooms start from £80 for two sharing (£10 discount for single occupancy) but if you really want to push the boat out, for £130 you could treat yourself to their Richmond Suite which has an open fire and a four-poster bed with freestanding bath and separate en suite with shower. The attention to detail here is evident, from the complementary glass of wine on arrival to the drying room for wet clothes.

## Where to eat and drink

Disregarding fast-food outlets which you won't necessarily have walked across the country to visit, there are lots of good places to eat in Richmond.

On the marketplace, *Cross View Tearoom & Restaurant* (☎ 01748 825897; Mon-Sat 9am-5pm, Sun 10am-5pm) is friendly and good value. Their beef pot pie is £7.75.

If pink is your colour head to *Cobbles Café* (☎ 01748 826707, Mon & Wed-Sat 9.30am-3.30pm, Sun 10.30am-3.30pm) in the centre of the marketplace. It's a popular little place.

*Lily's Café* (☎ 01748 822633; Mon 9.30am-3pm, Tue-Sun 9.30am-4pm), on Rosemary Lane, does great coffee and tea, scones and a scrumptious range of cakes and cupcakes as well as light lunches.

On Queens Rd, German dishes sit alongside roast beef and Yorkshire pudding at *The Bread Bowl Café* (☎ 01748 850625; Mon-Wed 11am-7.30pm, Thur-Sat 11am-8.30pm). It's very good value, too; jager schnitzel is £6.95.

For the biggest selection of sandwiches in the shire, *Tasty Macs* (☎ 01748 822597; Mon-Sat 9am-3pm), on Finkle St, is recommended. They also have a great range of milkshakes – Crunchie, Oreo Cookie or After Eight flavours are £2.20.

Richmond is well served by fish and chipperies, the most popular of which is *Richmond Fisheries* (☎ 01748 822937; Mon-Sat daily 11am-9pm, Sun 11.30am-8pm) at 4 Newbiggin or try *Castle Fisheries* (daily 5-11.30pm) or *Barker's Fish & Chips* both on the market square.

If you can't face the thought of more fish and chips or another pub meal, a top class curry is the only cure. Point yourself confidently towards *Amantola Tandoori*

ROUTE GUIDE AND MAPS

(☎ 01748 826070; 🖳 www.amontola-restaurant.co.uk; Sun-Thur 5-11.45pm, Fri-Sat 5pm-12.15am) up on Queen's Rd; we think it's the best value curry house on the Coast to Coast. There's plenty of space, the service is great, there's a three-course deal for £9.50 and on Thursdays an all you can eat buffet for £8.95. There's another curry house, *Tandoori Night* (☎ 01748 826677) south of the marketplace, which also gets good reviews.

For Italian try *La Piazza 2* (☎ 01748 825008, daily 5-10pm, Fri-Sun also noon-3pm) which is on Dundas St. There are pizzas from £7.95.

The *Black Lion* (☎ 01748 826217; food daily noon-2.30pm and 5.30-9.30pm) on Finkle St near the marketplace, does good pub grub. Their steak pie (£7.50) has been recommended.

*New Treasure Garden* (☎ 01748 825827; Sun, Mon, Wed & Thur 6-10.30pm, Fri & Sat 6-11pm), 7 Castle Hill, is a Cantonese restaurant with an interesting Szechuan selection; if you're unfamiliar with this spicy Chinese fare, you may care to try the Szechuan House Special (around £9 to eat in) which has a sample of every dish including chicken, squid, bean curd, duck and pork, much of it covered with a special sauce made with chillies, garlic, 'five spicy powder' and yellow bean sauce.

*A Taste of Thailand* (☎ 01748 829696; daily 5-11pm), on King St, is a quirky little place that's nevertheless popular. They do excellent red and green curries.

The **restaurant** at *The Kings Head* (see Where to stay; daily 7-9pm, Sun noon-2pm) is very smart but pricey. They also do meals at the **bar** (daily noon-2pm & 6-9.15pm) which are less expensive.

One of the best places to eat in Richmond is *Rustique* (☎ 01748 821565, 🖳 www.rustiquerestaurants.co.uk, daily noon-9pm), on Finkle St and French-run. For the full Gallic experience start with half a dozen snails for £6.95. It's all good value and you can get an excellent three-course set meal for £13.95.

Also highly recommended is *Richmond Grill & Brasserie* (☎ 01748 822602, 🖳 www.richmondgrillandbrasserie .co.uk; Tue-Sun noon-2pm and 6-10pm) on the marketplace. Main dishes are around £13.95 on the imaginative menu (eg braised ox cheek with horseradish mash or Asian marinated swordfish) and you can kick off the evening with a stylish RG&B martini for £7.50. You'll probably need to book.

*Frenchgate Restaurant & Hotel* (see Where to stay; daily noon-2pm & 7-9pm) is another good, if expensive, choice for a relaxed evening's dining. Venison, turbot and your old friend, Swaledale lamb, may be on the regularly changing menu. Their three-course set meal costs £39; booking recommended.

For drinking, there are some pubs lining Market Place, but they can be extremely noisy with a couple catering largely to groups of local lads looking for a fight. A safe option is *The Buck Hotel* (see Where to stay; food Mon & Wed-Fri noon-3pm & 4-8pm, Sat noon-7pm, Sun noon-4pm), on Newbiggin, which, though it still has live music some Saturday nights, is a lot more friendly and relaxed, with great views across the river.

If you need something for your lunchbox before you set off, on the marketplace try *Taylor's Noted Pie Shop* for their famous pies or the deli, *Jefferson's*, which also has a small café. And you could round it all off with a visit to *Frenchgate Fudge & Chocolate Makers*, at 1 Frenchgate.

## What to see and do
Richmond is a great town to walk around, with plenty of twisting 'wynds' to explore and plaques installed here and there pointing out places of historical interest. The following sights are all on 🖳 www.richmond.org.
● **Richmond Castle** (☎ 01748 822493; 🖳 www.english-heritage.org.uk; daily 10am-4pm; £4.80/4.30 adult/concs, English Heritage members free) Without Richmond Castle it's arguable there would be no Richmond and while it ceased performing its castellian duties centuries ago, in the middle of the 1800s it found a new purpose as a tourist attraction and has been welcoming visitors ever since.

Visitors are advised not to rush headlong at the ruins like a troupe of marauding barbarians, but instead first acquaint themselves with the **exhibition** in the reception building; it gives a thought-provoking account of the history of the castle and the town as well as a display on how the castle was originally built. There's also an interesting section on World War I conscientious objectors (absolutists) who were held captive here. Their poignant graffiti still exists on the cell walls, though for protection these cells are today kept locked; copies of the graffiti can be seen in the exhibition.

Now advancing to the ruins in an orderly and newly informed manner, you may be a little disappointed at first by the lack of surviving structures within the castle walls, though by reading the information boards dotted around, you should get a reasonable idea of how the castle once looked.

Scholars may be similarly entranced by the ruins of **Scolland Hall**, the finest ruins surviving from Alan the Red's time; most visitors, however, will find the views from the **keep** overlooking the town far more engrossing.

● **Georgian Theatre Royal** (☎ 01748 825252, ☐ www.georgiantheatreroyal.co .uk) Built in 1788 by actor-manager Samuel Butler and now beautifully restored, this is the most complete Georgian theatre in the country as well as being the oldest working theatre in its original form. It's well worth a visit for a performance (check the website for what's on) or a fascinating backstage tour. From mid-Feb to mid Nov (after the pantomime season) small guided tours run on the hour from 10am until 4pm; suggested donation £3.50. You'll get to see the oldest surviving painted scenery in Britain as well as the theatre museum.

● **Richmondshire Museum** (☎ 01748 825611, ☐ www.richmondshiremuseum .org.uk; Easter to end Oct daily 10.30am-4.30pm; £3) Another surprisingly absorbing local museum, similar in content to Reeth's Swaledale Museum (see p188), though bigger and with even more impressive exhibits. Highlights include **Cruck House**, a 15th-century building moved wholesale from Ravensworth in 1985, an exhibition tracing the history of transport (including an original penny farthing bicycle), and tellingly,

most popular of all, the set of the vet's surgery from the TV series of *All Creatures Great and Small*.

● **Green Howards Museum** (☎ 01748 826561; ☐ www.greenhowards.org.uk; closed for refurbishment until late 2014) Richmond has a long military association and is the garrison town of Catterick, now many times larger than Richmond itself. The town's regiment, the Green Howards, have their own museum and headquarters in this former Holy Trinity Church. With a history spanning the Crimean and Boer wars, as well as military engagements on the North-West Frontier of India and current operations in neighbouring Afghanistan, the story of the regiment is a fascinating one. Highlights include the staggering 3750-strong medal collection awarded to members of the regiment.

● **Easby Abbey** Formerly and more properly known as **St Agatha's Monastery**, Easby Abbey lies about a mile to the east of Richmond Castle. You may get a distant view of it from across the Swale during the next stage of the walk, but if you've got the time we strongly advise you make a detour and pay a proper visit. Like those at Shap, the ruins at Easby were once part of a Premonstratensian Abbey, this one built in 1152, just 31 years after the founding of the order by St Norbert in Prémontré in Picardy, northern France. The monastery served the community for almost 400 years because, unlike many other orders who chose to cut themselves off from the outside world, the Premonstratensians saw it as their duty to minister to and serve the laity until Henry VIII brought about the dissolution. Unwilling to bow to Henry's demands, they joined the Pilgrimage of Grace in 1536, the most popular rebellion against Henry. Many monasteries were briefly restored by the rebels – St Agatha's at Easby among them. They were subsequently defeated and Henry set about exacting a chilling revenge on those who had dared to defy his orders, instructing his forces in the north to '*cause such dreadful execution upon a good number of inhabitants, hanging them on trees, quartering them and setting their heads and quarters* *in every town, as shall be a fearful warn-ing'*. While visiting, be sure to check out the **parish church** here at Easby, which has survived in remarkable condition and plays host to some wonderful 13th-century **wall paintings**. Look, too, for the 12th-century **panel of glass** depicting St John.

**Other sights**  There are a couple of magnificent ruined towers in town. The first you'll come across is **Grey Friars Tower**, in the gardens behind the tourist office. This was once part of a Franciscan monastery, founded in 1258, though the tower itself wasn't built until sometime around 1500. The second, clearly visible to the west of town from Richmond Castle, is **Culloden Tower**, a folly dating back to 1746. Amazingly, it's now a novelty holiday cottage let out by the Landmark Trust ( www.landmarktrust.org.uk).

**Transport**          **(see also pp52-5)**
The nearest **railway station** is in Darlington, but there are plenty of **buses** from Market Place. Arriva's buses (X26, 26a, X27) run to Darlington and take around 45 mins. Dales & District's bus No 29 goes to Darlington, as does the No X34 (via Catterick), taking about an hour. Their No 30 service runs up Swaledale (Mon-Sat), calling at Reeth, Gunnerside and Keld, and their No 54 and No 55 go to Northallerton.

Those who wish to skip some of the next section can catch one of the many buses to Catterick Bridge or the No 55 to Bolton-on-Swale – your conscience may torment you but the truth is you won't have missed much.

For a **taxi** call Amalgamated ( 01748 825112 or  07552 160547).

## STAGE 10: RICHMOND TO INGLEBY CROSS          MAPS 61-72

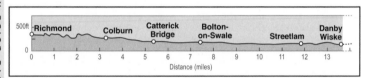

## Introduction
This is the longest stage in this book but it's also the flattest so there's something to be said for Wain-

wright's suggestion of traversing the **Vale of Mowbray** in one fell day, rather than overnighting at Danby Wiske. It's a fairly uneventful trudge by the standards of the Coast to Coast, much of it conducted on back roads and with barely a hill to grimace at, so the **22½ miles (36km, 8½hrs)** to Ingleby Cross are actually achievable. What you may want to factor in is the pounding your trail-weary feet may get along the roads as well as the following stage; a notably more gruelling 21-miler to Blakey Ridge. There's more on p221 to help make up your mind how you stage the next couple of days.

The Lakeland fell-loving Wainwright lost little love on this tepid agricultural tract, not least the innocent hamlet of Danby Wiske, cruelly claiming it to be a low point in his project in more than just elevation. Things have obviously changed for the better (and were probably never that bad), and now there are two B&Bs, and a pub to tempt you. So, in our opinion, there's a lot to be said for spending a morning ticking off a couple of sights in Richmond before setting out on the $13^{1}/_{2}$ miles to Danby Wiske in the afternoon.

## The route

Starting off from **Richmond Bridge** with a stroll along the Swale's southern bank, you leave the river for a terrace of houses and join the A6136, leaving it in turn along a lane to the left that passes alongside a sewage works and subsequently a dark, muddy stretch of riverside woodland. Slithering about over this clammy mush, you pop out of the trees, quite possibly to the sound of gunfire from the nearby garrison at Catterick, and traipse over or around more fields and farms to Catterick Bridge.

### COLBURN, CATTERICK BRIDGE & BROMPTON-ON-SWALE
#### MAP 63 p207, MAP 64 p208

A little further on is the village of **Colburn** (Map 63), with little to distract the east-bound hiker apart from *The Hildyard Arms* (☎ 01748 832353, 🖳 thehildyardarms.word press.com; food daily noon-3pm and 6-9pm; 🐾; ⒧). As well as Richmond ales on tap, they do soup and sandwiches outside the main food times and will make up packed lunches and breakfasts for campers. **Camping** is free if you phone ahead. They plan to convert the barn into a bunkhouse. The Hildyard comes recommended.

From Colburn at one point the path skirts past the former site of St Giles Hospital that flourished alongside the river some 800 years ago, although if any trace of it remains today, it's best observed following a prolonged session at the Hildyard Arms.

More conspicuous is *St Giles Farm* (☎ 01748 811372; 1T/1D/1Tr; all en suite; 🖜; ⒧ £variable) providing **B&B** (booking essential) from £37.50pp, and **camping** for £6pp including shower/toilet facilities.

From here the path continues above the river past *Thornborough Farm* (Map 64; ☎ 01748 811421; 🐾) where very basic **camping** (£5pp inc toilet/washing facilities, no shower; booking appreciated) is offered, and under the throbbing A1 trunk road to **Catterick Bridge**. Famed for its racecourse and army camp, the name Catterick reaches back 2000 years when a strategic Roman garrison and town developed where Dere Street (today's A1 or

Great North Road) bridged the Swale. By today's busy bridge you'll see *The Bridge House Hotel* (Map 64; ☎ 01748 818331; 🖳 www.thebridgehousehotelcatterick.co.uk; 3S/9D/3T; all en suite; 🖜; WI-FI; ⒧ £3.50-4), with origins dating back to the 15th-century coaching era. Rooms cost £35-49.95pp (sgl £39.95); breakfast £6pp (book in advance). Food served daily noon-3pm & 6-9pm.

There are other pubs offering accommodation in **Brompton-on-Swale**, as well as *Brompton Camping Barn* (arrivals confirmation ☎ 01748 818326; 🐾). The barn has three rooms (each sleeping four) with bunk beds including bedding (sleeping sacks cost £1); the rate is £10pp. There's a fully equipped kitchen, dining/lounge area and shower facilities (10p). Electricity is metered (£1 coins only). There's also **camping** (£4pp inc shower) for half a dozen tents. Book through the YHA (see p22; ☎ 0800 019 1700, 🖳 www.yha.org.uk/barn/bromp ton-camping-barn) or direct. Right opposite the Barn there's a mini **supermarket** open very early till late. To get to the Barn continue north once over the bridge, turn left down Bridge Rd, passing under the A1 and join West Richmond Rd; it's on the right; a 15-minute walk from the bridge. Or take a daring short cut by scrambling down to the small bridge over the Swale river by Colburn Beck Woods (see Map 63); you won't miss much.

Dales & District's No 55 **bus** stops in Brompton-on-Swale (Mon-Sat), and the No 54 goes via Catterick Bridge; see pp52-5.

Five miles from Richmond bridge cross back over the river at **Brompton-on-Swale** and continue along the north bank of the river. You then leave the Swale for good as you march into the hamlet of **Bolton-on-Swale** (Map 65). The only refreshments here are the drinks, cakes and crisps left outside the house opposite the church (a system that seems to be popular along this stage, but don't rely on it). If you can be bothered, you could walk the 400 metres north to **Scorton** where *Joan's Tearooms* (off Map 65; Mon-Fri 10am-4pm) serves bacon sandwiches, scones and cakes and other treats. In Bolton-on-Swale it's worth visiting the churchyard, famous for its **monument to Henry Jenkins**, a local man who lived an unremarkable life except for its length. (*cont'd on p212*)

BRIDGE                          80 MINS TO COLBURN (MAP 63) ⟶

**MAP 62**

DON'T TAKE THIS LOWER PATH TO THE BIG GATE; INSTEAD AIM FOR THE SMALLER KISSING GATE ABOVE RIGHT BY SHEDS

AFTER PASSING SHEDS, PASS BY FIVE HOUSES ON THE RIGHT – 'PRIORY VILLAS'

IGNORE THIS GATE

TURN RIGHT ONTO MAIN ROAD - A6136

CASTLE

RIVER SWALE

A6136

EASBY ABBEY

'L SIGN'

61

PLAYING FIELD

KISSING GATE

GO BETWEEN SHEDS TO 2ND GATE

TOILET

118

SEWAGE WORKS

LEFT OFF THE ROAD BY 'RICHMOND FC' SIGN

MUDDY PATH - PAST GREEN PERIMETER RAILINGS

GATE

BRIDGE

SMALL WOODEN BRIDGES

WOODS

63

TO HIPSWELL, ¾ MILE/1KM

A6136

0        ¼ mile
0    APPROX SCALE    500m

★ trailblazer

SIGN WARNING THAT YOU ARE NOW ENTERING A MILITARY TRAINING AREA

ROUTE GUIDE AND MAPS

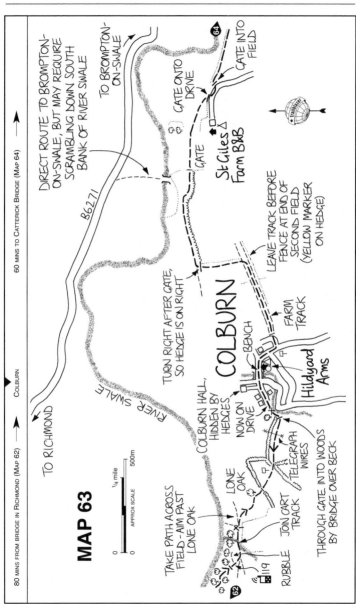

MAP 63

¼ mile

500m

APPROX SCALE

TO RICHMOND

RIVER SWALE

TO BROMPTON-ON-SWALE

DIRECT ROUTE TO BROMPTON-ON-SWALE, BUT MAY REQUIRE SCRAMBLING DOWN SOUTH BANK OF RIVER SWALE

B6271

COLBURN HALL, HIDDEN BY HEDGES

NOW ON DRIVE

TURN RIGHT AFTER GATE, SO HEDGE IS ON RIGHT

GATE

St Giles Farm B&B

GATE ONTO DRIVE

GATE INTO FIELD

LEAVE TRACK BEFORE FENCE AT END OF SECOND FIELD (YELLOW MARKER ON HEDGE)

FARM TRACK

BENCH

COLBURN

Hildyard Arms

TELEGRAPH WIRES

THROUGH GATE INTO WOODS BY BRIDGE OVER BECK

JOIN CART TRACK

LONE OAK

RUBBLE

119

TAKE PATH ACROSS FIELD - AIM PAST LONE OAK

62

64

ROUTE GUIDE AND MAPS

60 MINS FROM COLBURN (MAP 63) → CATTERICK BRIDGE → 40 MINS TO BOLTON-ON-SWALE (MAP 65)

# BROMPTON-ON-SWALE

## MAP 64

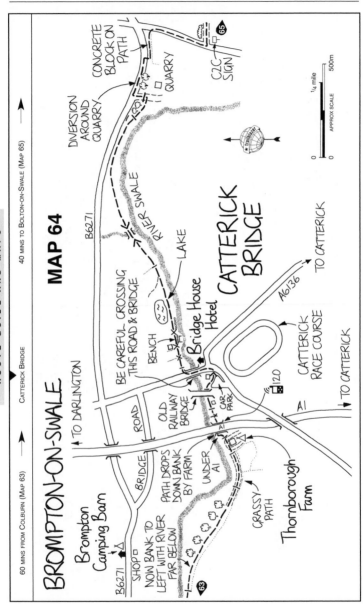

Brompton Camping Barn

SHOP

B6271

↑ TO DARLINGTON

NOW BANK TO LEFT WITH RIVER FAR BELOW

BRIDGE

ROAD

OLD RAILWAY BRIDGE

PATH DROPS DOWN BANK BY FARM

BE CAREFUL CROSSING THIS ROAD & BRIDGE

BENCH

Bridge House Hotel

LAKE

CAREFUL CROSSING BRIDGE

CAR PARK

UNDER A1

p120

Thornborough Farm

GRASSY PATH

A1

CATTERICK BRIDGE

CATTERICK RACE COURSE

A6136

TO CATTERICK

↑ TO CATTERICK

RIVER SWALE

B6271

DIVERSION AROUND QUARRY

CONCRETE BLOCK ON PATH

QUARRY

C2C SIGN

65

¼ mile

0          500m

0

APPROX SCALE

MAP 65

TO SCORTON, ¼ MILE/400M & JOANS TEAROOMS

B6271

BOLTON-ON-SWALE

OLD PUMP HOUSE - REFRESHMENTS OFTEN LEFT OUTSIDE. ALSO DRINKS IN THE CHURCH

BENCH

CHURCH
PHONE

MEMORIAL TO HENRY JENKINS

NOW IN FIELD FOLLOWING BECK

CRUMBLING BRIDGE OVER BECK

21

Laylands Farm

GATES

KEEP TO RIGHT SIDE OF FIELD BY BECK

B6271

TO GREAT LANGTON, 4¾ MILES/7.5KM

RED BRICK BRIDGE

LONG BUT QUIET ROAD WALK TO STREETLAM BEGINS

JOHN & JOHN'S CAR GARAGE

PLANTATION FARM

66

¼ mile

APPROX SCALE
0    500m

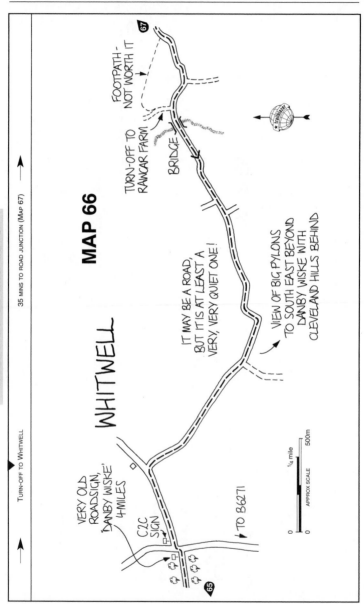

TURN-OFF TO WHITWELL          35 MINS TO ROAD JUNCTION (MAP 67)

MAP 66

WHITWELL

VERY OLD
ROADSIGN,
'DANBY WISKE'
4 MILES

C2C
SIGN

TO B6271

IT MAY BE A ROAD,
BUT IT IS AT LEAST A
VERY, VERY QUIET ONE!

VIEW OF BIG PYLONS
TO SOUTH EAST BEYOND
DANBY WISKE WITH
CLEVELAND HILLS BEHIND

TURN-OFF TO
RAWCAR FARM

BRIDGE

FOOTPATH -
NOT WORTH IT

¼ mile
APPROX SCALE
0        500m

STREETLAM

ROAD JUNCTION AT STREETLAM

40 MINS TO DANBY WISKE (MAP 68)

PHONE

BLUE GARAGE

122

MUDDY & OVERGROWN

EMERGE FROM MUD; VIEWS OF THE CLEVELAND HILLS

GREEN/ YELLOW TUB LID MARKERS

UNDER CABLES OF ELECTRICITY PYLONS

68

WEST FARM

STILE, BRIDGE, STILE

PARK HILL

CROSS STILE BY CATTLE GRID TO JOIN DRIVEWAY LEADING ONTO ROAD

FENCE TO RIGHT BETWEEN STILES

SMALL POND

HORSE ENCLOSURE

TREEHOUSE YARD

66

NOTE: GO BEHIND BLUE 2-DOOR GARAGE INTO THE YARD AND AROUND HORSE ENCLOSURE TO FOLLOW FENCE. THEN NORTH-EAST TO STILE IN CORNER OF FIELD (WPT 138)

1/4 mile          500m

0          APPROX SCALE

0

MAP 67

ROUTE GUIDE AND MAPS

(*cont'd from p206*)   He claimed he was 169 when he died, a fact which may explain the popularity of the village with retirees. The church itself is of course older, dating back to the 14th century, with Norman and Saxon ancestors; you can see various bits of masonry from these earlier churches inside, including part of an Anglo-Danish cross shaft in the vestry and part of a pointed arch in the vestry roof. If you need a break Dales & District's No 55 **bus** calls here (Mon-Sat) en route from Richmond to Northallerton; see p55.

More unexceptional field-tramping ensues, with **camping** at *Laylands Farm* (Map 65; ☎ 01748 811491; £4.50pp inc toilet/shower facilities; Mar-Oct/Nov), followed by a 3½-mile stretch of road-walking, the longest on the entire trail (Maps 65-68). With an OS map you might string together a network of footpaths but here in the Vale, is it worth it? The roads are nearly as quiet as they were in Wainwright's day, while the intrusive odours and hum of intensive farming will be present whichever route you take.

At **Streetlam** (Map 67) there's an opportunity to hack along an overgrown footpath towards more fields of pasture and livestock so if you're on the long haul to Ingleby Cross, stick to the roads where indicated; it's a pleasant chance to switch to autopilot. You'll shortly rejoin the road and march on to see what awaits in Danby Wiske.

## DANBY WISKE                 MAP 68

Chances are you'd never heard of Danby Wiske before you set your sights on the Coast to Coast, but this tiny village with an 11th-century Norman church and a tidy village green is a renowned staging post on your trek. Having long outgrown the hurtful comments in Wainwright's guide, the proud villagers seem to go out of their way to greet trail-weary Coasters, and with a bit of luck your transit will coincide with a lavish array of cakes laid on in the village hall.

*The White Swan* (☎ 01609 775131, 🖥 www.thewhiteswandanbywiske.co.uk) does **B&B** (2T/1Qd en suite; 2T shared facilities; WI-FI; ⓛ £5) for £38-42.50pp (sgl occ £45-50) and **camping** (£6pp inc shower; breakfast from £7.50 if prebooked) is also available in a field. They also have drying facilities. **Food** is available in the bar (Apr-Oct Sun-Wed noon-10pm, Thur-Sat noon-11pm; Nov-Mar Mon & Wed-Fri 7-11pm Sat & Sun noon-3pm & 6-10pm. Snacks are available most of the day.

The previous owners of the pub now run *The Old School* (☎ 01609 774227, 🖥 oldschooldanbywiske@yahoo.co.uk; 1D en suite/2T; shared facilities; ➡; ⓛ from £4; Easter to end Sep). A 19th-century school-house as its name implies, all the rooms are bright, neat and smart; if only two people book a twin room it is effectively en suite. Rates are from £36pp (sgl occ £45).

The other choice is *Ashfield* (☎ 01609 771628, 🖥 jeannorris@btinternet.com; 2T/1Tr, all with private facilities; ➡; ⓛ from £2; Apr-Sep) where B&B is from £36pp (sgl occ £40). Evening meals (£10 for two courses) are available and they also offer drying facilities.

As for the **church** – one of the very few in England that has no known dedication – only the solid oak door and the font are 11th-century originals, though much of the north aisle is only slightly younger. Look above the main door at the tympanum and you should be able to make out the outlines of three weathered figures. They've been interpreted as follows: the Angel of Judgement is weighing the soul of the figure on the right using the scales that he holds in his other hand, and though the evil deeds in one of the scale's pans outweigh the other, the third figure, the Angel of Mercy (Jesus Christ), has slipped his fingers under the pan containing the bad deeds, thus causing the good deeds to seem heavier.

DANBY WISKE

100 MINS TO RAILWAY (MAP 69) →

69

TAKE STILE BY GATE INTO LEFT HAND FIELD

Lovesome Hill Farm

TRACK FLANKED BY ARMCO WITH THREE STILES

Oaktree Hill B&B

OVER STILE NEXT TO GATE AND ONTO DIRT TRACK. HEDGES TO LEFT & RIGHT

124

OAK TREE FARM

CAR DEALERS

A167

TO NORTHALLERTON, 2 MILES/3KM

OAKTREE HILL

MAP 68

CROSS FIELD DIAGONALLY

THROUGH TREES

¼ mile

500m

0          APPROX SCALE          0

LAZENBY GRANGE FARM

WOODSIDE

LEAVE ROAD

123

DRIVE TO LAZENBY HALL FARM & COTTAGE

LONDON–EDINBURGH MAINLINE

RIVER WISKE

OAK DENE HOUSE

Ashfield B&B

White Swan

Old School

DANBY WISKE

CHURCH

PHONE

BENCH

67

ROUTE GUIDE AND MAPS

From the bridge crossing the River Wiske outside the village, you can see the outline of the Cleveland Hills in the distance. Unfortunately the other half of the Vale of Mowbray still lies before you (it's 8½ miles from Danby to Ingleby Cross), much of it as before on roads, but with a nifty back route sneaking up on Oaktree Hill

### OAKTREE HILL        MAP 68

This is not much more than a car dealership and a string of houses lining the A167 but there are a couple of accommodation options. Right by the trail is the eponymous *Oak Tree Hill B&B* (01609 761658; www.oaktreehillbedandbreakfast.co.uk; 1D/1T; shared bathroom; ☛; WI-FI; Ⓛ) a friendly B&B charging £32pp (£42 sgl occ). Evenings meals are £12 by prior arrangement, and there's a laundry service (£5). Half a mile further north is *Lovesome Hill Farm* (Map 68; ☎ 01609 772311, ☐ www.lovesomehillfarm.co.uk; 1S/1D/2D or T/1Tr; all en suite; ☛; WI-FI; Ⓛ from £3).

Despite the noise of the road, it's been praised by walkers for the quality of its accommodation, the food and the opportunity to take a tour of the 165-acre farm. **B&B** rates are £37-45pp (sgl £42). They also have a luxury cottage (1D) with spa bath (£40-45pp); a **bunk barn** with two rooms each sleeping four (from £11pp inc shower; bedding £4; 🐾) and offer **camping** (£5pp). Both **evening meals** (from £14) and breakfast (£6.50) for campers are provided if requested in advance. They also have a hot tub (30 mins/£10 + £5pp inc towels) so bring your swim wear. It's run by keen walkers.

Here more tracks and quiet backroads link a series of busy farms as you cross a railway line and a beck or two to finally meet the busy A19 (Map 71) at **Exelby Services**. Campers should note that, unless you pop into Osmotherley, from here on there are no village shops along the path until Glaisdale, two days and over 30 miles away. However, if you traipsed all the way from Richmond, a more pressing concern will be finding the energy to dash across four lanes of the A19 without causing a pile-up.

### INGLEBY CROSS       MAP 72, p219
### & INGLEBY ARNCLIFFE

Sandwiched between two busy 'A' roads, Ingleby Cross and its twin Ingleby Arncliffe are actually surprisingly peaceful places if you're not camping. Ingleby Cross is said to be named after its war memorial and has nothing more than the **post office** (Mon-Wed 9.30am-noon), situated in the Blue Bell Inn. Abbots No 80 and No 89 **bus** services stop here en route between Northallerton and Stokesley; see pp52-5.

If you've walked from Danby Wiske and have the time, spend it visiting **Mount Grace Priory** (see box p218), the best of the ruined abbeys on the Coast to Coast. When a heritage site advertises itself by saying that it has one of the most remarkable medieval drainage systems in the country, you'd be forgiven for thinking that there's not much point in visiting. But you'd be wrong.

### Where to stay and eat

In **Ingleby Arncliffe**, *Elstavale* (☎ 01609 882302, ☐ www.elstavale.co.uk; 1D or T/1Tr; en suite; WI-FI; laundry service available £6; Ⓛ from £5) is situated right on the path and offers B&B at £32.50pp (sgl occ rate on request, £90 for three in room). The rooms are in a separate annexe and come with foot spas. There are great breakfasts and a most welcome cream tea on arrival.

Conveniently located near the path is *Ingleby House Farm* (☎ 01609 882500, www.inglebyhousefarm.co.uk; 1S or D/1T/ 1D en suite; ☛; WI-FI; laundry service; Ⓛ; 🐾) where B&B in the twin and double rooms is £32.50pp in a separate building; the single is £45. Run by friendly people you'll be welcomed with a cream tea on arrival here, too, and given an excellent breakfast next day.

(cont'd on p218)

ROUTE GUIDE AND MAPS

100 MINS FROM DANBY WISKE (MAP 68)

RAILWAY

## MAP 69

TO DEIGHTON, 1¼ MILES/2KM

CONTINUE STRAIGHT ON TO NEXT STILE

NOW ON DRIVE

NORTHFIELD FARM

125

LONG LANE

WRAY HOUSE FARM

70

CROSS RAILWAY VIA STILE AT FAR END OF FIELD

GATE & SIGN FOR WRAY HOUSE

REFRESHMENTS OFTEN LEFT OUT

TO BROMPTON, 3MILES/5KM

STILE, BRIDGE, STILE

MOOR HOUSE FARM

MOOR HOUSE

¼ mile

APPROX SCALE

500m

0          0

SIGNPOSTS ASK WALKERS TO GO LEFT ROUND BACK OF HOUSE. REFRESHMENTS LEFT OUT BY BARN

TURN RIGHT AT SIGN FOR MOOR HOUSE

LEFT ON DEIGHTON LANE

C2C SIGN

WHITE HOUSE FARM

TO BROMPTON, 2½ MILES/4KM

NOW IN TREE ALLEY WITH FARM TO RIGHT

68

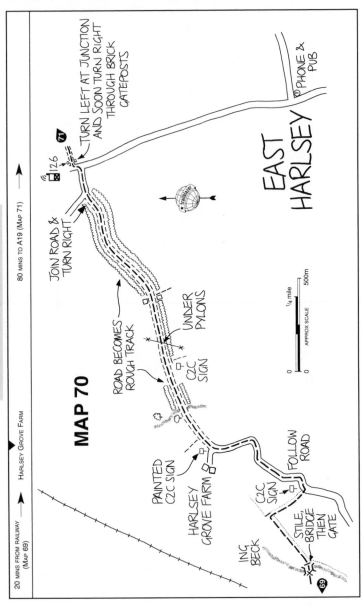

ROUTE GUIDE AND MAPS

20 MINS FROM RAILWAY (MAP 69)

HARLSEY GROVE FARM

80 MINS TO A19 (MAP 71)

MAP 70

TURN LEFT AT JUNCTION AND SOON TURN RIGHT THROUGH BRICK GATEPOSTS

126

71

PHONE & PUB

EAST HARLSEY

JOIN ROAD & TURN RIGHT

ROAD BECOMES ROUGH TRACK

UNDER PYLONS

C2C SIGN

PAINTED C2C SIGN

HARLSEY GROVE FARM

FOLLOW ROAD

C2C SIGN

STILE BRIDGE THEN GATE

ING BECK

69

¼ mile

500m

APPROX SCALE

80 MINS FROM HARLSEY GROVE FARM (MAP 70)

A19

¼ mile

500m

0

0

APPROX SCALE

A19

EXELBY SERVICES
(CAFÉ, TOILET &
SMALL SHOP IN GARAGE)

72

TO SOMERSET
HOUSE FARM,
¼ MILE/ SCOM

A19

C2C SIGN

VERY FAST TRAFFIC
ON DUAL CARRIAGEWAY.
TAKE YOUR TIME
THEN DASH!

LONGLANDS
FARM

UNDER
ELECTRICITY
CABLES

C2C SIGN

BRECKEN
HILL FARM
(RUIN)

MAP 71

POST

C2C SIGNS

SYDAL
LODGE

LEAVE DRIVE TO SYDAL
LODGE AND GO STRAIGHT
AHEAD AND OVER STILE

CLEVELAND HILLS CLEARLY
VISIBLE IN DISTANCE COVERED
BY A PATCHWORK OF TREES

70

218 Ingleby Arncliffe & Ingleby Cross

(cont'd from p214) **Somerset House Farm** (☎ 01609 882555, 🖳 www.somersethouse farm.co.uk; 2T/2D/1D or T; all en suite; ☛; small 🐾£5; WI-FI; ⓛ £6) charges £35-37.50pp (sgl occ £60). They also do laundry (£4); evening meals are available (from about £12 for two courses) if booked 48 hours in advance; they are also licensed. To get there, at the water tower in the village walk south, or walk down the A19 (see Map 71) for five minutes though this is not recommended; the farm's on the left.

*The Blue Bell Inn* (☎ 01609 882272, 🖳 www.the-blue-bell-inn.co.uk; 2S/2T/1D; en suite; 🐾 in bar area only; WI-FI; ⓛ £5) in the centre of **Ingleby Cross** serves real ales and standard **bar meals** (daily noon-2pm & 6-9pm) sometimes including the Middlesborough staple: chicken parmesan which is less Italian than it sounds. You can

also **camp** in the field out back for just £5 including shower; breakfast (£7.50) is available in the mornings if booked the night before. **B&B** is from £30pp (sgl £40).

Although it's just over a mile further along the path and agonisingly uphill too, from what readers tell us *Park House* (☎ 01609 882899, 🖳 www.parkhousebb.co .uk; 2D/2T/2Tr; all en suite; WI-FI downstairs; 🐾£10; ⓛ £5.50) is well worth the effort. With a lovely lounge and grounds that hopefully you'll have the energy to appreciate, there's also a laundry service (about £5) and drying facilities. If enough people have requested they will provide an evening meal (book 24 hrs in advance, main courses £7-11); this is a good option as they are also licensed. If they are not cooking they will take guests to a local pub. B&B costs £37.50pp (sgl occ £55).

---

### ❏ Mount Grace Priory                                                   Map 72
April-Oct Mon & Thur-Sun 10am-6pm, Nov-Mar Sat-Sun 10am-4pm; £5.40/4.90 adult/concessions, free for English Heritage and NT members.

Mount Grace Priory was built in 1398, by the ascetic **Carthusian** order, founded in 1084 by St Bruno, a canon of the Cathedral Church of Rheims. He established a religious community that settled at La Grande Chartreuse near Grenoble, from which the name Carthusian (and also the word for all Carthusian monasteries, which are known as charterhouses) comes. St Bruno and his followers saw the world as inherently wicked so lived as hermits undistracted by temptation. The monastic order that evolved from this community followed much the same principles. The prior was the only person in the monastery allowed access to the outside world, while each monk lived an essentially solitary existence, eating his meals alone and spending much of his life in his cell. The monk's day was fairly hard, rising at 5.45am and returning to bed only at 2.30am the next morning, following a day spent mainly in prayer or contemplation.

There are two people to thank for the preservation of Mount Grace. Following the priory's dissolution on 18 December 1539, James Strangways bought the land from the government but did not destroy the church as required by law at that time. Instead he let it stand as it was, intact save for the roof, possibly because his parents and grandparents had all been buried on the site. In 1899, 260 years later, Sir Lowthian Bell bought the adjoining 17th-century house, and during the course of his 30-year residency did some restoration to the priory, including the first attempt to rebuild cell number 8, one of 25 cells in total.

The priory today, though definitely a ruin, is an absorbing one, and one that clearly shows in its foundations the basic layout of the place. The restoration of **cell number 8** also makes clear that, for their time, these cells were remarkably comfortable, built on two floors with cabinets, a loom, a small bed, water closet and a small garden.

And the **drainage system**? Well with latrines fitted and clean water piped into every cell, the plumbing was indeed ahead of its time. Little of the system remains today save for the channels in which the water flowed around the priory.

INGLEBY ARNCLIFFE

A172

TO SWAINBY, 2 MILES/3KM

71

Elstavale.

Ingleby House Farm

INGLEBY CROSS

PHONE

WATER TOWER

WAR MEMORIAL

127

TO SOMERSET HOUSE FARM B&B

Blue Bell Inn & PO

INGLEBY CRICKET CLUB

CHURCH

HALL-FLAPJACKS FOR SALE

LEAVE ROAD HERE AND TURN RIGHT ONTO FOREST TRACK INTO ARNCLIFFE WOOD

C2C SIGN

A172

TO OSMOTHERLEY, 4 MILES/6.5KM

ARNCLIFFE WOOD

73

0   ¼ mile
0   APPROX SCALE   500m

Park House B&B

TRAIL FOLLOWS A LONG, WIDE AND WINDING TRACK THAT SNAKES ITS WAY THROUGH THE WOODS

TELECOM TOWERS

CLEVELAND WAY

PATHS OFF TO LEFT & RIGHT

★ trailblazer

SHORTCUTS FROM OSMOTHERLEY

SWAINSTYE FARM TRACK

MOUNT GRACE PRIORY

TO OSMOTHERLEY (FOLLOW CLEVELAND WAY SIGN), 20 MINS

CLEVELAND WAY SIGN

RELENTLESSLY UPHILL

128

TO OSMOTHERLEY, 20 MINS

MAP 72

ROUTE GUIDE AND MAPS

## OSMOTHERLEY
### OFF MAP 72 p219/MAP 73, p223

Though a 20-minute walk off the Coast to Coast trail, Osmotherley is a delight and energetic walkers may want to visit, even if they're not staying there. In the centre stands a **market cross** and a **barter table**, believed to be the same one from which John Wesley preached. Indeed, in Chapel Yard you can find what's believed to be Britain's oldest practising **Methodist chapel**, constructed in 1754.

There's also the church, **St Peter's**, built on Saxon foundations. The most distinctive things about Osmotherley, however, are its beautiful, **stone terraced cottages**, built for the workers who laboured at the flax mill that now houses the hostel. Another sight, **Thompson's**, for years a dusty, empty shop that's been in the same family since 1786 is currently being renovated and may soon reopen.

In the village there's a **post office** (Mon & Fri 9am-noon, Wed 1-4pm) inside the village hall and the small **village store** (Mon-Sat 8.30am-5.30pm, Sun 9am-5pm) where they sell basic provisions and sandwiches. If your boots are on their uppers, visit the **Osmotherley Boot & Coffee Shop** (☎ 01609 883818; Wed-Sun 10am-4pm), selling walking boots, wax, socks – and coffee and cakes!

To rejoin the trail, you needn't return to the junction with the Cleveland Way, but can take a short-cut up along Swainstye Farm track (on the left as you walk from the village towards Cote Ghyll caravan park), meeting up with the Cleveland and Coast to Coast paths at the Telecom Tower (see Map 72) or at Scarth Wood Moor (Map 73).

### Where to stay

YHA Osmotherley (🖳 www.yha.org.uk) is now operated by the owners of Cote Ghyll Caravan Park (see below) as part of their franchise Enterprise scheme. It has also been renamed: *Cote Ghyll Mill* (☎ 01609 883425, 🖳 www.coteghyll.com; 72 beds, 1x2-, 2x3-, 1x4-, 5x6-, 3x10-bed rooms; beds £20.40, rooms from £51 for two; ⓛ £4.75; breakfast £5; Feb-Oct). Virtually all beds are bunk beds; some 6-bed rooms are

en suite and have a double bed. Meals are available but check in advance. The hostel is licensed and accepts credit cards. Coming from Arncliffe Wood, at the top end of the village turn left when you hit the road, rather than right down the hill into town.

Just before the hostel, *Cote Ghyll Caravan Park* (contact details as above; dogs; WI-FI £3/day; book in advance in summer; Mar-Oct) has **camping** for £8-9.50pp inc toilet/shower facilities. Breakfast may be available at Cote Ghyll Mill. As its name suggests, its main business is caravans and during the school holidays it can be crammed with sugar-high kids, though they do have a few places to pitch a tent on the far side of the site.

Across the road from Osmotherley Walking Shop, *Queen Catherine Hotel* (☎ 01609 883209, 🖳 www.queencatherine hotel.co.uk; 1S/1D/2T; all en suite; 🐾; WI-FI; ⓛ £3.95), 4 West End, charges £35pp (sgl £35, sgl occ £50) for B&B. The pub is actually named after Henry VIII's wife, Catherine of Aragon, who is believed to have sheltered with monks at Mount Grace Priory (see box p218). It is, surprisingly, the only pub in England named after her.

Back up the hill a little way is charming *Vane House* (☎ 01609 883448, 🖳 www.vanehouse.co.uk; 4T/3D/1Qd; all en suite; 🐾£10; WI-FI; ⓛ around £7), 11A North End, with B&B from £42.50pp (sgl occ £60). They are happy to do laundry (wash and dry £10).

*The Three Tuns* (☎ 01609 883301, 🖳 www.threetunsrestaurant.co.uk; 3D/1T; all en suite; ☛; 🐾£10; WI-FI; ⓛ £7.50) is a restaurant that offers pleasant rooms. B&B starts at £42.50pp (sgl occ £65).

*The Golden Lion* (☎ 01609 883526, 🖳 www.goldenlionosmotherley.co.uk; 1D/4D or T, all en suite; 🐾; WI-FI) charges £45-50pp (sgl occ £65) for B&B.

### Where to eat and drink

We've had good reports about the food at *The Golden Lion* (see above). The bar is open Mon-Tue 5-11pm & Wed-Sun noon-11pm, food is served Wed-Sun noon-2.30pm & daily 6-9pm.

*Queen Catherine Hotel* (see Where to stay) has the most popular bar in town, with live blues or jazz music every Sunday evening. It also has some great homemade meals (daily noon-2.30pm & 6-9pm) including Mexican chicken for £9.50.

Down the road, *The Three Tuns* (see Where to stay; food served Mon-Sat noon-2.30pm & 5.30-9.30pm, Sun noon-6pm), opposite The Green, is a surprisingly smart establishment with starters from around £6.50 and mains from £10.75 for leek, spinach and goat's cheese risotto up to £16.95 for venison steak.

For something lighter try *The Coffee Pot* (☎ 01609 883536; Mar-Oct Mon-Thur 10.30am-2.30pm, school hols and Fri-Sun 10.30am-5pm, Nov-Feb Fri lunchtime only), a pleasant little café which also does soups and light lunches.

Cheapest of all is *Osmotherley Fish and Chip Shop* (☎ 01609 883557; summer Thur-Sat noon-2.30pm, Wed & Thur 5.30-9pm, Fri & Sat 5-9.30pm, winter Fri & Sat noon-2.30pm, Thur & Sat 5.30-8.30pm, Fri to 9pm), where it's £5.80 for a large haddock and chips or £1.40 for a chip bun.

**Transport**          **(see also pp52-5)**
Abbott's No 80/89 **bus** services stop here en route to Stokesley and Northallerton. Moorsbus's M9 service to Helmsley and M10 to Guisborough via Stokesley also call here (Apr-Oct).

## STAGE 11: INGLEBY CROSS TO BLAKEY RIDGE          MAPS 72-81

### Introduction
At **21 miles (34km, 8hrs)**, this is another stage that many walkers consider splitting in two. Unfortunately,

unless wild camping, it's less easily done than Stage 10 which is one reason you might want to spare yourself if coming from Richmond; you'll need to be in good shape to arrive at Blakey Ridge without looking like an extra from a George Romero zombie movie.

If you do divide the walk at **Clay Bank Top** and spend the night in one of the nearby villages, such as Great Broughton to the north or Urra to the south, the next day (having returned to Clay Bank Top) is a relatively effortless 8½ miles (14km) to Blakey Ridge so you can easily add the 9½ downhill miles to Glaisdale so needn't lose much time. Providing you book in advance, the B&Bs at Great Broughton, Urra and the other nearby villages are more than happy to collect you at Clay Bank Top and return you there next morning.

Weather and willpower depending, the all-in-one option has its plus points, however. For one thing, although the first half is a bit of a rollercoaster as the gradient profile reveals, once you've climbed one last time onto Urra Moor, some 12 miles (19.5km) from Ingleby Cross and following well over 1000 metres (nearly 3800ft) of accumulated ascent, the second half feels blessedly level and straightforward. Furthermore, many consider the Lion Inn at Blakey to be one of the more memorable pubs on the route, an isolated but busy tavern stranded atop a mist-bound moor with camping for Coast to Coasters only.

Thus our advice is as follows: if your feet are in good shape and there's room at the Inn (or elsewhere, see p232), grab it and attempt the 21 miles in a day. If that doesn't suit your schedule, organise a B&B near Clay Bank Top and if necessary catch up by pushing on to Glaisdale – an 18-mile day.

One final thing: campers should note that there's **camping** at Lord Stones Café (see p224 though it's no longer free but they do also have some pods) and the Lion Inn has camping for Coast to Coasters only.

As for the walk itself, this stage takes us into the **North York Moors National Park**, the third national park on the route with, it is said, the world's largest expanse of heather. Depending on the weather, this could be a pleasant stage as you tramp merrily along, stopping only to admire the iridescent plumage of the clucking pheasant or savour the views south to the valleys of Farndale and north to the industrial glories of Teeside and your first view of the North Sea. Or it could be a miserable, claggy rain-soaked trudge with all views obscured by a bone-chilling mist while paramotors buzz menacingly overhead. Let's hope it's the former but either way, on the bright side the waymarking is good so you're unlikely to get lost.

## The route

From Ingleby Cross the walk begins with a climb up past the **church** (note the triple-decker pulpit and purple box pews) and on up into **Arncliffe Wood**, where the path takes a turn to the south.

Having passed the turn-off for Park House (see Map 72, p219) you come to the junction for **Mount Grace Priory** (see box p218); take the right-hand fork for the priory and don't be tempted to duck out of paying, even though the path from the Coast to Coast trail takes you to the gate at the back of the priory, while the ticket office is by the front.

Stay on the Path if not visiting the priory and at the southernmost point of the wood a hairpin bend sees Wainwright's climbing trail meet the Cleveland Way, established a couple of years before Wainwright's original book was published and which you'll follow for almost the entire way to Blakey Moor. Those wishing to visit Osmotherley should turn off south through the gate.

The route continues steeply up through Arncliffe Wood (get used to it, there's plenty more of it on this stage), with cleared forestry providing views back to the Vale of Mowbray as you pass a humming telecoms station to emerge onto the heather-clad **Scarth Wood Moor** (Map 73). You soon join the Lyke Wake Walk (see box p263) in **Clain Wood** before joining the road briefly to pretty **Huthwaite Green**. Here, haul yourself up a steep, wooded climb onto

**Live Moor** (Map 74), duly noting the first appearance of a number of stone boundary markers along the wayside.

The path now drops slightly and then ascends to **Carlton Moor** (Map 75), with its gliding club, runway and paragliders. At the far end of the moor is a trig point and another boundary marker, from where you may see the **North Sea** beyond the industrial installations of Teeside, and where the path drops steeply around a quarry to a road. Crossing this and its adjacent stile, by a car park *Lord Stones Café, Grill & Camping* (Map 76; ☎ 01642 778482, 🖥 www.lord stones.com; summer daily 8am-9pm or to 4pm Sun, winter 9am-5pm or to 4pm Sun; 🐾; WI-FI;) is well staged for a break, a busy hub serving both day and dog walkers who you'll meet and greet between here and Clay Bank Top. Old hands will rue the changes here since redevelopment in 2013. Camping is no longer free but the facilities are much improved. The shop is more of a deli and there's now a swanky **restaurant**. There are 15 **camping** pitches at £17 per pitch, five furnished **pods** (sleep 4) with loo and basin en suite for £60-74 and ablutions block. It's also the only place on this stretch where **tap water** is available.

Another steep climb follows – this time up to **Cringle Moor** (Map 76), with the superbly situated **Alec Falconer Memorial Seat** from where you can take

ROUTE GUIDE AND MAPS

→ HUTHWAITE GREEN          55 MINS TO TRIG POINT (MAP 75) →

FENCES TO LEFT & RIGHT ON STEEP CLIMB UP STEPS THROUGH WOOD

PATH DESCENDS SLIGHTLY AFTER SECOND HUGE CAIRN

LIVE MOOR

131

POSTBOX, GATE & SIGNPOST: 'C.W. & L.W.W.'

NOW LESS STEEP AS YOU CROSS LIVE MOOR. PATH IS LARGELY PAVED

OLD WAGON

**MAP 74**

FARM

HUTHWAITE GREEN

0 ____ ¼ mile
0 ____ APPROX SCALE ____ 500m

130

SECOND BRIDGE

BENCH

CLEVELAND WAY SIGNPOST

OLD BRIDGE OVER STREAM COLLAPSED, BUT CAN CROSS ON NEW WOODEN ONE OR FORD THE STREAM— IT'S RARELY DEEP in more views over the smokestacks of Teeside, the outlying cone of Roseberry Topping, and just ahead of it, an obelisk on Easby Moor commemorating locally born Captain James Cook.

Follow the bends south then east (towards and then away from the summit of Cringle Moor), skirt the cliffs of **Kirby Bank** and then tackle a steep descent.

The **Wain Stones** are clearly visible on top of your next moor, the outcrops (a favourite of Wainwright's) resembling cake decorations atop **Hasty Bank** (Map 77). If staying at Great Broughton (see p228), you may wish to divert from the path on the signposted low-level trail before the climb up to the stones as the road walk is said to be no fun. Otherwise, from the Wain Stones the path continues east to **Clay Bank Top** steeply dropping one more time to the B1257 and, for those staying in the nearby villages, a possible rendezvous with your hosts. Moorsbus's M2 Sunday service calls here (Apr-Oct); see p55 for details.

ROUTE GUIDE AND MAPS

55 MINS FROM HUTHWAITE GREEN (MAP 74) ⟶    TRIG POINT    ⟶

**MAP 75**

GATE BY SIDE
OF BRIDLE-
WAY

76

SKIRT ROUND
OLD ALUM QUARRY
WITH FENCE
TO LEFT

TRIG POINT BY BOUNDARY
MARKER - GREAT VIEWS EAST
& NORTH TO MIDDLESBROUGH
& **THE NORTH SEA !!**

PATH FROM
RIGHT

★ trailblazer

VIEWS

↓ WEATHER
□ STATION
GLIDING
CLUB

CARLTON
MOOR

BOUNDARY
MARKERS

74

CAIRN

0          1/4 mile

0    APPROX SCALE    500m

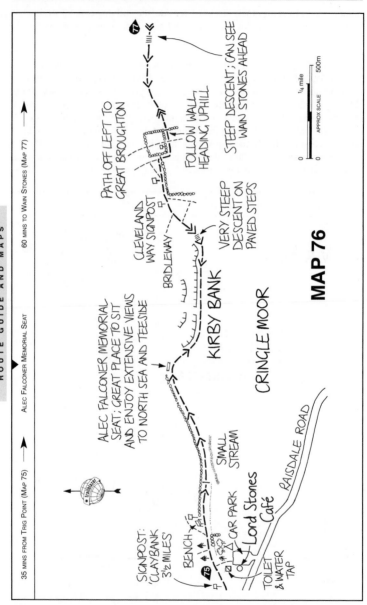

SIGNPOST: 'CLAYBANK 3½ MILES'

BENCH

CAR PARK

Lord Stones Café

TOILET & WATER TAP

SMALL STREAM

ALEC FALCONER MEMORIAL SEAT; GREAT PLACE TO SIT AND ENJOY EXTENSIVE VIEWS TO NORTH SEA AND TEESIDE

CRINGLE MOOR

KIRBY BANK

RAISDALE ROAD

BRIDLEWAY

VERY STEEP DESCENT ON PAVED STEPS

CLEVELAND WAY SIGNPOST

PATH OFF LEFT TO GREAT BROUGHTON

FOLLOW WALL HEADING UPHILL

STEEP DESCENT; CAN SEE WAIN STONES AHEAD

MAP 76

¼ mile

APPROX SCALE

500m

MAP 77

CLAY BANK TOP

45 MINS TO BOUNDARY MARKER WITH FACE (MAP 78)

CLAY BANK TOP

35 MINS

WAIN STONES

THROUGH GATE WITH SIGNPOST

CARR RIDGE

CAIRN

78

PAVED SLABS & STEPS

CLEVELAND WAY FINGERPOST

CAR PARK

B1257

TO GREAT BROUGHTON, 2½ MILES/4KM

BENCH

STEEP!

TO URRA, ¾ MILE/1.25KM & CHOP GATE 3 MILES/4½ KM

PATH PAVED AGAIN BUT NOW FLAT

HASTY BANK

WAIN STONES

TO GREAT BROUGHTON

TO CHOP GATE

76

¼ mile

500m

0

0

APPROX SCALE

## NEAR CLAY BANK TOP     MAP 77
### (Urra, Chop Gate & Great Broughton)

Accommodation-wise the nearest place to Clay Bank Top, where the B1257 bisects the Coast to Coast path, is **Urra** a mile to the south. Gerry and Wendy have been running *Maltkiln House* (☎ 01642 778216; 2T/1D; en suite/shared; ✆; ✖; wi-fi; Ⓛ£5) for many years and charge from £33pp for B&B, from £16 for dinner. One of the twin rooms is en suite and the other rooms share a shower room. They'll also show you the short cut from the back of the house directly onto Urra Moor the next morning. The house is currently on the market but hopefully will continue as a B&B.

**Chop Gate** is three miles (4.5km) south of Clay Bank Top but there are free lifts (after 4pm) offered by *The Buck Inn* (☎ 01642 778334, ▣ www.the-buck-inn.co.uk; 1S/2D/3T/1Tr or Qd, en suite; ✖£5; wi-fi; Ⓛ). B&B is from £32.50pp (sgl £55). **Camping** is £5pp. Run by a German-English couple, we've had great reports about this place from readers, about the local beer and the food (noon-9pm in summer, shorter hours in winter) in particular. Their game casserole (£10.95) is especially good. They will take walkers back up to Clay Bank next morning after 8.15am.

Near the pub and also offering free lifts to and from Clay Bank there's the very hospitable *Forge House* (☎ 01642 778166, ▣ rjsmithwilson@hotmail.co.uk; ▣ www.coast2coast.co.uk/forgehouse; 1S/2T/1D, shared/private facilities; ✆; ✖; wi-fi; Ⓛ £4). B&B is from £30pp (sgl £35).

**Great Broughton** lies 2½ miles to the north of Clay Bank Top. There's a **shop** (9.30am-5.30pm but closed Wed/Sat pm) and **post office** (same opening hours). Most B&Bs offer lifts to/from Clay Bank Top. *Newlands House* (☎ 01642 712619, ▣ www.newlandshouse.co.uk; 1D/1T/1Tr; all en suite; ✆; well-behaved ✖; wi-fi; Ⓛ) is at 7 Ingleby Rd; B&B starts at £40pp (sgl occ £50). *The Wainstones Hotel* (☎ 01642 712268, ▣ www.wainstoneshotel.co.uk; 3S/14D/7T; all en suite; ✆; wi-fi; Ⓛ £5.50) is more upmarket: B&B is £62.50-75pp (sgl £89.50, sgl occ £99-105), DB&B £77.50pp (sgl/sgl occ £105-125). *(cont'd on p232)*

45 MINS FROM CLAY BANK TOP (MAP 77) ⟶     BOUNDARY MARKER WITH FACE

**MAP 78**

NOW ON WIDE PAVED TRACK THROUGH THE HEATHER

CAIRNS

PATH LEFT

0     ¼ mile
0    APPROX SCALE    500m

URRA MOOR

BOUNDARY MARKER WITH HAND CARVED UPON IT

BOUNDARY STONES

TRIG POINT 445M

BOUNDARY MARKER WITH FACE

trailblazer

132

**MAP 79**

80

EASY, SANDY LEVEL TRACK

GREAT VIEWS DOWN FARNDALE

CLEVELAND WAY SIGN POINTS LEFT. CONTINUE STRAIGHT AHEAD

JOIN DISUSED RAILWAY TRACK

BLOWORTH CROSSING

MAIN TRACK TURNS LEFT. CONTINUE AHEAD ON SMALLER PATH TO JOIN DISUSED RAILWAY TRACK

FORMER ROSEDALE IRONSTONE RAILWAY

POND

78

¼ mile

500m

APPROX SCALE

0

0

ROUTE GUIDE AND MAPS

60 MINS FROM BLOWORTH CROSSING (MAP 79)

PATH ACROSS TRACK

MAP 80

GROUSE BUTTS
TO LEFT OF PATH

SIGN
POST

TO
CASTLETON

PATH IS AS STRAIGHT
AS AN ARROW HERE

FARNDALE MOOR

¼ mile

APPROX SCALE

500m

79

81

50 MINS FROM PATH ACROSS TRACK (MAP 80)

LION INN

BLAKEY RIDGE

FROM THE INN, TAKE THE ROAD NORTH, PAST THE COCKPIT - A TUMULUS ONCE USED AS A HOLLOW FOR COCKFIGHTING

Lion Inn 134

82

BOGGY

SMALL SHED

'WELCOME TO BLAKEY' INFO BOARD

LEAVE TRACK HERE GOING UP HILL, EAST, WITH WALL TO RIGHT. IF MIST IS THICK, LISTEN FOR CARS ON ROAD

HIGH BLAKEY MOOR

133

PATH TO FEVERSHAM ARMS INN, 1½ MILES/2KM CHURCH HOUSES & FARNDALE EAST

HOPEFULLY CAN SEE THE LION INN FROM HERE

MAP 81

WOODEN BOUNDARY POSTS

80

¼ mile

500m

APPROX SCALE

0

0

ROUTE GUIDE AND MAPS

**NEAR CLAY BANK** *(cont'd from p228)*
**(Great Broughton)** *The Wainstones
Hotel* (Mon-Sat noon-2pm & 5-10pm, Sun
noon-9pm) is a good place to eat, with
some main courses under £10. There's also
the walker-friendly *Bay Horse* (☎ 01642
712319; 🖳 www.thebayhorse-greatbrough
ton.co.uk; food Mon-Sat 11.30am-2pm &
6-9pm, Sun noon-9pm), on the High St.

Abbotts No 89 **bus** stops in Great
Broughton en route between Stokesley and
Northallerton; see p55 for details.

Just under a mile west of Great
Broughton at **Kirkby** there's more accommodation at *Dromonby Bridge B&B* (☎
01642 712226, 🖳 www.dromonbybridge
.com; 1D/2Tr/2Qd; all with private facilities; ➴; 🐾; WI-FI; Ⓛ) where B&B costs
£31-43pp (sgl occ from £36). They also
have laundry facilities and will pick
booked guests up at Clay Bank (and drop
off the next day) and also take them to the
pub for an evening meal.

From Clay Bank Top the penultimate climb the Coast to Coast follows is paved
with steps and after 20 minutes the top of **Urra Moor** is reached where the gradient relents to what feels like nothing. A wide track unrolls over the moor past
a **trig point** (Map 78) and after the **boundary marker with a face** carved onto
it, you arrive at a junction of tracks. It's here that the Cleveland Way breaks away
to the north, to return as you reach the sea cliffs north of Robin Hood's Bay,
while you continue on the wide track of the former Rosedale Ironstone Railway
(Map 79) that used to serve the nearby iron mines a century and a half ago.

Passing above the head of pretty **Farndale**, renowned for its daffodils in
spring, the track curves round High Blakey Moor towards your probable destination, the isolated Lion Inn.

**BLAKEY RIDGE**        **MAP 81, p231**
For everybody, be they a walker or a
motorist, Blakey Ridge *is* the *Lion Inn* (☎
01751 417320, 🖳 www.lionblakey.co.uk;
1T private bath/8D/4Tr; all en suite; ➴;
🐾£5; WI-FI; Ⓛ £5.25), the fourth highest
inn in Britain (the highest, the Tan Inn, lies
near Keld) and one of the most charming on
the route. The inn is nothing much to look
at on the outside. Indeed, its orange-tiled
roofs are rather disappointing for those
expecting the rustic image suggested by the
website. But inside, with its dark time-worn
beams and open fires, it looks like the inn
back nearly 500 years and is a great place to
end the day. The (small) twin is from
£24pp, but most other rooms cost £40-45pp
(sgl occ £47.50-90) for **B&B**.

The **food**, served at the bar or in the
restaurant (daily noon-10pm), is tailor-
made for walkers, being hearty and tasty.
Most dishes, such as the sumptuous steak
and mushroom pie, cost about £11.50.

**Camping** is allowed in the adjacent
field for £2.50pp, with a bit of shelter
offered by the walls; toilet and showers are

accessible when the pub's open. They prefer you book your pitch in advance to help
filter out beery louts intent on mischief, but
as long as you rock up in a suitably
drenched cagoule and not a Middlesbrough
FC outfit, they'll probably let you stay.

As the Lion Inn is often booked up,
readers have recommended an alternative.
*Feversham Arms Inn* (☎ 01751 433206, 🖳
www.fevershamarmsinn.co.uk;   3D   or
T/cottage sleeping four; all en suite; 🐾; Ⓛ
about £6.50) in **Church Houses**, down the
hill in **Farndale**, can be reached by following a path south from where the Lion Inn
comes into view (Map 81, WPT 133) for
about 1½ miles (an OS map or an OS print-
out of this section may help). B&B costs
£34.50-40pp (sgl occ £45); the cottage
costs from £105/£125 for two/four sharing.
Note that guests can check-in only when
the pub is open (see below). The **food**
(Mon-Sat noon-2pm, to 3pm on Sun, daily
6-9pm; daffodil season daily all day) is
reportedly excellent and the owner will
drive walkers back up the hill in the morning if convenient; or they can arrange a taxi.

30 MINS TO TROUGH HOUSE (MAP 83)

JUNCTION WITH FAT BETTY

PATH OFF TO THE LEFT (CONTINUATION OF BRIDLEWAY) WITH SHORT, SQUAT WHITE CROSS (FAT BETTY) TO LEFT. TRADITION REQUIRES THAT YOU LEAVE A FOOD OFFERING & TAKE ONE

83

¼ mile

500m

APPROX SCALE

0        0

PATH OFF TO LEFT

FAT BETTY

SHORTCUT ON BRIDLEWAY THOUGH TIME SAVED IS NEGLIGIBLE

81

SIGNPOST RIGHT TO ROSEDALE ABBEY; CAN SEE YOUNG RALPH CROSS UP THE ROAD AHEAD

MAP 82

JUNCTION WITH FAT BETTY

30 MINS FROM LION INN (MAP 81)

## STAGE 12: BLAKEY RIDGE TO GROSMONT            MAPS 81-87

### Introduction

For those who enjoy cosy English villages hidden amongst the gentlest, most bucolic scenery this fine country has to offer, the **13½-mile (22km, 5hr)** stroll down the **Esk Valley** to Glaisdale and on to Grosmont may be the best section of this walk. For charm, only the lakeland villages of Borrowdale and Grasmere come close to matching Egton Bridge and Grosmont, and it comes as no surprise that the nostalgic '60s village bobby TV show, *Heartbeat*, was filmed nearby.

As a final destination on this stage, either Egton Bridge or Grosmont will do nicely. But first you have to get to the valley, and that means getting down off the moors.

### The route

The walk begins by following the tarmac north towards **Young Ralph Cross** (off Map 82), which just pokes its head over the horizon as you turn off right onto another road, this one signposted to Rosedale Abbey.

Soon you pass the stumpy white landmark known as **Fat Betty** off the path to the left, where tradition requires you both take and leave a snack or a sweet; here's your chance to finally cash in those galling muesli bars! Suitably revived, you then turn north-east into the wonderfully named **Great Fryup Lane** (Map 83 and where one suspects Betty spent too much time) and leave the road to pass **Trough House**. The path can clearly be made out continuing eastwards round the southern side of Great Fryup Dale until the end of **Glaisdale Moor** where, on rejoining the road, the **North Sea** ought to be obvious at the far end of the valley.

After a mile of road-walking, Coast-to-Coasters take to the track along **Glaisdale Rigg** (Map 85) past various standing stones (and a particularly well-hewn **boundary marker** to the right of the path).

Continue on down to a gated junction by a small pool. Descend through farmland to the houses of Glaisdale.

### GLAISDALE            MAP 86, p238

Ten miles (16km) from Blakey, the village of Glaisdale sprawls across its lofty perch above the Esk Valley.

The terraced houses that are a feature of the town were originally built for the workers in the ironstone mines of the late 19th century. Today the **Robinson Institute** is a village hall that also acts as a small theatre. The late 18th-century **Church of St Thomas the Apostle**, near the upper end of

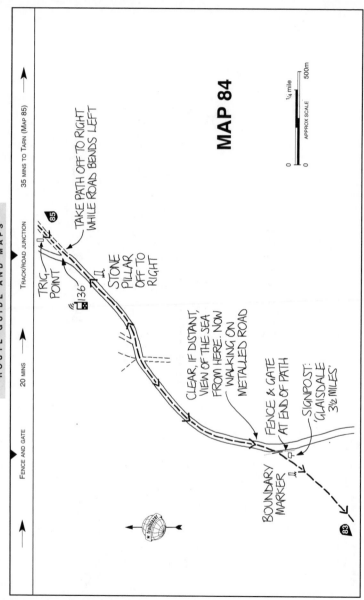

MAP 84

FENCE AND GATE     20 MINS     TRACK/ROAD JUNCTION     35 MINS TO TARN (MAP 85)

85

TAKE PATH OFF TO RIGHT WHILE ROAD BENDS LEFT

TRIG POINT

136

STONE PILLAR OFF TO RIGHT

CLEAR, IF DISTANT, VIEW OF THE SEA FROM HERE. NOW WALKING ON METALLED ROAD

FENCE & GATE AT END OF PATH

SIGNPOST: 'GLAISDALE 3½ MILES'

BOUNDARY MARKER

83

APPROX SCALE
0 ___ ¼ mile
0 ___ 500m

30 MINS FROM TARN (MAP 85) →

GLAISDALE STATION →

45 MINS TO EGTON BRIDGE (MAP 87) →

GLAISDALE

TO LANESIDE B&B

ROBINSON INSTITUTE

PO & SHOP

Tea Garden

PHONE

BARN TO RIGHT THEN HOUSES

85

CHURCH OF ST THOMAS THE APOSTLE

BENCH

TENNIS COURT

Red House Farm B&B

Arncliffe Arms

CROSS SMALL FOOTBRIDGE AND CLIMB STEPS TO ENTER EAST ARNCLIFFE WOOD

STATION

TOILET

Beggar's Bridge B&B

BEGGAR'S BRIDGE GO UNDER RAILWAY TO VIEW IT

BENCH LEFT IN MEMORY OF TWO DOGS

SMALL STREAM CROSSES PATH

ASCENDING ON RAILWAY SLEEPERS

SIGN POST

JOIN ROAD HERE  137

FORD (DRY)

87

RIVER ESK

BENCH

Broom House

MAP 86

0          ¼ mile
0    APPROX SCALE    500m

trailblazer

Glaisdale, is notable for its 16th-century wooden font cover and communion table. (Don't be fooled by the '1585' date stone in the side of the steps leading to the tower, it's from an earlier chapel). The church also contains a picture of Thomas Ferris, the beggar made famous in Glaisdale's other main sight, the **Beggar's Bridge** at the other end of the village. In the 17th century, Ferris, a humble pauper, was courting the daughter of the wealthy local squire. In order to win her hand Ferris thought he needed to improve his standing in the community so with this in mind he struck upon a plan to set sail from Whitby and seek his fortune on the high seas. The night before he put this plan into action, Ferris went to visit his beloved who lived across the river. Unfortunately, the river was swollen by heavy rains and Ferris's dreams of a romantic farewell were dashed. The story, however, does have a happy ending: Thomas returned from his adventures on the sea a wealthy man and married his sweetheart, and with part of his fortune built the Beggar's Bridge so that other young lovers from the neighbourhood would not suffer the same torment as he had that stormy night.

As for facilities, the **shop** (Mon-Sat 7am-6pm, Sun 9am-noon) is also home to the **post office** (Mon-Fri 9am-12.30pm & 1.30-5.30pm, Sat 9am-12.30pm). There is also a **public phone** at the top of the hill, and a **public toilet** near the station.

### Where to stay and eat
On the path as you enter Glaisdale you'll find *Glaisdale Tea Garden* (☎ 01947 897521; daily 10am-5pm) which serves hot and cold drinks, sandwiches, home-made cakes and pastries.

About half a mile north of the path is *Laneside B&B* (☎ 01947 897272, 💻 www.lanesidebedandbreakfast.co.uk; 1T/1D/1Tr; en suite; WI-FI; Ⓛ). B&B is from £32.50pp (sgl occ £40). Free transport to the pub for supper is provided if required.

Down near the railway station *The Arncliffe Arms* (☎ 01947 897555; 💻 www.arncliffearms.com; 2S/1D/1T/1D or T/1Tr; all en suite; 🐾£5; WI-FI; Ⓛ £6) charges from £35pp (sgl £42, sgl occ £52, three in triple £105). It also lays on **food** (Mon-Fri noon-2.30pm & 6-8.30pm, Sat noon-9pm, Sun noon-8pm). They accept credit cards and can do cashback as long as you buy a drink; they serve tea, coffee & cakes noon-6pm and have drying facilities.

Half a mile from the village centre is the award-winning 17th-century **Red House Farm** (☎ 01947 897242, 💻 www.redhousefarm.com; 2D/1Tr; en suite; 🐾; WI-FI; Ⓛ £6 if requested 24hrs in advance). Once a working farm and still the home of a number of farm animals, it's been tastefully converted to retain many of the original features to the point where it would be a shame to spend only one night here. B&B costs from £37.50pp (sgl £50).

At the very end of the village just across the tracks from the railway station is *Beggar's Bridge* (☎ 01947 897409, 💻 www.beggarsbridge.co.uk; 2D/1T; en suite; 🐾; Ⓛ £5), close to the lovelorn bridge. B&B rates are from £35pp (sgl occ £45).

### Transport                    (see also pp52-5)
M&D's **Bus** No 99 (Mon-Sat) travels up and down the Esk Valley from Lealholm to Whitby.

**Trains** stop here en route between Middlesbrough and Whitby.

From Glaisdale you enter East Arncliffe Wood, walking along the river until the path winds up at a road where a left leads down the hill and into Egton Bridge.

### EGTON BRIDGE          MAP 87, p241
A strong competitor for the accolade of prettiest village on the Coast to Coast, Egton Bridge is a delight, a hamlet of grand houses surrounding an uninhabited island on the Esk. Everything about the place is charming, from the bridge itself – a 1990s'

copy of the original 18th-century structure washed away in a flood in 1930 – to the stepping stones that lead across to the island and the mature trees that fringe the settlement. The Catholic **St Hedda's Church**, too, is incredibly grand given the tiny size of

**Egton Bridge**. On the exterior are a series of friezes while inside, behind glass to the right of the altar, are the relics of Nicholas Postgate, a local Catholic priest and martyr hung, drawn and quartered for continuing to practise his faith in 1679. See box below for details about St Hedda himself.

There are public **toilets** and a **telephone** in the village centre.

### Where to stay and eat

It would be a surprise indeed if somewhere like Egton Bridge didn't have decent accommodation, and the village doesn't disappoint. *The Horseshoe Hotel* (☎ 01947 895245, 🖥 www.egtonbridgehotel.co.uk; 4D/2T; all en suite; 🛒; 🐾; WI-FI; Ⓛ), right on the walk at the start of the village, fulfils every expectation of a country inn, with an expansive beer garden, a lavish array of local ales and a snug interior. Main courses are around £10 (hot baguettes cost £5-7) and are served daily noon-2pm & 6-9pm. B&B costs from £37.50pp (sgl occ £65).

A little way to the west of the village, the four-star *Broom House* (Map 86, p238; ☎ 01947 895279, 🖥 www.broom-house .co.uk; 2S/1T/5D/1Tr; all en suite; 🛒; WI-FI; Ⓛ £6.95; Feb-Oct) is a 19th-century farmhouse described by one reader as more of a country house hotel with a touch of class. They charge £41.50-70pp (sgl £65) for B&B and have a bistro, *White's Restaurant* (Mar-Oct Tue-Sat 6-9pm, Sun lunch noon to about 4pm), which is open to non-residents; advance booking preferred.

*The Postgate Inn* (☎ 01947 895241, 🖥 www.postgateinn.com; 1D/1D or T/1Qd; all en suite; 🛒; 🐾; WI-FI; Ⓛ) is another top choice with **food** served daily (light lunches daily noon-2.30pm, meals 6.30-9pm), and **B&B** from £42.50pp, £25-30pp for four/three in the quad. To get there, head up the hill from the church past the point where the Coast to Coast path turns down the track.

On Broom House Lane by the banks of the Esk is *The Old Mill* (☎ 01947 895351; 🖥 theoldmillegtonbridge@live.co .uk; 1D or T en suite, 1D or T private facilities; 🛒; Ⓛ). B&B is from £37.50pp (sgl occ £64).

### Transport                (see also pp52-5)

Egton Bridge is on the **railway** line between Whitby and Middlesbrough. In addition, M&D's **bus** No 99 travels from Whitby up the Esk Valley to Glaisdale and Lealholm.

---

❏ **St Hedda**

The seventh-century British saint, Hedda, crops up a few times on the Coast to Coast walk, even though he is these days more closely associated with Winchester, Hampshire. He began his episcopal career at Whitby Abbey (whose striking remains you'll have spied from Glaisdale Moor), where he was educated and rose to become abbot.

His big break came in 676AD when he was consecrated as the Bishop of Wessex by St Theodore of Tarsus, at that time the Archbishop of Canterbury. He ruled over the diocese for thirty years, during which time he moved the see from Dorchester to Winchester and became chief advisor to King Ina. Described by the Venerable Bede as 'a good and just man, who in carrying out his duties was guided rather by an inborn love of virtue than by what he had read in books', he died in 705AD and is buried at Winchester Cathedral.

---

The next mile or so from Egton Bridge to Grosmont takes you past the elegant **Egton Manor** along an old toll road (the original toll charges are still written on a board hanging from **Toll Cottage**, halfway along). It's an easy walk now, taking you under the railway and along the Esk, past Priory Farm (see p242), and into Grosmont.

EGTON BRIDGE

TO BROOM HOUSE

Postgate Inn

Old Mill

STATION

SCHOOL

ST HEDDA'S CHURCH

EGTON MANOR

SEWAGE WORKS

RIVER ESK

Horseshoe Hotel

86

TURN RIGHT DOWN EGTON ESTATES DRIVEWAY. SIGNPOSTED GROSMONT 1½ MILES'

UNDER THE RAILWAY

TOLL COTTAGE

FARMHOUSE

MAP 87

Priory Farm Camping

REJTON ROAD

GROSMONT

SEE MAP

p243

BENCH

CRICKET PITCH

38

88

0    ¼ mile
0    500m
APPROX SCALE

EGTON BRIDGE    30 MINS    GROSMONT

## GROSMONT      MAP 87, p241

After the quaint, picture-perfect settlements of the preceding few miles, Grosmont emerges as a grittier and more distinctive sibling. Indeed literally so as from the rail crossing in the village centre, a row of soot-stained terraces claw their way up the hill, caked by the acrid fumes that once belched from three ironstone smelting furnaces 150 years ago. These days this less glamorous heritage is all but forgotten as tourists and steam rail enthusiasts alike flock to ride the locomotives of the **North York Moors Railway**. Featured as the 'Hogwarts Express' in the original *Harry Potter* movie, it's definitely worth hanging about to see at least one loco in motion before leaving Grosmont, if not timing your arrival to take a return ride to Pickering or Whitby. By now you deserve to take the weight off your feet; for full details see 'Transport' opposite.

While you're waiting, follow the alleyway leading through a long train tunnel to the **sidings and loco sheds** to gain an insight into what it takes to keep these engines on track. The tunnel is thought to be the oldest passenger train tunnel in the world, hewn out around 1829 to serve a horse-drawn railway designed by no less than George Stephenson. Regarded as the 'Father of Railways', it was Stephenson who foresaw a future in a network of inter-linked rail lines along which engines powered by steam would go on to span and help consolidate the riches of the British Empire. During the tunnel excavations viable quantities of iron ore were unearthed, leading to the ironstone mining boom along the Esk Valley.

There's a **church**, too, with a boulder of Shap granite outside the west door, deposited here by a glacier which lost its way back in the Ice Age.

The settlement, originally known as 'Tunnel', went on to gain the name Grosmont and is today a one-street village where both modern and heritage rail lines intersect, and that has all of the essentials a weary trekker needs: a **store**, **pub** (the Station Tavern, of course!), several **tea-rooms** and a few B&Bs.

The **Co-op** (Mon-Fri 7.30am-5pm. Sat 8am-5.30pm, Sun 9am-5.30pm) is one of the oldest community-run village shops in the country. It's also home to the **post office** (Mon-Fri 9am-noon). As well as the post office, the Station Tavern does **cashback**.

### Where to stay and eat

A little before the village, **campers** stop at *Priory Farm* (Map 87, p241; ☎ 01947 895324, 💻 prioryfarmwhitby.wordpress .com) offering basic facilities for just £4pp including a small room alongside the farmhouse with a toilet, sink and a kettle.

B&B is now on offer above the *Geall Gallery* (☎ 01947 895007, 💻 www.chris geall.com; 2D/1T en suite; WI-FI) on Front St. The comfortable rooms (from £38pp) are decorated with atmospheric artwork from the gallery downstairs. The Art Café, also downstairs, is an excellent place to eat.

Just over the rails *Linten House* (☎ 01947 895386; 1D or T with private bathroom; 🐾; WI-FI; Apr-Oct) offers plain B&B accommodation in an old terrace house from £32.50pp (sgl occ £40).

Over the road is *The Station Tavern* (☎ 01947 895060, 💻 www.stationtavern-grosmont.co.uk; 1S/1D/1T or Tr; all with private facilities; 🐾; 🐾£10; WI-FI; 🄻 £variable) which serves **pub grub** (daily Easter to late Oct noon-3pm & 6.30-8.45pm, Nov to Easter weekends noon-3pm, daily 6.30-8.45pm) and has become something of a venue for spontaneous Coast to Coast banquets before people go their separate ways at Robin Hood's Bay. B&B costs £37.50-42.50pp (sgl from £43).

Just up the hill and left down Office Row, *Lisvane* (☎ 01947 895969, 💻 www .lisvane.me.uk; 1S/1T shared facilities; 1D or T en suite; WI-FI; 🐾; Mar-Oct) does B&B from £39pp.

Further on, *Grosmont House* (☎ 01947 895539, 💻 www.grosmonthouse.co .uk; 7D en suite/1T/1Tr or Qd; shared bathroom; 🐾; WI-FI; 🄻 about £5) is a delightfully quirky old place whose gardens also have wonderful views down over the railway. The two double rooms on the top floor are particularly good for a group of four people. Rates are from £35pp (sgl occ £40).

**Dinner** (daily around 7pm) is available if you pre-book (even if you're not staying there); the fresh lobster salad is said to be divine. One reader pointed out that Grosmont House 'needs a bit of a declutter' and another remarked that the 'shower wasn't very modern'. But the general consensus of opinion seems to be that this is a grand old place full of character run by a charming and hospitable couple.

Grosmont boasts several excellent tearooms. Long-running *Hazelwood House* (☎ 01947 895292; daily Easter to Oct 10.30am-5pm) is on the right before the rail crossing. Nearby is the *Art Café & Geall Gallery* (see above; daily Apr-Nov 11am-4pm, Dec-Mar Thur-Sun 11am-4pm, may also open in the evenings in summer; WI-FI) with an interesting menu (eg harissa salmon trout tagine) in addition to teatime favourites. The *Old School Coffee Shop* (☎ 01947 895754, 🖥 www.grosmontcoffee shop.co.uk; daily Easter to Oct 10.30am-4.30pm but closed some Fridays; 🐾; WI-FI) was formerly the village primary school and has a great view of the steam railway. They welcome walkers, don't mind muddy boots and even have shower facilities as well as a flask-filling service. There's also *Signals Tea Room*, on the railway platform.

**Transport**                    **(see also pp52-5)**
North York Moors Railway's **steam train** (☎ 01751 472508, 🖥 www.nymr.co.uk) to Pickering (70 mins), or Whitby (25 mins)

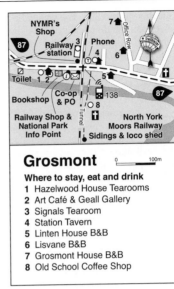

**Where to stay, eat and drink**
1  Hazelwood House Tearooms
2  Art Café & Geall Gallery
3  Signals Tearoom
4  Station Tavern
5  Linten House B&B
6  Lisvane B&B
7  Grosmont House B&B
8  Old School Coffee Shop

leaves Grosmont between four and eight times a day depending on the season. Some of the trains are drawn by a diesel engine rather than a steam engine, so if you want that authentic chuff-chuff sound check the timetable or give them a call. Northern Rail's **trains** go to Whitby (20 mins) and to Middlesbrough (70 mins).

M&D's **Bus** No 99 also travels to Whitby (15 mins) from the railway station.

## STAGE 13: GROSMONT TO ROBIN HOOD'S BAY        MAPS 87-95

### Introduction

Time to saddle up for the last stage, but don't be fooled into thinking this is a mere formality as the savage climb out of Grosmont will soon demonstrate. It's a long stretch totalling **15½ miles (25km, 6hrs)** with enough ups and downs, lefts and rights and ins and outs to ensure that you arrive in Robin Hood's Bay suitably dishevelled. The scenery is largely similar to what's gone before: desolate moorland punctuated with short road stages and a superior echo of the first leg, a grand finale along the sea cliffs prior to the final descent to the Bay. The most pleasant surprise, especially on a hot day, is the transit of Little Beck Wood, a narrow belt of the most heavenly woodland in north Yorkshire.

## The route

First, there's that backbreaking 700ft (230m) climb up to **Sleights Moor**, part of the intriguingly named Eskdaleside Cum Ugglebarnby, which is how you may feel if you missed breakfast. With views north-east to the well-ventilated ruins of **Whitby Abbey** or back down into misty Eskdale, you pass the **High Bride Stones** – five ancient standing monoliths – to the right of the road. (Incidentally, the confusing jumble of the Low Bride Stones stands just below them on a terrace, to your right as you passed over the cattle grid.)

Opposite a car park turn left onto a path (Map 88, WPT 139) and cut a corner down to the A169 where you turn left again for a few hundred metres until a Coast to Coast sign heralds the path dropping down through more heather to Littlebeck.

## LITTLEBECK                    MAP 89, p246

Littlebeck is another tiny hamlet with a lengthy past, it's hard to imagine today's picturesque rural idyll was actually once a centre of alum-mining in the 17th to 19th centuries. Alum, by the way, is used in dyeing as well as tanning leather. A hundred tons of shale would be produced in order to extract just one ton of alum, so it seems remarkable the surrounding land appears so unscarred.

The village has one other minor claim to fame as the home of master woodcarver Thomas Whittaker who died in 1991 (his house, now called **Woodcarver's Cottage**, is on the bend above the **Old Mill**). Whittaker exclusively used English oak and would 'sign' every piece of his furniture with a gnome; in German folklore the oak tree's guardian. Above the cottage is **Kelp House**, where kelp, used in the processing of alum, was stored.

Fifteen minutes south of the village and half a mile from the path, staying at *Intake Farm* (☎ 01947 810273, 💻 intakefarm.com; 2D/1T/1Tr; one en suite, others private/shared facilities; 🛏; 🐾; WI-FI; Ⓛ) is regularly and warmly recommended by readers who want to spin out the last day into an easy 12-miler. **B&B** costs £27.50-32.50pp (sgl occ £35, £25pp for three in the triple) – and £5 to **camp**. It's a way to the nearest pub but they'll happily lay on an evening meal (£15, three courses, book in advance). Whilst you can reach the farm from the centre of the village, it's quicker to join the track to the right (south) of the Coast to Coast path heading off the A169 via both High Quebec Farm and Low Quebec Farm.

Pretty as Littlebeck is, it's nothing when compared to the beauty that awaits in **Little Beck Wood**. This really is a stunning 65 acres of woodland, filled with oak trees, deer, badgers, foxes and birdlife galore. There are also a couple of man-made features to see on the way including the mysterious **Hermitage** (Map 89), a boulder hollowed out to form a small cave. Above the entrance is etched the year '1790'. More delights await as the path from the Hermitage leads you down to **Falling Foss** (Map 90), a 20m-high waterfall alongside the former ruins of **Midge Hall**, now enterprisingly converted into the *Falling Foss Tea Garden* (☎ 07723 477929, 💻 www.fallingfossteagarden.co.uk; Apr-Sept daily 10.30am-5pm, closed Oct-Mar), a great place for a coffee and cake, an ice cream or a light lunch before you leave the woods for the final hike to the sea. (*cont'd on p248*)

45 MINS FROM GROSMONT (MAP 87) →

CAR PARK

Trailblazer

87

TURN RIGHT ONTO
ROAD AS MAIN ROAD
TURNS LEFT

BENCHES

TO LOW
FAIRHEAD

STILL
STEEP

GLIMPSES OF
WHITBY ABBEY
TO THE NORTH

VERY STEEP
ROAD CLIMB FOR
OVER A MILE. NO
WAY TO START THE
LAST STAGE!

CATTLE
GRID

BENCH

LOW BRIDE
STONES
NOT VISIBLE
FROM ROAD

DISUSED
QUARRIES

FOLLOW THE
ROAD TO
WAYPOINT 139

HIGH BRIDE
STONES

SLEIGHTS MOOR

MAP 88

DISUSED CAR PARK

LEAVE ROAD ON
NARROW FOOT
PATH LEFT

SIGNPOST:
'LITTLEBECK
2 MILES'

139

TO A169

89

¼ mile

500m

APPROX SCALE

0

0

ROUTE GUIDE AND MAPS

40 MINS FROM CAR PARK (MAP 88) →  LITTLEBECK  40 MINS TO FALLING FOSS (MAP 90)

MAP 89

LITTLEBECK

WOODCARVER'S COTTAGE

KELP HOUSE

VILLAGE HALL

OVER TWO TRIBUTARIES

CAVE – OLD ALUM WORKS – GO OVER IT TO THE RIGHT

THROUGH GAP IN WALL

A FEN STEPS

HERMITAGE (CAVE)

90

LITTLE BECK WOOD

IGNORE RED ARROW SIGNS

AT HERMITAGE TAKE UPPER (LEFT-HAND) ROUTE. THEN TAKE RIGHT PATH WALKING PAST WALLS OF (UNSEEN) NEWTON HOUSE AND DOWN

WRONG WAY!

BENCH

OLD MILL

FOOTBRIDGE

WELL CLOSE

VIEW NORTH TO WHITBY ABBEY

JOIN MAIN LANE DOWN TO VILLAGE

FOOTPATH TO RIGHT

JOIN TRACK

Intake Farm

LOW QUEBEC FARM

UNDER ELECTRICITY CABLES

¼ mile
APPROX SCALE    500m
0          0

HIGH QUEBEC FARM

THE PATH JOINS THE ROAD HERE. TURN LEFT AND CONTINUE ON MAIN ROAD UNTIL YOU COME TO ANOTHER C2C SIGN POINTING ACROSS THE ROAD

TO SLEIGHTS, 2 MILES/3KM

A169

GATES

88

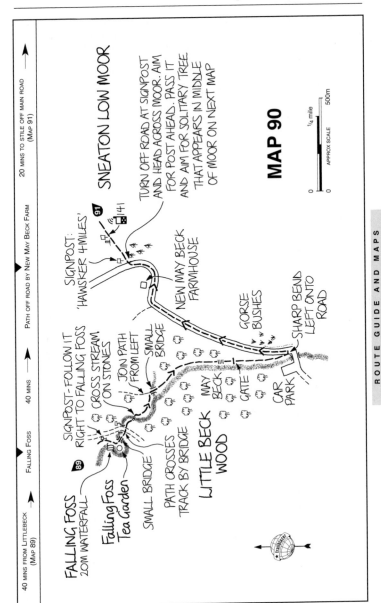

40 MINS FROM LITTLEBECK (MAP 89) →    FALLING FOSS    ◄    ← 40 MINS →    PATH OFF ROAD BY NEW MAY BECK FARM    ►    20 MINS TO STILE OFF MAIN ROAD (MAP 91) →

SNEATON LOW MOOR

TURN OFF ROAD AT SIGNPOST AND HEAD ACROSS MOOR. AIM FOR POST AHEAD. PASS IT AND AIM FOR SOLITARY TREE THAT APPEARS IN MIDDLE OF MOOR ON NEXT MAP

SIGNPOST: 'HAWSKER 4 MILES'

91

141

NEW MAY BECK FARMHOUSE

GORSE BUSHES

SHARP BEND LEFT ONTO ROAD

SIGNPOST - FOLLOW IT RIGHT TO FALLING FOSS

CROSS STREAM ON STONES

JOIN PATH FROM LEFT

SMALL BRIDGE

MAY BECK

GATE

CAR PARK

LITTLE BECK WOOD

FALLING FOSS 20M WATERFALL

89

Falling Foss Tea Garden

SMALL BRIDGE

PATH CROSSES TRACK BY BRIDGE

MAP 90

0   ¼ mile
0   APPROX SCALE   500m

(*cont'd from p244*). Suitably refreshed, head along **May Beck** to the car park at the southern extremity of the wood. Here you turn back north and walk along the road, looking back over the valley you've just walked through and the moors beyond. A traverse of two other moors, Sneaton Low Moor and the innocuously named Graystone Hills, follows; the rather lean waymarks and confusing paths across Graystone Hills to Normanby Hill Top (north of the B1416) can require a good sense of direction or some luck, even in bright sunshine; see box p93.

ROAD JUNCTION      30 MINS TO HIGH HAWSKER (MAP 93) ⟶

LOW HAWSKER

93

FIRST 'ROBIN HOOD'S BAY' SIGN - 3½ MILES (BY ROAD)

BACK LANE

MITTEN HILL FARM

RIGHT AT JUNCTION

**MAP 92**

Rigg Farm

JOIN ROAD

INITIALLY NO CLEAR PATH ON ROUGH PASTURE. HEAD NORTH THEN CURVE WEST

NOW IN MUDDY/STONY DITCH BETWEEN HEDGES

GORSE ⟶

POST

147

0      ¼ mile
0      APPROX SCALE      500m

A171

ALTERNATIVE TRAIL

146

VERY BOGGY

HILL TOP

RAISED BOARD-WALK OVER A MIRE

★ trailblazer

145

91

ROAD JUNCTION

55 MINS FROM STILE OFF MAIN ROAD (MAP 91) ⟶

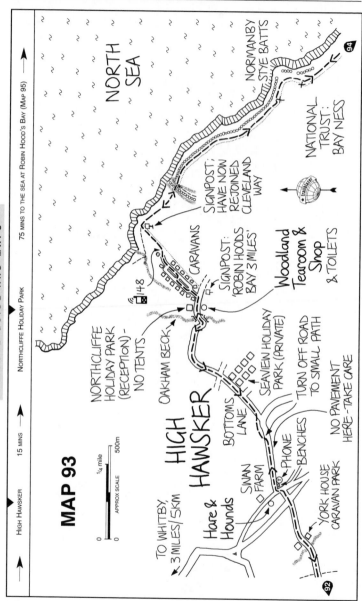

← High Hawkser  15 MINS →  Northcliffe Holiday Park  75 MINS TO THE SEA AT ROBIN HOOD'S BAY (MAP 95) →

MAP 93

¼ mile

500m

0

0

APPROX SCALE

TO WHITBY; 3 MILES/5KM

Hare & Hounds

HIGH HAWKSER

Swan Farm

PHONE

BENCHES

NO PAVEMENT HERE – TAKE CARE

YORK HOUSE CARAVAN PARK

BOTTOMS LANE

OAKHAM BECK

NORTHCLIFFE HOLIDAY PARK (RECEPTION) – NO TENTS

SEAVIEW HOLIDAY PARK (PRIVATE)

TURN OFF ROAD TO SMALL PATH

CARAVANS

SIGNPOST: 'ROBIN HOODS BAY 3 MILES'

Woodland Tearoom & Shop & TOILETS

SIGNPOST; HAVE NOW REJOINED CLEVELAND WAY

NORMANBY STYE BATTS

NATIONAL TRUST: BAY NESS

NORTH SEA

the trailmaster

You soon emerge on a road and should turn left here if planning to camp at Rigg Farm (see below). If not, continue down the road where before long you will no doubt be thrilled to spot the first road sign to Robin Hood's Bay indicating it's only '3½ miles' by road. But for you, my friend, the walk is not over; turn right to follow Back Lane past York House Caravan Park and into the village of **High Hawsker** (Map 93) on the A171 Whitby road.

### HIGH HAWSKER          MAP 93

In the village the *Hare & Hounds* (☎ 01947 880453, 🖳 www.hareandhound shawsker.co.uk; Mon-Thur noon-3pm & 5-9pm, Fri-Sun noon-9pm) serves hot meals as well as sandwiches. You'll have passed York House Caravan Park on the way there, a large complex with expensive camping and more regulations than the Highway Code. If you're set on **camping**, the smaller

*Rigg Farm Caravan Park* (Map 92; ☎ 01947 880430, 🖳 www.riggfarmcaravan park.co.uk; 🐾; Mar-Oct), a couple of minutes' walk west from where you rejoined the road, charges £12 per pitch to camp. There's limited space so phone in advance. The site has toilet/shower facilities but no shop.

Arriva's **bus** No 93 (daily) calls here; see pp52-5 for details.

ROUTE GUIDE AND MAPS

75 MINS FROM NORTHCLIFFE HOLIDAY PARK (MAP 93) TO THE SEA AT ROBIN HOOD'S BAY (MAP 95)

★ trailblazer

**MAP 94**

0       ¼ mile
0  APPROX SCALE  500m

GOOD PLACE TO WATCH SEABIRDS ON CLIFFS

LOOKOUT HUT

ROCKET POST FIELD

GATES IN & OUT OF FIELD TO AVOID ERODED SECTION OF PATH

BENCH BY INFORMATION BOARD

ROCKET POST

MOUNT PLEASANT NORTH ROAD

STATION ROAD

WHITBY ROAD

GATE

HOUSES BY PATH

NORTH SEA

From Hawsker, the remains of your eastward marathon takes you down past sprawling caravan parks and **Woodland Tearoom and Shop** (Map 93; Mon-Thur 9am-2pm, Fri 9am-2pm & 5-10pm-ish, Sat 9am-10pm-ish, Sun 9am-4pm), where you can get a last-minute snack for the final stretch.

And so you arrive at the **North Sea** to rejoin the Cleveland Way and stride weary but unbeaten along the blustery clifftops towards Robin Hood's Bay. Though the tiny beach at Robin Hood's Bay appears half an hour before you actually set foot on it, the village itself, tucked away by the headland, is concealed until the very last moment. But eventually, having passed a coastguard station and **Rocket Post Field** (Map 94) from which coastguards used to practise aiming their rescue rockets, you join Mount Pleasant North Rd at the top end of Robin Hood's Bay. Take a left at the end of the road and at the roundabout follow either the cliff path or the steep street down, down, down to the bay.

You arrive at the slipway, or Dock as it's known, and all that remains is to liberate that pebble you've carried from St Bees beach and then toast your fine achievement in Wainwright's Bar at Bay Hotel (see p254 for opening hours), not forgetting to sign their book.

And that's it. Your Coast to Coast walk is over. Congratulations: you've walked the width of England, quite probably some 200 miles, which is certainly something to be pleased about. But not quite as satisfying as knowing there's no more walking on the agenda for a while.

## ROBIN HOOD'S BAY    MAP 95, p255

Robin Hood's Bay is the perfect place to finish: a quaint, cosy little fishing village that in high summer becomes a busy seaside resort that is entirely in keeping with the picturesque theme of the walk. Though fishing has declined since its heyday in the 19th century, there's been a revival thanks to its crab grounds, said to be amongst the best in the north.

The old town huddles around the Dock, row after row of terraced, stone cottages arranged haphazardly uphill with numerous twisting interconnecting alleyways and paths to explore. Within them are a number of pubs and tearooms where you can celebrate. There are also gift, souvenir and antique shops aplenty, as well as certificates (see Bay Hotel, p254) for newly ennobled Coast to Coasters. If that's not enough to commemorate your achievement you could get a personalised plaque (from £45) from **Cromwells** (🖥 www.cromwells plaques.com), opposite the Bay Hotel.

The **Old Coastguard Station National Trust Visitor Centre** (☎ 01947 885900; Easter-Sep daily 10am-5pm, Oct-Easter weekends only 11am-4pm) sits right by the end of the trail and has some great displays including a mini wind machine and an aquarium of marine life. There's also a small **museum** (June & Sep Sun only noon-4pm, July-Aug Sun-Fri noon-4pm).

### Services

The official tourist information **website** (🖥 www.robin-hoods-bay.co.uk) has plenty of useful information, including a comprehensive list of **accommodation**. The **post office and general store** (Mon-Fri 9am-5.30pm, Sat 9am-12.30pm) offers **cashback**. There's another **general shop** in the lower town. If you've any aches and pains after the walk visit **Treat Therapy** (🖥 www.treattherapy.co.uk) for their Coast to Coast Massage (£20).

### Where to stay

Robin Hood's Bay is divided into Upper Bay, the development dating from the Victorian era at the top of the hill, and the quainter and more congested 17th-century Lower Bay or 'Old Town' down by the sea, where there are fewer accommodation options and rooms are less spacious. Not since Grasmere have you paused to stay in such a busy tourist 'honeypot', and as most Coasters end their walk on a Thursday or Friday, it's worth knowing that rooms at weekends and in holiday periods may be hard to come by and some places may even insist on a **minimum of two nights stay** for advance bookings.

There are two **campsites** and both can be pretty crowded in summer with families, dogs and caravans. The first, *Middlewood Farm Holiday Park* (☎ 01947 880414, 🖥 www.middlewoodfarm.com; ☞; 🐾£2; Easter-Oct) is a smart and efficient operation with a laundry room and, according to some, the finest ablutions block north of the 52nd parallel. Camping costs from £8pp; showers and toilets are free but for £1 you can even take a bath. They are very 'pro' Coast to Coasters and will always endeavour to accommodate campers arriving on foot even at busy times, but prefer 24 hours warning of your arrival if possible. To get there, from the end of the walk by the Bay Hotel head up Albion Rd past the chippy for 10 minutes along the path.

High on a hill above the town, you may want to check into the no less popular *Hooks House Farm* (☎ 01947 880283, 🖥 www.hookshousefarm.co.uk; 🐾on a lead; Mar-Oct) before walking the last mile or two down to the sea as the walk back can be quite an effort. **Camping** here costs £7-9pp including showers and use of kitchen.

*YHA Boggle Hole* (☎ 0845 371 9504, 🖥 www.yha.org.uk/hostel/boggle-hole; 85 beds, 1xsingle, 2-/4-/6-/8-/10-bed rooms; beds £17-18.50, 4-bed rooms £55-84; WI-FI; Ⓛ £5.50; Mar-Oct daily, Nov-Feb weekends only) is a former corn mill located in a ravine about a mile south of the village and reachable either along the shore or the inland road which passes Middlewood Farm Holiday Park. The hostel serves meals and has a bar. Credit cards are accepted, there is internet access (£1/20 mins) and a drying room.

Back in town there are nearly three dozen hotels, guesthouses and B&Bs to choose from; the official town website mentioned above has a fuller list. Accommodation is most prolific in Upper Bay, the top of the village, where

*Thackwood* (☎ 01947 880858, 🖥 www.thackwood.com; 2D/1T, all en suite; ☞; WI-FI; Ⓛ £variable) is the first B&B you spot as the trail comes into town. B&B is from £35pp (sgl occ £50).

This is followed by *Northcliff* (☎ 01947 880481, 🖥 www.north-cliff.co.uk; 2D/1T; all en suite; WI-FI) a Victorian villa also on Mount Pleasant North Rd. B&B rates are from £32.50pp (sgl occ £40-65).

On the same street is *Manning Tree* (☎ 01947 881042, 🖥 www.manningtreebnb.co.uk; 2D/1T; all en suite) offering a similar standard of accommodation; B&B costs from £32.50pp (sgl occ £40).

On Mount Pleasant Rd there's more of the same with the pick of the bunch including *Lee-Side* (☎ 01947 881143, 🖥 leeside.rhbay.co.uk; 2D/1T as well as a suite with 1D/1T; all with private facilities; ☞; WI-FI) with B&B starting at £40pp (sgl occ £50), and *Streonshalh* (☎ 01947 881065, 🖥 www.streonshalh.co.uk; 2S/2D/2D or T; all en suite; WI-FI), costing £37.50-40pp for B&B (sgl £43). Credit cards are accepted.

On Station Rd, at the junction with Whitby Rd, is *The Grosvenor Hotel* (☎ 01947 880320, 🖥 www.thegrosvenor.info; 6D/1T/3Tr; all en suite; ☞; 🐾; WI-FI) with B&B from £35pp (sgl occ £50, three in triple £85); while still on Station Rd, *The Villa* (☎ 01947 881043, 🖥 www.thevillarhb.co.uk; 2D/2D or T, all en suite; ☞; WI-FI) is another Victorian property. They have retained the period features such as the cast-iron fireplaces and the servant bells. B&B rates are from £37.50pp (sgl occ £50). All dietary requirements, coeliac in particular, catered for by these friendly people.

Below, a further string of B&Bs on Station Rd leads down towards the old town. They're all pretty similar. Readers have recommended the rooms – and the food – at *The Wayfarer* (☎ 01947 880240, 🖥 www.wayfarerbistro.co.uk; 4D/1D or T; all en suite; WI-FI; Feb-Dec). B&B costs £35-43pp (sgl occ £45-50).

Opposite this is the purpose-built *Glen-Lyn* (☎ 01947 880391, 🖥 www.glenyn.co.uk; 3D/1Tr; all en suite; WI-FI) with B&B from £37.50pp (sgl occ £75).

The elegant *West Royd* (☎ 01947 880678, 🖥 www.westroyd.co.uk; 2D/1Tr;

all en suite; ✆; WI-FI) comes next, built in 1897 and maintaining its Victorian charm. Rates start at £75pp (sgl occ £50).

This is followed by: *Devon House* (☎ 01947 880062, ☐ www.devonhouserhb.co .uk; 1S/3D; all en suite; ✆; WI-FI) with B&B from £37.50pp (sgl occ £50); *Birtley House* (☎ 01947 880566, ☐ www.birtley housebedandbreakfast.co.uk; 3D/1T/1Tr, all with private facilities; ✆; WI-FI) charging £32.50-40pp (sgl occ £45) and *Lynnfield* (☎ 01947 881253, ☐ www.lynn fieldbedandbreakfast.co.uk; 3D/1T; en suite; ✆; WI-FI), said to be the first house in Upper Bay to offer B&B way back in 1955, but totally renovated in 2012. B&B in the bright rooms is from £35pp.

Alongside these *The Victoria Hotel* (☎ 01947 880205, ☐ www.victoriarhb.com; 10D/2D or T; all en suite; ✆; WI-FI) charges £40-60pp (sgl occ from £60).

Take the alleyway next to The Victoria and it leads onto a road with great views down to the old town. This is where you'll find *Raven House* (☎ 01947 880444, ☐ ravenhouse.rhbay.co.uk; 1S/3D/1Tr; all en suite; WI-FI), which more than one reader has recommended. Edwardian rather than Victorian, most of the rooms enjoy great panoramas. B&B starts at £35-37.50pp (sgl/sgl occ from £40).

In the **old town**, most of the accommodation has been given over to self-catering holiday apartments for those intending to stay for a week or more, such as *Ingleby House* (☎ 01947 880887, ☐ www.ingleby houseinrobinhoodsbay.com; 1D en suite; WI-FI) although it does also have a room available for one-night stays for £27.50-32.50pp (sgl occ £45). Tea, coffee, milk and cereal are provided in the room. They also have an en suite room with basic cooking facilities that could accommodate two singles; contact them for details. There's a similar arrangement at *The Locker* (☎ 07768 813135, ☐ www.stayatthebay.co.uk, 1D en suite) where one-night stays are possible from Mon-Thur from £35pp, continental breakfast is an extra £15. The room is compact but it does have a little garden.

Of the B&Bs, many request a minimum stay of two nights. If you can't stay that long, try the *The Boathouse* (☎ 01947 880099, ☐ boathouserhb.co.uk; 2D/2T/ 1Tr, studio and apartment both with 1D; all en suite; WI-FI). Right in the centre of the action, B&B is from £40pp (sgl occ £65). Most rooms can be booked for a single-night stay other than over bank holiday weekends.

Close to the Dock, *Bramblewick* (☎ 01947 880187, evenings ☎ 01947 881186, ☐ www.bramblewick.org; 4D; all en suite), 2 King St, retains the feel of its 17th-century origins with B&B from £40pp (sgl occ £60); and finally, as close to the walk's end as the tides will allow, *Bay Hotel* (☎ 01947 880278, ☐ www.bayhotel.info; 3D all with private facilities; ✆; WI-FI; 🐾) where B&B is £35-42.50pp (sgl occ £70-85).

## Where to eat and drink

It has to be said that Robin Hood's Bay is not the easiest place to celebrate your monumental achievement with fine dining. The cuisine here seems strictly seaside traditional: pubs, takeaways and bucket 'n' spade snackeries, but there are a few notable exceptions.

There are plenty of good tea rooms to relax in should you arrive early and need to spin down. *Swell* (☐ www.swellcafe.co.uk; 10am-3.30pm, to 4 or 5pm in summer), in the heart of the old-town alleyways, is the smartest place. Formerly a Wesleyan chapel it's now also a wedding venue. The *Old Bakery Tearoom* is a far more traditional place. 'You won't find a better cuppa anywhere', said one satisfied customer as he savoured his pot of Yorkshire tea (£1.40). Up near the top of the hill, *Candy's Café* has a flagstone terrace where you can devour a big breakfast, ice-cream or cake whilst admiring the great sea view.

A visit to the *Bay Hotel* (see Where to stay; food served daily noon-2pm & 6.30-9pm, 2.30-5pm soup & sandwiches) is almost obligatory. The main **bar** is upstairs (daily 11am-midnight) and in peak periods open the so-called **Wainwright's Bar** downstairs. The pub sells various mementos of the walk including certificates (£2.50); don't forget to sign their book to record your success (the log book will be in the upstairs bar if Wainwright's Bar is closed).

In the old town the best place to eat is *Smugglers Bistro* (see The Boathouse, opp;

ROUTE GUIDE AND MAPS

To Hooks House Farm
(for camping)

Mount Pleasant North Rd

94

Mount Pleasant Rd

**Where to stay**
1 Thackwood B&B
2 Northcliff B&B
3 Manning Tree B&B
4 Grosvenor Hotel
5 Lee-Side B&B
6 Streonshalh B&B
7 The Villa B&B
8 Glen-Lyn B&B
9 The Wayfarer B&B &
  Bistro
10 West Royd
11 Devon House
12 Birtley House
13 Lynnfield
14 Raven House
15 Victoria Hotel & Bay &
   Sea View Restaurant
16 Ingleby House B&B
17 The Bay Hotel &
   Wainwright's Bar
18 Bramblewick
19 Boathouse &
   Smugglers Bistro

Post Office
& shop

Bus
stop

Thorpe Lane

CP

Phone
Toilets

Candy's
Café

75 MINS FROM NORTHCLIFFE HOLIDAY PARK (MAP 93)

ROUTE GUIDE AND MAPS

0    50    100m

trailblazer

North
Sea

Shop

Old
Bakery
Tearoom

Swell

Treat Therapy

Museum

The
Dolphin

THE SEA AT ROBIN HOOD'S BAY

# Robin
# Hood's
# Bay
# MAP 95

Tysons
Steps

18    16

19    17

Mariondale fish & chips

THE
END    149

Toilets & phone
Cromwells

Old Coastguard
Visitor Centre

To Middlewood Farm
(camping), 5-10 mins

The
Locker

To YHA Boggle Hole,
10-15 mins on clifftop path

daily 5pm; booking advised). The menu includes lots of seafood dishes from £12.95.

The best place to eat at the top of town – and some reckon this to be the best place to eat in the whole area – is *The Wayfarer Bistro* (see p253; Feb-Oct Tue-Sun from 6pm; Nov-Dec Thur-Sun from 6pm) features grills and seafood; booking advised. Main courses cost £12-18.

Also in the higher part of town, Victoria Hotel's (see Where to stay) *Bay & Sea View Restaurant* is popular, as is *The Grosvenor Hotel* (see Where to stay, food served Apr-Oct daily noon-9pm, Nov-Mar Mon-Fri 6-9pm, Sat & Sun noon-9pm) which serves curries, steaks and burgers for £6.50-12.95. There's live music on Tue and most Sat nights, quiz night on Sunday.

Down in the old town, *Bramblewick* (see Where to stay; café from 9.30am; restaurant school summer holidays Wed-Sat 6-9pm; rest of year Fri & Sat only) serves a home-made prawn and crab cocktail (£7.95) and a variety of main courses for around £11-17. During the day their café menu includes all-day breakfast. Further up King St *The Dolphin* (food served noon-2pm & 6.30-9pm) serves local fish dishes, as well as boasting a good range of real ales and live music sessions on Fridays and Mondays.

Fish and chips under a mashed pea sludge never did Alfred Wainwright any harm, so the like-minded will queue expectantly at Mariondale Fisheries' **chippy** (daily noon-8pm) up an alleyway by the Boathouse. This is certainly one of the best chippies in the area.

## Transport                (see also pp52-5)

Arriva's **bus** No 93 runs daily, once an hour, north to Whitby (20 mins) and on to Middlesbrough (90 mins) for train connections to Darlington – or heads south to Scarborough (40 mins), the nearest place from where you can get a train to York. The bus stop is on Thorpe Lane, just north of the main car park.

For a **taxi**, call Bay Private Hire on ☎ 01947 880603.

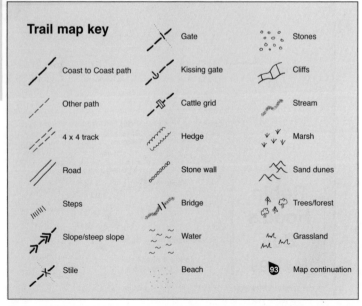

**Trail map key**

| Symbol | | Symbol | | Symbol | |
|---|---|---|---|---|---|
| | Coast to Coast path | | Gate | | Stones |
| | Other path | | Kissing gate | | Cliffs |
| | 4 x 4 track | | Cattle grid | | Stream |
| | Road | | Hedge | | Marsh |
| | Steps | | Stone wall | | Sand dunes |
| | Slope/steep slope | | Bridge | | Trees/forest |
| | Stile | | Water | | Grassland |
| | | | Beach | 93 | Map continuation |

# APPENDIX A – TAKING A DOG

## COAST TO COAST WITH A DOG

Many are the rewards that await those prepared to make the extra effort required to bring their best friend along the trail. You shouldn't underestimate the amount of work involved, though. Indeed, just about every decision you make will be influenced by the fact that you've got a dog: how you plan to travel to the start of the trail, where you're going to stay, how far you're going to walk each day, where you're going to rest and where you're going to eat in the evening etc.

If you're also sure your dog can cope with (and will enjoy) walking 12 miles or more a day for several days in a row, you need to start preparing accordingly. Extra thought also needs to go into your itinerary. The best starting point is to study the village and town facilities table on pp36-7 (and the advice below), and plan where to stop and where to buy food.

### Looking after your dog

To begin with, you need to make sure that your own dog is fully **inoculated** against the usual doggy illnesses, and also up to date with regard to **worm pills** (eg Drontal) and **flea preventatives** such as Frontline – they are, after all, following in the pawprints of many a dog before them, some of whom may well have left fleas or other parasites on the trail that now lie in wait for their next meal to arrive. **Pet insurance** is also a very good idea; if you've already got insurance, do check that it will cover a trip such as this.

On the subject of looking after your dog's health, perhaps the most important implement you can take with you is the **plastic tick remover**, available from vets for a couple of quid. These removers, while fiddly, help you to remove the tick safely (ie without leaving its head behind buried under the dog's skin).

Being in unfamiliar territory also makes it more likely that you and your dog could become separated. For this reason, make sure your dog has a **tag with your contact details on it** (a mobile phone number would be best if you are carrying one with you); you could also consider having it **microchipped** for further security.

### When to keep your dog on a lead

● **On mountain tops** It's a sad fact that, every year, a few dogs lose their lives falling over the edge of steep slopes.

● **When crossing farmland**, particularly in the lambing season (around May) when your dog can scare the sheep, causing them to lose their young. Farmers are allowed by law to shoot at and kill any dogs that they consider are worrying their sheep. During lambing, most farmers would prefer it if you didn't bring your dog at all. The exception to the dogs on

---

## Town plan key

| | | | |
|---|---|---|---|
| 🏠 Where to stay | 📖 Library/bookstore | ● Other | |
| ○ Where to eat and drink | Ⓝ Internet | CP Car park | |
| Λ Campsite | 🏛 Museum/gallery | 🕐 Bus station | |
| ✉ Post Office | 🚩 Church/cathedral | 🕐 Bus stop | |
| Ⓔ Bank/ATM | Ⓣ Public telephone | ━□━ Rail line & station | |
| ⓘ Tourist Information | ☑ Public toilet | ▭ Park | |
| | □ Building | 📱 082 GPS waypoint | |

leads rule is if your dog is being attacked by cows. A couple of years ago there were three deaths in the UK caused by walkers being trampled as they tried to rescue their dogs from the attentions of cattle. The advice in this instance is to let go of the lead, head speedily to a position of safety (usually the other side of the field gate or stile) and call your dog to you.

● **Around ground-nesting birds** It's important to keep your dog under control when crossing an area where certain species of birds nest on the ground. Most dogs love foraging around in the woods but make sure you have permission to do so; some woods are used as 'nurseries' for game birds and dogs are only allowed through them if they are on a lead.

## What to pack

You've probably already got a good idea of what to bring to keep your dog alive and happy, but the following is a checklist:

● **Food/water bowl** Foldable cloth bowls are popular with walkers, being light and taking up little room in the rucksack. You can get also get a water-bottle-and-bowl combination, where the bottle folds into a 'trough' from which the dog can drink.

● **Lead and collar** An extendable one is probably preferable for this sort of trip. Make sure both lead and collar are in good condition – you don't want either to snap on the trail, or you may end up carrying your dog through sheep fields until a replacement can be found.

● **Medication** You'll know if you need to bring any lotions or potions.

● **Bedding** A simple blanket may suffice, or you can opt for something more elaborate if you aren't carrying your own luggage.

● **Poo bags** Essential.

● **Hygiene wipes** For cleaning your dog after it's rolled in stuff.

● **A favourite toy** Helps prevent your dog from pining for the entire walk.

● **Food/water** Remember to bring treats as well as regular food to keep up the mutt's morale. That said, if your dog is anything like mine the chances are they'll spend most of the walk dining on rabbit droppings and sheep poo anyway.

● **Corkscrew stake** Available from camping or pet shops, this will help you to keep your dog secure in one place while you set up camp/doze.

● **Tick remover** See above.    ● **Raingear** It can rain!    ● **Old towels** For drying your dog.

When it comes to packing, I always leave an exterior pocket of my rucksack empty so I can put used poo bags in there (for deposit at the first bin we come to). I always like to keep all the dog's kit together and separate from the other luggage (usually inside a plastic bag inside my rucksack). I have also seen several dogs sporting their own 'doggy rucksack', so they can carry their own food, water, poo etc – which certainly reduces the burden on their owner!

## Cleaning up after your dog

It is extremely important that dog owners behave in a responsible way when walking the path. Dog excrement should be cleaned up. In towns, villages and fields where animals graze or which will be cut for silage, hay etc, you need to pick up and bag the excrement.

## Staying with your dog

In this guide we have used the symbol 🐕 to denote where a hotel, pub or B&B welcomes dogs. However, this always needs to be arranged in advance and some places make an additional charge (usually per night but occasionally per stay) while others may require a deposit which is refundable if the dog doesn't make a mess. Hostels (both YHA and independent) do not permit them unless they are an assistance (guide) dog; smaller campsites tend to accept them, but some of the larger holiday parks do not. Before you turn up always double check whether there is space for them; many places have only one or two rooms suitable for people with dogs. In some cases dogs need to sleep in a separate building.

When it comes to eating, most landlords allow dogs in at least a section of their pubs, though few restaurants do. Make sure you always ask first and ensure your dog doesn't run around the pub but is secured to your table or a radiator.

# APPENDIX B – GPS WAYPOINTS

Each GPS waypoint below was taken on the route at the reference number marked on the map as below. This list of GPS waypoints is also available to download from the Trailblazer website – 🖳 www.trailblazer-guides.com.

| MAP NO | WAY-POINT | OS GRID REF | DESCRIPTION |
|---|---|---|---|
| **Stage 1** | | **St Bees to Ennerdale Bridge (14 miles)** | |
| 1 | 001 | NX 96042 11791 | Mile Zero; Coast to Coast sign on St Bees beach |
| 3 | 002 | NX 97898 14269 | Gate on right, then downhill to railway tunnel |
| 3 | 003 | NX 98500 14189 | Plank bridge over stream |
| 4 | 004 | NX 98932 14175 | By woods continue N then E to disused railway/ cycle route |
| 4 | 005 | NX 99608 14346 | Cross A595 and pass Coast to Coast statue; east into Moor Row |
| 4 | 006 | NY 00768 13923 | Turn E into field |
| 5 | 007 | NY 01558 13494 | Cleator Stores, Main St; cross road into Kiln Brow |
| 5 | 008 | NY 02295 13356 | Black How Farm. Backroad N to Ennerdale or track E to Dent Hill |
| 5 | 009 | NY 03055 13338 | Stile in fence; follow wall ESE towards Dent Hill summit |
| 5 | 010 | NY 03743 13052 | Cairn along walls; not the summit |
| 5 | 011 | NY 04148 12893 | Dent Hill summit (353m), small cairn |
| 5 | 012 | NY 04352 12765 | Stile in fence, continue SE |
| 6 | 013 | NY 04535 12668 | Junction, follow track going ENE to tall stile |
| 6 | 014 | NY 05532 12979 | Having crossed over Kirk Beck continue NE along stream |
| 6 | 015 | NY 05744 13873 | Opposite gorse hillside head NE |
| 7 | 016 | NY 06942 15811 | Ennerdale Bridge over river |
| **Stage 2 Ennerdale Bridge to Borrowdale (Rosthwaite) low route (15 miles)** | | | |
| 9 | 017 | NY 12493 13874 | Bridge at eastern end of Ennerdale Water |
| 10 | 018 | NY 14564 14122 | Turn off north for high-level route via Red Pike |
| 10 | 019 | NY 17713 13216 | A path leads E up to Scarth Gap Pass (Hay Stacks) |
| 11 | 020 | NY 19118 12508 | Path comes down from Scarth Gap |
| 12 | 021 | NY 20278 12033 | Cross Loft Beck by two cairns and ascend |
| 12 | 022 | NY 20548 12383 | Top of Loft Beck at boggy saddle; turn E for stile in fence |
| 12 | 023 | NY 20802 12417 | Stile in fence |
| 12 | 024 | NY 21135 12465 | Cairns; now head NE |
| 13 | 025 | NY 21366 12632 | Join bigger track coming from Brandreth |
| 13 | 026 | NY 21593 13455 | Drum House |
| 14 | 027 | NY 25825 14939 | At bridge turn off by bus stop in Rosthwaite |
| **Stage 3 Borrowdale to Grasmere (9 miles)** | | | |
| 16 | 028 | NY 28313 11202 | Top of Lining Crag; bogs & cairns to Greenup Edge |
| 16 | 029 | NY 28602 10526 | Greenup Edge; twin cairns just after fence post |
| 17 | 030 | NY 29558 10287 | Top of Easedale; two routes separate |
| 17 | 031 | NY 30160 10411 | Top of Calf Crag (538m) |
| 18 | 032 | NY 32744 09202 | Near Helm Crag summit |
| 18 | 033 | NY 32712 08536 | Gate on left for Poet's Walk route |

| MAP NO | WAY-POINT | OS GRID REF | DESCRIPTION |
|---|---|---|---|
| **Stage 3** (*cont'd*) | | | |
| 18 | 034 | NY 33260 08458 | At road just E of Thorney How Hostel |
| **Stage 4 Grasmere to St Sunday Crag to Patterdale (8½ miles)** | | | |
| 19 | 035 | NY 33952 09817 | Two Tongue paths separate |
| 19 | 036 | NY 34908 11680 | Grisedale Hause |
| 21 | 037 | NY 36932 13393 | Summit of The Cape (841m); head N briefly to cairn |
| 21 | 038 | NY 36975 13678 | Cairn; descent NE from St Sunday Crag begins |
| 24 | 039 | NY 37927 14728 | Wall joins from E |
| 24 | 040 | NY 38680 15699 | Turn right (SE) at oak tree |
| **Stage 5 Patterdale to Shap (15½ miles)** | | | |
| 25 | 041 | NY 40053 16146 | Behind Rooking, path heads off SE uphill to Boredale Hause |
| 25 | 042 | NY 40793 15619 | Boredale Hause; grassy flat by two drain covers |
| 25 | 043 | NY 41104 14953 | Paths diverge but soon join up near Angle Tarn |
| 26 | 044 | NY 42550 13650 | Wall ends; continue E on path |
| 26 | 045 | NY 42761 13574 | By wall, turn SE |
| 26 | 046 | NY 43106 13121 | Cross stream before gap in wall |
| 27 | 047 | NY 43629 12849 | Walls meet; path becomes track and curves to the S |
| 27 | 048 | NY 43924 12259 | Turn left (NE) at cairn for track to Kidsty Pike |
| 27 | 049 | NY 44735 12583 | Kidsty Pike summit (784m) |
| 28 | 050 | NY 45912 58881 | Minor path to N; continue E to start of steep descent |
| 28 | 051 | NY 46839 11894 | End of descent at Haweswater reservoir |
| 30 | 052 | NY 50559 16134 | E of the dam, a gate leads through the trees to Burnbanks |
| 30 | 053 | NY 51132 16000 | Out of woods; ladder stile near stream |
| 30 | 054 | NY 52026 16221 | Turn right up side of field by gully |
| 31 | 055 | NY 53372 16466 | After bog, turn right, SE, just before Rosgill Bridge |
| 32 | 056 | NY 53868 15625 | Head E here across fields to Shap Abbey |
| 33 | 057 | NY 56210 15555 | Shap (northern end by The Hermitage) |
| **Stage 6 Shap to Kirkby Stephen (20½ miles)** | | | |
| 34 | 058 | NY 56801 39500 | Path turns SE away from motorway |
| 34 | 059 | NY 57916 13829 | Cross wall by farm and head E across farm drive |
| 35 | 060 | NY 58568 13573 | Steps to and from quarry access road |
| 36 | 061 | NY 59961 11826 | Southern corner of plantation. Head ESE towards twin tree landmark |
| 36 | 062 | NY 60406 11733 | Limestone pavement near two isolated trees; track soon curves to S |
| 36 | 063 | NY 60836 10784 | E at wall corner then NE past gully near Robin Hood's Grave |
| 39 | 064 | NY 67383 07661 | Join road near Sunbiggin Tarn |
| 40 | 065 | NY 67138 07336 | Leave road to S |
| 40 | 066 | NY 67101 06984 | Faint, unmarked junction; turn E across Ravenstonedale Moor |
| 40 | 067 | NY 67621 06930 | Wooden bridge |
| 40 | 068 | NY 69342 06501 | Drain by the road with a hilltop reservoir to the E |
| 41 | 069 | NY 72068 05957 | Smardale Bridge over Scandal Beck |
| 42 | 070 | NY 74695 07269 | Through gate to road |
| 42 | 071 | NY 75630 07479 | Head for corner of the field towards gully to Green Riggs Farm |

| MAP NO | WAY-POINT | OS GRID REF | DESCRIPTION |
|---|---|---|---|
| **Stage 6** (*cont'd*) | | | |
| 43 | 072 | NY 77423 08375 | Kirkby Stephen Market Square |
| 45 | 073 | NY 81047 06732 | Signpost for Nine Standards; Red and Blue routes go E, Green route goes S |

**Stage 7 Kirkby to Keld**
● **Green route (12½ miles)**

| | | | |
|---|---|---|---|
| 45 | 074 | NY 81305 05950 | Stone pens by wall |
| 45 | 075 | NY 81278 05146 | Head of Rigg Beck |
| 45 | 076 | NY 80800 04633 | Path joins from NW; continue S to road |
| 45 | 077 | NY 80810 04467 | Four paths meet, head S then SSE to B6270 |
| 48 | 078 | NY 83106 02787 | Leave road; or carry on a bit and take easier track left uphill. |
| 48 | 079/099 | NY 83542 02774 | Red route comes down from pillar cairn to N |

● **Blue route (13 miles)**

| | | | |
|---|---|---|---|
| 46 | 082 | NY 82495 06561 | Nine Standards |
| 46 | 083 | NY 82544 06111 | Trig point 662m |
| 47 | 084 | NY 82689 05836 | Signpost |
| 47 | 085/093 | NY 82736 05728 | Blue and Red routes diverge |
| 47 | 086 | NY 83608 05632 | Waypoint on Blue route |
| 47 | 087 | NY 84157 05563 | Waypoint on Blue route |
| 47 | 088 | NY 84635 05204 | Signpost at descent to Whitsundale Beck |
| 48 | 089 | NY 84873 03745 | Old shelter |
| 48 | 090 | NY 85250 03380 | Vicinity of blue post by fence |
| 49 | 091 | NY 85536 03263 | Turn S |

● **Red route (13 miles)**

| | | | |
|---|---|---|---|
| 46 | 082 | NY 82495 06561 | Nine Standards |
| 46 | 083 | NY 82544 06111 | Trig point 662m |
| 47 | 084 | NY 82689 05836 | Signpost |
| 47 | 093/085 | NY 82736 05728 | Blue and Red routes diverge |
| 47 | 094 | NY 82830 04950 | White stick nearby |
| 47 | 095 | NY 82823 04381 | Cairn. Can see pillar cairn S of here |
| 48 | 096 | NY 83098 03785 | Pillar cairn; head SE here |
| 48 | 097 | NY 83280 03636 | Footbridge; ignore 'no access' sign to E and head for next waypoint |
| 48 | 098 | NY 83352 03582 | White-topped pole; descent continues to Green route track |
| 48 | 099/079 | NY 83542 02774 | Point where Red route joins Green route; turn E on track |

● **All routes**

| | | | |
|---|---|---|---|
| 49 | 080/092 | NY 85583 03012 | Signpost; all three routes converge by beck and wall |
| 50 | 081 | NY 87689 01633 | Leave track for indistinct scar-top path (or descend to road) |

**Stage 8 Keld to Reeth**

| | | | |
|---|---|---|---|
| 51 | 100 | NY 90464 00863 | Fork; high route goes left, low route goes downhill |

● **High route (11 miles)**

| | | | |
|---|---|---|---|
| 51 | 101 | NY 90594 00864 | Crackpot Hall; turn N towards spoil heaps then E onto stony track |
| 51 | 102 | NY 91865 01300 | Climb out of East Grain ends and path joins track |

| MAP NO | WAY-POINT | OS GRID REF | DESCRIPTION |
|---|---|---|---|
| ● **High route (11 miles)** *(cont'd)* | | | |
| 52 | 103 | NY 93189 01309 | Leave track to NE; descent to Gunnerside Beck |
| 52 | 104 | NY 93782 01747 | Point above Blakethwaite ruins on zigzag path |
| 52 | 105 | NY 93988 01332 | Signpost for Surrender Bridge; turn E up Bunton Hush (gully) |
| 52 | 106 | NY 94709 01420 | Join track near wooden pen around mine shaft |
| 54 | 107 | NY 99363 00007 | Cairn after Surrender Bridge |
| 55 | 108 | SE 02712 99739 | Cairn; head ENE for wall corner |
| 55 | 109 | SE 03321 99494 | Cross field SE to the east side of the school buildings |
| 56 | 110 | SE 03813 99295 | Reeth village green |
| ● **Low route (11½ miles)** | | | |
| 51a | 200 | SD 91014 98674 | Main track goes left, take path to right |
| 51b | 201 | SD 92579 97809 | Fallen tree |
| 51b | 202 | SD 93295 97817 | Join road |
| 51b | 203 | SD 93600 97989 | Leave road in Ivelet, cross Shore Gill, head E |
| 51c | 204 | SD 94488 98054 | Direct route to Gunnerside unclear; take river path |
| 51c | 205 | SD 96355 98286 | Gully |
| 51d | 206 | SD 97385 98160 | Join concrete path |
| 51d | 207 | SD 98420 98436 | Leave road, follow muddy track |
| 51d | 208 | SD 99535 98999 | Leave main track for small path |
| 56 | 110 | SE 03813 99295 | Reeth village green |
| **Stage 9 Reeth to Richmond (10½ miles)** | | | |
| 56 | 111 | SE 04272 99087 | Leave main road to right, take path along river behind farm |
| 56 | 112 | SE 04647 98581 | Cross road by bridge and continue along northern side of Swale |
| 56 | 113 | SE 05412 98630 | Tap by gate; cross road and enter field to N |
| 56 | 114 | SE 05708 98625 | Head for this stile |
| 57 | 115 | SE 06622 97883 | Field path rejoins road at Marrick Abbey farm |
| 58 | 116 | NZ 10897 00916 | Leave road to right for path NE up to white cairn |
| 61 | 117 | NZ 17033 01012 | Turn right into Rosemary Lane |
| **Stage 10 Richmond to Ingleby Cross (22½ miles)** | | | |
| 62 | 118 | NZ 17494 00656 | Gate on right leads to sheds and path to houses |
| 63 | 119 | SE 18611 99429 | Continue SE past junction before stream; at the track head E then SE |
| 64 | 120 | SE 22732 99420 | North of bridge turn right (E) along river bank |
| 65 | 121 | SE 26050 98454 | Crumbling bridge over beck |
| 67 | 122 | SE 31230 98932 | Join muddy, overgrown path at stile |
| 68 | 123 | SE 34873 98550 | Leave the road and head ENE along edge of field |
| 68 | 124 | SE 36146 99166 | Turn E off the A167 |
| 69 | 125 | SE 38890 99773 | No obvious sign but turn S here onto road |
| 70 | 126 | NZ 41763 01057 | Brick gateposts |
| 72 | 127 | NZ 44962 00629 | Crossroads opposite Blue Bell Inn |
| **Stage 11 Ingleby Cross to Blakey Ridge (21 miles)** | | | |
| 72 | 128 | SE 45403 98603 | Footpath for Osmotherley |
| 73 | 129 | NZ 47460 00404 | Join track, leave woods, head ENE |
| 74 | 130 | NZ 48952 00288 | Leave track and turn NE down across field |
| 74 | 131 | NZ 50499 01301 | Cairn (324m) |
| 78 | 132 | NZ 59411 01512 | Near trig point (445m) |

| MAP NO | WAY-POINT | OS GRID REF | DESCRIPTION |
|---|---|---|---|

**Stage 11** *(cont'd)*

| 81 | 133 | SE 66677 99442 | A path leads S to Church Houses pub |
| 81 | 134 | SE 67914 99725 | Lion Inn pub |

**Stage 12 Blakey Ridge to Grosmont (13½ miles)**

| 83 | 135 | NZ 69990 01919 | Turn E off road for Glaisdale Moor |
| 84 | 136 | NZ 73998 04022 | Junction near trig point |
| 86 | 137 | NZ 79303 04644 | Path emerges from Arncliffe Wood by road |
| 87 | 138 | NZ 82819 05246 | Grosmont level crossing |

**Stage 13 Grosmont to Robin Hood's Bay (15½ miles)**

| 88 | 139 | NZ 85514 04255 | Leave moorland road here and take path E to A169 |
| 89 | 140 | NZ 86174 04720 | Turn E off A169 for descent to Littlebeck |
| 90 | 141 | NZ 89912 03519 | Coast to Coast signpost; solitary tree visible to NNE |
| 91 | 142 | NZ 90712 03993 | Turn NE off B1416 at stile |
| 91 | 143 | NZ 91309 04415 | White top post |
| 91 | 144 | NZ 91491 04509 | Old post |
| 92 | 145 | NZ 91778 04649 | Open moor |
| 92 | 146 | NZ 91992 04894 | Two-metre high Coast to Coast pole; soon tracks fork, go right |
| 92 | 147 | NZ 92088 05505 | Post by stile and gate |
| 93 | 148 | NZ 94062 08147 | NE end of caravan park, just before sea cliffs |
| 95 | 149 | NZ 95325 04849 | Slipway by Bay Hotel in Robin Hood's Bay |

❏ **The Lyke Wake Walk** **(see p222)**

The Lyke Wake Walk, which the Coast to Coast trail joins for part of the stretch across the moors, was the invention of one man. Local farmer and journalist Bill Cowley came up with the idea in 1955 when he claimed that, with the exception of one or two roads that run across the moors, one could walk the entire 40 miles over the North York Moors from east to west (or vice-versa) on **heather**. Several walkers were keen to see if Mr Cowley was right, and it was agreed that the trail should start on Scarth Wood Moor, near Osmotherley, and finish in Ravenscar. To make the challenge tougher, the whole 40 miles had to be completed in 24 hours.

The curious name comes from the Lyke Wake Dirge, possibly the oldest verse in the Yorkshire dialect and starts:

*This yah neet, this yah neet,*      *When thoo frae hence away art passed*
*Ivvery neet an' all,*      *Ivvery neet an' all,*
*Fire an' fleet an' cannle leet,*      *Ti Whinny Moor thoo cums at last*
*An' Christ tak up thy saul.*      *An' Christ tak up thy saul.*

'Lyke' was the local term for corpse and the song recounts the passage of the soul through the afterlife. Bill himself became the chief dirger and handed out black-edged cards to those who successfully completed the trail. There was also a Wake Club which he founded for those who completed the walk.

Unfortunately, the trail has suffered from hard times recently. Firstly, the popularity of the walk through the '60s and '70s, led to a fair amount of environmental damage. These days there are a number of different paths to choose from to limit the damage caused by the walkers. The death of Bill Cowley in 1994 dealt another blow to the trail and the demise of the original Lyke Wake Club in 2005 was a further setback. However, a New Lyke Wake Club (🖳 www.lykewake.org) has been set up to continue along much the same lines as the original organisation. See the website for details.

# INDEX

❏ **Norse names** We have the Vikings to thank for many names in the north of England. Unless otherwise stated the following are derived from Old Norse words.

| Place names | | Landscape features | |
| --- | --- | --- | --- |
| Borrowdale | Valley of the fort | Beck | Stream |
| Ennerdale | Valley of the River Ehen | Dale | Valley |
| Glaisdale | Valley of the River Glas | Fell | Mountain |
| Grasmere | Grass lake (Old English) | Force/ Foss | Waterfall |
| Grosmont | Big hill (Old French) | Garth | Enclosure |
| Grisedale | (Gris dalr) Valley of pigs | Ghyll/Gill | Ravine |
| Keld | Spring (of water) | Hause | Narrow neck of land |
| Kirkby | Village with church | Mere | Lake/ pond (Old English) |
| Marrick | Horse ridge | Ness | Headland |
| Marske | Marsh | Pike | Peak |
| Patterdale | Patrick's Valley | Rigg | Ridge |
| Richmond | Strong hill | Scar | Bare rocky cliff or crag |
| | (Old French: Riche monte) | Tarn | Lake |
| River Rothay | Trout river | Thwaite | Clearing or meadow |
| St Sunday Crag | St Dominic's Crag (Celtic) | | |

# TRAILBLAZER'S LONG-DISTANCE PATH (LDP) WALKING GUIDES

We've applied to destinations which are closer to home Trailblazer's proven formula for publishing definitive practical route guides for adventurous travellers. Britain's network of long-distance trails enables the walker to explore some of the finest landscapes in the country's best walking areas. These are guides that are user-friendly, practical, informative and environmentally sensitive.

● **Unique mapping features** In many walking guidebooks the reader has to read a route description then try to relate it to the map. Our guides are much easier to use because walking directions, tricky junctions, places to stay and eat, points of interest and walking times are all written onto the maps themselves in the places to which they apply. With their uncluttered clarity, these are not general-purpose maps but fully edited maps drawn by walkers for walkers.

● **Largest-scale walking maps** At a scale of just under 1:20,000 (8cm or 3$^1/_8$ inches to one mile) the maps in these guides are bigger than even the most detailed British walking maps currently available in the shops.

● **Not just a trail guide – includes where to stay, where to eat and public transport** Our guidebooks cover the complete walking experience, not just the route. Accommodation options for all budgets are provided (pubs, hotels, B&Bs, campsites, bunkhouses, hostels) as well as places to eat. Detailed public transport information for all access points to each trail means that there are itineraries for all walkers, for hiking the entire route as well as for day or weekend walks.

**Coast to Coast** *Henry Stedman*, 6th edition, £11.99
ISBN 978-1-905864-57-7, 256pp, 109 maps, 40 colour photos

**Cornwall Coast Path (SW Coast Path Pt 2)** 4th edition, £11.99
ISBN 978-1-905864-44-7, 352pp, 130 maps, 40 colour photos

**Cotswold Way** *Tricia & Bob Hayne* 2nd edition, £11.99
ISBN 978-1-905864-48-5, 192pp, 60 maps, 40 colour photos

**Dorset & South Devon (SW Coast Path Pt 3)** *Stedman & Newton*, £11.99
ISBN 978-1-905864-45-4, 336pp, 88 maps, 40 colour photos

**Exmoor & North Devon (SW Coast Path Pt I)** *Stedman & Newton*, £11.99
ISBN 978-1-905864-43-0, 192pp, 60 maps, 40 colour photos

**Hadrian's Wall Path** *Henry Stedman*, 3rd edition, £11.99
ISBN 978-1-905864-37-9, 224pp, 60 maps, 40 colour photos

**North Downs Way** *John Curtin*, 1st edition, £9.99
ISBN 978-1-873756-96-6, 192pp, 80 maps, 40 colour photos

**Offa's Dyke Path** *Keith Carter*, 3rd edition, £11.99
ISBN 978-1-905864-35-5, 240pp, 98 maps, 40 colour photos

**Peddars Way & Norfolk Coast Path** *Alexander Stewart*, £11.99
ISBN 978-1-905864-28-7, 192pp, 54 maps, 40 colour photos

**Pembrokeshire Coast Path** *Jim Manthorpe*, 4th edition, £11.99
ISBN 978-1-905864-51-5, 224pp, 96 maps, 40 colour photos

**Pennine Way** *Keith Carter & Chris Scott*, 3rd edition, £11.99
ISBN 978-1-905864-34-8, 272pp, 138 maps, 40 colour photos

**The Ridgeway** *Nick Hill*, 3rd edition, £11.99
ISBN 978-1-905864-40-9, 192pp, 53 maps, 40 colour photos

**South Downs Way** *Jim Manthorpe*, 4th edition, £11.99
ISBN 978-1-905864-42-3, 192pp, 60 maps, 40 colour photos

**West Highland Way** *Charlie Loram*, 5th edition, £11.99
ISBN 978-1-905864-50-8, 208pp, 60 maps, 40 colour photos

'The same attention to detail that distinguishes its other guides has been brought to bear here'.
THE
SUNDAY TIMES